The Dairy Book of
HOME COOKERY

New edition for the 90's

Brockhampton Press

ACKNOWLEDGEMENTS

Original recipes by Sonia Allison have been updated, tested and prepared for photography by the Nutrition and Education Department of the Milk Marketing Board.

Editors: Sheelagh Donovan, Helen Mott.

Additional Contributions: Susanna Tee, Meat & Livestock Commission, Seafish Authority.

Home Economists: Helen Mott, Ruth Povey, Lynne Riddle, Jennie Shapter.

Microwave Conversions: Annette Yates.

Design: Amber Designs.

Photography: Mike Kay, Graham Langridge of Darius Photography, Edward Allwright.

Stylists: Maria Kelly, Marion McLornan, Sue Russell.

Index: Julie Beesley.

Production: John Vanner.

First Edition 1968

Second Edition 1978

Third Edition 1992

Reprinted 1995

This edition published 1996 by Brockhampton Press, a member of Hodder Headline PLC Group

ISBN 1-86019-485-0

© 1995 Milk Marque
Lower Wick Worcester WR2 4YB

The Dairy Book of
HOME COOKERY

New edition for the 90's

FOREWORD

The Milk Marketing Board published the first edition of the Dairy Book of Home Cookery, by Sonia Allison, in 1968. This was followed by a metricated version in 1978.

Both editions proved extremely popular, selling over 1 million copies each. In fact, it was continued requests for the 'out of print' second edition that prompted work to start on this, the 'new edition for the '90's'.

Many of the original recipes have been retained. However, changes in the range of foods available, cooking methods and eating habits have given rise to new 'basic' recipes in the British repertoire. These we have endeavoured to include too.

A major feature of this edition is the inclusion of instructions, within the basic method, for cooking many of the recipes in a microwave oven. With over 50% of households owning a microwave oven, we considered this essential in a basic cookbook of this nature.

Despite changes in our way of life since publication of the first edition, appreciation of the taste and nutritional value of milk and milk products has not diminished. There is in fact a wider range of English and Welsh dairy products to choose from than ever before – many of which are featured in recipes throughout this book.

It is our sincere hope that like the previous editions, this third edition adds to your knowledge and enjoyment of preparing meals for every occasion.

CONTENTS

EGGS

LIGHT MEALS & SNACKS

SAUCES, STUFFINGS & MARINADES

PUDDINGS & DESSERTS

HOME BAKING

PRESERVES, CONFECTIONERY & DRINKS

GLOSSARY

INDEX

USEFUL INFORMATION

USEFUL INFORMATION

WEIGHTS AND MEASURES FOR COOKS

TEMPERATURE CONVERSION CHART

°F	°C		°F	°C
212	100		59	15
122	50		50	10
113	45		41	5
104	40		32	0
95	35		23	−5
86	30		14	−10
77	25		5	−15
68	20		−4	−20

OVEN TEMPERATURE CHART

°C	°F	Gas Mark	Description
110	225	¼	very slow
120/130	250	½	very slow
140	275	1	slow
150	300	2	slow
160/170	325	3	moderate
180	350	4	moderate
190	375	5	moderately hot
200	400	6	moderately hot
220	425	7	hot
230	450	8	hot
240	475	9	very hot

LIQUID MEASURES

Approximate millilitre (ml) conversion	Recommended millilitre (ml) equivalent	Imperial pint	Imperial fluid ounce (fl oz)
568	575–600	1	20
284	300	½	10
142	150	¼	5

SPOON MEASURES

1 tablespoon	= 3 teaspoons
1 level tablespoon	= 15 ml
1 level teaspoon	= 5 ml

If great accuracy is not required:

1 rounded teaspoon	= 2 level teaspoons
1 heaped teaspoon	= 3 level teaspoons or 1 tablespoon

DRY WEIGHTS

Approximate gram (g) conversion to nearest round figure	Recommended gram (g) conversion to nearest 25 g	Imperial ounce (oz)
28	25	1
57	50	2
85	75	3
113	100–125	4 (¼ lb)
142	150	5
170	175	6
198	200	7
227	225	8 (½ lb)
255	250	9
284	275	10
311	300	11
340	350	12 (¾ lb)
368	375	13
396	400	14
425	425	15
453	450	16 (1 lb)

HANDY MEASURES

The following ingredients measured in **level tablespoons** give approximately 25 g/1 oz weight

3	Semolina, flour, custard powder, cornflour and other powdery starches
4	Porridge oats
2	Rice
6	Breadcrumbs (fresh)
3	Breadcrumbs (dry)
5	Grated cheese
2	Granulated and caster sugar
3	Demerara sugar, icing sugar (sifted)
5	Desiccated coconut
1	Syrup, honey, treacle and jam
4	Ground almonds, hazelnuts and walnuts
2	Dried fruits (currants, sultanas and raisins)
4	Cocoa powder
1	Salt

NOTES ON RECIPES

Preparation and cooking times at the beginning of each recipe are approximate timings only. Where a second recipe is required, for example, pastry, these timings have *not* been added to the recipe in case you should choose to use the ready made alternative.

☐ Cooking times may vary slightly depending on individual ovens. The oven and grill should be pre-heated to the specified temperature. Use the centre of the oven for baking.

☐ For **fan assisted ovens**, adjust cooking times in accordance with the Manufacturer's handbook.

> **Ⓕ** This symbol indicates that the recipe is suitable to freeze.

☐ For all recipes, ingredients are shown in metric and imperial measures. Follow either metric or imperial measures but do not mix them.

☐ When measuring milk, the **actual** metric conversion has been used. For example 568 ml (1 pint).

☐ Use sets of measuring spoons, available in both metric and imperial sizes, to give accurate measurements.

☐ All spoon measurements are level. Abbreviations used are 'tsp' for teaspoon and 'tbsp' for tablespoon.

☐ Size 3 eggs should be used unless otherwise stated.

☐ All vegetables are taken as trimmed, washed and peeled where appropriate. Weights are prepared weights.

☐ Where a weight of an ingredient is expressed as **75 g (3 oz) rice, cooked,** this means 75 g (3 oz) weighed raw, then cooked. If **75 g (3 oz) cooked rice** this means 75 g (3 oz) weighed after cooking.

☐ Use **plain** flour unless otherwise stated.

☐ White or brown breadcrumbs and white or brown sugar can be used unless otherwise stated.

☐ Wholemeal alternatives for flour, rice and pasta, can be used where desired. Extra liquid may be needed when using wholemeal flour as it may absorb more liquid.

☐ When using wholemeal rice or pasta, follow the instructions on the packet.

Low fat, low sugar, low salt variations of traditional products

There is now a wide range of milks and milk products available, with varying fat contents. Space does not allow us to list them as alternatives in the recipe ingredients but you may choose whether to use whole, semi-skimmed or skimmed milk in a recipe.

Note: When heating skimmed milk in a saucepan, take care and use a moderate heat as it has a tendency to scorch if placed over a high heat.

☐ Hard cheeses and yogurts with differing fat contents are also interchangeable.

☐ Low fat spreads are usually unsuitable for frying and baking because of their high water content. Check their packaging as this should highlight their limitations.

☐ Low sugar, low fat or low salt varieties of products such as jams, baked beans, sausages and mayonnaise are now available. These can be used in the recipes instead of the traditional products.

Microwave instructions

Microwave instructions have been given for recipes when appropriate, that is when the result is considered to be just as good as when cooked conventionally. The colour or consistency may be slightly different but this is not considered to impair the quality. Recipes tested have been using a **700 watt oven based on the 1992 rating assessment of the power output** of ovens (see page 10).
All cooking is on HIGH (100%) or full power, unless otherwise stated.

HIGH means 100% full power output
MEDIUM means 50% full power
MEDIUM LOW means 30% full power

☐ If your oven has a lower or higher wattage, you may need to increase or shorten the cooking times accordingly. Even microwave ovens with the same wattage vary in their performance and therefore, like conventional ovens, the time to cook a dish may vary from one oven to another. All cooking times are therefore approximate.
☐ Whatever the wattage of your oven, always check the food before the end of the cooking time to see that it is not over-cooking. When in doubt, always undercook as you can always cook a dish for a few minutes longer, whereas over-cooked food is often spoilt.
☐ Follow the instructions in the method that follow the words *To microwave:*
☐ Always read through the method before cooking as many of the recipes use the hob or grill as well as the microwave. Use the two to get the best results in the quickest and most convenient time. Where there is no microwave instruction, follow the conventional method.
☐ Boiling water or stock is used in many of the recipes to save time. Boil the water in a kettle for speed and convenience.
☐ It is unnecessary to cover the dish, unless stated.
☐ If you need to cover a dish but it does not have a lid, use a plate.
☐ If using special **non-PVC microwave film, direct contact between the food and film should be avoided.**
☐ If possible, stir the food and reposition the dish in the oven during cooking to ensure that it is cooked evenly.

☐ Stir liquids in mugs before and halfway through cooking to help avoid them erupting in or after being removed from the oven (see Points to Remember page 10).
☐ Some recipes benefit if the dish is placed on a low rack during cooking. This is indicated in the recipes.
☐ Observe any recommended standing times.

Always check cooking results in the traditional way, i.e. make sure it is cooked thoroughly and is piping hot right through.

Freezing information Ⓕ

☐ Freezing does not kill bacteria but stops them from multiplying as long as the freezer is kept at the correct temperature of 0°C (−18°F) or below.
☐ It is important to only freeze fresh food because if the food contains bacteria before it is frozen, it will do so once it has been thawed.
☐ Remember to defrost your freezer regularly to ensure it is working efficiently and effectively.

 **STAR SYMBOLS**

All freezers carry this star symbol which indicates that fresh food can be frozen in it. In addition the three small stars illustrate the ability to store commercially frozen foods for up to 3 months.

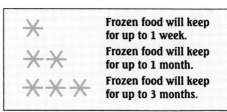

A frozen food compartment in a refrigerator with three stars or less is only suitable for storing commercially frozen food.

✳	**Frozen food will keep for up to 1 week.**
✳✳	**Frozen food will keep for up to 1 month.**
✳✳✳	**Frozen food will keep for up to 3 months.**

USING A MICROWAVE OVEN

A microwave oven, used in conjunction with the other appliances in your kitchen, can be a great asset.

There is usually a great time saving in using the microwave method. However, you will notice there are some recipes that take as long as they do conventionally. For example, rice and dried pasta need to rehydrate before they start cooking and less tender cuts of meat, used in casseroles, still need long slow cooking in order for the meat to tenderise and for the flavours to develop. Nevertheless, the microwave is economical and if this is your only means of cooking, you can prepare a wide range of dishes.

POINTS TO REMEMBER

☐ For even cooking, choose straight not sloping sides and round rather than rectangular dishes.

☐ Heat can transfer from the food to the dish, so use oven gloves to remove containers from the oven.

☐ Prick potatoes and other whole vegetables with skins all over before baking.

☐ Cut vegetables and meat into small, uniform pieces for even cooking.

☐ Place thinner parts of a food towards the centre and thicker parts towards the outer edge of the cooking container.

☐ **Always stir liquids before placing in a microwave and part way through heating,** eg, a reheated cup of coffee, milk for a sauce. This minimises the chance of a 'superheated' layer of liquid forming, and causing an eruption of hot liquid once the container is removed from the oven. Though rare, this could cause a serious burn.

As a precaution
– always choose mugs with sloping sides
– avoid mugs with vertical sides as these promote spillover.

☐ Eggs can be baked in a plastic poached egg type container, but the yolks must first be pricked with a cocktail stick – otherwise they will explode.

NEW MICROWAVE OVEN LABELS

☐ A new voluntary labelling scheme for ovens and retail food packs is being introduced in 1992.

☐ It has been developed by oven manufacturers, food manufacturers, retailers and consumer organisations in partnership with the Ministry of Agriculture, Fisheries and Food.

☐ It has been designed to help consumers microwave food more successfully, particularly when heating smaller quantities of food such as ready meals for one or two.

☐ It will lead to important changes in the way new ovens and microwaveable foods are labelled.

NEW MODELS OF OVEN in the scheme will be labelled with two pieces of information
a) the IEC 705 **power output**, which is more relevant to larger food loads, and
b) a **heating category letter**, from A to E, to indicate how much power the oven will deliver into a **small food pack**.

Example of label on new domestic microwave ovens

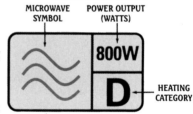

MICROWAVE SYMBOL   POWER OUTPUT (WATTS)

800W

D   HEATING CATEGORY

IF YOU ALREADY HAVE A MICROWAVE OVEN and want to know the power output of your oven under the new scheme, **a free booklet 'The New Microwave Labels'** is available from most supermarkets and microwave oven retailers as well as from Food Sense, London SE99 7TT.

This booklet explains the new system and **contains a list of existing models of domestic microwave ovens and,** where manufacturers have been able to determine the information, **their new IEC 705 power output.** It also tells you what to do if your current oven is not listed in the booklet.

Food packs in the scheme will be marked with the new microwave symbol and the appropriate instructions for heating. Matching the information on the food pack with that on the oven will give the heating time needed.

DAIRY PRODUCTS IN THE MICROWAVE

Milk

☐ Use a container large enough to hold **twice** the amount of liquid to prevent milk from boiling over when cooking, for example, soups, sauces and custards.

☐ The microwave is ideal for heating a mug of milk, a drink or soup containing milk. To heat milk, pour into a mug **with sloping sides, stir** and cook on HIGH until hot.
1 cup will take about 1½ minutes,
2 cups will take 2–3 minutes,
3 cups will take 4–5 minutes.

☐ **Do not heat milk in a baby's feeding bottle/cup in the microwave.** It could get hotter than you think and burn the baby's mouth – even though the container is cool.

☐ Never attempt to heat milk in narrow necked bottles as the glass may shatter.

Cheese

☐ If possible, add cheese to a dish just before the end of cooking to avoid over-cooking it. Cook for seconds not minutes as it should only be allowed to melt. If over-cooked it will become tough and stringy.

☐ Use grated hard cheese, rather than sliced, for a smooth result.

Cream

☐ In general, stir cream into a dish after it has been cooked.

Butter

☐ To soften cold hard butter, remove foil wrapping, place the block on a plate or in a dish and cook on MEDIUM–LOW (30%) for 30 seconds to 1 minute until a spreading consistency.

☐ To melt butter, cut quantities over 25g (1oz) in cubes and put in a small bowl. Cook on HIGH until melted.
15g (½oz) takes about 30 seconds,
25g (1oz) takes about 45 seconds,
50–75g (2–3oz) takes about 1 minute and
100g (4oz) takes 1½–2 minutes.

Yogurt

☐ Yogurt should be stirred into a dish after it has been cooked.

MILK

Most fresh milk in the UK comes from Friesian cows and has been heat treated – pasteurised, sterilised or ultra heat treated. This has a negligible effect on its nutritional value but destroys harmful bacteria and prolongs its keeping qualities.
Milk sold in cartons or plastic bottles will be appropriately labelled.
Pasteurised milk in glass bottles is easily recognised by its coloured foil cap.
Please don't forget to return bottles to your milkman!

PASTEURISED MILK

WHOLE MILK (silver top)
This is ordinary pasteurised milk which means that it has been heated to not less than 72°C (161°F) for 15 seconds and then rapidly cooled. Most of the cream rises to the top of the milk which gives it a noticeable cream line. It contains an average 3.9% fat.

HOMOGENISED (red top)
This is whole milk but processed so that the cream is evenly distributed throughout.

SEMI-SKIMMED (red and silver striped top)
This is milk from which a little over half the cream has been removed to give an average fat content of 1.6%.

SKIMMED (blue and silver checked top)
This is milk from which almost all the cream has been removed to give an average fat content of 0.1%.

CHANNEL ISLAND (gold top)
This is milk from the Guernsey or Jersey breeds of cow. It has an average 5.1% fat.

STANDARDISED MILK
The EC is proposing to introduce a milk which has been standardised to give a fat content of 3.5%.

UNTREATED MILK

WHOLE MILK (green top)
This is raw milk which has not been pasteurised. It must be sold under licence and labelled 'This milk has not been heat-treated and may therefore contain organisms harmful to health'. It contains an average 3.9% fat.

STERILISED MILK

This is homogenised milk which has been heated to boiling point or above for 20 to 30 minutes and vacuum sealed to sterilise it. It is available as whole, semi-skimmed and skimmed milk and is sold in tall bottles with a crown cap or in plastic bottles.

ULTRA-HEAT TREATED MILK

Known as UHT or long-life milk, this is homogenised milk which has then been ultra-heated to 132°C(270°F) for at least 1 second then aseptically packaged in foil-lined cartons. It is available as whole, semi-skimmed and skimmed milk.

Storing milk

PASTEURISED MILK
☐ Wipe containers and refrigerate as soon as possible. Refer to the date stamped on the bottle cap or carton for the storing time.

☐ Milk keeps best in the container in which you bought it. If you do pour milk into a jug, do not pour it back into the container.

☐ Do not mix milk from different containers unless it is to be cooked at once.

STERILISED MILK
☐ Unopened it should keep for several weeks, particularly if stored in a cool place. **Once opened, refrigerate and treat as pasteurised milk.**

UHT MILK
☐ Its treatment produces a milk with a 6 month shelf life – check the carton for details. Store in a cool place if possible. **Once opened, refrigerate and treat as pasteurised milk.**

Freezing milk

☐ Freeze milk in cartons or plastic containers, not in a bottle.

☐ **Homogenised** milk freezes successfully but pasteurised milk tends to separate on thawing. Freeze for up to 1 month.

☐ Milk should be thawed slowly in the refrigerator but thawing can be accelerated if the milk is to be used in cooking.

☐ If you have spare pasteurised milk, it is better use of freezer space to make it into a sauce or quiche before freezing.

SPECIALIST MILKS

ENRICHED REDUCED FAT MILK
Removing some or all of the cream affects the flavour and mouth feel of milk. Some brands have therefore added skimmed milk powder to give the milk more 'body'. These milks may be pasteurised or UHT, and may be fortified with vitamins A and D. Check the carton for details of such modifications.

CALCIUM ENRICHED MILK

Milk is, in its own right, an excellent source of calcium. However, there are pasteurised reduced fat milks on the market with added calcium. Check cartons for details. These could prove useful for those with small appetites or breastfeeding mothers whose need for calcium is high.

LACTOSE REDUCED MILK

These are whole and reduced fat milks designed for the small number of people in the UK unable to digest quantities of lactose. They are UHT products and can be found with UHT milk.

MILK FOR CEREAL

For those who like 'cream off the top of the milk' on their breakfast cereal, look for 'milk with added cream' or breakfast milk – which is homogenised Channel Island Milk.

FLAVOURED MILKS AND THICK SHAKES

Milk is available in a variety of flavours including chocolate, strawberry and banana. These may be pasteurised, sterilised or UHT and as whole, semi-skimmed or skimmed. There are also special liquids or powders for making flavoured milks or thick shakes at home.

MILK CAN

This is UHT semi-skimmed milk in a can. Look for it with other canned soft drinks.

NUTRITIONAL VALUE

Milk is a valuable source of calcium, riboflavin and protein in the UK diet. For vegetarians it can be a valuable source of vitamin B_{12}. However, vegetarians should not rely on sterilised or UHT milks for vitamin B_{12} as they contain less than pasteurised milk.

The carbohydrate in milk is called lactose. It caramelises during the sterilisation process and changes to lactic acid during the production of yogurt.

The figures below show how skimming milk reduces its fat content. As a consequence, the energy and vitamin A are reduced, while the calcium, protein and B vitamins increase slightly.

THE EFFECT OF THE SKIMMING PROCESS ON KEY MILK NUTRIENTS

WHOLE MILK per pint		SEMI-SKIMMED per pint		SKIMMED per pint	
Energy Kcal	386	Energy Kcal	273	Energy Kcal	193
Fat g	23	Fat g	10	Fat g	1
Protein g	19	Protein g	19	Protein g	19
Calcium mg	676	Calcium mg	693	Calcium mg	704
Vitamin A μg	329	Vitamin A μg	136	Vitamin A μg	6

Milk and milk products are an excellent source of calcium

Milk, hard cheese and yogurt are major sources of calcium in the UK diet.

A pint of milk daily would meet the needs of all groups of the population, apart from adolescents who would need the equivalent of 1⅓ pints and breastfeeding mothers, the equivalent of 1½ pints.

As you can see from the table below, there are other sources of calcium. However, milk and milk products are by far the most concentrated sources consumed on a **regular** basis.

PRINCIPAL SOURCES OF CALCIUM

200ml	⅓ pint whole milk	225mg
200ml	⅓ pint semi-skimmed milk	230mg
200ml	⅓ pint skimmed milk	235mg
25g	1oz Cheddar type chese	210mg
150g	5oz pot yogurt	270mg
112g	4oz carton cottage cheese	90mg
56g	2oz sardines including bones	310mg
100g	3 large slices bread	100mg
112g	4oz spring cabbage	34mg
112g	4oz baked beans	50mg

FRESH CREAM

Fresh cream can turn a simple dish into something special – be it a couple of tablespoons in a quiche or the small carton topping that special trifle.

Most cream has been pasteurised or ultra heat treated. Look for this symbol as your guarantee of **fresh dairy cream**.

PASTEURISED CREAM

HALF CREAM
This may be called 'top of the milk' or coffee cream. It is a thin pouring fresh cream suitable for fruit, cereal or coffee.
It is usually homogenised and may be pasteurised or ultra heat treated. It contains 12% butterfat and cannot be whipped.

SINGLE CREAM
This is a pouring fresh cream which is pasteurised or ultra heat treated and may be homogenised to give a thicker consistency. It does not contain sufficient fat (18% butterfat) to whip successfully but is ideal for coffee, on cereal, swirled into soup, stirred into casseroles and with fresh fruit.

EXTRA THICK SINGLE CREAM
This fresh cream contains 18% butterfat and is homogenised to produce a spoonable cream. It is ideal for spooning over fresh fruit or on to fruit pies. It will not whip.

SOURED CREAM
This is homogenised single cream which is cultured to give a pleasant acidic flavour. It enhances the flavour and creaminess of many savoury dishes and is delicious spooned over baked jacket potatoes and fresh fruit.

HOME-MADE SOURED CREAM
Stir 5 ml (1 tsp) lemon juice into 150 ml (¼ pint) fresh single cream and leave for 10–15 minutes.

CRÈME FRAICHE
This fresh cream has a slightly soured taste and thick consistency. It contains 30–35% butterfat and is suitable for spooning over puddings and desserts.

WHIPPING CREAM
This fresh cream contains 35–40% butterfat and can be whipped to produce a soft 'airy' foam and double its original volume. It can be used for piping on desserts, in cheesecakes, topping trifles and filling cakes and pastries.

DOUBLE CREAM
This versatile fresh cream is a rich pouring cream and will float on the top of coffee or soup. It contains 48% butterfat and therefore can be whipped successfully. **Double cream gives a firmer result than whipping cream and so is the preferred choice for decorating a gateau.**
If the cream is not required for piping, you

may add 15 ml (1 tbsp) milk to every 150 ml (¼ pint) cream. This slightly lowers the butterfat content, which will increase the volume of the whipped cream.

EXTRA THICK DOUBLE CREAM
This is fresh double cream which is homogenised to produce an extra thick cream. **It will not whip successfully** but is a rich spoonable cream ideal for puddings, desserts and on fruit.

EXTENDED LIFE DOUBLE CREAM
This double cream is heat treated, homogenised and vacuum sealed in glass bottles or jars. Unopened, it will keep for 2 to 3 weeks in a refrigerator. It is usually used for pouring or spooning but may be lightly whipped.

CLOTTED CREAM
Clotted fresh cream originates from Devon, Cornwall and Somerset and is often called Cornish or Devonshire cream. It has a butterfat content of 55% and its own traditional granular texture, special 'nutty' flavour and golden yellow colour. It spreads easily and is delicious in cakes, with scones and jam, pastries and fruit.

UHT CREAM

This cream is ultra heat treated and so has a shelf life of up to 3 months without refrigeration. Check the date stamp. **Treat as pasteurised cream once opened**.

Half, single, whipping and double cream are available. It is ideal for picnics and holidays.

AEROSOL CREAM

This is whipped UHT cream which is packed into aerosol cans with up to 13% added sugar, stabilizers and a propellant to make it flow from the can. It has a short shelf life so check the date stamp and refrigerate once opened. Use just before serving as it has a tendency to collapse within minutes of contact with air.

COMMERCIALLY FROZEN CREAM

This is available as single, whipping, double and clotted cream in chip or stick form.

STERILISED CREAMS

Sterilised creams are available in cans and have been heat treated and homogenised. **Sterilised Half Cream** is a pouring cream with a slight caramel flavour since the high temperature used in processing caramelises the lactose. **Sterilised Cream** is a thicker, caramel flavoured cream that can be spooned but will not whip. If unopened, sterilised creams should keep for up to two years but once opened they have the same keeping quality as fresh cream. Check the can for its 'best before' date.

Storing fresh cream

When buying cream check the date stamp and refrigerate as soon as possible. Take advantage of re-sealable lids as these prevent an opened carton picking up taints from other foods.

Home freezing cream

☐ Cream needs a fat content of 35% to freeze successfully in a domestic freezer.

☐ **Double and whipping cream are therefore suitable for freezing.**

☐ For best results, double and whipping cream should be partially whipped to the 'floppy' stage and then frozen in rigid plastic containers or, for small quantities, in ice cube trays.

☐ Take care when whipping thawed cream as it thickens very quickly.

☐ Whipped cream can also be piped into rosettes, then 'open frozen', before packing into a rigid container to store (see page 22).

☐ **Do not freeze cream after its use by date.**

☐ Freeze **double and whipping cream** for up to 2 months.

Thawing cream

☐ Thaw cream slowly in the refrigerator for several hours.

☐ Place rosettes in position as decoration **before thawing** as they cannot be handled once thawed. Allow 30 minutes to thaw.

☐ Frozen cubes of cream can be simply dropped into a warm sauce or soup.

THE WHIPPING OF CREAM

1 Use double or whipping cream. Chill the cream, bowl and all the utensils for

30 minutes before whipping. You can use an electric whisk but the chances of over-whipping the cream are greater as the blades revolve very quickly. You have more control using a hand whisk and a **spiral whisk produces the greatest volume.**

2 Pour the cream into the bowl. Adding 15 ml (1 tbsp) milk to 150 ml (¼ pint) double cream will help to achieve more volume. Whip quickly until a matt finish is reached then continue whipping more slowly until the cream stands in soft peaks. Over-whipping gives a granular, buttery texture.

3 When piping freshly whipped double cream, force the cream into the end of a large piping bag fitted with a nozzle.

4 Hold the piping bag at the end above the cream, not in the centre as this will cause the cream to lose volume and possibly have a granular texture. Use your forefinger to guide the nozzle as you pipe.
Note: When using UHT whipping cream, it is particularly important to ensure the cream is **cold** before whipping.

BUTTER

Butter is a natural product made by churning fresh cream and has a unique and luxurious flavour. It is ideal in everyday cooking such as grilling, roasting, frying, in sauces and in baking cakes, biscuits and pastries. As a spread on bread, toast, crumpets, muffins, buns and scones it has no rival.

BUTTER
Butter, like hard and soft margarines, contain about 81% fat, so all these products have the same number of calories. Butter naturally contains vitamins A and D, the amounts varying slightly with the season. No preservatives or colourings are added, although salt (at about 2% in salted butter) and/or lactic acid cultures may be added for extra flavour. It is available, salted, slightly salted and unsalted.

CONCENTRATED BUTTER
As the name suggests, concentrated butter contains less water than butter, giving it a minimum fat content of 96% whereas for ordinary butter it is 80%. It has been developed for cooking use only. Refer to the packet for instructions on using.

HALF FAT BUTTER
This is a product with half the fat of butter and hence a greater percentage of water. It still has a buttery taste and can be used for spreading, all-in-one sauces, vegetables and grills and in some baking.

Spreads
There is an ever increasing range of spreads on the market so always check the label for details of fat content and usage.

DAIRY SPREADS
These are a blend of milk fat from butter or cream and vegetable oils. This produces a butter flavoured spread which can be used for spreading, grilling, frying, roasting, sauces, vegetables, baking and pastry.

LOW FAT AND VERY LOW FAT SPREADS
These are made from vegetable oils and various dairy ingredients such as buttermilk. Low fat spreads can be used for spreading, all-in-one sauces and some baking. Very low fat spreads are only suitable for spreading.

Storing butter
Butter should be kept closely covered or wrapped and stored in the refrigerator away from foods with strong flavours or smells. It will keep for 2–3 weeks but check the 'use by' date.
Concentrated butter can be stored for up to 6 months in the refrigerator. See use by date.

Freezing butter
Overwrap blocks in foil before freezing. 'Open freeze' butter curls or pats before layering with greaseproof paper in a rigid container. Salted butter freezes for up to 3 months and unsalted for 6 months. Thaw butter in the refrigerator – a 225g (8oz) block takes about 4 hours.

THE CHEESES OF ENGLAND AND WALES

There are many varieties of cheese produced in England and Wales, all different in flavour and texture and well worth making a point of trying. This guide highlights some of them and is designed to whet your appetite!
The nine regional varieties of cheeses are:

HARD AND SEMI-HARD CHEESES

CAERPHILLY
Creamy white, with a moist and crumbly texture and a mild flavour.

CHEDDAR – MILD, MEDIUM OR MATURE
Creamy yellow, close and smooth textured, the flavour ranges from mild when young to full flavoured and nutty when mature.

CHESHIRE
White, red or blue veined, Cheshire has a loose and crumbly texture, with a slightly salty, tangy flavour.

DERBY
Pale honey colour with a firm texture and mild flavour. Sage Derby is green marbled and flavoured with sage.

DOUBLE GLOUCESTER
Golden coloured, smooth textured and full flavoured.

LANCASHIRE
Today most Lancashire is mild and crumbly but there is also a more mature traditional variety which is moist with a sharp tang.

LEICESTER
Bright, reddish colour, smooth open texture and mellow flavour.

STILTON
Most famous is the blue veined Stilton with a soft and moist texture. White Stilton is, as the name suggests, white and is a young version of Blue Stilton without the mould. Blue is rich and creamy, white has a fresh and milder flavour.

WENSLEYDALE
Creamy white with a flaky texture and a mild, creamy flavour.

FARMHOUSE CHEESES

Cheeses such as Cheddar, Lancashire and Cheshire are still made by traditional methods, using milk produced on the maker's farm or known local farms. Some of the cheeses are independently graded and carry the Farmhouse cheese mark as a guarantee of quality.

KEY TO CHEESES
1. Caerphilly
2. White Cheshire
3. Red Cheshire
4. Derby
5. Sage Derby
6. Double Gloucester
7. English Cheddar
8. Mild Cheddar
9. Lancashire
10. Leicester
11. Blue Stilton
12. Wensleydale

CHEESES MADE ON THE FARM

Renewed interest in cheese making has resulted in the development of new cheeses and the re-appearance of some traditional ones. Made on farms or smallholdings, they are often only available locally or from specialist cheese shops. For example Pencarreg and Teifi from Wales, Exmoor and Coleford Blue from the West Country, and Beamish and Swaledale from the North.

BLUE VEINED CHEESES

BLUE STILTON
This is Britain's most celebrated blue cheese and world famous, but there are other blue cheeses produced in Britain with different flavours and textures.

BLUE CHESHIRE
This blue variety of Cheshire is matured longer than ordinary white Cheshire and although softer and less crumbly, has the same characteristic saltiness.

BLUE WENSLEYDALE
Relatively mild this is probably the best one for new 'Blue cheese eaters' to try!

BLUE SHROPSHIRE
This strong, rich cheese is deep orange with blue veins.

BLUE VINNEY
This hard, skimmed milk Dorset cheese is almost legendary. However, it is now made commercially in the Melton Mowbray area.

HINTON BLUE
A new English blue veined cheese. It is a two curd cheese which gives it an attractive golden white marbled effect. It has a smooth, nutty flavour and is made on a Shropshire farm.

BUXTON BLUE
This blue veined, russet coloured cheese has a mellow flavour.

REDUCED FAT HARD CHEESES

These have approximately half the fat of traditional cheeses – between 14–23% instead of 32%. Check the labels for information on individual brands. Mild or mature Cheddar types and other traditional varieties are available.

VEGETARIAN CHEESES

Nutritionally identical to ordinary hard cheese, these are made with rennet of fungal origin rather than animal rennet. Cheddar and other varieties are available from supermarkets and health food shops.

FLAVOURED CHEESES

As well as the traditional cheeses there are a great variety of flavoured ones now available. These will add interest to your cheeseboard.

THE CHEESEBOARD

A cheeseboard can make a quick nutritious lunch as well as an after dinner course.

Selecting the cheese

☐ Allow 50g (2oz) per person if serving as part of a meal

☐ Allow up to 100g (4oz) if a meal in itself.

☐ Select cheeses to give variety and colour, flavour and texture – include one of the flavoured cheeses listed.

☐ When eating, start with a mild cheese and finish with the strongest.

Serving cheese

☐ Bring cheese to room temperature for about an hour before serving.

☐ Don't overcrowd the board – leave room for cutting.

☐ Serve with a selection of sweet and savoury biscuits, breads, fresh fruit and celery.

☐ Offer the cheeseboard before the dessert and you can continue drinking your main course wine.

ADMIRALS
Cheddar with port layered with Blue Stilton.
APPLEWOOD or CHARNWOOD
Smoked Cheddar coated with paprika.
BELLSHIRE
Wensleydale with chives.
BEAUCHAMP
Double Gloucester with herbs and garlic.
COTSWOLD or ABBEYDALE
Double Gloucester with chives and onions.
GLENPHILLY
Mature Cheddar with Scotch Whisky.
HUNTSMAN or COUNTY
Double Gloucester layered with Blue Stilton.
NUTCRACKER
Cheddar with walnuts.
PENMILL
Cheddar with peppercorns
ROMANY
Double Gloucester layered with Caerphilly, onions and chives.
SOMERTON or RUTLAND
Cheddar with beer, garlic and parsley.
WALGROVE
Red Leicester and walnuts.
WINDSOR RED
Cheddar marbled with elderberry wine.
YEOMAN
Cheddar with sweet pickle.

KEY TO CHEESES
1. Blue Shropshire
2. Bellshire
3. Windsor Red
4. Swaledale
5. Farmhouse Cheddar
6. Red Cheshire
7. Cheddar with fruit cake
8. Smoked Caerphilly
9. Pencarreg
10. Huntsman
11. Lancashire

KEY TO CHEESES

1. Cambridge Blue
2. Somerset Brie
3. Somerset Camembert
4. Cream Cheese

5. Natural Fromage Frais
6. Cottage Cheese
7. Fruit Fromage Frais
8. Curd Cheese

RIPENED SOFT CHEESES

Continental style mould-ripened cheeses can now be produced in England. Mould-ripened cheeses are identified by their white outer rind, which is edible – though not enjoyed by everyone! They have a characteristic flavour and texture which develops as the cheese matures to give a soft cheese with a mellow creamy flavour.

Check the 'use by' date as this will indicate the ripeness of the cheese. The longer the time before expiry of the date, the firmer and milder the cheese will be. Names to look for are **Cambridge Blue** and **Somerset Brie**.

UNRIPENED SOFT CHEESES

Fresh or unripened soft cheeses are characterised by a mild, sometimes slightly acidic flavour and a soft, spreadable texture. They are made from pasteurised milk or cream to which a special culture is added.

CREAM CHEESE

Made from single or double cream with a rich, creamy texture and flavour.
Available as:
'full fat soft cheese': minimum fat content 20%,
'cream cheese': minimum fat content 45%.
Use in cheesecakes, dips and sandwiches.

CURD CHEESE

A 'medium fat' or 'skimmed milk' soft cheese with a mild flavour. It can be used as a lower fat alternative to cream cheese in recipes. The 'medium fat' variety has a fat content of 10–20%, while the 'skimmed milk' soft cheese has a fat content of less than 2%. Check individual labels for fat content. Use as for cream cheese and in flans or spread on crispbreads and biscuits.

COTTAGE CHEESE

Made from skimmed milk, the curds are cut and cooked, to give the characteristic texture. Available as:
'low fat': with a fat content of 2–10%,
'very low fat': with less than 2% fat.
It is sold plain or with added herbs, fruit or vegetables. Use as a baked potato filling or with salads.

FROMAGE FRAIS

In French this means 'fresh cheese' and it is made using whole or skimmed milk. It has a soft texture and looks and tastes more like Greek-style yogurt. It is sold as low fat (less than 1%) and medium fat (8%). Both are available as plain or fruit flavoured. Use as a topping in the same way as fresh cream, stirred into sauces or with fruit.

Other soft cheeses available are **Fromage Blanc** and **Quark**. Both are very similar to fromage frais, though a little firmer.

Storing cheese

The success of storing cheese lies in keeping it cool. A cool larder or the door of the refrigerator is ideal.

☐ Exposure to the air causes cheese to dry out and crack. Keep cheese in plastic airtight containers or closely wrapped in foil.

☐ Greaseproof paper is not suitable as it does not give an airtight seal.

☐ Bring cheese to room temperature for at least 1 hour if storing in a refrigerator to allow its true flavour to develop.

☐ To hasten ripening of a mould ripened cheese, leave at room temperature for several hours before eating. However, store in a refrigerator.

Cooking with cheese

Cheese is easy to prepare, just slice, crumble, grate or dice it, but more care is needed when cooking with it.

☐ Too high a heat and too much cooking causes it to separate and become tough and stringy. Cheese must therefore not be allowed to boil and should melt rather than bubble when under the grill.

☐ Add cheese to a sauce **off the heat** so that the heat of the sauce melts it. **Do not allow a sauce to boil once the cheese has been added.**

☐ In general, the hard cheeses are more versatile for cooking and mature cheeses give the best flavour. Even adding more of, for example, a less expensive mild Cheddar to a dish will not impart more flavour and will therefore not be an economy.

☐ If using mild Cheddar, you may add a little mustard for additional flavour.

☐ When a recipe specifies a certain cheese it usually does so because of its particular flavour, texture or colour. By substituting another variety of cheese, the taste of the dish will obviously be altered, but may be improved!

Freezing cheese

☐ For best results choose a rectangular block rather than a wedge shape and not too large a piece – 225g (8oz) pieces are ideal.

☐ The cheese should be well wrapped in foil to prevent it from drying out.

☐ Alternatively, grate the cheese, 'open freeze' to ensure a free-flowing product, and pack in useable quantities.

☐ Freeze for up to 4 months.

☐ **Blue Stilton** can be frozen but the rind tends to be soft on thawing. The cheese is not therefore of cheeseboard quality but can be used in cooking minus the rind.

☐ It is not recommended that you freeze **mould ripened** cheese. The thawed product lacks the quality of a freshly bought piece.

☐ Freeze **medium or full fat soft cheese** in their cartons. Freeze medium fat soft cheese for up to 3 months and full fat soft cheese for up to 1 month.

Freeze **fromage frais** in rigid cartons. It separates slightly on thawing so stir well to reconstitute. Freeze for up to 1 month.

Note: 'Open freezing' is designed to ensure items are separate and do not freeze together in a solid mass, e.g. grated cheese, cream rosettes. To open freeze, spread the grated cheese sparsely over a baking sheet and place uncovered in the freezer. After about 30 minutes the 'shavings' of cheese will be frozen and can be poured into a freezer bag/plastic box.

Thawing cheese

Thaw cheese slowly in the refrigerator (a 225g (8oz) block will take about 24 hours), then allow to come to room temperature before serving. Grated cheese can be used straight from frozen.

Nutritional value

Cheese is a concentrated form of milk containing most of the nutrients found in milk. 25g (1oz) cheese contains as much calcium as 200ml (⅓pint) milk or one pot of yogurt. Reduced fat hard cheeses and mould ripened cheeses are good sources of calcium too, but soft cheeses contain much less.

KEY NUTRIENTS IN CHEESE (Per 100g/4oz)				
	ENERGY cal	PROTEIN g	FAT g	CALCIUM mg
Cheddar type	412	25.5	34.4	720
Reduced fat Cheddar type*	261	31.5	15	840
Brie type	319	19.3	26.9	540
Cottage cheese*	98	13.8	3.9	73
Cream cheese	439	3.1	47.4	98
Full fat soft cheese	313	8.6	31.0	110
* Check packaging for the basic nutritional value of different branded products.				

Yogurt

Yogurt is a cultured product made from whole or skimmed milk. To improve its flavour and texture, skimmed milk solids or cream may be added. It is slightly acidic in taste, refreshing to eat and very versatile. It is available natural, in a variety of flavours and with pieces of fruit added.

Yogurt, whilst delicious eaten straight from the carton, teams well with both sweet and savoury dishes.

'LIVE' YOGURT

Regardless of whether labelled 'live' or not, all yogurt contains living bacteria – Lactobacillus bulgaricus and Streptococcus thermophilus – unless it has been pasteurised **after** manufacture. Most commercially produced yogurt is 'live'. It should therefore be kept in the refrigerator and eaten within the 'use by' date.

Method of manufacture
SET YOGURT

Known as 'French Recipe' by some manufacturers, this yogurt is incubated in the individual cartons in which it is sold and has a junket-like texture. It is available in natural and fruit flavours and has a smoother, firmer texture than stirred yogurt.

STIRRED YOGURT

This yogurt is incubated in bulk quantities then transferred into cartons. It is available natural or with whole fruit and has a soft texture and appearance.

Fat content
VERY LOW FAT YOGURT

Has a fat content of less than 0.5% and is often sweetened artificially for slimmers.

LOW FAT YOGURT

This has a fat content between 0.5–2.0%.

CREAMY YOGURT

This is made from whole milk, and may also be enriched with cream. It is available flavoured and with fruit and has a thick and creamy texture. Check the label for nutritional information.

GREEK-STYLE YOGURT

This is made from either cows' or ewes' milk. It has a thick, creamy consistency and a fat content between 1.8–10.5%.

FLAVOURED YOGURT

There are many varieties of yogurt flavoured with fruit juice and other flavourings such as honey and chocolate.

FRUIT YOGURT

These contain at least 5% of the whole fruit as pieces or purée.

'BA YOGURT'/BIO YOGURT

This yogurt is made with alternative cultures (bifidus and acidophilus cultures) which are said to aid efficient digestion. It is available in natural and fruit flavours and is less tart than ordinary yogurt.

DRINKING YOGURT

Drinking yogurt is made from yogurt with added milk and fruit juice to give a drinking consistency. It is available in a variety of flavours as a fresh or UHT product.

CULTURED BUTTERMILK

This is another cultured milk product which is made from pasteurised skimmed milk. The added buttermilk culture gives it a slightly thick consistency and acid taste. It makes a refreshing drink and can be used in some baking recipes.

Storing yogurt

Yogurt should be bought from a refrigerated cabinet, always stored in a refrigerator and eaten before the 'use by' date.

Freezing yogurt

Freeze whole fruit, fruit flavoured and stirred-type natural yogurt in rigid containers.

☐ Fruit yogurt freezes for up to 3 months and natural yogurt for 2 months.

☐ Do not freeze Greek-style yogurt as it separates on thawing.

☐ Thaw yogurt slowly in the refrigerator.

Nutritional value

The nutritional value of yogurt is similar to that of the milk from which it is made. It is therefore a good source of protein and calcium. Some low fat natural varieties have vitamins A and D added but check the label. For the nutritional value of 'Bio yogurts' see the individual cartons.

Making yogurt at home

There are various appliances on the market for making yogurt at home. However, it can be just as easy to make your own in a wide-necked vacuum flask.

☐ The best results are obtained if you use UHT or sterilised milk. Whole milk gives the best result, the yogurt becoming progressively thinner, the lower the fat content of the milk.

☐ If using fresh pasturised milk, choose homogenised milk. Pasteurised milk must be boiled first, covered and allowed to cool to 42°C (106°F), approximately blood heat.

☐ Most commercially produced natural yogurt, except that which is pasteurised after manufacture, can be used as a 'starter' for making yogurt at home.

☐ Do *not* use a tablespoon of your home-made yogurt as the 'starter' for your next batch. It may be contaminated and the two bacteria essential for development of the flavour and texture may not be present in the right proportions.

☐ Ensure that the bought yogurt is fresh by checking the 'use by' date.

☐ Individual brands of yogurt have their own distinct flavour, so 'start' your yogurt using your favourite brand.

First sterilise all equipment with boiling water or a sterilising solution used for sterilising babies bottles.

1 Heat 568ml (1 pint) milk, less 30ml (2 tbsp), to 42°C (106°F), approximately blood heat.

2 Blend the reserved milk with 15ml (1 tbsp) natural yogurt until smooth then stir into the warm milk.

3 Pour into a pre-warmed, wide-necked, flask and leave for 6–8 hours until slightly thickened. At this stage it will not be as thick as commercially produced yogurt.

4 Turn yogurt into a bowl, stand bowl in cold water and whisk the yogurt until cool.

5 Cover the bowl, place in the refrigerator and leave for at least 4–6 hours. During this time the yogurt will thicken considerably.

6 Serve plain or flavoured. When adding flavour such as fruit, add as little juice as possible as the more juice you add, the more runny the yogurt becomes.

☐ Keeps for up to 1 week in the refrigerator.

ICE CREAM

Ice cream makes a perfect dessert for any occasion. It comes in all shapes and sizes, flavours and textures and can be divided into three different types.

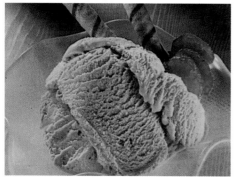

STANDARD
Vanilla, ripples, neapolitans and basic flavours are characteristic of this type of ice cream. Standard ice cream is usually vegetable fat or butter based and generally relatively low in fat and high in air content.

PREMIUM
Most of these ice creams are based on dairy products such as milk and/or cream, although some are made with higher quality vegetable fat. These ice creams are classified by the quality of their ingredients.

SUPER PREMIUM
These ice creams have developed along American lines, with a high cream content and very little air. They are deliciously rich and creamy and contain high quality ingredients such as fruit pieces, toffee, nuts, liqueurs and real chocolate.

ICE CREAM MADE WITH DAIRY CREAM

This can now bear the special mark which is awarded to ice cream that contains double cream and meets the high standards specified by the Milk Marketing Board. It must contain at least 10% butterfat, half of which must come from English or Welsh double cream.

Storing ice cream
Dairy cream ice cream will keep in the freezer for up to three months.

☐ If you have a part full container, place greaseproof paper over the ice cream to exclude the air and stop ice crystals forming.

☐ Always seal the container tightly to avoid the ice cream absorbing other flavours.

☐ Once thawed, do not refreeze.

RUM 'N' RAISIN & ORANGE SAUCE

Choosing the Best Cut

1 FORERIB
Traditionally sold on the bone but now often sold boned and rolled. A moist, succulent cut as it is "marbled" with fat.
Suitable as a joint to roast, steaks to grill, fry.

2 TOPSIDE
A very lean cut often sold with a layer of fat tied around it.
Suitable as a joint to roast, pot roast
steaks to fry, grill, stir fry.

3 FLASH FRY STEAKS
Thick flank, topside or silverside beef. Good value but not as tender and succulent as rump or sirloin.
Suitable to grill, fry, stir fry.

4 SIRLOIN
Sold boned and rolled.
Suitable as a joint to roast.

5 BRAISING STEAK
Chuck, blade or thick rib.
Suitable to braise, stew, casserole.

6 STEWING BEEF
Shin, leg, neck or clod. Cheaper than braising steak, it requires long, slow cooking for best results.
Suitable to braise, stew, casserole.

7 & 10 MINCE (Coarse or fine)
Clod, neck, thin rib, thin flank. Sometimes called 'ground' beef. Extra lean mince is also available. Choose coarse for Shepherd's Pie, fine for burgers.
Suitable to dry fry and in burgers.

8 BRISKET
Sold boned and rolled and may be salted.
Suitable to roast, pot roast. boil if salted.

9 RUMP STEAK
Usually cheaper than sirloin or fillet, it is often considered the best steak for flavour, though not as tender as fillet.
Suitable to grill, fry, barbecue, stir fry.

11 FILLET STEAK
Has little or no fat and ideal for those who like 'tender' steak. The cut for tournedos or Châteaubriand.

Suitable to grill, fry, in Beef Wellington.

12 THICK FLANK (top rump)
Similar to topside, though topside is a better choice for roasting.
Suitable as a joint to roast; as steaks slowly
fried over a low heat or braised.

13 SIRLOIN STEAK
The cut for 'T' bone, Porterhouse and Entrecôte.
Suitable to grill, fry, barbecue, stir fry.

14 SILVERSIDE
Traditionally a salted joint for boiling. Today a very lean joint, usually sold unsalted.
Suitable to pot roast and roast. Must be
basted frequently and cooked
slowly if roasting.

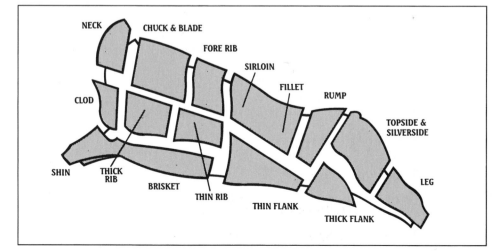

CHOOSING THE BEST CUT

1 & 5 DOUBLE LOIN/LOIN CHOP
Suitable to grill, fry, roast.

2 BEST END OF NECK
Sold as individual cutlets or a roasting joint.
Two joints are used for a Crown Roast.
Suitable to grill, fry, roast.

3 LEG JOINT
Sold as a whole leg, the fillet end or the
knuckle end. Boneless joints are also
available.
Suitable to roast.

4 NOISETTE
A boneless loin chop.

6 LEG STEAK
A relatively expensive cut but cooks quickly
and is very lean and tender. It may be
necessary to brush lightly with oil to keep it
moist when cooking.
Suitable to grill, fry, barbecue.

7 BREAST RIBLET
Excess fat should be trimmed off before
cooking.
Suitable to marinate then grill, barbecue or
          roast.
May also be sold as a boned, rolled and
stuffed joint.
Suitable to roast or braise – fat should be
          skimmed off during cooking.

8 CHUMP CHOP
Lambs' equivalent to rump steak. May be
sold with or without bone. May be more
expensive than loin chops but chump chops
are larger and meatier.
Suitable to grill, fry. barbecue or bake in
          foil parcels.

9 VALENTINE STEAK
Cut from a boneless single loin

10 KIDNEY
Suitable to grill, fry, braise, on kebabs.

11 NECK FILLET
A boneless, lean, tender cut. Good value for
stir fry or cubes.
Suitable to grill, fry, stir fry, on kebabs.

12 LIVER
Milder than ox or pigs; cheaper than calves.

13 ROLLED SHOULDER
May also be sold with the bone in. Least
expensive of the roasting joints but fattier.
Unless rolled it is difficult to carve. May be
sold ready stuffed.
Suitable to roast.

14 MINCED/GROUND
Ideal for meat loaf, burgers, meat balls,
stuffed vegetables.

15 CUBES
Usually cut from the shoulder, leg or chump.
For kebabs, marinate first to help tenderise
the meat.
Suitable to casserole, on kebabs.

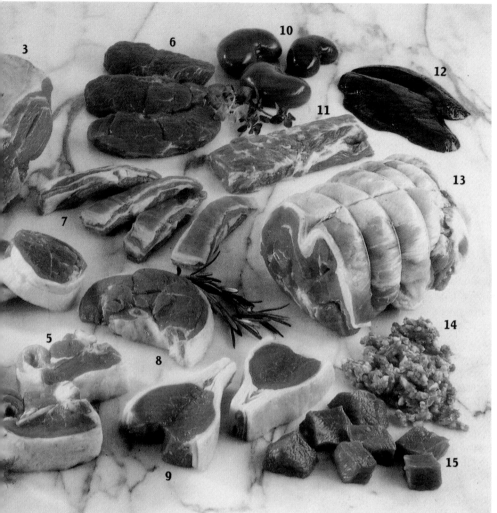

PHOTOGRAPHER ALAN NEWNHAM

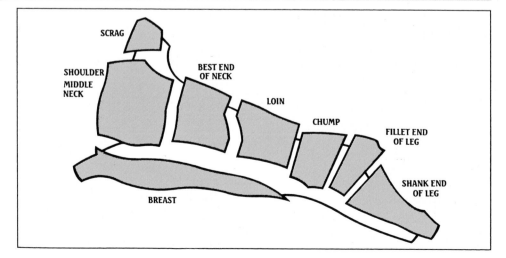

CHOOSING THE BEST CUT

1 NECK END
Sold boned and rolled as a joint or as meaty spare rib chops. As chops, not quite as lean as loin or chump, but very succulent.
Suitable as a joint to roast, pot roast.
chops to grill or cut up in pie filling.

2, 13, 15 LOIN CHOPS/JOINT
Sold with or without the bone, singly, double or as a full loin. Chops may have the kidney attached. A roasting joint and the choice for Crown Roast.
Suitable to grill, fry, barbecue, roast.

3 BELLY SLICE
Sold with or without the bone, with more fat trimmed off than traditional belly pork.
Suitable to grill, barbecue, casserole, roast.

4 CUBES
Cut from trimmed shoulder or leg. It has little natural fat so may need to marinate or brush lightly with oil if grilling or for kebabs.
Suitable to grill, casserole, on kebabs.

5 CHUMP CHOPS
Sold with or without bone.
Suitable to grill, fry, barbecue, casserole.

6 & 7 LEG/SHOULDER STEAK
Very lean, so need to brush lightly with oil or bake in foil to keep succulent.
Suitable to grill, fry, barbecue, stir fry.

8 LEG (JOINT)
Usually sold cut into two joints – prime fillet end and knuckle end.
Suitable to roast, pot roast.

9 MINCED/GROUND
Often cheaper than extra lean beef or lamb.
Suitable for burgers, meat loaf.

10 FILLET/TENDERLOIN
Very lean and tender. Best to marinate or stuff to keep moist.
Suitable to stir fry, marinate
or stuff then roast.

11 LIVER
Stronger flavour than lambs or calves.

12 ESCALOPE
Usually taken from the leg; very lean and tender, requiring minimal cooking.
Suitable to grill, fry, stir fry.

14 SPARE RIB
May be called barbecue, Chinese style or American cut ribs. Allow 3–4 ribs per person. Marinate or cook in a barbecue sauce.
Suitable to grill, barbecue, casserole, bake.

16 KIDNEY

17 SHOULDER
May be called the Hand. Boned and rolled it is a good roasting joint, also cubed for stews or minced.
Suitable to roast, stew, in burgers.

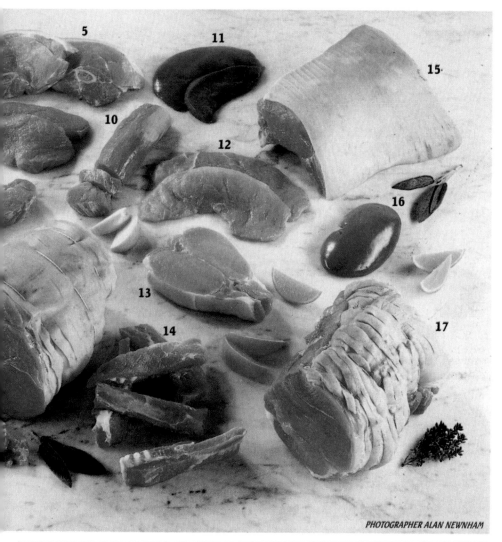

PHOTOGRAPHER ALAN NEWNHAM

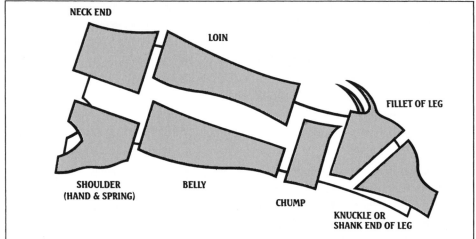

31

YOUR GUIDE TO SEAFISH

The following guide will help you to recognise the different varieties of fish offered by your fishmonger or wet fish counter in the local supermarket.
We have given guidelines on seasonality but many varieties are available all year round in frozen form .
Fish is classified into 3 main groups
White round and flat fish, Oily fish, Shellfish.

FISH	SEASON
SEA BASS	August–March
CATFISH (Rockfish)	February–July
COD	June–February
CONGER EEL	March–October
COLEY (Saithe)	August–February
HADDOCK	May–February
HAKE	June–March
HUSS (Dogfish, Flake, Rigg)	All year
JOHN DORY	All year
MONKFISH	All year
GREY MULLET	September–February
RED MULLET	May–November
SWORDFISH	All year
WHITING	June–February

To scale a fish

Some recipes call for whole fish to be scaled, but this is not necessary for a barbecue.

1 Wash fish in cold water. Working from tail to head, scrape off the scales, holding a small knife at right angles to the fish. Hold under a cold running tap, washing and scraping as you go.

2 Finish by using kitchen scissors to cut off the fins, head and tail – these can be used in stocks or sauces.

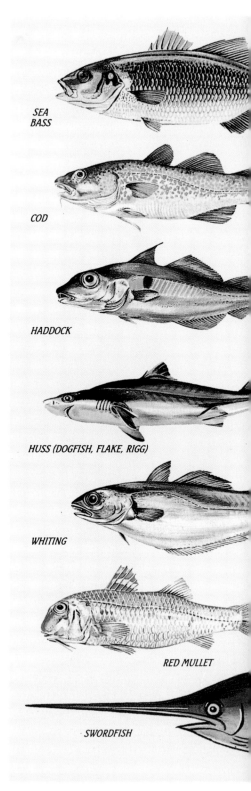

SEA BASS

COD

HADDOCK

HUSS (DOGFISH, FLAKE, RIGG)

WHITING

RED MULLET

SWORDFISH

CATFISH (ROCKFISH)

CONGER EEL

COLEY (SAITHE)

HAKE

GREY MULLET

MONKFISH

JOHN DORY

FLAT & OILY FISH

FLAT FISH	SEASON
HALIBUT	June–March
PLAICE	May–February
SKATE	May–February
LEMON SOLE	May–March
DOVER SOLE	May–February
TURBOT	April–February
WITCH	May–February
OILY FISH	SEASON
ANCHOVY	June–December
HERRING	May–December
MACKEREL	All year
SARDINE	Nov–Feb, April
SPRAT	October–March
TUNA	All year
WHITEBAIT – the fry of herring, mackerel or sprat	All year – frozen form

SKATE

WITCH

TURBOT

HERRING

Skinning fish

Skin flat fish (eg. sole) before it is filleted. A round and large flat fish such as turbot is easier to skin after filleting.

1 **To skin a flat fish:** place it dark side up and cut through the skin above the tail. Ease up skin, grip tail and firmly pull off the skin towards the head with the other hand. If fish is slippery, rub salt between your fingers.

2 **To skin fish fillets:** place fish on a board, skin side down. Cut about 1 cm (½ inch) of flesh away from the skin at the tail end, then hold down this piece of skin as you ease the flesh from the skin, holding the knife at a low angle and using short, sawing strokes.

Filleting fish

Four fillets can be cut from flat fish, such as plaice or sole.

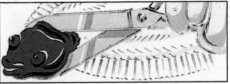

1 Place the skinned fish with its eyes facing up and the tail towards you. Cut off the head and fins with scissors.

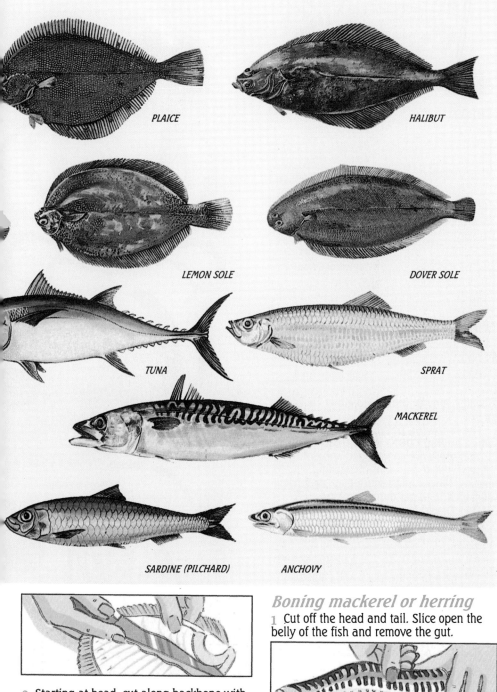

PLAICE

HALIBUT

LEMON SOLE

DOVER SOLE

TUNA

SPRAT

MACKEREL

SARDINE (PILCHARD)

ANCHOVY

2 Starting at head, cut along backbone with a sharp knife. Keeping knife close to the bone, push out from central bone with long, firm strokes, keeping the blade under the flesh and close to bone until the fillet can be lifted off. Remove all fillets.

Boning mackerel or herring

1 Cut off the head and tail. Slice open the belly of the fish and remove the gut.

2 Lay skin side up and press along the backbone with your thumb to loosen it. Turn over. Ease out the backbone with a knife.

SHELLFISH	SEASON
COCKLES	May–December
CLAMS	All year
BROWN CRAB	April–December
SPIDER CRAB	April–October
CRAWFISH	April–October
DUBLIN BAY PRAWNS	April–November
LOBSTER	April–November
MUSSEL	September–March
OCTOPUS	May–December
NATIVE OYSTER	September–April
PACIFIC OYSTER	All year
PRAWN	All year
SCALLOP	September–March
SHRIMP	February–October
SQUID (Calamari)	May–October
WHELK	February–August
WINKLE	September–April

Shellfish may be purchased either cooked or live.

The following points should be noted when buying COOKED shellfish:
1 That shells are undamaged and tightly closed without any signs of cracking – if cracked flavour and texture may have been damaged by water during cooking.
2 They should feel heavy for their size – cooked shellfish which feels light or which have soft shells may have moulted recently and will be in poor condition.
3 Freshly cooked prawns and shrimps should be firm to the touch and chilled.

If you buy LIVE shellfish make sure:
1 The fishmonger sells live shellfish from a reliable source or buy direct from a fish market or port as the catch is landed.
2 With crab or lobster, that the main claws are present.
3 The shellfish is packed and sold in moist and cool conditions and that they are reasonably lively.
4 That lobster tails spring back into place when uncurled.
5 The shells remain closed or shut rapidly when touched.

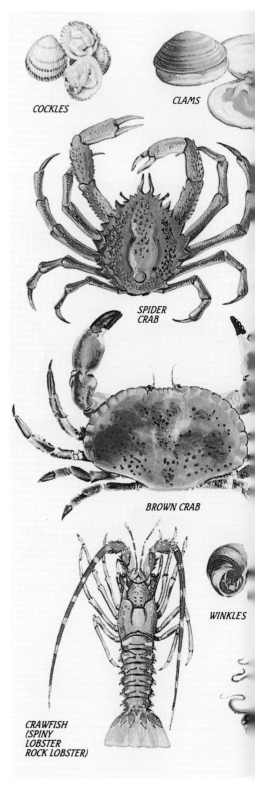

COCKLES

CLAMS

SPIDER CRAB

BROWN CRAB

WINKLES

CRAWFISH (SPINY LOBSTER ROCK LOBSTER)

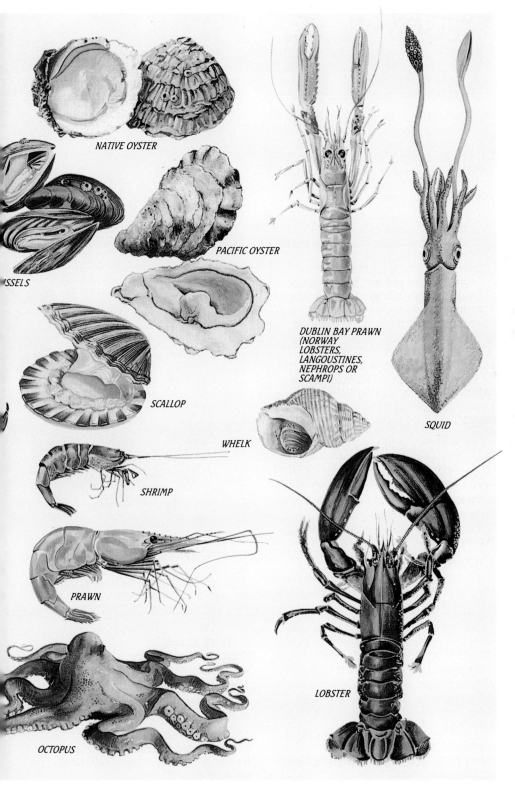

NATIVE OYSTER

PACIFIC OYSTER

MUSSELS

SCALLOP

WHELK

SHRIMP

PRAWN

OCTOPUS

DUBLIN BAY PRAWN
(NORWAY
LOBSTERS,
LANGOUSTINES,
NEPHROPS OR
SCAMPI)

SQUID

LOBSTER

PULSES

Many pulses are available in cans and so can be simply added to a dish towards the end of its cooking time or used in salads. Buying them raw is cheaper but – apart from lentils – they require several hours soaking then several hours cooking – unless you cook them in a pressure cooker.

> Red kidney, black kidney, aduki, black-eyed, and borlotti beans need pre-boiling (see page 398 in Glossary). This is particularly important for red and black kidney beans as they contain toxins in the outer skin, when raw. Boiling vigorously for 15 minutes destroys these toxins.

Soaking time depends on the length of time the beans have been stored, the older the bean the longer the soaking time. Follow soaking and cooking times suggested on the packet.

1 CHICK PEAS
Chick peas need more soaking than any other pulses. They are an essential ingredient in humus and can also be used in casseroles.

2 BROWN LENTILS
These are especially good in lentil and bacon soup, in salads or as a vegetable flavoured with bacon.

3 YELLOW SPLIT PEAS
These cook quickly and need little soaking, if any. They make excellent soups, particularly those flavoured with ham or bacon.

4 PINTO BEANS
These were the original ingredient of Mexican refried beans.

5 FLAGEOLETS
Serve as a main vegetable to accompany a roast leg of lamb. Their delicate flavour makes them a perfect ingredient in a mixed bean salad.

6 HARICOT BEANS
These can be used in casseroles, bean salads and vegetable soups.

7 ADUKI BEANS
Delicious in salads, mixed with other vegetables and due to their small size can be used in stuffings.
They are also the basis of red bean paste used in Chinese cooking.

8 MUNG BEANS
These cook well in soups and casseroles and are suitable for making into purées.

9 RED KIDNEY BEANS
These are excellent in mixed bean salads and stews such as chilli con carne.

10 BLACK-EYED BEANS
These are used in Indian cooking and add fragrance to a spicy curry. They can also be eaten mixed with rice.

11 GREEN SPLIT PEAS
These can be used in soups flavoured with ham or bacon, for pease pudding or mushy peas.

12 BLACK KIDNEY BEANS or BLACK BEANS
These are an essential ingredient of a traditional Brazilian stew and in black bean soup with ground cumin and coriander.

13 CANNELLINI BEANS
These are good all purpose beans in soups, salads and casseroles.

14 GREEN LENTILS
Use in soups, salads or as a vegetable.

15 SPLIT RED LENTILS
Use in soups, salads or as a vegetable

16 BORLOTTI BEANS
These can be used in Italian recipes, such as a pasta and bean or minestrone soup and in mixed bean salads. Mainly available canned.

17 SOYA BEANS
These beans are very dense and take longer than other pulses to cook. They have little flavour of their own and so need other flavours – garlic, spices to produce tasty dishes. They form the basis of soya milk, tofu and soya bean paste.

18 BUTTER BEANS
These are very good added to mixed bean salads or rich meaty stews.

FOOD SAFETY

Bacteria are all around us, although only a few types are harmful and cause illness. However, contaminated food which causes food poisoning quite often looks, tastes and smells perfectly normal. It is therefore important to know how to reduce the risk of food poisoning.

---

3 MAIN WAYS OF BREAKING THE FOOD POISONING CHAIN

☐ protect food from contamination.
☐ prevent bacteria in food from multiplying, this means depriving them of warmth and moisture.
☐ destroy bacteria present in the food by cooking/reheating food thoroughly.

This is where you can play your part, when shopping, storing, preparing and cooking food.

THE FOOD SAFETY ACT
For many years we have had legislation aimed at protecting the consumer from harmful food but more recently, under the Food Safety Act 1990, food safety has been extended to provide greater protection by including farms, food factories, catering establishments and shops. Food handlers in such establishments are now required by law to have hygiene training and legislation governs the temperature at which food must be kept during distribution and display. It is therefore important that this good work is not undone by the consumer.

When buying food

☐ Check the 'use by' or 'best before' date marks to ensure they are still current.

USE BY	BEST BEFORE

'USE BY' DATE
This is used on **highly perishable** foods such as prepared salads, soft mould ripened cheese, cooked meat, paté, poultry, fish and fresh meat. Eating food after this date could put your health at risk unless you have frozen or cooked it to increase its life. It is illegal to sell foods after their 'use by' date.

'BEST BEFORE' DATE
This indicates the time during which a food should remain in peak condition. It is used on foods that are not microbiologically highly perishable. If stored according to manufacturers instructions, the food should still be safe to eat after the date. However, its appearance and quality could have suffered, eg biscuits could be 'soft'.
It is not illegal to sell food after this date as long as it is considered fit for human consumption and the store makes it clear the date has expired.

'BEST BEFORE END' DATE
This is used on longer life food, eg all canned food should be marked this way after June 1992. It is an indication of quality and is not used on highly perishable food.

When shopping

☐ Do not buy food in shops where raw and cooked meats are displayed together.
☐ Beware of frozen and chilled food cabinets which are over-loaded and where the food does not feel cold.
☐ Do not buy damaged cans which have 'blown', that is where the ends are bulging.

☐ Do not buy dirty or cracked eggs. Check the date on the box. All carry a 'packing' date and may carry a 'display until' date.
☐ Make sure each piece of meat and poultry is wrapped separately so that they do not touch each other.
☐ Buy frozen and chilled food last.

Taking food home

☐ Pack frozen and chilled food together and take them home as quickly as possible, particularly in warm weather. Do not leave them in a warm car, office or carry them around for too long. If left for just 1 hour, their temperature can rise and may encourage bacteria to grow.

☐ If you cannot take food home immediately or you have a long journey home, especially during a hot summer, pack frozen and chilled foods in an insulated bag. This will keep it at the correct temperature.

> Put perishable foods in the refrigerator or freezer as soon as you get home.
> This advice is particularly important for foods such as cook/chill ready prepared meals, paté, mould ripened cheeses such as Brie, and ready washed salads which are susceptible to contamination by Listeria organisms.

Storing food safely at home

☐ Keep cupboards clean and wipe up any spillages immediately.

☐ Avoid keeping dried foods in potentially damp cupboards, such as those above a steaming kettle.

☐ Store packaged dry ingredients, such as flour, semolina, oatmeal, suet, and nuts in their original packets, in a cool, dry, airy cupboard. Once opened, transfer the packet to an airtight container, remembering to retain the date mark or noting down when the contents should be used.

☐ Use cans and packets in rotation.

☐ Store dried herbs and spices in wood, earthenware or dark-coloured glass away from the light so that they do not lose their colour or aroma.

☐ Store dried fruit in an airtight container once opened as it will shrink in warm conditions.

☐ Check flour, semolina and other cereal products for insect infestation and immediately throw away any affected foods.

☐ Store root vegetables, such as potatoes and carrots, preferably unwashed, in a cool but frost-free, dry, dark, airy place. **Do not store in polythene bags**. If they must be kept in the refrigerator, keep in a paper bag

or put in a polythene bag with absorbent kitchen paper around them to absorb moisture.

A Germometer

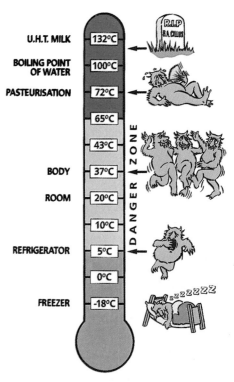

U.H.T. MILK	132°C
BOILING POINT OF WATER	100°C
PASTEURISATION	72°C
	65°C
	43°C
BODY	37°C
ROOM	20°C
	10°C
REFRIGERATOR	5°C
	0°C
FREEZER	-18°C

Refrigerator storage

☐ The best place to keep perishable foods, such as dairy products, meat, fish and cooked dishes containing these foods, is in a refrigerator.

☐ Refrigeration does not kill bacteria, but slows down their growth. Keep the refrigerator at 5°C (41°F) – buy a fridge thermometer so you can check the temperature – as bacteria multiply quickly above 5°C.

☐ Perishable foods should not be stored beyond their 'use by' date, as the chance of bacteria multiplying is increased. It is therefore sensible to buy perishable foods frequently and in realistic quantities.

☐ Perishable foods can often be frozen at home but this must be done when they are in peak condition **not** just before the expiry of the 'use by' date!

Remember

☐ Do not site the refrigerator next to a heat source such as the oven, dishwasher or central heating boiler as it will not work efficiently.

☐ Do not overload the refrigerator. This will ensure it keeps cold at all times.

☐ Defrost the refrigerator regularly unless it does this automatically. This helps it to keep cooler and use less energy.

☐ Keep the refrigerator clean and wipe up spills immediately.

☐ Do not leave the refrigerator door open as this warms the internal temperature.

☐ Do not put warm food straight into the refrigerator. You should cool it quickly (see Good Cooking Rule No 6).

☐ Cover all foods before putting in the refrigerator.

Organising your refrigerator

☐ Put cooked meat and cooked dishes at the top, which is the coldest part, under the frozen food compartment if you have one.

☐ Ensure that meat and poultry are wrapped so that they cannot contaminate other foods.

☐ Put raw foods such as meat, poultry and fish and thawed foods in a dish, cover and store on the lowest shelf. Place underneath any cooked food so that juices cannot drip on to other food and pass on bacteria.

☐ Put fruit, vegetables and salad ingredients at the bottom, preferably in the salad box.

☐ Put milk, fruit juices, butter and eggs in the door.

☐ Store raw foods separately from cooked foods to avoid cross contamination.

☐ Do not store cooked foods for longer than 2 days.

☐ Store eggs in the refrigerator.

☐ Store soft fruits and apples in the salad box of the refrigerator.

☐ Keep mushrooms in a **paper** bag and store in the salad box.

☐ Once opened, **store low sugar jams and sauces such as tomato ketchup in the refrigerator**. If jams or marmalades grow mould or ferment, throw entire contents away.

☐ Do not store opened canned foods in their can. Transfer to a container, cover and store in the refrigerator.

TOP SHELF
BACON
HAM
PATÉ

MIDDLE SHELF
PASTRY PRODUCTS
CREAM

MIDDLE SHELF
YOGURT
PASTRY PRODUCTS
DESSERTS-
WITH CREAM

BOTTOM SHELF
MEAT (Raw)
POULTRY (Raw)
FISH (Raw)

SALAD DRAWER
VEGETABLES
AND
SOFT FRUIT

TOP DOOR
EGGS, BUTTER
MARGARINE
COTTAGE CHEESE
CHEESE

INSIDE DOOR
FRUIT JUICE
Reduced Sugar JAM
MAYONNAISE
SALAD CREAM

INSIDE DOOR
MILK
MINERAL WATER
WHITE WINE

The kitchen hygiene guide

☐ **Cleanliness is the key.** Keep the kitchen clean, crumb free and dry. As well as dishes and utensils, this includes the refrigerator, microwave oven, work surfaces, small appliances including their working parts such as blades and whisks, and the floor. When washing up, use hot water and detergent, rinse under very hot water and let it drip dry. Try not to use a tea-towel as this can harbour bacteria. A dishwasher is the most hygienic method of washing as it uses very hot water and also dries the dishes.

☐ Change and wash tea-towels, towels, dishcloths, aprons and oven gloves often. Absorbent kitchen paper is a hygienic alternative for drying your hands, work surfaces, chopping boards and utensils.

☐ Hang dishcloths and tea-towels to dry after use. Bacteria multiply rapidly in damp conditions.

☐ Cover cuts and grazes.

☐ Always wash your hands with soap and hot water before preparing food and after touching raw meats and vegetables, pets, dirty washing, dirty nappies, the dustbin, a handkerchief or going to the lavatory.

☐ Wash your hands and utensils between preparing raw and cooked foods.

☐ Clean and dry the work surface and chopping board before preparing food.

☐ Use plastic polyboards in preference to wooden ones. If possible, have separate boards for raw meat, vegetables and cooked meat.

☐ Do not prepare cooked food on a board just used for raw food and vice versa.

☐ Always wash vegetables, salad ingredients and fruit before preparing them.

☐ Do not smoke in the kitchen.

☐ Do not allow pets on work surfaces and try to keep them out of the kitchen, especially when preparing food. Keep pet dishes and serving utensils separate from the family's dishes and utensils.

☐ Use rubbish bin liners and empty bins regularly. Keep dustbins outside the house away from the kitchen, children and pets.

GOOD COOKING RULES

1 Make sure meat and poultry is thawed thoroughly before cooking.

2 Make sure large joints of meat and poultry are thoroughly cooked in the centre. To ensure poultry is cooked, push a skewer into the thigh and if the juices run clear, the poultry is cooked.

3 Once thawed, do not refreeze raw food unless you have cooked it first.

4 Cooked, frozen then thawed food should not be refrozen.

5 Follow the recipe or manufacturer's instructions but always check food is piping hot throughout before serving. Ovens can vary. If the temperature in the centre of the food reaches 70°C for 2 minutes, most harmful bacteria are killed.

6 **Do not keep meals warm. Keep them piping hot or cool quickly.** If cooling large quantities, for example a casserole, stand the container in cold water, stir the food occasionally and change the water frequently. Steam should be allowed to escape during cooling, so place a paper towel over the container if there is the likelihood of insect or fly contamination. Once cool, cover and store in the refrigerator or freezer for serving later.

7 Do not reheat cooked dishes, whether prepared at home or purchased, more than once. Heat them until piping hot.

8 If making recipes such as mayonnaise or ice cream, in which eggs are not thoroughly cooked, ensure you have stored the eggs in the refrigerator and they are within their 'use by' date. **'At risk' groups such as pregnant women, babies, elderly sick individuals are advised not to eat lightly cooked eggs/egg dishes.**

SOUPS AND STARTERS

AVOCADO DIP PAGE 55 · CARROT & MINT SOUP PAGE 47
LEEK & SWEETCORN SOUP PAGE 46 · STUFFED TOMATOES PAGE 62

SOUPS

CREAM OF POTATO SOUP ⓕ

Preparation 15 mins **Cooking** 35 mins *Serves 4*

450 g (1 lb) potatoes, diced
1 large onion, thinly sliced
2 medium celery sticks, sliced
25 g (1 oz) butter
450 ml (¾ pint) water
salt and freshly ground pepper
300 ml (½ pint) fresh milk
45 ml (3 tbsp) fresh double cream (optional)
30 ml (2 tbsp) chopped parsley

1. In a saucepan fry vegetables gently in butter for 10 minutes without browning.
To microwave: Cook vegetables and butter covered for 5 minutes.
2. Add water and season to taste.
To microwave: Add BOILING water and season to taste.
3. Bring to the boil, cover and simmer gently for 25 minutes.
To microwave: Cover and cook for 15 minutes, stirring once or twice, until vegetables are tender.
4. Liquidise or rub through a sieve, return to pan and stir in milk.
5. Bring to the boil, stirring, and simmer for 5 minutes.
To microwave: Cook for 5–10 minutes covered until boiling, stirring once or twice.
6. Ladle into warm soup bowls. Whirl on fresh cream if used and sprinkle with parsley.

Variations

CREAM OF CAULIFLOWER SOUP ⓕ

Follow recipe and method for cream of potato soup (above). Use 450 g (1 lb) cauliflower (divided into small florets) instead of potatoes. Add a large pinch of nutmeg with seasoning.

CREAM OF CELERY SOUP ⓕ

Follow recipe and method for cream of potato soup (left). Use a large head of celery, sliced, instead of potatoes. Stir in 45 ml (3 tbsp) fresh double cream just before serving.

CREAM OF LENTIL SOUP ⓕ

Preparation 15 mins
Cooking 1 hr 10 mins *Serves 4*

1 large carrot, thinly sliced
1 large onion, thinly sliced
1 celery stick, thinly sliced
½ small turnip, finely diced
1 medium potato, finely diced
40 g (1½ oz) butter
100 g (4 oz) split red lentils
handful of parsley
568 ml (1 pint) fresh milk
300 ml (½ pint) chicken stock or water
pinch of ground nutmeg
salt and freshly ground pepper
150 ml (5 fl oz) fresh single cream
15 ml (1 tbsp) chopped parsley to garnish

1. In a saucepan fry vegetables gently in butter for 7–10 minutes.
To microwave: Cook vegetables and butter covered for 5 minutes.
2. Add lentils, parsley, milk and stock or water.
To microwave: Add lentils, 300 ml (½ pint) milk and BOILING stock or water.
3. Bring to the boil, lower heat, cover and simmer gently for 1 hour.
To microwave: Cover and cook for 20 minutes until lentils are cooked, stirring once or twice. Add remaining milk.
4. Liquidise or rub through a sieve and return to pan. Add nutmeg and season to taste.
5. Reheat gently. Stir in cream just before serving. Ladle into warm soup bowls and sprinkle each with parsley.

CREAMY CARROT SOUP Ⓕ

Preparation 20 mins **Cooking** 40 mins   *Serves 4*

25 g (1 oz) butter
225 g (8 oz) carrots, grated
1 large potato, grated
1 medium onion, grated
568 ml (1 pint) water
568 ml (1 pint) fresh milk
25 g (1 oz) rice
large pinch of ground nutmeg
salt and freshly ground pepper
10 ml (2 tsp) lemon juice
45 ml (3 tbsp) fresh single cream

1. Melt butter and fry vegetables gently for
5 minutes without browning.
*To microwave: Cook butter and vegetables
covered for 5 minutes.*

2. Add water, milk, rice, nutmeg and
seasoning.
*To microwave: Stir in BOILING water, milk,
rice, nutmeg and seasoning.*

3. Bring to the boil, cover and simmer gently
for 30 minutes or until rice is cooked.
*To microwave: Cover and cook for 8 minutes
or until boiling, then simmer on MEDIUM
(50%) for 15 minutes, stirring once or twice,
until rice is cooked.*

4. Stir in lemon juice and cream.

5. To serve, reheat without boiling.

FRENCH ONION SOUP Ⓕ

Preparation 15 mins **Cooking** 1 hr   *Serves 4*

350 g (12 oz) onions, thinly sliced
40 g (1½ oz) butter
900 ml (1½ pint) beef stock
salt and freshly ground pepper
10 ml (2 tsp) dry sherry (optional)
4 slices French bread,
  each 2.5 cm (1 inch) thick
50 g (2 oz) English Cheddar, grated

1. In a saucepan fry onions gently in butter
until golden.
*To microwave: Cook onions and butter
covered for 5 minutes, stirring once.*

2. Pour on stock.
To microwave: Pour on BOILING stock.

3. Season to taste.

4. Bring to the boil, lower heat, cover and
simmer for 45 minutes.
*To microwave: Cover and cook for
15–20 minutes.*

5. Add sherry. Pour into a flameproof dish,
float bread on top and sprinkle with cheese.

6. Brown under a hot grill and serve.

LEEK & SWEETCORN SOUP

Preparation 20 mins **Cooking** 25 mins   *Serves 4*

25 g (1 oz) butter
450 g (1 lb) leeks, sliced
1 medium onion, sliced
2 celery sticks, sliced
198 g (7 oz) can sweetcorn, drained
450 ml (¾ pint) vegetable stock
25 g (1 oz) cornflour
450 ml (¾ pint) fresh milk
50 g (2 oz) Sage Derby cheese, grated

1. Melt butter and fry leeks, onion and celery
until soft.
*To microwave: Cook butter, leeks, onion and
celery covered for 5 minutes until soft.*

2. Add sweetcorn and stock, bring to the
boil, cover and simmer for 10–15 minutes.
*To microwave: Add sweetcorn and BOILING
stock, cover and cook for 15 minutes, stirring
once.*

3. Blend cornflour with milk, add to soup
and stir until thickened.

4. Simmer for 5 minutes.
To microwave: Cover and cook for 5 minutes.

5. Remove from heat and stir in half of the
cheese.

6. Serve topped with remaining cheese.

CHICKEN & CORN SOUP

Preparation 10 mins **Cooking** 30 mins   *Serves 4*

1 bunch spring onions, sliced
15 g (½ oz) butter
400 g (14 oz) can creamed sweetcorn
100 g (4 oz) frozen sweetcorn
175 g (6 oz) cooked chicken meat, shredded
750 ml (1¼ pint) chicken stock
1 egg, beaten
prawn crackers to serve

1. Fry spring onions in butter for 30 seconds.
To microwave: Cook butter and spring onions covered for 1 minute.

2. Add creamed and frozen sweetcorn, chicken and stock.
To microwave: Add creamed and frozen sweetcorn, chicken and BOILING stock.

3. Bring to the boil, cover and simmer for 5 minutes.
To microwave: Cover and cook for 10 minutes, stirring once.

4. Bring almost to the boil, add beaten egg slowly, while gently stirring soup, to form egg threads.
To microwave: Bring just to the boil, then stir in beaten egg slowly to form egg threads.

5. Cook until egg has set – do not boil.
To microwave: Allow to stand for a minute or two.

6. Serve immediately with prawn crackers.

CARROT & MINT SOUP Ⓕ

Preparation 15 mins **Cooking** 25 mins   *Serves 4*

25 g (1 oz) butter
700 g (1½ lb) carrots, sliced
1 medium onion, chopped
568 ml (1 pint) vegetable stock
568 ml (1 pint) fresh milk
30 ml (2 tbsp) chopped fresh mint
few drops of Worcestershire sauce
salt and freshly ground pepper
natural yogurt and fresh mint to garnish

1. Melt butter, add carrots and onion and cook for 5 minutes.
To microwave: Cook butter, carrots and onion covered for 5 minutes.

2. Add stock and milk, cover and simmer gently for 15–20 minutes until vegetables are soft.
To microwave: Stir in BOILING stock, cover and cook for 15 minutes, stirring once or twice, until vegetables are soft. Add milk.

3. Purée until smooth. Add chopped mint, Worcestershire sauce and seasoning.

4. Serve hot or well chilled, garnished with natural yogurt and fresh mint.

CHICKEN & CORN SOUP

COURGETTE & CUMIN SOUP

Preparation 15 mins **Cooking** 25 mins *Serves 4*

25 g (1 oz) butter
1 onion, chopped
1 garlic clove, crushed
10 ml (2 tsp) ground cumin
150 g (5 oz) potatoes, cubed
350 g (12 oz) courgettes, thickly sliced
450 ml (¾ pint) chicken stock
300 ml (½ pint) fresh milk
freshly ground pepper
thinly sliced courgettes to garnish

1. Melt butter and fry onion and garlic for 5 minutes until soft.
To microwave: Cook butter, onion and garlic covered for 3 minutes until soft.

2. Add cumin. Stir in potatoes and courgettes.

3. Cook gently for 2 minutes.
To microwave: Cover and cook for 2 minutes.

4. Add stock, milk and pepper, bring to the boil.
To microwave: Add BOILING stock, milk and pepper.

5. Cover and simmer for 15 minutes until vegetables are soft.
To microwave: Cover and cook for 15 minutes, stirring once.

6. Purée the soup.

7. Serve hot or cold, garnished with sliced courgettes.

WATERCRESS SOUP

Preparation 10 mins **Cooking** 20 mins *Serves 4*

2 bunches watercress (about 225 g (8 oz))
1 medium onion, chopped
1 medium potato, diced
25 g (1 oz) butter
450 ml (¾ pint) fresh milk
300 ml (½ pint) chicken stock
salt and freshly ground pepper
60 ml (4 tbsp) fresh double cream (optional)

WATERCRESS SOUP

1. Shred watercress, reserving some sprigs for garnish.

2. In a saucepan fry vegetables gently in butter for 5 minutes without browning.
To microwave: Cook vegetables covered for 5 minutes.

3. Add milk and stock. Bring to the boil, stirring continuously, cover and simmer for 10–15 minutes.
To microwave: Add BOILING stock only, cover and cook for 10 minutes, stirring once or twice. Add milk.

4. Liquidise or rub through a sieve and return to pan.

5. Season to taste and reheat.
To microwave: Season to taste and cook for about 5 minutes or until reheated.

6. Ladle into warm soup bowls, whirl on a tablespoon of cream if used, and garnish with watercress.

Variation
LETTUCE SOUP   F

Follow recipe and method for watercress soup (left). Use 1 large lettuce (shredded) instead of watercress.

MINESTRONE SOUP   F

Preparation 15 mins
Cooking 1 hr 25 mins   *Serves 4*

1 medium leek, sliced
1 large onion, thinly sliced
1 medium carrot, sliced
2 large celery sticks, sliced
175 g (6 oz) white or green cabbage, shredded
225 g (8 oz) frozen green beans
400 g (14 oz) can tomatoes
50 g (2 oz) haricot beans, soaked overnight
30 ml (2 tbsp) chopped parsley
5 ml (1 tsp) dried basil
salt and freshly ground pepper
5 ml (1 tsp) sugar
900 ml (1½ pint) stock
50 g (2 oz) macaroni
75 g (3 oz) English Cheddar, grated

1. Put vegetables in a large pan with drained haricot beans, herbs, seasoning, sugar and stock.
To microwave: Put vegetables in a large dish with drained haricot beans, herbs, seasoning, sugar and BOILING stock.

2. Bring to the boil and boil rapidly for 10 minutes.
To microwave: Cover and cook for 30 minutes, stirring two or three times.

3. Lower heat, cover and simmer for 1 hour.
To microwave: Cover, cook on MEDIUM (50%) for 20–30 minutes, stirring once or twice.

4. Add macaroni and simmer for 10 minutes or until cooked.
To microwave: Add macaroni, cover and cook for 10 minutes or until cooked.

5. Ladle into warm soup bowls and sprinkle each thickly with cheese.

VEGETABLE BROTH   F

Preparation 15 mins
Cooking 1 hr 40 mins   *Serves 4*

25 g (1 oz) butter
1 medium carrot, diced
1 small parsnip, diced
½ small turnip, diced
1 medium onion, chopped
2 large celery sticks, chopped
1 large leek, finely sliced
900 ml (1½ pint) vegetable stock
30 ml (2 tbsp) pearl barley
salt and freshly ground pepper
15 ml (1 tbsp) chopped parsley

1. Melt butter in a saucepan. Add vegetables, cover and fry gently for 7 minutes without browning.
To microwave: Cook butter and vegetables covered for 5 minutes, stirring once.

2. Pour in stock, add barley and season to taste. Bring to the boil.
To microwave: Pour in BOILING stock, add barley and season to taste. Cook covered for 5 minutes or until boiling.

3. Lower heat, cover and simmer gently for 1½ hours.
To microwave: Cover and cook on MEDIUM (50%) for 30–40 minutes.

4. Ladle into warm soup bowls and sprinkle each with parsley.

TOMATO SOUP ⒡

Preparation 5 mins **Cooking** 25 mins   *Serves 4*

1 onion, finely chopped
3 medium celery sticks and leaves,
    finely chopped
25 g (1 oz) butter
1 litre (1¾ pint) tomato juice
1 bay leaf
3 cloves
2.5 ml (½ tsp) dried basil
15 ml (1 tbsp) chopped parsley
15 ml (1 tbsp) lemon juice
salt and freshly ground pepper

1. In a saucepan fry onion and celery in
butter for 7 minutes without browning.
*To microwave: Cook onion, celery and butter
covered for 5 minutes.*

2. Pour in tomato juice and add bay leaf,
cloves, basil and parsley.

3. Bring to the boil, lower heat, cover and
simmer gently for 15 minutes.
*To microwave: Cover and cook for
10 minutes, stirring once or twice.*

4. Remove and discard bay leaf and cloves.
Add lemon juice and season to taste.

5. Reheat for 1 or 2 minutes if necessary.

CHEESE & VEGETABLE SOUP

Preparation 15 mins **Cooking** 40 mins   *Serves 4*

4 medium carrots, finely diced
2 medium onions, finely chopped
2 celery sticks, finely chopped
450 ml (¾ pint) water
25 g (1 oz) flour
300 ml (½ pint) fresh milk
100 g (4 oz) English Cheddar, grated
25 g (1 oz) butter
salt and freshly ground pepper

1. Put vegetables into a saucepan with
300 ml (½ pint) water. Bring to the boil, cover
and simmer for 20–30 minutes or until
vegetables are tender.
*To microwave: Cook vegetables with
300 ml (½ pint) BOILING water for
15–20 minutes until vegetables are
tender, stirring once or twice.*

2. Pour in remaining water.

3. Blend flour to a smooth paste with milk
and add to vegetables.

4. Cook, stirring, until soup boils, then
simmer for 5 minutes.
*To microwave: Cook uncovered for 5 minutes
or until soup thickens, stirring once or twice.*

5. Remove from heat, add 75g (3oz) cheese and butter. Stir until both have melted.

6. Season to taste and ladle into warm soup bowls. Sprinkle with remaining cheese.

MULLIGATAWNY SOUP Ⓔ

Preparation 25 mins **Cooking** 55 mins *Serves 4*

1 large onion, thinly sliced
1 small carrot, finely diced
1 large celery stick, finely chopped
50g (2oz) butter
25g (1oz) flour
10ml (2tsp) curry powder
900ml (1½ pint) stock or water
1 large cooking apple, peeled, cored, and diced
10ml (2tsp) lemon juice
25g (1oz) cooked rice
  (about 15g (½oz) uncooked)
25g (1oz) cooked chicken meat, finely chopped
salt and freshly ground pepper
60ml (4tbsp) fresh single cream, to serve

1. In a saucepan fry vegetables gently in butter for 7 mins. Do not allow to brown.
To microwave: Cook vegetables and butter, covered for 5 mins, stirring once.

2. Stir in flour and curry powder. Cook for 2 mins then blend in stock or water.
To microwave: Stir in flour and curry powder and cook uncovered for 2 mins. Gradually blend in BOILING stock or water.

3. Cook stirring, until soup comes to the boil and thickens slightly. Lower heat and cover pan.
To microwave: Cook for 5 mins, or until soup boils and thickens slightly. Stir well.

4. Simmer very slowly for 30 mins, stirring occasionally.
To microwave: Cover and cook for 10 mins, stirring once.

5. Add apple, lemon juice, rice and chicken to soup. Season to taste.

6. Simmer for a further 15 mins.
To microwave: Cover and cook for 10 mins.

7. Remove from heat.

8. Ladle into 4 warm soup bowls.

9. Whirl on fresh cream to serve.

CHICKEN SOUP Ⓔ

Preparation 10 mins **Cooking** 35 mins *Serves 4*

1 chicken carcass
1 medium onion, chopped
1 bay leaf
1 clove
900ml (1½ pint) fresh milk
1 chicken stock cube
60ml (4tbsp) boiling water
15ml (1tbsp) cornflour
60ml (4tbsp) cold water
1.25ml (¼tsp) ground nutmeg
100g (4oz) cooked chicken meat, chopped
salt and freshly ground pepper
25g (1oz) toasted, flaked almonds to garnish

1. Break up carcass and put into a saucepan.
To microwave: Break up carcass and put into a large dish.

2. Add onion, bay leaf, clove, milk and stock cube dissolved in BOILING water.

3. Simmer gently for 20 minutes.
To microwave: Cook uncovered for 10 minutes. Allow to stand for 3 minutes.

4. Strain and return liquid to pan. Blend cornflour to a smooth paste with cold water and add to soup.

5. Cook, stirring, until soup boils and thickens slightly.
To microwave: Cook for 5 minutes, stirring frequently.

6. Add nutmeg and chicken. Season to taste.

7. Cover and simmer for 15 minutes.
To microwave: Cover and cook for 5 minutes.

8. Ladle into warm soup bowls and sprinkle each with almonds.

Variation

TURKEY SOUP Ⓔ

Follow recipe and method for chicken soup (above). Use a turkey carcass and cooked turkey meat in place of chicken.

Spicy Lentil Soup ⓕ

Preparation 15 mins **Cooking** 20 mins *Serves 4*

15 g (½ oz) butter
1 onion, chopped
1 garlic clove, crushed
5 ml (1 tsp) ground ginger
10 ml (2 tsp) ground cumin
1 green pepper, seeded and chopped
1 red pepper, seeded and chopped
1 bay leaf
175 g (6 oz) split red lentils
568 ml (1 pint) vegetable stock
450 ml (¾ pint) fresh milk
fresh coriander to garnish

1. Melt butter in a non-stick pan, add onion and cook until soft. Add garlic and spices and fry for 1 minute, stirring.
To microwave: Cook butter, onion, garlic and spices covered for 3 minutes.

2. Stir in peppers, bay leaf, lentils and stock.
To microwave: Stir in peppers, bay leaf, lentils and BOILING stock.

3. Bring to the boil, cover and simmer for 15 minutes or until lentils are cooked.
To microwave: Cover and cook for 15–20 minutes, stirring once or twice, until lentils are cooked.

4. Remove and discard bay leaf. Stir in milk and reheat without boiling.

5. Garnish with a sprig of coriander.

Blue Cheese & Leek Soup

Preparation 20 mins **Cooking** 30 mins *Serves 4*

25 g (1 oz) butter
1 onion, chopped
175 g (6 oz) leeks, sliced
25 g (1 oz) flour
450 ml (¾ pint) chicken stock
1 bouquet garni
450 ml (¾ pint) fresh milk
100 g (4 oz) Blue Cheshire cheese, crumbled
freshly ground pepper
75 ml (3 oz) natural yogurt

1. Melt butter in a saucepan. Add onion and leeks and fry for 5 minutes until soft.
To microwave: Cook butter, onion and leeks, covered for 5 minutes.

2. Stir in flour and stock then heat, whisking continuously, until soup thickens.
To microwave: Stir in flour then gradually blend in BOILING stock.

3. Add bouquet garni and simmer over a low heat for 20 minutes.
To microwave: Add bouquet garni, cover and cook for 5 minutes, then stir well.

4. Cool slightly, remove bouquet garni and liquidise soup. Return to pan or dish.

5. Add milk and heat until almost boiling.
To microwave: Add milk, cover and cook for 3–5 minutes, stirring once, until almost boiling.

6. Remove from heat. Add cheese, pepper and yogurt and stir until cheese has melted.

7. Serve hot or chilled.

Sweetcorn Soup ⓕ

Preparation 20 mins **Cooking** 30 mins *Serves 4*

1 rasher streaky bacon, chopped
1 medium onion, finely chopped
25 g (1 oz) butter
2 large potatoes, sliced
2 celery sticks, sliced
300 ml (½ pint) chicken stock
salt and freshly ground pepper
198 g (7 oz) can sweetcorn, drained
50 g (2 oz) peeled prawns (optional)
15 ml (1 tbsp) cornflour
568 ml (1 pint) fresh milk
croûtons to serve

1. Fry bacon and onion in butter until soft.
To microwave: Cook bacon, onion and butter covered for 3 minutes.

2. Add potatoes, celery, stock and seasoning and simmer for 15–20 minutes until vegetables are soft.
To microwave: Stir in potatoes, celery, BOILING stock and seasoning. Cover and cook for 10–15 minutes, stirring once or twice, until vegetables are soft.

3. Add sweetcorn and prawns, if used. Blend cornflour with milk and add to soup.

PRAWN & CORN CHOWDER

4. Bring to the boil and simmer for 5 minutes.
To microwave: Cover and cook for 5 minutes.

5. Sieve or purée the soup.

6. Serve with croûtons.

Variation

MIXED VEGETABLE SOUP ⑤

Follow recipe and method for sweetcorn soup
(left). Omit sweetcorn and prawns, add
225g (8oz) frozen mixed vegetables at step 3.
Do not sieve or liquidise before serving.

PRAWN & CORN CHOWDER

Preparation 10 mins **Cooking** 20 mins   *Serves 4*

1 large onion, finely chopped
15g (½oz) butter
450g (1 lb) potatoes, diced
300ml (½pint) stock
salt and freshly ground pepper
175g (6oz) peeled prawns
198g (7oz) can sweetcorn, drained
568ml (1pint) fresh milk
75g (3oz) English Cheddar, grated

1. Fry onion in butter until soft but not
coloured.
*To microwave: Cook onion and butter
covered for 3 minutes.*

2. Add potatoes, stock and season to taste.
*To microwave: Add potatoes and BOILING
stock.*

3. Bring to the boil, cover and simmer gently
for 10–15 minutes, or until potatoes are just
cooked.
*To microwave: Cover and cook for
10 minutes or until potatoes are just cooked.
Season to taste.*

4. Add prawns, sweetcorn and milk.

5. Reheat, remove from heat and stir in
cheese.
*To microwave: Cook for 3–5 minutes to
reheat, then stir in cheese.*

6. Serve immediately.

ICED CUCUMBER & YOGURT SOUP

Preparation 10 mins **plus chilling** *Serves 4–6*

1 large unpeeled cucumber
275 g (10 oz) natural yogurt
½ small green pepper,
    seeded and finely diced
1 garlic clove, crushed
30 ml (2 tbsp) wine vinegar
15 ml (1 tbsp) chopped chives
salt and freshly ground pepper
300 ml (½ pint) fresh milk, chilled
30 ml (2 tbsp) chopped parsley to garnish

1. Grate cucumber on a medium grater. Transfer to a bowl and stir in yogurt, green pepper, garlic, vinegar and chives.

2. Season to taste. Chill thoroughly.

3. Just before serving stir in milk. Ladle into soup bowls and sprinkle each with chopped parsley.

VICHYSSOISE SOUP Ⓕ

Preparation 15 mins
Cooking 30 mins **plus chilling** *Serves 4–6*

2 medium leeks, chopped
1 small onion, chopped
25 g (1 oz) butter
350 g (12 oz) potatoes, thinly sliced
568 ml (1 pint) chicken stock
salt and freshly ground pepper
1 blade of mace
150 ml (5 fl oz) fresh double cream
30 ml (2 tbsp) chopped chives or finely
    chopped watercress to garnish

1. In a saucepan fry leeks and onion gently in butter for 7–10 mins without browning.
To microwave: Cook leeks, onion and butter covered for 5 mins.

2. Add potatoes, stock, seasoning and mace.
To microwave: Add potatoes, BOILING stock, seasoning and mace.

3. Bring to the boil, lower heat, cover and simmer gently for 20–30 mins or until vegetables are tender.
To microwave: Cover and cook for 10 mins, stirring once or twice, until vegetables are tender.

4. Remove and discard mace. Liquidise or rub soup through a fine sieve. Chill thoroughly.

5. Just before serving, stir in cream. Pour into soup bowls and sprinkle each with chives or watercress.

Variation

LEEK & POTATO SOUP Ⓕ

Follow recipe and method for vichyssoise soup (left) but serve hot not cold.

CHUNKY FISH SOUP

Preparation 30 mins **Cooking** 20 mins *Serves 4*

25 g (1 oz) butter
1 large onion, chopped
2 garlic cloves, crushed
2 medium leeks, sliced
450 ml (¾ pint) fish stock
397 g (14 oz) can chopped tomatoes
1 bay leaf
1 bouquet garni
350 g (12 oz) assorted fish fillets,
    skinned and cut into bite-size pieces
100 g (4 oz) peeled prawns
salt and freshly ground pepper
4 slices French bread, toasted

1. Melt butter in a large saucepan and fry onion, garlic and leeks for 5 mins.
To microwave: Cook butter, onion, garlic and leeks, covered, for 5 mins.

2. Add stock, tomatoes, bay leaf and bouquet garni. Bring to the boil and cook for 10 mins.
To microwave: Add BOILING stock, tomatoes, bay leaf and bouquet garni. Cover and cook for 6 mins.

3. Add fish, bring back to the boil and simmer for 5 mins.
To microwave: Add fish, cover and cook for 5 mins.

4. Stir in prawns and cook for 2 mins.
To microwave: Stir in prawns, cover and cook for 2 mins.

5. Remove bay leaf and bouquet garni. Season to taste.

6. To serve, place bread in base of soup bowls and cover with soup.

STARTERS

ONION DIP

Preparation 10 mins **plus chilling**   *Serves 4*

½ packet of onion soup mix
150 g (5 oz) natural yogurt
150 ml (5 fl oz) fresh double cream
chopped parsley to garnish
vegetable sticks to serve

1. Blend onion soup mix with a little yogurt to make a smooth paste.
2. Add remaining yogurt and cream, stir to mix.
3. Whisk until thick and creamy.
4. Transfer to a serving bowl and chill for 2–3 hours.
5. Sprinkle with parsley before serving with vegetable sticks.

AVOCADO DIP

Preparation 15 mins   *Serves 6*

1 ripe avocado
lemon juice
225 g (8 oz) curd cheese
freshly ground pepper
2 garlic cloves, crushed
10 drops hot pepper sauce
15 ml (1 tbsp) fresh lime or lemon juice
vegetable sticks and whole baby
    sweetcorn to serve

1. Peel avocado, discard stone. Reserve and dip in lemon juice two slices of the flesh.
2. Mash remaining flesh with curd cheese until smooth.
3. Season to taste and stir in garlic, pepper sauce and lime juice.
4. Cover and refrigerate if not serving immediately.
5. Garnish with avocado slices and serve with vegetable sticks and whole baby sweetcorn.

BLUE CHEESE & POPPY DIP

Preparation 10 mins   *Serves 4–6*

150 g (5 oz) Blue Stilton cheese, crumbled
175 g (6 oz) cottage cheese
150 ml (5 fl oz) fresh soured cream
30 ml (2 tbsp) mayonnaise
15 ml (1 tbsp) poppy seeds
vegetable sticks and crisp biscuits to serve

1. Mix all ingredients together. Spoon into a serving dish.
2. Garnish with a few extra poppy seeds.
3. Serve with sticks of vegetables and crisp biscuits.

CURRIED CREAM CHEESE DIP

Preparation 10 mins   *Serves 4–6*

225 g (8 oz) cream cheese
60 ml (4 tbsp) mayonnaise
150 g (5 oz) natural yogurt
20 ml (4 tsp) curry powder
10 ml (2 tsp) finely grated onion
salt and freshly ground pepper
fresh coriander leaves to garnish
vegetable sticks to serve

1. Beat cheese until smooth with mayonnaise and natural yogurt.
2. Stir in curry powder and onion. Season to. taste.
3. Spoon into a serving bowl.
4. Garnish with fresh coriander leaves.
5. Serve with vegetable sticks.

STUFFED MUSHROOMS Ⓕ

Preparation 25 mins **Cooking** 12 mins *Serves 4*

8 medium open mushrooms
100 g (4 oz) garlic butter
8 spring onions, chopped
½ red pepper, seeded and finely chopped
100 g (4 oz) can sweetcorn, drained
175 g (6 oz) fresh breadcrumbs
100 g (4 oz) English Cheddar, grated
fresh parsley to garnish

1. Remove stalks from mushrooms. Reserve caps and chop stalks.

2. Melt 50 g (2 oz) garlic butter in a non-stick saucepan and fry chopped mushrooms, onions and pepper until soft.
To microwave: Melt 50 g (2 oz) garlic butter for 45 seconds and stir in mushrooms, onions and pepper. Cover and cook for 3 minutes.

3. Remove from heat and stir in sweetcorn, breadcrumbs and half the cheese. Mix well.

4. Spread remaining butter over rounded sides of reserved mushroom caps.

5. Put butter side down, in ovenproof dish.

6. Spoon filling into mushrooms and sprinkle with remaining cheese.

7. Bake at 180°C (350°F) Mark 4 for 20–25 minutes.
To microwave: Cook uncovered for 5–6 minutes. If liked brown under a hot grill before serving.

8. Serve hot, garnished with parsley.

MUSHROOM RAMEKINS

Preparation 30 mins **Cooking** 25 mins *Serves 4*

15 g (½ oz) butter
1 small onion, finely chopped
225 g (8 oz) button mushrooms, sliced
1 egg, beaten
60 ml (4 tbsp) fresh single cream
30 ml (2 tbsp) natural yogurt
2.5 ml (½ tsp) dried thyme
100 g (4 oz) Blue Cheshire cheese, crumbled
25 g (1 oz) fresh wholemeal breadcrumbs, toasted
parsley and slices of mushroom to garnish

1. Melt butter in a saucepan and lightly cook onion and mushrooms.
To microwave: Cook butter, onion and mushrooms covered for about 5 minutes, stirring once.

STUFFED MUSHROOMS

2. Beat together egg, cream, yogurt and thyme.

3. Divide vegetables and cheese between 4 ramekin dishes. Pour egg mixture over.

4. Place dishes in a baking tin containing enough hot water to come halfway up sides of dishes.
To microwave: Stand ramekin dishes in a circle on a low microwave rack in microwave.

5. Bake at 180°C (350°F) Mark 4 for 20 minutes or until set.
To microwave: Cook on DEFROST (30%) for 10 minutes or until set.

6. Sprinkle over breadcrumbs and garnish.

MUSHROOM & STILTON MOUSSES

Preparation 45 mins **Cooking** 2 mins   *Serves 6*

175 g (6 oz) button mushrooms, chopped
175 g (6 oz) Blue Stilton cheese, crumbled
90 ml (6 tbsp) mayonnaise
150 g (5 oz) natural yogurt
30 ml (2 tbsp) chopped parsley
1.25 ml (¼ tsp) cayenne pepper
15 g (½ oz) gelatine
salt and freshly ground pepper
2 egg whites
mushrooms and watercress to garnish

1. Mix mushrooms, cheese, mayonnaise, yogurt, parsley and cayenne pepper together in a bowl.

2. Place 45 ml (3 tbsp) of cold water in a small bowl and sprinkle in gelatine. Leave to stand for 10 minutes.

3. Stand bowl over a pan of hot water and gently heat until dissolved. Leave to cool.

4. Fold gelatine into mushroom and cheese mixture and season to taste.

5. Whisk egg whites until stiff and fold into mushroom mixture.

6. Spoon into 6 ramekin dishes and chill.

7. Garnish with mushroom and watercress.

SALMON MOUSSE

Preparation 20 mins **Cooking** 2 mins   *Serves 6*

1 sachet gelatine
45 ml (3 tbsp) water
198 g (7 oz) can red salmon, drained
2 eggs, hard-boiled, shelled and chopped
5 spring onions, finely chopped
275 g (10 oz) mayonnaise
salt and freshly ground pepper
150 ml (5 fl oz) fresh double cream,
    softly whipped
sliced cucumber and lemon to garnish

1. Sprinkle gelatine over water in a small bowl.

2. Leave to stand for 10 minutes.

3. Dissolve gelatine over hot water and cool slightly.

4. Remove and discard skin and bones from salmon. Flake remainder.

5. Combine salmon, eggs, onions and mayonnaise. Season to taste.

6. Stir gelatine into salmon mixture.

7. Fold in cream. Spoon into 6 small dishes.

8. Chill until set.

9. Serve garnished with cucumber & lemon.

PRAWN COCKTAIL

Preparation 15 mins   *Serves 4*

½ round lettuce, washed and dried
30 ml (2 tbsp) mayonnaise
60 ml (4 tbsp) natural yogurt
45 ml (3 tbsp) tomato ketchup
10 ml (2 tsp) Worcestershire sauce
10 ml (2 tsp) creamed horseradish
30 ml (2 tbsp) lemon juice
225 g (8 oz) peeled prawns
brown bread and butter to serve

1. Shred lettuce and use to half-fill 4 large wine glasses. Leave on one side.

2. Combine mayonnaise with natural yogurt, ketchup, Worcestershire sauce, horseradish and lemon juice.

3. Add prawns and mix well. Chill lightly.

4. Spoon equal amounts into glasses. Serve with brown bread and butter.

QUICK LIVER PÂTÉ 🄵

Preparation 15 mins
Cooking 10 mins   *Serves 4–6*

450g (1lb) chicken livers
25g (1oz) butter
1 medium onion, finely chopped
2 garlic cloves, crushed
10 drops hot pepper sauce
1.25 ml (¼ tsp) ground bay leaves
2.5 ml (½ tsp) tomato purée
60 ml (4 tbsp) natural yogurt
100g (4oz) curd cheese
30 ml (2 tbsp) sherry
sprigs of parsley to garnish
vegetable sticks and toast to serve

1. Remove and discard stringy parts of livers. Roughly chop remainder.

2. Melt butter in a non-stick pan, add livers, onion and garlic and cook, stirring, until livers are cooked.
To microwave: Melt butter for 30 seconds and stir in livers, onion and garlic. Cook uncovered for 6–8 minutes, stirring two or three times, or until livers are cooked.

3. Cool, then place in a blender or food processor with remaining ingredients.

4. Purée until smooth. Place in a serving dish, cover and chill.

5. Garnish with sprigs of fresh parsley and serve with vegetable sticks and toast.

FRENCH COUNTRY-STYLE PÂTÉ 🄵

Preparation 30 mins **Cooking** 1 hr   *Serves 6–8*

175g (6oz) pigs' liver, sliced
1 small onion
2 garlic cloves, crushed
100g (4oz) smoked bacon, chopped
100g (4oz) minced pork
100g (4oz) fresh breadcrumbs
15 ml (1 tbsp) chopped parsley
2 eggs, beaten
150 ml (¼ pint) fresh milk
salt and freshly ground pepper
3 bay leaves
crisp toast to serve

1. Place liver, onion and garlic in a food processor and process until finely chopped.

2. Turn into a bowl and add bacon and pork. Stir in breadcrumbs, parsley, eggs and milk. Season to taste.

3. Pack mixture into a well-greased 900g (2lb) loaf tin or terrine, put bay leaves on top and cover with aluminium foil.
To microwave: Pack mixture into a well-greased 900g (2lb) loaf dish, put bay leaves on top and cover with greaseproof paper or pierced film.

4. Bake at 170°C (325°F) Mark 3 for 1 hour.
To microwave: Cook on MEDIUM (50%) for 30 minutes until cooked through.

5. Leave in tin or dish for 5 minutes. Remove bay leaves then turn out.

6. Serve cold, cut into slices with toast.

AVOCADOS WITH SHELLFISH

Preparation 15 mins   *Serves 4*

2 ripe avocados
lemon juice
175g (6oz) peeled prawns or crab meat
120 ml (8 tbsp) Thousand Island
    mayonnaise
lemon slices to garnish

1. Cut avocados in half lengthways and remove stones. Brush avocado flesh with lemon juice to prevent discoloration.

2. Fill cavities with shellfish and spoon over the dressing.

3. Garnish with slices of lemon.

SALMON ROLL UPS

Preparation 15 mins   *Serves 4*

100g (4oz) medium fat soft cheese
60 ml (4 tbsp) fresh soured cream
2 spring onions, finely chopped
pinch of ground bay leaves
freshly ground pepper
100g (4oz) thinly sliced smoked salmon
frisée and lemon wedges to garnish

1. Mix together cheese, cream, onions and ground bay leaves. Season to taste.
2. Divide mixture between salmon and roll up. Chill.
3. Serve garnished with frisée and lemon.

LEICESTER FISH PÂTÉ

Preparation 25 mins   *Serves 4*

198g (7oz) can tuna, drained
200g (7oz) Red Leicester cheese, grated
10ml (2tsp) lemon juice
150g (5oz) natural yogurt
30ml (2tbsp) chopped parlsey
freshly ground pepper
parsley to garnish
toast, crispbreads or French bread to serve

1. Place tuna in a bowl and mash with a fork.
2. Add cheese and lemon juice and mash together.
3. Add yogurt, chopped parsley and season to taste. Mix well.
4. Spoon mixture into a serving dish or 4 ramekin dishes and chill.
5. Garnish with parsley and serve with toast, crispbreads or French bread.

SMOKED MACKEREL PÂTÉ

Preparation 20 mins   *Serves 6*

275g (10oz) smoked mackerel fillets
grated rind and juice of ½ lemon
salt and freshly ground pepper
225g (8oz) fromage frais
10ml (2tsp) chopped fresh tarragon
lemon slices and parsley to garnish
crusty bread or melba toast to serve

1. Remove skin and bones from mackerel, flake flesh and mash in a bowl.
2. Add lemon rind and juice, seasoning, fromage frais and tarragon.
3. Mix well, transfer to individual serving dishes.
4. Garnish with a slice of lemon and a sprig of fresh parsley.
5. Serve with crusty bread or melba toast.

SMOKED MACKEREL PÂTÉ

SALMON & CHEESE TRIANGLES

SALMON & CHEESE TRIANGLES

Preparation 40 mins **Cooking** 10 mins   *Makes 8*

100 g (4 oz) curd cheese
100 g (4 oz) Wensleydale cheese, grated
198 g (7 oz) can pink salmon, drained and
    flaked
5 ml (1 tsp) lemon juice
15 ml (1 tbsp) chopped parsley
8 sheets of filo pastry
50 g (2 oz) unsalted butter, melted

1. Mix together cheeses, salmon, lemon juice
and parsley.

2. Brush a sheet of filo pastry with butter,
fold in half lengthways, brush with butter.

3. Place a spoonful of filling in corner of
pastry and fold over repeatedly to make a
triangle.

4. Repeat with remaining pastry and filling.

5. Place on a greased baking sheet and
brush with melted butter.

6. Bake at 200°C (400°F) Mark 6 for 10 min.

7. Serve hot.

Keep filo pastry covered to prevent it from
drying out and breaking up.

EGG MAYONNAISE

Preparation 15 mins   *Serves 4*

1 box mustard and cress
4 eggs, hard-boiled, shelled and halved
120 ml (8 tbsp) mayonnaise
paprika
4 anchovy fillets,
    each halved lengthways to garnish

1. Line 4 serving plates with mustard and
cress.

2. Arrange 2 hard-boiled egg halves on
each, cut side down.

3. Spoon mayonnaise over eggs. Sprinkle
lightly with paprika.

4. Garnish each serving with 2 strips of
anchovy.

Variation

EGG & SMOKED SALMON MAYONNAISE

Follow recipe and method for egg
mayonnaise (above). Garnish each serving
with strips of smoked salmon.

STILTON-FILLED EGGS

Preparation time 25 mins　　　　*Serves 4*

4 eggs, hard-boiled and shelled
50g (2oz) Blue Stilton cheese
5ml (1tsp) paprika
30ml (2tbsp) fresh single cream
salt and freshly ground pepper
60ml (4tbsp) mustard and cress
8 small slices of tomato to garnish

1. Halve eggs lengthways and carefully remove yolks

2. Place yolks in a bowl. Mash finely with Stilton and stir in paprika and cream then season to taste.

3. Pile back into egg white halves. Cover 4 serving plates with mustard and cress and place 2 egg halves on each.

4. Garnish each with slices of tomato. Chill lightly before serving.

BLUSHING FRUIT STARTER

Preparation 25 mins　　　　*Serves 4*

½ medium melon, seeded
1 medium pink grapefruit
1 medium paw paw
1 ripe avocado
lemon juice
frisée lettuce
fresh coriander to garnish

1. Peel melon and cut into chunks. Place in a bowl.

2. Peel and segment grapefruit. Remove all pith – catch any juice and reserve. Cut segments into chunks.

3. Halve paw paw, remove and discard seeds. Peel and cut into strips.

4. Halve avocado and remove stone. Peel and cut flesh into strips. Dip into lemon juice.

5. Add prepared fruit and avocado to melon. Add any reserved grapefruit juice and stir gently to mix.

6. Arrange frisée lettuce on individual plates and spoon fruit mixture on top.

7. Garnish with coriander.

BLUSHING FRUIT STARTER

STILTON & GRAPE AVOCADOS

Preparation 30 mins | *Serves 4*

2 ripe avocados, halved and stoned
juice of ½ lemon
100 g (4 oz) Blue Stilton cheese, crumbled
75 g (3 oz) black seedless grapes, halved
freshly ground pepper
45 ml (3 tbsp) fresh soured cream
25 g (1 oz) toasted breadcrumbs
salad and grapes to garnish

1. Scoop flesh from avocados, chop and mix with lemon juice.

2. In a bowl mix Stilton, grapes, pepper and soured cream with avocado.

3. Spoon back into avocado shells, sprinkle over breadcrumbs.

4. Serve with a salad and grape garnish.

STUFFED TOMATOES

Preparation 25 mins | *Serves 4*

4 large tomatoes
50 g (2 oz) English Cheddar, diced
225 g (8 oz) cottage cheese, drained
2 spring onions, chopped
¼ cucumber, diced
freshly ground pepper
lettuce or frisée to garnish

1. Slice top from each tomato and scoop out flesh.

2. Drain pulp, discarding juice and core. Chop remaining flesh.

3. Combine remaining ingredients with flesh and season to taste.

4. Pile into tomato shells.

5. Serve on a bed of lettuce or frisée.

CURRIED EGG & PRAWN COCKTAIL

Preparation 25 mins **plus chilling** | *Serves 4*

½ round lettuce, washed and dried
2 eggs, hard-boiled and shelled
45 ml (3 tbsp) mayonnaise
60 ml (4 tbsp) natural yogurt
10 ml (2 tsp) curry powder
60 ml (4 tbsp) chutney
30 ml (2 tbsp) lemon juice
15 ml (1 tbsp) sultanas
100 g (4 oz) peeled prawns

1. Shred lettuce and use to half-fill 4 large wine glasses. Leave on one side.

2. Coarsely chop eggs.

3. Combine mayonnaise with yogurt, curry powder, chutney and lemon juice.

4. Stir in sultanas, prawns and eggs.

5. Mix well and chill lightly.

6. Spoon equal amounts into glasses to serve.

FRIED WHITEBAIT

Preparation 5 mins **Cooking** 5 mins | *Serves 4*

450 g (1 lb) whitebait
50 g (2 oz) flour
salt and freshly ground pepper
deep fat or oil for frying
sprigs of parsley to garnish
lemon wedges and brown bread and
    butter to serve

1. Carefully rinse and dry whitebait. Coat in seasoned flour.

2. Half-fill a deep pan with fat or oil and heat until temperature is 180°C (350°F) or until a cube of day-old bread browns in 30 seconds.

3. Fry whitebait in batches for 2–3 minutes, until crisp.

4. Drain on absorbent kitchen paper.

5. Arrange on 4 individual plates and garnish with parsley.

6. Serve with lemon wedges and brown bread and butter.

PRAWN & PINEAPPLE SALAD

Preparation 15 mins   *Serves 4*

1 Webb or Cos lettuce
227 g (8 oz) can pineapple rings,
   drained and chopped
175 g (6 oz) peeled prawns
175 g (6 oz) Derby or Wensleydale cheese,
   diced
soured cream with Stilton dressing made
   with 50 g (2 oz) Stilton (page 197)
30 ml (2 tbsp) fresh single cream
paprika and cucumber slices to garnish
   (optional)

1. Wash lettuce and shake leaves dry.

2. Tear into bite-size pieces and use to cover 4 individual plates.

3. Mix pineapple with prawns and cheese.

4. Pile equal amounts on top of lettuce.

5. Mix dressing with cream.

6. Pour dressing over salad.

7. Garnish lightly with paprika and cucumber slices, if wished.

CHEESE & GARLIC BREAD   Ⓕ

Preparation time 15 mins **Cooking** 10 mins
Makes 2 × 30.5 cm (12 inch) loaves

100 g (4 oz) butter
3 garlic cloves, crushed
15 ml (1 tbsp) chopped parsley
100 g (4 oz) Double Gloucester cheese,
   grated
2 × 30.5 cm (12 inch) French sticks

1. Blend together butter, garlic and parsley.

2. Stir in cheese and mix well.

3. Make cuts down the loaves at 1 cm (½ inch) intervals almost to the base.

4. Spread mixture over each side of the bread slices.

5. Wrap loaves in aluminium foil.

6. Cook at 200°C (400°F) Mark 6 for 15 minutes, open up foil after 10 minutes.

7. Serve cut into slices.

MAIN MEALS

VEGETABLE CASSEROLE PAGE 132 · PORK PIE PAGE 100
STIR-FRIED CHICKEN PAGE 118

FISH

GRILLED WHOLE PLAICE

Preparation 5 mins **Cooking** 25 mins   *Serves 4*

4×175g (6oz) whole plaice, cleaned
50g (2oz) butter, melted
salt and freshly ground pepper
lemon wedges and parsley to garnish

1. Line grill pan or rack with aluminium foil. Arrange 2 plaice on top, brush with melted butter and season to taste.

2. Grill for 5–6 minutes.

3. Turn over, brush with more butter and season to taste.

4. Grill for a further 5–6 minutes. Transfer to a warm platter and keep hot.

5. Cook remaining plaice in the same way.

6. Garnish with lemon and parsley.

DEEP FRIED FISH

Preparation 5 mins **Cooking** 10 mins   *Serves 4*

deep fat or oil for frying
4 cutlets or 8 medium fillets of fish
   (about 750g/1½lb)
coating batter (page 209)
lemon wedges to garnish

1. Half-fill a deep pan with melted fat or oil.

2. Heat until a faint haze rises from it (or until bread cube sinks to bottom of pan, rises to top immediately and turns golden in 50 seconds).

3. Coat 2 pieces of fish with batter. Lift into pan with fork or kitchen tongs.

4. Fry until crisp and golden, allowing about 6–8 minutes for cutlets and 4–5 minutes for fillets. Remove from pan.

5. Drain on absorbent kitchen paper.

6. Repeat with remaining fish.

7. Garnish with lemon.

TROUT WITH ALMONDS

Preparation 5 mins **Cooking** 15 mins   *Serves 4*

75g (3oz) butter
10ml (2tsp) oil
50g (2oz) blanched and halved almonds
4 medium trout, cleaned
60ml (4tbsp) flour
salt
cayenne pepper
lemon wedges and parsley to garnish

1. Melt butter and oil in a large frying pan.
To microwave: Melt butter with oil in a shallow heatproof dish for 1 minute.

2. Add almonds and fry gently until golden brown. Remove and drain.
To microwave: Stir in almonds. Cook for about 5 minutes, stirring frequently, until golden brown. Lift out almonds and drain.

3. Wash trout and wipe dry with absorbent kitchen paper.
To microwave: Wash and dry trout and slash skin in a few places.

4. Season flour with salt and cayenne pepper and coat fish well.
To microwave: Omit flour and seasonings.

5. Fry trout in remaining butter in pan, until cooked through and golden (about 4–5 minutes each side).
To microwave: Arrange trout, head to tail, in a large shallow dish and brush with butter and oil mixture. Cover and cook for 6–7 minutes, rearranging trout half way through cooking.

6. Remove to serving dish and keep warm.

7. Pour hot butter and almonds over fish.
To microwave: Season fish with salt and cayenne pepper if wished, and scatter almonds over.

8. Garnish with lemon and parsley. Serve immediately.

TROUT WITH WATERCRESS SAUCE

Preparation 15 mins **Cooking** 20 mins *Serves 4*

4×100g (4oz) trout fillets
1 garlic clove, crushed
15 ml (1 tbsp) lemon juice
salt and freshly ground pepper
1 bunch of watercress, finely chopped
2.5 ml (½ tsp) French mustard
150 ml (5 fl oz) fresh soured cream

1. Lay a large piece of aluminium foil on a baking sheet. Arrange trout on foil.
To microwave: Arrange trout in a large shallow dish.

2. Spread garlic and 10 ml (2 tsp) lemon juice over fish. Season to taste.
To microwave: Spread garlic and 10 ml (2 tsp) lemon juice over fish. Season with pepper only.

3. Fold foil over and seal.
To microwave: Cover dish.

4. Bake at 180°C (350°F) Mark 4 for 20 mins.
To microwave: Cook on MEDIUM (50%) for 5–7 mins.

5. Stir watercress, mustard and remaining lemon juice into soured cream. Season and chill.

6. Remove fish from oven. Transfer fish to a serving plate and serve sauce separately.

SALMON WITH AVOCADO SAUCE

Preparation 5 mins **Cooking** 30 mins *Serves 4*

1 ripe avocado
15 ml (1 tbsp) lemon juice
450 ml (¾ pint) fish stock
150 ml (¼ pint) white wine
4×150g (5oz) salmon steaks or fillets
5 ml (1 tsp) cornflour
150 ml (5 fl oz) fresh double cream
2.5 ml (½ tsp) dried dill
freshly ground pepper
fresh dill to garnish

1. Peel avocado and mash with lemon juice.

2. Place stock and wine in a large frying pan. Bring to the boil and add salmon.

To microwave: Arrange salmon in a shallow dish and pour over BOILING stock and wine.

3. Cover and simmer for 5 minutes. Remove from heat and keep warm.
To microwave: Cover and cook for 5 minutes.

4. Pour 300 ml (½ pint) of cooking liquid into a pan and boil rapidly until reduced to 150 ml (¼ pint).
To microwave: Pour 300 ml (½ pint) of cooking liquid into a jug and cook uncovered for about 10 minutes until reduced to 150 ml (¼ pint).

5. Blend cornflour with cream, dill and pepper. Stir in reduced stock.

6. Pour sauce back into pan and heat gently until thickened.
To microwave: Cook for about 2 minutes, stirring once, until thickened.

7. Remove from heat and stir in avocado.

8. Remove and discard skin from fish.

9. Garnish with fresh dill and serve with avocado sauce.

SALMON FISH CAKES   Ⓕ

Preparation 30 mins **Cooking** 10 mins *Serves 4*

450g (1 lb) potatoes
75g (3 oz) butter
213g (7.5 oz) can red salmon, drained
15 ml (1 tbsp) chopped parsley
5 ml (1 tsp) grated lemon rind
onion salt to taste
freshly ground pepper
15 ml (1 tbsp) oil
parsley and lemon slices to garnish

1. Cook potatoes in boiling water until tender.

2. Drain and mash with 25g (1 oz) butter, salmon, parsley and lemon rind.

3. Season to taste with onion salt and pepper. Leave mixture to cool.

4. Turn out on to floured board. Divide into 8 equal-sized pieces and shape into cakes.

5. Fry in a non-stick frying pan in remaining butter and oil until crisp and golden, allowing about 3–4 minutes each side.

6. Drain on absorbent kitchen paper.

7. Garnish with parsley and lemon.

FISH & SOURED CREAM BAKE

Preparation 15 mins **Cooking** 35 mins *Serves 4*

25 g (1 oz) flour
salt and freshly ground pepper
450 g (1 lb) white fish fillets or steaks
150 ml (5 fl oz) fresh soured cream
150 g (5 oz) mayonnaise
2 spring onions, finely chopped
5 ml (1 tsp) dried dill
5 ml (1 tsp) lemon juice
50 g (2 oz) smoked Cheddar cheese, grated

1. Season flour and coat fish. Place in a greased ovenproof dish.

2. Mix together soured cream, mayonnaise, onions, dill and lemon juice.

3. Spoon over fish.

4. Sprinkle with cheese.
To microwave: Omit cheese.

5. Cook at 180°C (350°F) Mark 4 for 30–35 minutes until fish flakes with a fork.
To microwave: Cover and cook for 5–6 minutes until fish flakes with a fork. Sprinkle with cheese and brown lightly under a hot grill.

DANISH-STYLE COD

Preparation 15 mins **Cooking** 30 mins *Serves 4*

100 g (4 oz) streaky bacon, chopped
100 g (4 oz) mushrooms, halved if large
100 g (4 oz) frozen peas
4 × 150 g (5 oz) cod cutlets or fillets
salt and freshly ground pepper
25 g (1 oz) butter

1. Arrange bacon, mushrooms and peas in a greased shallow ovenproof dish.
To microwave: Cook bacon in a shallow flameproof dish for 5 mins, stirring once or twice, until it crisps and browns. Scatter mushrooms and peas over top.

2. Season cod and place on top of bacon and vegetables.
To microwave: Sprinkle cod with pepper only, place on top of bacon and vegetables.

3. Put a piece of butter on each cutlet.
To microwave: Melt butter for 45 seconds and brush it over cutlets.

4. Cover and bake at 180°C (350°F) Mark 4 for 20 mins. Remove lid, bake for a further 10 mins.
To microwave: Cover and cook for about 8 mins until fish is tender. If wished, season with salt and brown lightly under a hot grill.

DANISH-STYLE COD

COD WITH ORANGE & WALNUTS

Preparation 15 mins **Cooking** 35 mins *Serves 4*

25 g (1 oz) butter
75 g (3 oz) fresh wholemeal breadcrumbs
1 garlic clove, crushed
25 g (1 oz) finely chopped walnuts
finely grated rind and juice of 1 medium
  orange
4 × 175 g (6 oz) cod cutlets
salt and freshly ground pepper
watercress to garnish

1. Melt butter in a pan. Stir in breadcrumbs, garlic, walnuts and orange rind.
To microwave: Melt butter for 45 seconds. Stir in breadcrumbs, garlic, walnuts and orange rind.

2. Cook over a low heat, stirring frequently, until breadcrumbs absorb butter.
To microwave: Cook for 30 seconds and stir well.

3. Season fish and place in a greased shallow ovenproof dish.
To microwave: Sprinkle fish with pepper only and place in a shallow flameproof dish.

4. Pour orange juice over fish and cover with breadcrumb mixture.

5. Bake, uncovered, at 180°C (350°F) Mark 4 for 20–30 minutes, or until fish is tender.
To microwave: Cook uncovered for 6–8 minutes then brown lightly under a hot grill.

6. Garnish with watercress.

CHEESY FISH BAKE

Preparation 40 mins **Cooking** 50 mins *Serves 4*

450 g (1 lb) cod fillet, skinned
300 ml (½ pint) fresh milk
1 bay leaf
25 g (1 oz) flour
25 g (1 oz) butter
100 g (4 oz) English Cheddar, grated
salt and freshly ground pepper
700 g (1½ lb) new potatoes, cooked and
  sliced
50 g (1.8 oz) can anchovy fillets, drained

1. Place fish in a saucepan with milk and bay leaf.
To microwave: Place fish in a dish with milk and bay leaf.

2. Bring to the boil and simmer for 15 minutes or until fish flakes easily.
To microwave: Cover and cook for 5 minutes or until fish flakes easily.

3. Drain, reserving liquid. Flake fish. Discard bay leaf.

4. Make fish liquid up to 300 ml (½ pint) with extra milk.

5. Place fish liquid, flour and butter in a pan, heat whisking continuously until sauce thickens, boils and is smooth.
To microwave: Whisk together fish liquid, flour and butter in a large jug. Cook for 3 minutes, whisking frequently, until sauce thickens, boils and is smooth.

6. Stir in fish and half the cheese. Season.

7. Arrange half the potatoes in a greased overproof dish.

8. Pour over sauce and cover with remaining potatoes.

9. Sprinkle with remaining cheese. Arrange anchovies in a lattice pattern over cheese.

10. Bake at 200°C (400°F) Mark 6 for 30 minutes.

BUTTERED PLAICE WITH BANANAS

Preparation 10 mins **Cooking** 20 mins *Serves 4*

4 × 175 g (6 oz) plaice fillets
salt and freshly ground pepper
40 g (1½ oz) butter
25 g (1 oz) salted cashew nuts
2 medium bananas, peeled and sliced
juice of 1 lemon

1. Arrange plaice fillets in a greased shallow ovenproof dish. Season to taste.
To microwave: Fold fillets in half widthways and arrange in a shallow dish, thin ends to the centre.

2. Melt 25g (1oz) butter and pour over fish.
To microwave: Melt 25g (1oz) butter for 30 seconds and brush over fish.

3. Cover and cook at 180°C (350°F) Mark 4 for 20 minutes.
To microwave: Cover and cook for 4–5 minutes.

4. After 15 minutes, melt remaining butter in a pan.
To microwave: Melt remaining butter in a shallow heatproof dish for 30 seconds.

5. Add nuts and bananas and fry gently for 3 minutes.
To microwave: Stir in nuts and cook for about 4 minutes, stirring frequently. Lift out and drain. Stir bananas into hot butter, coating them well and pushing them to outer edge of dish. Cook for ½–1 minute until bananas are soft.

6. Arrange nuts and bananas on top of fish.

7. Sprinkle with lemon juice and serve immediately.

PORTUGUESE PLAICE

Preparation 25 mins **Cooking** 30 mins   *Serves 4*

120g (4.2oz) can sardines in oil, drained
40g (1½oz) fresh breadcrumbs
30ml (2tbsp) chopped parsley
grated rind and juice of 1 medium lemon
5ml (1tsp) finely grated onion
salt and freshly ground pepper
beaten egg to bind
8×75g (3oz) plaice fillets, skinned
25g (1oz) butter, melted

1. Mash sardines well and combine with breadcrumbs, parsley, lemon rind, onion and seasoning. Bind loosely with egg.

2. Spread sardine mixture over skinned side of plaice fillets and roll up.

3. Arrange in a greased shallow ovenproof dish.
To microwave: Place around edge of a shallow dish.

4. Stir lemon juice into melted butter and brush over fish.

5. Cover and cook at 180°C (350°F) Mark 4 for 30 minutes.
To microwave: Cover and cook for 4–5 minutes.

FAMILY FISH PIE

FAMILY FISH PIE

Preparation 40 mins
Cooking 15 mins   *Serves 4-6*

50 g (2 oz) butter
50 g (2 oz) flour
568 ml (1 pint) fresh milk plus extra for
    mashing
450 g (1 lb) smoked haddock,
    skinned and cubed
100 g (4 oz) frozen peas
198 g (7 oz) can sweetcorn, drained
2 eggs, hard-boiled, shelled and chopped
15 ml (1 tbsp) chopped parsley
350 g (12 oz) potatoes,
    diced and freshly cooked
225 g (8 oz) swede,
    diced and freshly cooked
50 g (2 oz) Red Leicester cheese, grated
parsley to garnish

1. Place butter, flour and milk in a
saucepan.
*To microwave: In a large jug, gradually
blend milk into flour. Add butter.*

2. Heat, whisking continuously until sauce
thickens, boils and is smooth. Cook for a
minute.

*To microwave: Cook for 6–8 minutes, stirring
frequently, until sauce thickens, boils and is
smooth.*

3. Add fish, peas, sweetcorn, egg and
parsley.

4. Cook for 2–5 minutes.
*To microwave: Cook for 3–4 minutes, stirring
once.*

5. Pour into a large flameproof dish.

6. Mash warm potato and swede with a little
extra milk. Spoon on to fish mixture.

7. Sprinkle cheese over and place under a
hot grill for a few minutes until cheese has
melted.

8. Garnish with a sprig of parsley.

Variation

MIXED FISH PIE

Follow recipe and method for family fish pie
(left). Use 225 g (8 oz) each white fish fillet
and smoked fish fillet and 50 g (2 oz) peeled
prawns.

Smoked Fish Terrine

Preparation 15 mins **Cooking** 2¼ hrs *Serves 6*

40 g (1½ oz) butter
40 g (1½ oz) flour
450 ml (¾ pint) fresh milk
550 g (1¼ lb) smoked cod fillets,
  skinned and chopped
150 ml (5 fl oz) fresh double cream
1 garlic clove, crushed
3 eggs
freshly ground pepper
45 ml (3 tbsp) chopped parsley
75 g (3 oz) peeled prawns
sprigs of parsley and
  lemon slices to garnish

1. Place butter, flour and milk in a saucepan.
To microwave: In a jug, gradually blend milk into flour. Add butter.

2. Heat whisking continuously until sauce thickens, boils and is smooth. Cook for a minute.
To microwave: Cook for about 6 minutes, stirring frequently, until sauce thickens, boils and is smooth.

3. In a food processor blend together sauce, fish, cream, garlic and eggs. Season with pepper.

4. Spoon half the mixture into a greased and base lined 900 g (2 lb) loaf tin.
To microwave: Spoon half the mixture into a greased and base lined 1.25 litre (2¼ pint) loaf dish.

5. Sprinkle with parsley and most of prawns. Cover with remaining fish mixture.

6. Cover with buttered greaseproof paper.

7. Place in a roasting tin with hot water to come half way up sides of loaf tin.
To microwave: Place in a large shallow dish with hot water to come half way up sides of loaf dish.

8. Bake at 150°C (300°F) Mark 2 for 2 hours.
To microwave: Cook on MEDIUM (50%) for 30 minutes. Allow to stand for 5–10 minutes in the dish of water.

9. Turn out on to a dish and drain off any juices.

10. Serve hot garnished with remaining prawns, parsley and lemon slices. To serve cold, allow to cool before garnishing.

Smoked Fish Florentine

Preparation 10 mins **Cooking** 20 mins *Serves 4*

450 g (1 lb) smoked cod or haddock fillets
450 ml (¾ pint) fresh milk
225 g (8 oz) frozen chopped spinach
25 g (1 oz) butter
25 g (1 oz) flour
75 g (3 oz) Double Gloucester cheese,
  grated
freshly ground pepper
parsley to garnish

1. Place fish in a large frying pan and pour over sufficient milk to cover.
To microwave: Arrange fish in one layer in a shallow dish. Pour over 150 ml (¼ pint) milk.

2. Bring to the boil and simmer gently for 10–12 minutes or until fish is tender.
To microwave: Cover and cook for 7–8 minutes.

3. Cook spinach as directed on packet.
To microwave: Cook spinach covered for 5 minutes, stirring once.

4. Drain well and use to cover base of a 700 ml (1½ pint) flameproof dish. Keep warm.

5. Drain fish and reserve milk. Remove and discard skin and bones. Flake the fish and keep warm.

6. Make up reserved milk to 300 ml (½ pint) and place in a saucepan with butter and flour.
To microwave: Make up reserved milk to 300 ml (½ pint) and blend gradually into flour. Add butter.

7. Heat, whisking continuously, until sauce thickens, boils and is smooth. Cook for a minute.
To microwave: Cook for 3–4 minutes, stirring frequently, until sauce thickens, boils and is smooth.

8. Remove from heat, add 50 g (2 oz) cheese and stir until melted. Season to taste.

9. Add fish to sauce and pour over spinach.

10. Sprinkle with remaining cheese and grill until it melts and browns.

11. Garnish with parsley.

CHEESE-BAKED HADDOCK ⒡

Preparation 10 mins **Cooking** 40 mins *Serves 4*

700 g (1½ lb) haddock fillets
salt and freshly ground pepper
1 medium onion, finely chopped
1 garlic clove, crushed
400 g (14 oz) can tomatoes
25 g (1 oz) butter
1.25 ml (¼ tsp) dried thyme
30 ml (2 tbsp) chopped parsley
25 g (1 oz) fresh breadcrumbs
50 g (2 oz) Lancashire cheese, crumbled

1. Skin fish and cut into 4 portions.

2. Arrange in a shallow ovenproof dish and season to taste.
To microwave: Arrange on a shallow flame-proof dish and season with pepper only.

3. Put onion and garlic into a saucepan with tomatoes, butter, thyme and parsley. Simmer slowly for 10 minutes.
To microwave: Cook onion, garlic, tomatoes, butter, thyme and parsley covered for 10 minutes, stirring once or twice. Season with salt.

4. Cover fish with tomato mixture and sprinkle with breadcrumbs and cheese. Bake at 180°C (350°F) Mark 4 for 30 minutes.
To microwave: Cover fish with tomato mixture and cook for 5–6 minutes. Sprinkle with breadcrumbs and cheese and brown under a hot grill.

SAVOURY HADDOCK CASSEROLE ⒡

Preparation 30 mins **Cooking** 45 mins *Serves 4*

700 g (1½ lb) haddock fillets
30 ml (2 tbsp) flour
salt and freshly ground pepper
25 g (1 oz) butter
juice of 1 small lemon
100 g (4 oz) mushrooms, chopped
1 medium onion, chopped
225 g (8 oz) tomatoes, chopped
1 small green pepper,
   seeded and chopped
5 ml (1 tsp) dried mixed herbs
10 ml (2 tsp) soft brown sugar

CHEESE-BAKED HADDOCK

1. Skin fish and cut into 4 portions.

2. Coat with seasoned flour. Fry quickly in butter in a non-stick pan until golden.
To microwave: Coat fish with flour and place in a 900ml (1½pint) dish.

3. Transfer to a 900ml (1½pint) greased ovenproof dish and sprinkle with lemon juice.
To microwave: Sprinkle with lemon & pepper.

4. Mix together vegetables & herbs, spread over fish. Scatter with brown sugar.
To microwave: Cook butter, vegetables, herbs and sugar covered for 8 mins, stirring once or twice. Pour over fish.

5. Cover and bake at 190°C (375°F) Mark 5 for 30–40 mins.
To microwave: Cover and cook for 5–6 mins.

BAKED HADDOCK WITH CREAM

Preparation 10mins **Cooking** 30mins   *Serves 4*

550g (1¼lb) haddock fillets
salt and freshly ground pepper
15g (½oz) butter, softened
30ml (2tbsp) lemon juice
5ml (1tsp) made mustard
1 small onion, grated
5ml (1tsp) Worcestershire sauce
10ml (2tsp) cornflour
150ml (5floz) fresh double cream
chopped parsley and paprika to garnish

1. Season haddock to taste then spread with butter. Arrange fish in a greased shallow ovenproof dish.
To microwave: Place haddock in shallow dish. Melt butter for 30 seconds and brush over fish.

2. Combine lemon juice with mustard, onion, Worcestershire sauce and cornflour. Stir in cream and pour over fish.
To microwave: Cook onion covered for 2 minutes. Combine lemon juice with mustard, Worcestershire sauce and cornflour. Stir into onion and add cream. Cook for 2–3 minutes until it just boils. Pour over fish.

3. Bake uncovered at 190°C (375°F) Mark 5 for 25–30 minutes or until fish is tender.
To microwave: Cover and cook for about 4–5 minutes or until fish is tender.

4. Sprinkle with parsley and paprika.

SOUSED HERRINGS

Preparation 25mins **Cooking** 1½hrs   *Serves 4*

4 large herrings, cleaned and filleted
1 large onion, thinly sliced
15ml (1tbsp) mixed pickling spice
2 small bay leaves, halved
75ml (5tbsp) water
150ml (¼pint) malt vinegar
5ml (1tsp) sugar
2.5ml (½tsp) salt

1. Wash and dry herrings.

2. Roll up from head to tail, with skin outside. Arrange in a 900ml (1½pint) ovenproof dish.

3. Scatter onion over herrings and sprinkle with pickling spice and bay leaves.

4. Combine water with vinegar, sugar and salt. Pour over fish.

5. Cover and bake at 170°C (325°F) Mark 3 for 45 minutes or until tender.
To microwave: Cover and cook for 8–10 minutes or until tender.

6. Leave herrings to cool in dish and chill thoroughly before serving.

FRIED HERRINGS SCOTS-STYLE

Preparation 5mins **Cooking** 10mins   *Serves 4*

4 large herrings, cleaned and filleted
100g (4oz) porridge oats or oatmeal
2.5ml (½tsp) salt
pepper
50g (2oz) butter
10ml (2tsp) oil
lemon wedges to garnish

1. Wash and dry herrings.

2. Season the oats with salt and a good shake of pepper. Coat the fish with the seasoned oats.

3. Fry in hot butter and oil, allowing 4–5 minutes each side.

4. Drain on kitchen paper.

5. Transfer to a serving dish and garnish.

KEDGEREE ⓕ

Preparation 20 mins
Cooking 15 mins   *Serves 4–6*

450 g (1 lb) smoked haddock fillets
3 eggs, hard-boiled and shelled
350 g (12 oz) cooked long-grain rice
   (about 150 g (5 oz) raw)
50 g (2 oz) butter, melted
30 ml (2 tbsp) chopped parsley
75 ml (3 fl oz) fresh single cream or milk
parsley to garnish

1. Place fish in a large frying pan and cover with water.
To microwave: Arrange fish in a single layer in a shallow dish.

2. Bring to the boil and simmer for 10–12 minutes, until fish is tender.
To microwave: Cover and cook for 5 minutes. Allow to stand for 3–5 minutes.

3. Drain fish, remove and discard skin and bones. Flake the flesh.

4. Chop 2 eggs. Slice third and reserve for garnish.

5. Mix together fish, rice, chopped eggs, butter, parsley and cream in a large saucepan.
To microwave: Mix together fish, rice, chopped eggs, parsley and cream in a large dish.

6. Cook, stirring, until heated through.
To microwave: Cover and cook for 3–5 minutes, stirring once, until heated through.

7. Serve garnished with parsley and slices of egg.

JUGGED KIPPERS

Preparation 5 mins **Cooking** 6–8 mins   *Serves 4*

4 medium kippers
40 g (1½ oz) butter

1. Put kippers into a tall jug and cover completely with boiling water.

2. Leave for 6–8 minutes and drain.

3. Serve immediately and top each with pieces of butter.

If kippers are very large it may be necessary to trim away the head.

NORMANDY WHITING

Preparation 10 mins **Cooking** 30 mins   *Serves 4*

550 g (1¼ lb) whiting fillets
1 small onion, finely chopped
15 ml (1 tbsp) French mustard
60 ml (4 tbsp) white wine or cider
juice of ½ medium lemon
25 g (1 oz) butter
15 ml (1 tbsp) chopped parsley

1. Arrange fish in a greased ovenproof dish.
To microwave: Arrange fish in a shallow dish.

2. Sprinkle onion over fish.
To microwave: Cook onion covered for 3 mins.

3. Heat mustard, wine or cider, lemon juice, butter and parsley in a small saucepan until butter melts. Pour over fish.
To microwave: Stir in mustard, wine or cider, lemon juice, butter and parsley. Cook for 1 minute until butter melts. Pour over fish, coating it well.

4. Cover and cook at 180°C (350°F) Mark 4 for 15 mins. Uncover and continue to cook for a further 10 mins.
To microwave: Cover and cook for 4–5 mins.

MARINATED MACKEREL

Preparation 25 mins plus 1 hr **marinade**
Cooking 30 mins   *Serves 4*

4 × 250 g (9 oz) mackerel,
   cleaned and filleted
15 ml (1 tbsp) honey
2.5 ml (½ tsp) chilli powder
2.5 ml (½ tsp) grated fresh ginger
30 ml (2 tbsp) vinegar
150 ml (¼ pint) fish stock
2 medium carrots, cut into matchsticks
2 celery sticks, finely sliced
4 spring onions, sliced

1. Place fish in a large ovenproof dish.
To microwave: Place fish in a casserole dish.

2. Mix together honey, chilli powder, ginger, vinegar and stock. Pour over fish.

3. Scatter vegetables over fish, cover and refrigerate for 1 hour.

4. Bake at 190°C (375°F) Mark 5 for 30 mins.
To microwave: Cover and cook for 10 mins.

SHELLFISH

MUSSELS

In season from September to March, but farmed mussels are available all year. Mussels should be purchased tightly closed or close when tapped, discard any open ones before cooking. Cut away beards with scissors, then put into a colander and wash under cold running water. Shake colander continuously to prevent mussel shells from opening. Scrub with stiff brush, wash again.

MOULES MARINIÈRE

Preparation 30 mins **Cooking** 20 mins   *Serves 4*

25 g (1 oz) butter
6 shallots or small onions, chopped
1 garlic clove, crushed
150 ml (¼ pint) dry white wine
1 small bay leaf
1.8 kg (4 lb) mussels,
   scrubbed and beards removed
45 ml (3 tbsp) chopped parsley

1. Melt butter in a large saucepan. Add shallots and garlic. Fry gently until pale gold.
To microwave: Cook butter, shallots or onions and garlic in a large bowl for 3 minutes.

2. Add wine and bay leaf and simmer gently for 7 minutes.
To microwave: Add wine and bay leaf, cover and cook for 3 minutes.

3. Add mussels and cook over a brisk heat, shaking pan frequently, until shells open (about 6–8 minutes).
To microwave: Add half the mussels, cover and cook for 3–5 minutes, shaking bowl occasionally and removing mussels from the top as they cook. Lift out with a draining spoon. Repeat, cooking remaining mussels in same way.

4. Discard any mussels which do not open.

5. Pour into warm serving dishes, sprinkle with parsley and serve immediately.

MOULES MARINIÈRE

Scallops

Scallops are in season during the winter months, from about November to March. If they have not already been opened and cleaned by the fishmonger, put them into a hot oven and leave for a few minutes until the shells open. Remove the dark frill (beard) from round the scallop, then carefully wash the white portion and bright orange roe.

Fried Scallops

Preparation 5 mins **Cooking** 8 mins *Serves 4*

8 scallops
salt and freshly ground pepper
15 ml (1 tbsp) lemon juice
45 ml (3 tbsp) flour
25 g (1 oz) butter
10 ml (2 tsp) oil
lemon wedges to garnish

1. Cut washed scallops in half. Pat dry with absorbent kitchen paper.
2. Season to taste and sprinkle with lemon juice.
3. Toss in flour.
4. Fry in hot butter and oil until golden, allowing about 4 minutes each side.
5. Serve immediately garnished with lemon wedges.

Coquille St-Jacques

Preparation 30 mins **Cooking** 40 mins *Serves 4*

4 scallops
60 ml (4 tbsp) white wine
100 g (4 oz) mushrooms, sliced
mornay sauce made with 300 ml (½ pint) fresh milk (page 233)
25 g (1 oz) English Cheddar, grated
25 g (1 oz) fresh breadcrumbs
225 g (8 oz) potatoes, boiled and mashed
15 g (½ oz) butter
lemon slices and parsley to garnish

1. Remove scallops from their shells. Discard darker intestine. Wash thoroughly.
2. Place scallops with their orange roes in a saucepan with wine and mushrooms and poach for 10 minutes.
To microwave: Cut off orange roes and reserve. Cook scallops, wine and mushrooms covered for 3–4 minutes. Add roes cover and cook for a further 1–2 minutes.
3. Make mornay sauce (page 233).
4. Drain scallops, add wine and mushrooms to sauce.
5. Place scallops and roes back in their shells or in individual flameproof dishes. Pour sauce over.
6. Mix together cheese and breadcrumbs and sprinkle over sauce.
7. Cream potatoes with butter and pipe a border around the edge of each shell or dish.
8. Brown under a hot grill. Garnish with lemon slices and parsley. Serve hot.

Prawn Stuffed Courgettes

Preparation 40 mins **Cooking** 40 mins *Serves 4*

4 medium courgettes, halved lengthways
50 g (2 oz) butter
1 medium onion, chopped
250 g (9 oz) cooked long grain brown rice, (about 75 g (3 oz) raw)
3 medium tomatoes, skinned, seeded and chopped
198 g (7 oz) can sweetcorn, drained
5 ml (1 tsp) made mustard
15 ml (1 tbsp) chopped parsley
100 g (4 oz) English Cheddar, grated
60 ml (4 tbsp) fresh single cream
100 g (4 oz) peeled prawns
25 g (1 oz) flour
300 ml (½ pint) fresh milk
salt and freshly ground pepper
50 g (2 oz) wholemeal breadcrumbs

1. Cook courgettes in boiling water for 10 minutes.
To microwave: Cook courgettes with 30 ml (2 tbsp) water, covered, for 6 minutes, rearranging once.

2. Drain courgettes and leave to cool. Scoop out flesh and reserve.

3. Place courgette cases in a greased ovenproof dish.
To microwave: Place courgette cases in a greased flameproof dish.

4. Melt 25g (1oz) butter in a saucepan and cook onion until soft.
To microwave: Cook 25g (1oz) butter and onion, covered, for 3 minutes.

5. Chop reserved courgette flesh and mix with onion, rice, tomatoes, sweetcorn, mustard, parsley, 50g (2oz) cheese, cream and prawns.

6. Spoon into courgette cases, adding any left over filling to dish.

7. Place remaining butter, flour and milk in a pan. Heat, stirring, until sauce thickens, boils and is smooth. Cook for a minute.
To microwave: Put flour in a jug and gradually blend in milk. Add remaining butter. Cook for 5 minutes, stirring frequently, until sauce thickens, boils and is smooth.

8. Season sauce to taste and pour over courgettes.

9. Mix breadcrumbs and remaining cheese and sprinkle over sauce.

10. Bake at 200°C (400°F) Mark 6 for 15–20 minutes, until golden brown.
To microwave: Cook uncovered for 5 minutes then brown under a hot grill.

PRAWN STIR-FRY

Preparation 5 mins **Cooking** 5 mins   *Serves 2*

25g (1oz) butter
1 garlic clove, crushed
pinch of ground ginger
225g (8oz) baby sweetcorn, halved
375g (13oz) pack fresh stir-fry vegetables
225g (8oz) peeled prawns
cooked rice to serve

1. Melt butter in a large frying pan or wok.

2. Add garlic, ginger and sweetcorn, cook for 2 minutes.

3. Add vegetables and prawns, stir-fry for 2–3 minutes, until prawns are hot.

4. Serve immediately with rice.

PRAWN STUFFED COURGETTES

BEEF

ROAST BEEF   Ⓕ

Preparation 5 mins **Cooking times**

20 mins **per 450g (1 lb) plus** 20 mins **RARE**
25 mins **per 450g (1 lb) plus** 25 mins **MEDIUM**
30 mins **per 450g (1 lb) plus** 30 mins **WELL-DONE**

Choose sirloin, fore rib, topside, silverside, thick flank or brisket

When buying allow, raw per person about

100–175g (4–6oz) meat without bone

175–350g (6–12oz) meat with bone

accompany with
gravy (page 236)
Yorkshire pudding (page 208)
creamed horseradish sauce or mustard
roast or boiled potatoes
vegetables

1. Tie or skewer joint into a neat shape if necessary and stand in a roasting tin.

2. Calculate cooking time allowing
20 minutes per 450g (1 lb) plus
20 minutes for rare beef.
25 minutes per 450g (1 lb) plus
25 minutes for medium beef.
30 minutes per 450g (1 lb) plus
30 minutes for well-done beef.

3. Cook at 180°C (350°F) Mark 4 for calculated cooking time.
A meat thermometer may be used to assess the final temperature which should be
60°C for rare
70°C for medium
80°C for well-done.

4. Remove from oven, stand joint on a board to carve. Remove string or skewers.

5. Carve and serve with accompaniments.

POT ROASTED BEEF   Ⓕ

Preparation 30 mins **Cooking** 2¼ hrs   *Serves 4*

40g (1½oz) butter
15ml (1 tbsp) oil
900g (2 lb) topside or thick flank of beef
1 medium onion, chopped
2 large carrots, sliced
2 large celery sticks, chopped
1 large tomato, chopped
300ml (½ pint) beef stock
150ml (¼ pint) red wine
salt and freshly ground pepper
12 small onions or shallots

1. Heat butter and oil in a large saucepan or flameproof casserole. Brown beef briskly on all sides. Lift out.

2. Add onion, carrots and celery to remaining butter in pan and fry until golden.

3. Replace meat. Add tomato, stock, wine and seasoning.
To microwave: Place meat and vegetables in a large casserole. Add tomato, BOILING stock and wine. Season with pepper only.

4. Bring to the boil, lower heat, cover and simmer gently for 1 hour, turning meat at least twice.
To microwave: Cover and cook for 10 minutes or until boiling. Turn meat over and push down into liquid. Cover and cook on MEDIUM–LOW (30%) for 30 minutes. Turn meat over and push back down into liquid.

5. Add whole onions, cover and continue to simmer for 45 minutes–1 hour or until meat is tender.
To microwave: Add whole onions, cover and cook on MEDIUM–LOW (30%) for 40–60 minutes until meat is tender.

6. Serve meat with vegetables.

GRILLED STEAK

Preparation 5 mins **Cooking** 15 mins   *Serves 4*

4×175 g (6 oz) fillet, rump or sirloin steaks,
trimmed of excess fat
25 g (1 oz) butter, melted (optional)
flavoured butter, if desired
   (page 254) to garnish
4 whole grilled tomatoes, watercress and
   fried mushrooms to garnish

1. Stand steak on grill rack. Brush with
butter if desired.

2. Stand under pre-heated hot grill.

3. Grill for 1 minute, turn over.

4. Brush with more butter. Grill for 1 minute.

5. Turn over. Grill for a further:
2–3 minutes each side for rare steak;
4–5 minutes each side for medium steak;
up to 6 or 7 minutes each side for well-done
steak.

6. Remove from grill. Top each with a piece
of flavoured butter if desired.

7. Garnish with tomatoes, watercress and
mushrooms.

Variation

GRILLED STEAK AU POIVRÉ

Follow recipe and method for grilled steak
(left). An hour before grilling, press
30 ml (2 tbsp) crushed black peppercorns (use
rolling pin for crushing) well into steaks with
palm of hand. Chill until ready to cook.

FRIED STEAK & ONIONS

Preparation 10 mins **Cooking** 15 mins   *Serves 4*

350 g (12 oz) onions, sliced
50 g (2 oz) butter
4×175 g (6 oz) rump steaks, trimmed of fat

1. Fry onions gently in butter until golden.
Transfer to a plate and keep warm.

2. Add steaks to pan. Fry briskly for 1 min
each side.

3. Lower heat. Continue to fry for a further
3–4 mins for rare steak; 4–5 mins for medium
steak; about 7–8 mins for well-done steak.

4. Turn steaks about every minute to ensure
even cooking.

5. Transfer to 4 individual warm plates and
serve with fried onions.

GRILLED STEAK AU POIVRÉ

STEAK & KIDNEY PLATE PIE   Ⓕ

Preparation 35 mins **Cooking** 2½ hrs   *Serves 4*

450g (1lb) lean stewing beef,
   trimmed and cubed
175g (6oz) ox kidney, cored and chopped
30ml (2 tbsp) flour
salt and freshly ground pepper
25g (1oz) butter
15ml (1 tbsp) oil
1 large onion, chopped
300ml (½ pint) beef stock
shortcrust pastry
   made with 350g (12oz) flour (page 364)
milk for brushing

1. Toss steak and kidney in seasoned flour.

2. Fry steak and kidney in hot butter and oil until well browned. Remove to a plate.
To microwave: Put butter into a casserole, (omit oil).

3. Add onion to remaining butter in pan and fry gently until pale gold.
To microwave: Add onion, cover and cook for 3 minutes.

4. Replace meat, pour in stock and bring to the boil.
To microwave: Stir in meat, pour in BOILING stock, cover and cook for 5 mins or until boiling.

5. Lower heat, cover and simmer gently for 1¾–2 hours, stirring occasionally, or until meat is tender.
To microwave: Cover and cook on MEDIUM (50%) for 45 minutes, stirring once or twice. Uncover and cook on MEDIUM (50%) for a further 15 mins or until meat is tender.

6. Leave until completely cold.

7. Roll out half of the pastry on a floured work surface. Use to cover a lightly greased 23cm (9 inch) ovenproof pie plate. Trim away surplus pastry.

8. Roll out remaining pastry to make a lid.

9. Pile cold meat with sufficient gravy in centre. Moisten edges of pastry with water.

10. Cover with lid, pressing edges together to seal and trim away surplus pastry. Flake by cutting with back of a knife. Flute and stand pie on a baking sheet.

11. Brush with milk and bake at 220°C (425°F) Mark 7 for 25–30 minutes or until golden brown.

STEAK & MUSHROOM PIE

Variation

STEAK & MUSHROOM PIE Ⓕ

Prepare meat filling as left, omitting kidney and adding 100g (4oz) sliced mushrooms with onions. Transfer to a 568ml (1pint) pie dish. Cover with puff pastry (page 366) and bake at 230°C (450°F) Mark 8 for 20–30 mins or until pastry is puffed and golden.

STEAK & KIDNEY PUDDING Ⓕ

Preparation 35 mins **Cooking** 4 hrs   *Serves 4*

suet crust pastry made with 225g (8oz) flour (page 367)
450g (1lb) stewing steak, trimmed cubed
175g (6oz) ox kidney, cored and chopped
15ml (1 tbsp) flour
salt and and freshly ground pepper
1 large onion, chopped
45ml (3 tbsp) cold water

1. Roll out two-thirds of pastry. Use to line a well-greased 900ml (1½ pint) pudding basin.

2. Toss steak and kidney in seasoned flour.

3. Layer in basin with onion. Add water.

4. Moisten edges of pastry with water. Cover with lid, rolled from remaining pastry.

5. Press pastry edges well together to seal.

6. Cover with double thickness of buttered greaseproof paper or single thickness of greased aluminium foil. Pleat once to allow pudding to rise.

7. Secure with string. Use extra string to make a handle for ease of removal.

8. Place in a steamer over a pan of hot water. Or place a metal trivet in a large saucepan and add boiling water to come halfway up the sides of basin. Add pudding and cover.

9. Steam steadily for 3½–4 hours. Replenish boiling water as necessary.

10. Remove from steamer, turn out to serve.

Alternatively cook filling as for steak and kidney plate pie (left) prior to making pastry. Then assemble and steam for 2 hours to cook pastry.

To microwave: Prepare and cook the filling as for steak and kidney plate pie (left), allow to cool and use to fill the suet crust pastry above. Cover the pudding with greaseproof paper, stand it on a plate and cook for about 10 mins or until pastry is cooked. Allow to stand for 5 mins before serving.

HAMBURGERS Ⓕ

Preparation 20 mins **Cooking** 10 mins *Serves 4*

450g (1lb) lean minced beef
1 small onion, finely chopped
2.5ml (½tsp) made mustard
5ml (1tsp) Worcestershire sauce
salt and freshly ground pepper
1 egg, beaten

1. Put all ingredients in a bowl and mix well.

2. Using dampened hands divide into 8 equal pieces and shape into 1cm (½inch) thick burgers.

3. Grill or dry fry in a non-stick frying pan for 8–10 minutes, or until cooked through. Turn once.

CHEESE BURGERS Ⓕ

Preparation 20 mins **plus** 30 mins **chilling**
Cooking 20 mins *Serves 4*

450g (1lb) lean minced beef
1 onion, chopped
5ml (1tsp) dried mixed herbs
100g (4oz) English Cheddar, grated
15ml (1tbsp) tomato purée
1 egg, beaten

1. Put all ingredients in a bowl and mix well.

2. Using dampened hands, shape mixture into 4 burgers. Chill for 30 minutes.

3. Grill or dry fry in a non-stick pan for 8–10 minutes on each side until golden brown and cooked through.

BEEF STROGANOFF

Preparation 25 mins **Cooking** 15 mins *Serves 4*

700g (1½lb) rump or fillet steak
1 onion, sliced
50g (2oz) butter
salt and freshly ground pepper
175g (6oz) button mushrooms, sliced
45ml (3tbsp) white wine
150ml (5floz) fresh soured cream
15ml (1tbsp) chopped parsley to garnish
cooked rice or noodles to serve

1. Cut steak into 1.5×5cm (¼×2inch) strips.

2. Fry onion in a non-stick pan in 25g (1oz) butter for 5 mins.
To microwave: Cook onion and butter, covered, for 5 mins, stirring once.

3. Add remaining butter and steak strips. Fry for a further 5 mins, turning constantly. Season to taste.
To microwave: Add steak strips and cook, uncovered, for 6–7 mins, stirring twice, until almost cooked.

4. Add mushrooms, fry for 3 mins, stirring.
To microwave: Add mushrooms and cook uncovered for 2 mins.

5. Stir in wine and cream and reheat gently without boiling.
To microwave: Stir in wine and cream, cook for 1 min, without boiling, until reheated.

6. Garnish with parsley to serve.

7. Serve with rice or noodles.

BEEF & BEER CASSEROLE Ⓕ

Preparation 30 mins **Cooking** 2¾ hrs *Serves 4*

700g (1½lb) lean stewing beef, trimmed and cubed
40g (1½oz) butter
3 medium onions, sliced
1 garlic clove, crushed
30ml (2tbsp) flour
300ml (½pint) brown ale
5ml (1tsp) wine vinegar
150ml (¼pint) beef stock
salt and freshly ground pepper
8 slices of French bread
60ml (4tbsp) wholegrain mustard

1. Fry beef in butter until brown. Transfer beef to an ovenproof casserole.
To microwave: Melt butter in a large flame-proof casserole for 45 seconds. Stir in beef.

2. Add onions and garlic to pan and fry in remaining butter until lightly browned.
To microwave: Add onions and garlic.

3. Add flour and cook, stirring, until it turns light brown.
To microwave: Stir in flour.

4. Gradually stir in liquids. Season to taste.

5. Bring to the boil and pour over meat.
To microwave: Cover and cook for 10 minutes or until BOILING.

6. Cover and cook at 170°C (325°F) Mark 3 for 2 hours.
To microwave: Continue cooking on MEDIUM–LOW (30%) for 1–1½ hours, stirring two or three times, until beef is tender. Remove lid for final 30 minutes of cooking.

7. Spread one side of bread with mustard. Push mustard side down, into casserole.

8. Return to oven and cook uncovered for 30 minutes.
To microwave: Brown under a hot grill.

COUNTRY BEEF BAKE   Ⓕ

Preparation 20 mins **Cooking** 50 mins   *Serves 4*

450 g (1 lb) lean minced beef
1 medium onion, sliced
100 g (4 oz) mushrooms, sliced
198 g (7 oz) can sweetcorn with peppers
225 ml (8 fl oz) beef stock
5 ml (1 tsp) dried mixed herbs
40 g (1½ oz) English Cheddar, grated
40 g (1½ oz) Sage Derby cheese, grated
450 g (1 lb) cooked potato, mashed
chopped parsley to garnish

1. Dry fry mince in a non-stick pan until browned. Add the onion and mushrooms and cook for 5 minutes, stirring occasionally.
To microwave: Cook onions, covered, for 3 minutes. Stir in mince, cover and cook for 5 minutes, stirring frequently to break up the meat. Add mushrooms, cover and cook for 2 minutes.

2. Add sweetcorn, stock and herbs.
To microwave: Stir in sweetcorn, BOILING stock and herbs.

3. Bring to the boil, cover and simmer for 15 minutes.
To microwave: Cover and cook for 10 minutes, stirring twice.

4. Transfer to an ovenproof dish.
To microwave: Transfer to a flameproof dish.

5. Mix together cheeses and stir half into potato.

6. Spoon or pipe potato on top of meat.

7. Sprinkle remaining cheese over potato.

8. Bake at 190°C (375°F) Mark 5 for 30 minutes.
To microwave: Cook on MEDIUM (50%) for 10–15 minutes then brown under a hot grill.

9. Sprinkle with chopped parsley to garnish.

COUNTRY BEEF BAKE

COCONUT BEEF CURRY

COCONUT BEEF CURRY

Preparation 10 mins **plus** 1 hr **marinade**
Cooking 2 hrs   *Serves 6*

150 g (5 oz) natural yogurt
1 garlic clove, crushed
15 ml (1 tbsp) curry powder
900 g (2 lb) lean stewing beef, cubed
50 g (2 oz) desiccated coconut
150 ml (¼ pint) fresh milk
300 ml (½ pint) beef stock
397 g (14 oz) can tomatoes
boiled rice to serve
accompany with mango chutney,
    diced cucumber and yogurt

1. Combine yogurt, garlic and curry powder.

2. Stir in beef and leave to marinade for
1 hour.

3. Meanwhile soak coconut in milk.

4. Place beef and marinade in a saucepan
with coconut, milk, stock and tomatoes.
*To microwave: Place beef and marinade in a
casserole with coconut, milk, stock and
tomatoes.*

5. Bring to the boil, cover and simmer for
2 hours or until meat is tender. Stir
occasionally.

*To microwave: Cover and cook for
10 minutes, stirring twice, or until boiling.
Cook on MEDIUM–LOW (30%) for 30 minutes.
Stir well. Continue cooking, uncovered, for
about 45 minutes, stirring once or twice, or
until beef is tender.*

6. Serve with boiled rice and
accompaniments.

FARMHOUSE MINCE **F**

Preparation 5 mins **Cooking** 46 mins   *Serves 4*

350 g (12 oz) lean minced beef
1 medium onion, chopped
50 g (2 oz) split red lentils
15 ml (1 tbsp) tomato purée
5 ml (1 tsp) paprika
5 ml (1 tsp) cayenne pepper
30 ml (2 tbsp) Worcestershire sauce
568 ml (1 pint) beef stock
450 g (1 lb) frozen mixed vegetables
mashed potato to serve

1. Dry fry mince and onion in a non-stick
pan until browned.
*To microwave: In a casserole, mix together
mince and onion. Cover and cook for 5 mins,
stirring twice to break up mince.*

2. Add lentils, tomato purée, spices, Worcestershire sauce and stock.
To microwave: Stir in lentils, tomato purée, spices, Worcestershire sauce and BOILING stock.

3. Bring to the boil, cover and simmer for 40 mins.
To microwave: Cover and cook for 15 mins, stirring once or twice.

4. Stir in mixed vegetables.

5. Bring back to the boil and cook for 6 mins.
To microwave: Cover and cook for 6–8 mins.

6. Serve with mashed potato.

HARVEST BAKE

Preparation 35 mins **Cooking** 1 hr   *Serves 4*

450 g (1 lb) lean minced beef
25 g (1 oz) flour
300 ml (½ pint) beef stock
15 ml (1 tbsp) dried mixed herbs
30 ml (2 tbsp) tomato purée
100 g (4 oz) leeks, sliced
175 g (6 oz) cauliflower florets
100 g (4 oz) carrots, diced
450 g (1 lb) potatoes, cooked and sliced
1 egg, beaten
275 g (10 oz) natural yogurt
50 g (2 oz) English Cheddar, grated

1. Dry fry mince in a non-stick pan until browned. Stir in flour. Gradually stir in stock. Heat, whisking continuously until sauce thickens, boils, and is smooth.
To microwave: Place mince in a casserole and stir in flour. Gradually blend in BOILING stock. Cover and cook for about 5 minutes, stirring once, until boiling.

2. Add 10 ml (2 tsp) herbs, tomato purée, leeks, cauliflower and carrots.

3. Bring to the boil, cover and simmer for 15 minutes. Stir occasionally.
To microwave: Cover and cook for 8 minutes, stirring once.

4. Transfer to an ovenproof dish. Cover with sliced potatoes.
To microwave: Transfer to a flameproof dish and cover with sliced potatoes.

5. Whisk together egg, yogurt and remaining herbs. Pour over potatoes and top with cheese.

6. Bake at 190°C (375°F) Mark 5 for 40 minutes.
To microwave: Cook on MEDIUM (50%) for 10 minutes then brown under a hot grill.

MEATBALL CASSEROLE Ⓕ

Preparation 30 mins **Cooking** 1 hr   *Serves 4*

450 g (1 lb) lean minced beef
1 medium onion, chopped
5 ml (1 tbsp) dried mixed herbs
1 egg, beaten
25 g (1 oz) butter
2 medium potatoes, diced
1 medium green pepper,
    seeded and sliced
1 medium carrot, thinly sliced
15 ml (1 tbsp) cornflour
300 ml (½ pint) stock
283 g (10 oz) can oxtail soup

1. Mix together meat, half the onion, herbs and egg.

2. Using dampened hands shape into 16 small balls.

3. Gently fry batches of meatballs in butter until browned on the surface. Remove meatballs to an ovenproof casserole.
To microwave: Arrange meatballs in a large casserole and cook, uncovered, for 6 minutes, rearranging them half way. Lift out.

4. Add remaining onion and vegetables to butter in pan and fry for 5 minutes.
To microwave: Add onion, vegetables and butter to casserole. Cover and cook for 5 minutes.

5. Blend cornflour with a little stock, then add to pan with remaining stock and soup.
To microwave: Blend cornflour with a little soup, then add to casserole with BOILING stock. Stir well.

6. Bring to the boil, stirring and cook for a minute. Pour into casserole.
To microwave: Return meatballs to casserole and push beneath the surface of the sauce.

7. Cover and cook at 190°C (375°F) Mark 5 for 40 minutes.
To microwave: Cover and cook for 5 minutes. Stir gently, cover and cook on MEDIUM (50%) for 15 minutes, stirring once or twice, until vegetables are tender.

SPICED BEEF & ORANGE Ⓕ

Preparation 30 mins **Cooking** 2¼ hrs   *Serves 4*

2.5 ml (½ tsp) *each*
  ground ginger,
  ground cinnamon,
  ground cloves,
  and ground nutmeg
5 ml (1 tsp) mixed spice
30 ml (2 tbsp) flour
450 g (1 lb) lean stewing beef, cubed
25 g (1 oz) butter
1 medium onion, sliced
4 celery sticks, sliced
grated rind of 2 oranges
450 ml (¾ pint) orange juice
2 medium oranges, peeled and segmented
25 g (1 oz) walnut pieces

1. Add spices to flour.

2. Add beef and coat in flour.

3. Melt butter in a saucepan, add beef and cook until browned. Lift out beef and place in an ovenproof casserole.
To microwave: Melt butter in a casserole for 30 seconds.

4. Add onion and celery to remaining fat in pan and cook for 3 minutes.
To microwave: Add onion and celery, cover and cook for 5 minutes.

5. Stir in any remaining flour and orange rind. Cook for a minute.
To microwave: Stir in beef, any remaining flour and orange rind.

6. Gradually stir in orange juice. Bring to the boil, stirring, and cook for a minute. Pour over beef and cover.
To microwave: Gradually stir in orange juice, cover and cook for 10 minutes, stirring twice, or until boiling.

7. Bake at 180°C (350°F) Mark 4 for 1½ hours.
To microwave: Cook on MEDIUM–LOW (30%), covered, for about 1 hour, stirring once or twice until the beef is tender.

8. Stir in orange segments and walnuts.

9. Return to oven and cook for a further 30 minutes.
To microwave: Cook, uncovered, for 5–10 minutes.

SPICED BEEF & ORANGE

CHILLI CON CARNE Ⓕ

Preparation 25 mins **Cooking** 1¼ hrs *Serves 4*

2 rashers streaky bacon, chopped
1 large onion, chopped
1 garlic clove, crushed
450 g (1 lb) lean minced beef
397 g (14 oz) can chopped tomatoes
30 ml (2 tbsp) tomato purée
1 green pepper, seeded and chopped
15 ml (1 tbsp) chilli powder
150 ml (¼ pint) beef stock
425 g (15 oz) can red kidney beans, drained
cooked rice or pasta to serve

1. Cook bacon in a non-stick pan for
5 minutes, stirring.
*To microwave: Cook bacon, uncovered, for
3 minutes.*

2. Add onion and garlic and cook until soft.
*To microwave: Stir in onion and garlic, cover
and cook for 3 minutes.*

3. Add beef and cook, stirring, until
browned.
To microwave: Stir in beef.

4. Stir in tomatoes, tomato purée, pepper,
chilli powder and stock.

5. Bring to the boil, cover and simmer for
45 minutes, stirring occasionally.
*To microwave: Cover and cook for
10 minutes or until boiling, stirring twice.
Continue cooking on MEDIUM (50%) for
15 minutes.*

6. Stir in beans and cook for 10 minutes.
*To microwave: Stir in beans and cook,
uncovered, for 10 minutes.*

7. Serve with cooked rice or pasta.

Variation
CHILLI COBBLER Ⓕ

Follow recipe and method for chilli con carne
(above). To make the cobbler topping rub
25 g (1 oz) butter into 100 g (4 oz) wholemeal
self raising flour. Stir in 65 ml (2½ fl oz) fresh
milk to form a soft dough. Roll out on a
floured work surface to 1 cm (½ inch) thick
and cut into 5 cm (2 inch) rounds. Place hot
chilli into an ovenproof dish, place scones
overlapping around the edge of the dish.
Brush with a little milk and bake at
200°C (400°F) Mark 6 for 10 minutes or
until scones are golden and cooked.

BEEF STEW Ⓕ

Preparation 30 mins **Cooking** 2½ hrs *Serves 4*

700 g (1½ lb) lean stewing beef,
    trimmed and cubed
30 ml (2 tbsp) flour
salt and freshly ground pepper
40 g (1½ oz) butter
2 medium onions, chopped
3 medium carrots, sliced
½ small swede, diced (optional)
450 ml (¾ pint) stock

1. Toss meat in seasoned flour.

2. Fry meat in butter until browned, turning
constantly. Remove to a plate.
*To microwave: Melt butter in a casserole for
45 seconds.*

3. Add vegetables to pan and fry for
7 minutes until golden.
*To microwave: Stir in vegetables, cover and
cook for 5 minutes (8 minutes if swede is
included).*

4. Add meat and stock. Bring to the boil,
cover and simmer gently for 2 hours or until
meat is tender, stirring occasionally.
*To microwave: Stir in meat and BOILING
stock. Cover and cook for 5 minutes or until
boiling, then continue cooking on MEDIUM–
LOW (30%) for 1–1½ hours, stirring two or
three times, until meat is tender.*

Variations
BEEF & TOMATO STEW Ⓕ

Follow recipe and method for beef stew
(above). Use 227 g (8 oz) can chopped
tomatoes and 200 ml (7 fl oz) tomato juice in
place of stock.

BEEF STEW & DUMPLINGS Ⓕ

Follow recipe and method for beef stew
(above), adding dumplings 20 minutes
before the end of cooking. To make
dumplings: Mix 100 g (4 oz) sifted self raising
flour with 50 g (2 oz) shredded suet and a
pinch of salt. Add sufficient water to make a
soft dough. Divide into 8 and roll into balls.
Arrange on top of stew and simmer for
15–20 minutes.
*To microwave: Arrange dumplings on top of
stew, cover and cook for 10 minutes.*

ROAST LAMB 🄵

Preparation 5 mins **Cooking times**
25 mins **per 450g (1 lb) plus** 25 mins **MEDIUM**
30 mins **per 450g (1 lb) plus** 30 mins **WELL-DONE**

Choose leg, shoulder, loin, best end of
neck or stuffed boned breast

When buying allow, raw per person about
100–175g (4–6oz) meat without bone
175–350g (6–12oz) meat with bone

accompany with
gravy (page 236)
mint sauce (page 237)
roast or boiled potatoes
vegetables

1. Tie or skewer joint into a neat shape if
necessary and stand in a roasting tin.

2. Calculate cooking time allowing
25 minutes per 450g (1 lb) plus
25 minutes for medium lamb.
30 minutes per 450g (1 lb) plus
30 minutes for well-done lamb.

3. Cook at 180°C (350°F) Mark 4 for
calculated cooking time.
A meat thermometer may be used to assess
the final temperature which should be
75°C for medium
82°C for well-done.

4. Remove from oven, stand joint on a board
to carve. Remove string or skewers.

5. Carve and serve with accompaniments.

GRILLED LAMB CUTLETS OR CHOPS

Cooking 10–20 mins　　　　**Serves 4**

8 best end neck cutlets or 4 loin chops

1. Stand chops in grill pan. Cook under
pre-heated hot grill for 1 minute.

2. Turn over. Grill for a further minute.
Continue to grill for a total of 7–9 minutes
for cutlets, or 10–18 minutes for loin chops.
Turning frequently.

3. Transfer to 4 individual plates or a warm
serving dish and serve.

CROWN ROAST OF LAMB

Preparation 1 hr
Cooking 30 mins **per 450g (1 lb) plus** 30 mins
　　　　　　　　　　　　　　　　Serves 6

1 crown roast of lamb
suitable stuffing
　(see stuffings on page 246)
paper cutlet frills
fresh rosemary to garnish

accompany with
the same as roast lamb (left)

1. Ask your butcher to prepare a crown from
2 best end necks of lamb, each with 6 or
7 cutlets.

2. Alternatively to make a crown yourself
buy 2 best end necks, already chined.

3. Trim away meat from upper parts of
bones, leaving 2.5cm (1 inch) of bone bare.

4. With skin side inside, curve both necks
round to form a crown. Hold together by
stitching ends together with fine string and a
trussing needle.

5. Place in a roasting tin and place stuffing
in centre of crown. Weigh with stuffing to
calculate roasting time, allowing 30 minutes
per 450g (1 lb) plus 30 minutes.

6. Cover tops of bones with pieces of
aluminium foil to prevent over browning.

7. Roast at 180°C (350°F) Mark 4 for
calculated cooking time.

8. Remove from oven. Transfer to a board or
serving dish.

9. Remove and discard foil. Place cutlet frills
on bones.

10. Garnish with rosemary and serve with
accompaniments.

BRAISED SHOULDER OF LAMB Ⓕ

Preparation 25 mins **Cooking** 2¼ hrs *Serves 4–6*

50 g (2 oz) butter
225 g (8 oz) onions, chopped
1 garlic clove, crushed
100 g (4 oz) lean bacon, chopped
225 g (8 oz) carrots, sliced
100 g (4 oz) turnip, diced
2 large celery sticks, chopped
150 ml (¼ pint) red wine
150 ml (¼ pint) water
5 ml (1 tsp) dried rosemary
5 ml (1 tsp) salt and freshly ground pepper
1.4 kg (3 lb) shoulder of lamb,
   boned and rolled

1. Heat butter in a large saucepan. Add onions, garlic, bacon, carrots, turnip and celery.

2. Cover pan. Fry gently for 10 minutes, shaking pan frequently.

3. Add wine, water, rosemary and season to taste.

4. Bring to the boil. Stand lamb on top.

5. Cover and simmer very gently for 2 hours or until meat is tender.

6. Transfer lamb to a warm serving dish and surround with vegetables from saucepan.

LAMB BARLEY CASSEROLE Ⓕ

Preparation 20 mins **Cooking** 55 mins *Serves 4*

2 medium onions, sliced
15 g (½ oz) butter
4 lamb chops
15 g (½ oz) wholemeal flour
175 g (6 oz) pearl barley
225 g (8 oz) mushrooms, halved
4 sticks celery, sliced
300 ml (½ pint) lamb stock
568 ml (1 pint) fresh milk

1. In a large saucepan fry onions in butter until soft.

2. Add lamb, cook until brown on both sides.

3. Add flour, cook for a minute.

4. Stir in barley, mushrooms, celery and stock.

5. Simmer gently without a lid for 45 mins or until lamb and barley are tender.

6. Add milk, bring to the boil and serve.

KOFTA CURRY

Preparation 20 mins **Cooking** 40 mins *Serves 4*

450g (1lb) minced lamb
1 medium onion, finely chopped
1cm (¾ inch) piece fresh root ginger,
    peeled and grated
2 garlic cloves, crushed
1 fresh green chilli,
    seeded and finely chopped
30ml (2 tbsp) fresh chopped coriander
1 egg, beaten
15g (½ oz) butter
10ml (2 tsp) ground coriander
5ml (1 tsp) ground cumin
2.5ml (½ tsp) turmeric
2.5ml (½ tsp) ground cinnamon
450ml (¾ pint) fresh milk
15ml (1 tbsp) tomato purée
50g (2 oz) blanched almonds
150g (5 oz) natural yogurt
cooked rice to serve

1. Mix together meat, half the onion, ginger, garlic, chilli, fresh coriander and egg.

2. Shape into 16 small balls with dampened hands.

3. In a non-stick frying pan, fry meatballs in butter in batches until evenly browned. Lift out and drain off excess fat from pan.
To microwave: Arrange meatballs in a large shallow dish. Cook uncovered for 5 minutes. Lift out.

4. Place remaining onion in pan and fry lightly.
To microwave: Put remaining onion and butter in dish, cover and cook for 3 minutes.

5. Add spices and cook for 1 minute, stirring.
To microwave: Stir in spices and cook for 1 minute.

6. Add milk and tomato purée and bring to the boil.
To microwave: Stir in milk and tomato purée, cover and cook for 5 minutes or until boiling.

7. Return meatballs to pan, cover and simmer gently for 30 minutes.
To microwave: Return meatballs and their juices to dish, coating them with sauce. Cook uncovered on MEDIUM (50%) for 15 minutes, rearranging meatballs half way.

8. Add almonds and stir in yogurt gradually. Do not boil.
To microwave: Stir in almonds and yogurt and cook for ½–1 minute to reheat if necessary. Do not boil.

9. Serve with rice.

EASTERN LAMB

Preparation 25 mins **Cooking** 1 hr *Serves 4*

50g (2 oz) butter
350g (12 oz) lamb neck fillet,
    cut into strips
100g (4 oz) onion, chopped
227g (8 oz) can chopped tomatoes
175g (6 oz) long grain rice
50g (2 oz) raisins
10ml (2 tsp) brown sugar
60ml (4 tbsp) vinegar
5ml (1 tsp) turmeric
5ml (1 tsp) ground ginger
2 garlic cloves, crushed
300ml (½ pint) stock
salt and freshly ground pepper
50g (2 oz) peeled prawns
unpeeled prawns to garnish

1. Melt butter in a saucepan and fry lamb until browned. Remove meat and place in an ovenproof casserole.
To microwave: Melt butter in a casserole for 45 seconds.

2. Add onion to pan and fry for 3 minutes.
To microwave: Stir onion into butter, cover and cook for 3 minutes.

3. Put onions in casserole with tomatoes, rice, raisins, sugar, vinegar, spices, garlic and stock. Stir to mix.
To microwave: Stir in lamb and cook, uncovered, for 3 minutes. Stir in tomatoes, rice, raisins, sugar, vinegar, spices, garlic and BOILING stock.

4. Cover and cook at 190°C (375°F) Mark 5 for 50 minutes or until rice and meat are tender.
To microwave: Cover and cook for 10 minutes, stirring once. Uncover and cook for a further 5 minutes until rice and meat are tender.

5. Remove from oven, season to taste and stir in peeled prawns.

6. Garnish with unpeeled prawns to serve.

LAMB KORMA

Preparation 25 mins **Cooking** 35 mins *Serves 4*

25 g (1 oz) butter
1 medium onion, chopped
2 garlic cloves, crushed
5 cm (2 inch) piece fresh root ginger,
  peeled and grated
10 ml (2 tsp) ground coriander
10 ml (2 tsp) ground cumin
5 ml (1 tsp) ground turmeric
2.5 ml (½ tsp) ground cinnamon
275 g (10 oz) natural yogurt
450 g (1 lb) lamb (leg or shoulder),
  trimmed and cubed
50 g (2 oz) cashew nuts
30 ml (2 tbsp) fresh chopped coriander
cooked basmati rice to serve

1. Melt butter in a large saucepan and fry onion and garlic until soft.
To microwave: Cook butter, onion and garlic covered, for 3 minutes.

2. Add ginger and spices and cook for a few minutes.
To microwave: Add ginger and spices and cook for 1 minute.

3. Gradually stir in yogurt, then add lamb, nuts and half the coriander.

4. Cook on low heat for 30 minutes.
To microwave: Cover and cook for 5 minutes, stirring once, then continue cooking on MEDIUM (50%) for about 20 minutes, stirring occasionally.

5. Garnish with remaining coriander.

6. Serve accompanied with boiled basmati rice.

Variation

CHICKEN KORMA

Follow recipe and method for lamb korma (left). Omit lamb and use 450 g (1 lb) boneless chicken breast fillet, cubed.

EASTERN LAMB

LAMB KEBABS

LAMB KEBABS

Preparation 30 mins **plus** 3 hrs **marinading**
Cooking 26 mins   *Serves 4*

450 g (1 lb) boneless leg of lamb, cubed
yogurt marinade made with 300 g (10 oz)
   yogurt (page 253)
4 shallots or small onions
8 rashers streaky bacon
8 small tomatoes
8 button mushrooms
40 g (1½ oz) butter, melted
350 g (12 oz) freshly boiled rice
   (about 175 g (6 oz) raw)
fresh coriander to garnish

1. Add lamb to yogurt marinade and
refrigerate for 3 hours.

2. Cook shallots in boiling water for 10 mins.
Drain and halve.

3. Cut bacon rashers in half. Roll up each
one like a Swiss roll.

4. Thread lamb on to 4 skewers alternately
with halved onions, bacon rolls, tomatoes
and mushrooms.

5. Stand in grill pan. Brush well with melted
butter.

6. Cook under pre-heated hot grill for 8 mins.

7. Turn and brush with more butter.

8. Grill for a further 8 mins or until cooked.

9. Serve on bed of rice.

10. Garnish with coriander.

SHEPHERD'S PIE   Ⓕ

Preparation 15 mins **Cooking** 1¾ hrs   *Serves 4*

450 g (1 lb) minced lamb *or* beef
1 medium onion, chopped
30 ml (2 tbsp) flour
300 ml (½ pint) lamb *or* beef stock
15 ml (1 tbsp) tomato purée
2.5 ml (½ tsp) dried mixed herbs
salt and freshly ground pepper
700 g (1½ lb) potatoes, chopped
25 g (1 oz) butter
45 ml (3 tbsp) fresh milk

1. Dry fry lamb in a non-stick pan until
browned. Add onion and cook for 5 minutes,
stirring occasionally.
*To microwave: Cook lamb and onion for
5 minutes, stirring once or twice to break up
meat.*

2. Add flour and cook, stirring for 1 minute. Gradually blend in stock, tomato purée, herbs and season to taste.
To microwave: Stir in flour, BOILING stock, tomato purée and herbs. Season to taste.

3. Cook, stirring, until mixture thickens and boils. Cover and simmer for 25 minutes.
To microwave: Cover and cook for 15 minutes, stirring twice.

4. Turn mince mixture into a 1.1 litre (2 pint) ovenproof dish.
To microwave: Turn mince mixture into a 1.1 litre (2 pint) flameproof dish.

5. Meanwhile, cook potatoes in boiling water for 20 minutes until tender.
To microwave: Cook potatoes with 60 ml (4 tbsp) water, covered for about 15 minutes, stirring twice, until tender.

6. Drain well, mash with butter and milk.

7. Cover mince mixture with potato.

8. Bake at 190°C (375°F) Mark 5 for 1¼ hrs.
To microwave: Cover and cook on MEDIUM (50%) for 15–20 minutes then brown under a hot grill.

LAMB & MINT PASTY Ⓕ

Preparation 20 mins **Cooking** 40 mins *Serves 4*

350 g (12 oz) minced lamb
1 medium onion, finely chopped
15 ml (1 tbsp) mint jelly
75 g (3 oz) cooked peas
375 g (13 oz) puff pastry
beaten egg to seal and glaze

1. Dry fry lamb until browned, add onion and cook for 5 minutes.
To microwave: Cook lamb for about 5 minutes, stirring twice. Add onion and cook for 5 minutes.

2. Remove from heat and stir in mint jelly and peas.

3. Roll out pastry on a floured work surface to a 30.5 cm (12 inch) square, cut in half. Place one half on a baking sheet.

4. Spoon lamb mixture into centre of pastry on baking sheet. Brush edges with egg.

5. Fold remaining pastry in half lengthways and cut slits to within 2.5 cm (1 inch) of edge, spaced 1 cm (½ inch) apart. Unfold.

6. Place cut pastry over filling and seal edges. Brush with beaten egg.

7. Bake at 200°C (400°F) Mark 6 for 30 minutes.

LAMB CHOPS WITH HERBY CHEESE SAUCE

Preparation 10 mins **Cooking** 20 mins *Serves 4*

8 lamb loin chops
15 g (½ oz) butter
1 medium onion, chopped
60 ml (4 tbsp) beer
150 ml (5 fl oz) fresh double cream
65 g (2½ oz) Cheddar cheese with garlic
   and herbs, grated

1. Grill chops for 5–10 minutes on each side, depending on thickness. Remove and keep warm.

2. Meanwhile melt butter in a non-stick pan, add onion and cook until soft.

3. Add beer and boil for 2 minutes.

4. Stir in cream and heat through.

5. Remove from heat, add cheese and stir until melted.

6. Serve chops with sauce.

GOLDEN LANCASHIRE LAMB Ⓕ

Preparation 25 mins **Cooking** 30 mins *Serves 4*

225 g (8 oz) cold cooked lamb, chopped
450 ml (¾ pint) basic white coating sauce
   (page 231)
225 g (8 oz) cooked diced carrots and peas
50 g (2 oz) Lancashire cheese, grated

1. Add lamb to sauce with carrots and peas.

2. Turn into a 900 ml (1½ pint) greased ovenproof dish.
To microwave: Turn into a 900 ml (1½ pint) greased flameproof dish.

3. Sprinkle cheese over top.

4. Bake at 200°C (400°F) Mark 6 for 30 minutes.
To microwave: Cook on MEDIUM (50%) for about 10 minutes then brown under a hot grill.

MEDITERRANEAN LAMB CASSEROLE Ⓔ

Preparation 30 mins **Cooking** 1½ hrs   *Serves 4*

1 medium aubergine, halved and sliced
salt and freshly ground pepper
25 g (1 oz) butter
450 g (1 lb) lamb neck fillet, cubed
1 medium onion, sliced
1 garlic clove, crushed
100 g (4 oz) mushrooms, sliced
15 g (½ oz) flour
150 ml (¼ pint) stock
397 g (14 oz) can tomatoes
2.5 ml (½ tsp) dried rosemary
225 g (8 oz) courgettes, sliced

1. Sprinkle aubergine with salt and leave to stand for 30 minutes.

2. Rinse and drain well.

3. Melt butter in a frying pan and brown lamb. Remove to an ovenproof dish.
To microwave: Melt butter for 30 seconds.

4. Add onion, garlic and mushrooms to pan and cook for 3 minutes.
To microwave: Add onion, garlic and mushrooms. Cover and cook for 3 minutes.

5. Add flour and cook, stirring, for 1 minute.
To microwave: Stir in flour.

6. Stir in stock, tomatoes and aubergines.
To microwave: Stir in lamb, stock, tomatoes and aubergines.

7. Bring to the boil, stirring, and cook for a minute.
To microwave: Cover and cook for 10 minutes, stirring twice, or until boiling.

8. Add rosemary and courgettes.

9. Cover and cook at 190°C (375°F) Mark 5 for 1¼ hours or until lamb is tender.
To microwave: Cover and cook on MEDIUM (50%) for about 20 minutes, stirring once.

LANCASHIRE HOT POT Ⓔ

Preparation 30 mins **Cooking** 1¾ hrs   *Serves 4*

700 g (1½ lb) best end neck of lamb
2 lambs' kidneys
450 g (1 lb) potatoes, thinly sliced
225 g (8 oz) onions, thinly sliced
salt and freshly ground pepper
150 ml (¼ pint) stock or water
25 g (1 oz) butter, melted

MEDITERRANEAN LAMB CASSEROLE

1. Cut lamb into cutlets. Remove surplus fat.

2. Remove and discard skin and core from kidneys. Cut into slices.

3. Cover base of a 1.7 litre (3 pint) ovenproof casserole with some of the potato slices.

4. Stand lamb on top, cover with kidneys and onions. Season to taste.

5. Arrange overlapping rings of remaining potatoes on top.

6. Pour in stock or water.

7. Brush with butter. Cover dish with lid or aluminium foil.

8. Bake at 180°C (350°F) Mark 4 for 1¼ hrs.

9. Uncover and continue to cook for a further 30 mins or until potatoes are golden brown.

Variation

TRADITIONAL LANCASHIRE HOT POT

Follow recipe and method for Lancashire hot pot (above) adding 8 shelled oysters.

LAMB STEW   Ⓕ

Preparation 20 mins **Cooking** 2 hrs   *Serves 4*

1.1 kg (2½ lb) middle neck of lamb
30 ml (2 tbsp) flour
salt and freshly ground pepper
25 g (1 oz) butter
1 large onion, chopped
30 ml (2 tbsp) pearl barley
450 ml (¾ pint) stock or water

1. Divide lamb into neat pieces. Cut away surplus fat.

2. Toss in seasoned flour.

3. Fry briskly in hot butter until crisp and brown. Transfer to plate.

4. Add onion to remaining butter in pan. Fry slowly until pale gold.

5. Replace lamb. Add barley, stock or water and season to taste.

6. Bring slowly to the boil. Lower heat and cover pan.

7. Simmer gently for 1½–2 hours or until meat is tender.

FRUITY LAMB STEW   Ⓕ

Preparation 15 mins **Cooking** 1½ hrs   *Serves 4*

700 g (1½ lb) boneless leg of lamb, trimmed and cubed
1 medium onion, chopped
2.5 ml (½ tsp) each ground ginger, ground coriander and ground cinnamon
900 ml (1½ pint) stock
50 g (2 oz) no-soak dried prunes, stoned and halved
50 g (2 oz) no-soak dried apricots, halved
cooked rice to serve

1. Place lamb, onion, spices and stock in a saucepan.
To microwave: Place lamb, onion, spices and BOILING stock in a casserole and stir well.

2. Bring to the boil, cover and simmer for 1¼ hours or until the meat is tender.
To microwave: Cook for 10–12 minutes, stirring twice, until boiling. Cover and cook on MEDIUM (50%) for 20 minutes, stirring once.

3. Add fruit and bring back to the boil.
To microwave: Stir in fruit and cover.

4. Simmer for 15 minutes.
To microwave: Cook on MEDIUM (50%) for 15 minutes.

5. Serve with cooked rice.

Variation

FRUITY PORK STEW

Follow recipe and method for fruity lamb stew (above). Use 700 g (1½ lb) cubed boneless pork in place of lamb.

MOUSSAKA ⓕ

Preparation 15 mins **plus** 30 mins **standing**
Cooking 1 hr 20 mins   *Serves 4*

2 medium aubergines
salt and freshly ground pepper
75 g (3 oz) butter
30 ml (2 tbsp) oil
2 large onions, sliced
450 g (1 lb) minced lamb or beef
150 ml (¼ pint) water
15 ml (1 tbsp) tomato purée
1 egg, beaten
cheese coating sauce made with
    300 ml (½ pint) fresh milk (page 232)
50 g (2 oz) English Cheddar, grated

1. Cut aubergines into 0.5 cm (¼ inch) thick slices. Sprinkle with salt and leave for 30 minutes.

2. Rinse and drain thoroughly. Fry quickly in butter and oil until golden on both sides.

3. Remove from pan and leave on one side.

4. Fry onions in remaining butter and oil until pale gold.

5. Add meat and cook until browned. Add water and tomato purée. Season to taste.

6. Line base of an oblong or square ovenproof dish with half the aubergine slices.

7. Cover with meat mixture and onions. Arrange remaining aubergine slices on top.

8. Gradually beat egg into cheese sauce. Pour over aubergine slices.

9. Sprinkle with cheese.

10. Bake at 180°C (350°F) Mark 4 for 45 minutes–1 hour.

Variation

LAMB & POTATO BAKE ⓕ

Follow recipe and method for moussaka (left). Omit aubergines and steps 1 to 3. Use 700 g (1½ lb) potatoes, cooked and sliced in place of aubergines.

MOUSSAKA

LAMB BURGERS

CHESHIRE LAMB CRUMBLE   Ⓕ

Preparation 20 mins **Cooking** 1¼ hrs   *Serves 4*

450g (1lb) minced lamb
1 medium onion, chopped
75g (3oz) wholemeal flour
15ml (1tbsp) tomato purée
300ml (½pint) beef stock
salt and freshly ground pepper
50g (2oz) butter
50g (2oz) Cheshire cheese, grated
25g (1oz) oats
2.5ml (½tsp) dried mixed herbs

1. Dry fry meat and onion in a non-stick pan for 10 minutes.

2. Mix in 15g (½oz) flour, tomato purée, stock and seasoning.

3. Turn into a shallow ovenproof dish.

4. In a bowl, rub butter into remaining flour, then stir in cheese, oats, herbs and seasoning.

5. Spoon crumble over meat.

6. Bake at 190°C (375°F) Mark 5 for 45 minutes–1 hour.

7. Serve immediately.

LAMB BURGERS   Ⓕ

Preparation 15 mins **Cooking** 15 mins   *Serves 4*

1 onion, chopped
1 garlic clove, crushed
15g (½oz) butter
450g (1lb) minced lamb
15ml (1tbsp) chopped parsley
2.5ml (½tsp) dried mint
1 egg, beaten
4 rashers streaky bacon

1. Fry onion and garlic in butter until soft.

2. Place lamb, onion, garlic and herbs in a bowl.

3. Add egg and mix well.

4. Cut bacon rashers in half giving 8 long thin strips.

5. Divide lamb mixture into 8 equal pieces.

6. Shape into burgers using dampened hands.

7. Wrap a piece of bacon around sides of each burger.

8. Secure bacon with wooden cocktail sticks.

9. Cook under a hot grill until brown and cooked through. Turn twice.

ROAST PORK Ⓕ

Preparation 10 mins
Cooking 30 mins per 450g (1lb) **plus** 30 mins

Choose shoulder, loin, leg or belly
When buying allow, raw per person about
100–175g (4–6oz) meat without bone
175–350g (6–12oz) meat with bone

accompany with
gravy (page 236)
apple sauce (page 236)
mustard
mashed or boiled potatoes
vegetables

1. Tie or skewer joint into a neat shape if necessary and stand in a roasting tin.
2. Calculate cooking time allowing 30 minutes per 450g (1lb) plus 30 minutes.
3. Cook at 180°C (350°F) Mark 4 for the calculated cooking time.
A meat thermometer may be used to assess the final temperature which should be 85°C.
4. Remove from oven, stand joint on a board to carve. Remove string or skewers.
5. Carve and serve with accompaniments.

PORK CHOPS WITH CHEESE & BEER

Preparation 10 mins **Cooking** 25 mins *Serves 4*

4×175g (6oz) pork chops
175g (6oz) Lancashire cheese, grated
10ml (2tsp) made mustard
60ml (4tbsp) beer

1. Stand chops in grill pan. Grill for 8–10 minutes, depending on thickness.
2. Turn over and grill for a further 8–10 minutes.
3. Mix cheese with mustard and beer.
4. Spread equal amounts over chops.
5. Grill until brown.

COTSWOLD CHOPS

Preparation 25 mins **Cooking** 50 mins *Serves 4*

50g (2oz) Double Gloucester cheese
  with onion and chives, grated
75g (3oz) reduced fat soft cheese
25g (1oz) fresh breadcrumbs
15ml (1tsp) creamed horseradish sauce
10ml (2tsp) chopped parsley
4×150g (5oz) pork chops
25g (1oz) butter
45ml (3tbsp) sherry
45ml (3tbsp) fresh double cream

1. Mix together cheeses, breadcrumbs, horseradish and parsley.
2. Cut a pocket in flesh of each chop, fill with cheese mixture.
3. Melt butter in a roasting tin, add chops and fry to brown on both sides.
4. Cover and bake at 190°C (375°F) Mark 5 for 30 minutes, uncover and cook for a further 10 minutes.
5. Remove from oven, take out chops and keep warm.
6. Add sherry to tin, scrape up any sediment and heat on hob, boil until syrupy.
7. Remove from heat and stir in cream.
8. Spoon over chops to serve.

SOMERSET PORK CHOPS Ⓕ

Preparation 15 mins **Cooking** 50 mins *Serves 4*

4×150g (5oz) pork chops, trimmed of fat
25g (1oz) butter
1 medium onion, thinly sliced
25g (1oz) flour
150ml (¼ pint) cider
75ml (3fl oz) water
1 garlic clove, crushed
salt and freshly ground pepper
pinch of dried sage
30ml (2tbsp) fresh single cream (optional)

1. Fry chops in butter with onion.

2. When chops are brown, remove from pan.

3. Continue cooking onion until soft.

4. Add flour to pan and cook gently until brown.

5. Stir in cider, water, garlic, seasoning and sage.

6. Place pork chops and onion in a shallow ovenproof dish. Pour sauce over.

7. Cover and bake at 190°C (375°F) Mark 5 for 30–40 minutes.

8. Pour cream over chops and serve immediately.

Variation

HAWAIIAN PORK CHOPS Ⓕ

Follow recipe and method for Somerset pork chops (left). Omit cider, garlic and sage. Use 75 ml (3 fl oz) pineapple juice, 50 ml (2 fl oz) water, 10 ml (2 tsp) soy sauce and 4 rings of canned pineapple, chopped.

BRAISED PORK CHOPS Ⓕ

Preparation 40 mins **Cooking** 1½ hrs *Serves 4*

4 × 175 g (6 oz) pork chops, trimmed of fat
30 ml (2 tbsp) flour
salt and freshly ground pepper
25 g (1 oz) butter
1 large onion, chopped
4 medium potatoes, sliced
2 large celery sticks, chopped
225 g (8 oz) tomatoes, chopped
10 ml (2 tsp) sugar
5 ml (1 tsp) Worcestershire sauce

1. Toss chops in seasoned flour.

2. Fry in butter until crisp and golden on both sides. Transfer to a plate, keep warm.

3. Add onion to remaining butter in pan. Fry until golden.

4. Cover the base of a fairly shallow ovenproof dish with potatoes.

5. Add celery, tomatoes, sugar and Worcestershire sauce to onion in pan.

6. Mix well. Pour over potatoes.

7. Arrange chops on top.

8. Cover and bake at 180°C (350°F) Mark 4 for 1–1¼ hours.

PORK PIE

Preparation 1¼ hrs **Cooking** 2 hrs   *Serves 4–6*

hot water crust pastry
    made with 350 g (12 oz) flour (page 368)
350 g (12 oz) lean diced pork
3 rashers of bacon, chopped
5 ml (1 tsp) dried sage
pinch of ground nutmeg
freshly ground pepper
beaten egg for brushing
75 ml (3 fl oz) water
7.5 ml (1½ tsp) gelatine

1. Roll out two-thirds of pastry. Keep remaining pastry covered.

2. Place inside a 15 cm (6 inch) round cake tin and draw pastry up sides to completely cover base and sides.

3. Mix pork with bacon, sage, nutmeg and pepper.

4. Pack into pastry case. Moisten edges of pastry with water.

5. Roll out remaining pastry into a lid. Cover pie, pressing pastry edges well together to seal.

6. Make a hole in top to allow steam to escape.

7. Brush with beaten egg.

8. Decorate with pastry leaves, cut from trimmings. Brush with more egg.

9. Bake at 200°C (400°F) Mark 6 for 15 minutes.

10. Reduce temperature to 180°C (350°F) Mark 4 and bake for a further 1¾ hours.

11. Remove from oven.

12. Heat water. Add gelatine and stir briskly until dissolved.

13. Pour into hot pie through the hole on top, using a small funnel.

14. Leave until completely cold before removing from tin and cutting.

PEPPERED ULSTER PORK

Preparation 30 mins **Cooking** 20 mins   *Serves 4*

450 g (1 lb) pork fillet, cut into strips
freshly ground pepper
25 g (1 oz) butter
225 g (8 oz) carrots, cut into strips
1 large onion, chopped
100 g (4 oz) mushrooms, sliced
45 ml (3 tbsp) Irish whiskey
150 ml (5 fl oz) fresh soured cream
chopped parsley to garnish

1. Liberally sprinkle pork with pepper.

2. Melt butter in a large frying pan, add pork and carrots, stir-fry for 5 minutes.

3. Add onion and mushrooms and cook until soft.

4. Stir in whiskey and soured cream and heat through, do not boil.

5. Serve garnished with chopped parsley.

PORK IN CREAM SAUCE Ⓕ

Preparation 30 mins **Cooking** 30 mins   *Serves 4*

4 × 100 g (4 oz) pork escalopes
75 g (3 oz) butter
1 celery stick, sliced
50 g (2 oz) leeks, chopped
½ eating apple, peeled, cored & chopped
freshly ground pepper
25 g (1 oz) English Cheddar, grated
1 medium onion, chopped
15 g (½ oz) flour
300 ml (½ pint) fresh milk
100 g (4 oz) mushrooms, sliced
30 ml (2 tbsp) fresh double cream

1. Place escalopes between 2 sheets of greaseproof paper. Beat until thin with a rolling pin.

2. Melt 25 g (1 oz) butter in a large frying pan and fry celery, leeks and apple. Season.

3. Remove from pan and cool. Mix in cheese.

4. Place some stuffing on to each escalope, roll up. Secure with wooden cocktail sticks.

5. Melt remaining butter in pan. Add pork and brown. Remove from pan.

6. Add onion to pan and cook until soft.

7. Stir in flour and cook for 2 minutes. Add milk, stirring, and bring back to the boil.

8. Add pork and simmer, covered, for 10 mins.

9. Add mushrooms and simmer for 5 mins.

10. Stir in cream and serve.

PORK & VEGETABLE CRUMBLE Ⓕ

Preparation 30 mins **Cooking** 50 mins   *Serves 4*

65 g (2½ oz) butter
450 g (1 lb) lean pork, trimmed and cubed
150 g (5 oz) wholemeal flour
450 ml (¾ pint) fresh milk
salt and freshly ground pepper
10 ml (2 tsp) fresh chopped sage
2 medium leeks, sliced
100 g (4 oz) mushrooms, sliced
½ red pepper, seeded and diced
5 ml (1 tsp) dry mustard
5 ml (1 tsp) paprika
50 g (2 oz) Red Leicester cheese, grated
25 g (1 oz) porridge oats
fresh sage to garnish

1. Melt 15 g (½ oz) butter in a non-stick pan and fry pork until browned.

2. Add 25 g (1 oz) flour and cook for a minute. Gradually stir in milk and cook stirring until sauce thickens, boils and is smooth. Season and add sage.

3. Add vegetables, bring to the boil and simmer for 10 minutes.

4. Pour pork mixture into an ovenproof dish.

5. Rub remaining butter into remaining flour until mixture resembles fine breadcrumbs.

6. Stir in remaining ingredients and sprinkle over pork mixture.

7. Bake at 200°C (400°F) Mark 6 for 30 minutes.

8. Garnish with fresh sage.

Variation

GARLIC PORK CRUMBLE Ⓕ

Follow recipe and method for pork and vegetable crumble (left). Omit butter, sage, mustard and paprika. Use 65 g (2½ oz) garlic butter and add 5 ml (1 tsp) dried mixed herbs to sauce.

PORK & VEGETABLE CRUMBLE

BAKED PORK CREOLE

BAKED PORK CREOLE   ⓕ

Preparation 40 mins **Cooking** 1½ hrs   *Serves 4*

450 g (1 lb) pork fillet, thinly sliced
60 ml (4 tbsp) flour
salt and freshly ground pepper
25 g (1 oz) butter
1 large onion, chopped
225 g (8 oz) tomatoes,
    skinned and chopped
1 large celery stick, chopped
1 small green pepper,
    seeded and chopped
60 ml (4 tbsp) tomato juice
boiled rice to serve

---

1. Coat pork in seasoned flour.

2. Fry in butter until golden. Transfer meat to a casserole dish.

3. Add onion to remaining butter in pan and fry gently until pale gold. Add to casserole with tomatoes, celery and green pepper.

4. Season to taste and add tomato juice.

5. Cover and bake at 180°C (350°F) Mark 4 for 1 hour.
To microwave: Cover and cook for 10–12 minutes, stirring twice.

6. Uncover and cook for a further 15 minutes.
To microwave: Uncover and cook for a further 5 minutes.

7. Serve with boiled rice.

Variation

CHILLI PORK CREOLE   ⓕ

Follow recipe and method for baked pork creole (left). Add 10 ml (2 tsp) chilli powder at step 4.

NORMANDY PORK & RICE   ⓕ

Preparation 25 mins **Cooking** 30 mins   *Serves 6*

25 g (1 oz) butter
350 g (12 oz) pork fillet, cut into strips
100 g (4 oz) onion, chopped
1 eating apple, cored and cut into slices
300 ml (½ pint) cider
568 ml (1 pint) stock
225 g (8 oz) long grain rice
60 ml (4 tbsp) fresh double cream (optional)
chopped parsley to garnish

1. Melt butter in a frying pan and cook pork until brown and almost cooked through.
To microwave: Cook butter and onion covered for 3 minutes.

2. Add onion and cook until soft.
To microwave: Stir in pork, cover and cook for 3 minutes.

3. Add apple, cider, stock and rice. Bring to the boil, cover and simmer for about 30 minutes or until rice is cooked, stirring occasionally and adding more liquid if needed.
To microwave: Add cider, 450ml (¾ pint) BOILING stock and rice. Cover and cook for 15 minutes. Stir in the apple and cook uncovered for 5 minutes or until the rice is tender.

4. Stir cream into rice, if used and sprinkle with chopped parsley.

PORK & PINEAPPLE CURRY   Ⓕ

Preparation 25 mins **Cooking** 1½ hrs   *Serves 4*

2 large onions, chopped
1 garlic clove, crushed
40g (1½oz) butter
550g (1¼lb) lean pork, diced
15ml (1 tbsp) flour
15–30ml (1–2 tbsp) curry powder
   (depending on strength preferred)
227g (8oz) can pineapple rings,
   drained and chopped
15ml (1 tbsp) tomato purée
50g (2oz) raisins or sultanas
15ml (1 tbsp) lemon juice
1 bay leaf
5ml (1 tsp) ground ginger
300ml (½ pint) stock or water
150ml (¼ pint) fresh milk
boiled rice to serve

1. Fry onions and garlic in butter until pale gold.
To microwave: Cook onions, garlic and butter, covered, for 5 minutes.

2. Add pork and fry briskly for 5 minutes, turning constantly.
To microwave: Stir in pork.

3. Stir in flour and curry powder.

4. Add remaining ingredients and bring to the boil.
To microwave: Stir in remaining ingredients, cover and cook for 10 minutes or until boiling, stirring once.

5. Lower heat, cover and simmer gently for 1–1½ hours or until pork is tender. Stir frequently.
To microwave: Continue cooking on MEDIUM (50%) for 10 minutes, then uncover and cook on MEDIUM (50%) for a further 15 minutes, or until pork is tender.

6. Serve with boiled rice.

PEKING PORK STIR-FRY   Ⓕ

Preparation 35 mins **Cooking** 25 mins   *Serves 4*

25g (1oz) butter
275g (10oz) pork fillet, cut into strips
225g (8oz) carrots, cut into thin strips
225g (8oz) courgettes, cut into thin strips
1 red, green or yellow pepper,
   seeded and cut into strips
4 spring onions, sliced
425g (15oz) can baby sweetcorn,
   drained and cut in half
100g (4oz) hoi sin or barbecue sauce
boiled rice to serve

1. Melt butter in a large frying pan or wok, add pork and stir-fry for 5 minutes.
To microwave: Melt butter for 30 seconds, stir in pork and cook uncovered for 4 minutes, stirring once or twice.

2. Add carrots and continue stir-frying for 3 minutes.
To microwave: Add carrots and cook uncovered for 3 minutes.

3. Add remaining vegetables and stir-fry for 3–4 minutes.
To microwave: Stir in remaining vegetables and cook for 4 minutes, stirring once.

4. Stir in hoi sin or barbecue sauce and heat through.
To microwave: Stir in hoi sin or barbecue sauce and cook for 3 minutes. Stir well.

5. Serve with boiled rice.

CHINESE-STYLE PORK Ⓕ

Preparation 35 mins **plus marinading**
Cooking 20 mins   *Serves 4*

15 ml (1 tbsp) soy sauce
5 ml (1 tsp) brown sugar
15 ml (1 tbsp) dry white wine
15 ml (1 tbsp) flour
450 g (1 lb) pork fillet, cut into thin slices
25 g (1 oz) butter
1 medium onion, chopped
100 g (4 oz) mushrooms, sliced
2 large tomatoes, skinned and chopped
50 g (2 oz) frozen peas
boiled noodles to serve

1. Mix soy sauce, sugar and wine with flour. Add pork and mix well. Leave to marinade for 30 minutes.

2. Melt 15 g (½ oz) butter in a non-stick frying pan, add onion and fry until soft but not brown. Remove from pan.

3. Melt remaining butter in pan, add pork and cook for 5 minutes, stirring.

4. Add fried onion, and remaining vegetables and cook for 5–10 minutes, or until pork is cooked. Stir frequently.

5. Serve with boiled noodles.

ORIENTAL PORK Ⓕ

Preparation 20 mins **plus marinading**
Cooking 35 mins   *Serves 4*

30 ml (2 tbsp) soy sauce
15 ml (1 tbsp) Worcestershire sauce
60 ml (4 tbsp) tomato ketchup
15 ml (1 tbsp) honey
5 ml (1 tsp) made mustard
450 g (1 lb) pork fillet, sliced
25 g (1 oz) butter
1 medium onion, chopped
150 ml (¼ pint) stock
1 red or green pepper, seeded and sliced
75 g (3 oz) mushrooms, sliced
boiled rice to serve

1. Mix together sauces, ketchup, honey and mustard. Add pork and marinade for 30 mins.

2. Melt butter and fry onion and meat (reserve marinade) until coloured.
To microwave: Cook butter and onion covered for 3 minutes. Stir in meat (reserve marinade) and cook uncovered for 6 mins.

3. Add stock and marinade, cover and simmer for 20 mins until pork is cooked.
To microwave: Add stock and marinade and cook uncovered for 5 mins.

ORIENTAL PORK

4. Add vegetables and cook for 3 mins or until sauce has reduced.
To microwave: Add vegetables and cook uncovered for 5 mins.

5. Serve with boiled rice.

PARTY GAMMON Ⓕ

Preparation 30 mins **Cooking** 3 hrs *Serves 12–14*

1.6–1.8 kg (3½-4 lb) piece boned corner or middle cut of gammon
cloves
75 g (3 oz) soft brown sugar
10 ml (2 tsp) dry mustard
50 g (2 oz) butter, melted
30 ml (2 tbsp) cider or apple juice
5 ml (1 tsp) Worcestershire sauce

1. Put gammon into a large pan, cover with cold water and bring to the boil. Discard water.
To microwave: Put gammon into a large casserole, pour over enough BOILING water to come up to the top of the gammon. Cover and cook for 5 minutes then discard water. Turn gammon over.

2. Cover with fresh water. Bring slowly to the boil and remove any scum. Cover and simmer gently for 1¾–2 hours.
To microwave: Pour over enough BOILING water to come to the top of the gammon. Cover and cook for 15 minutes, then lower power to MEDIUM (50%) and cook for about 1¼ hours, turning the meat at least once, or until cooked through.

3. Drain and cool slightly.

4. Strip off skin. Score fat into a diamond pattern with a sharp knife.

5. Press a clove into each alternate diamond.

6. Put gammon into a roasting tin.

7. Mix together sugar, mustard, butter, cider or apple juice and Worcestershire sauce. Coat fat with mixture.

8. Cook at 190°C (375°F) Mark 5 for 30 minutes or until fat is golden brown, basting three or four times.

9. Serve hot or cold.

BAKED GAMMON STEAKS WITH APPLES Ⓕ

Preparation 30 mins **Cooking** 50 mins *Serves 4*

30 ml (2 tbsp) soft brown sugar
5 ml (1 tsp) dry mustard
freshly ground pepper
4 × 150 g (5 oz) gammon steaks, trimmed of fat
12 very small onions or shallots, halved
150 ml (¼ pint) apple juice or cider
2 medium cooking apples, cored and sliced
3 cloves
15 g (½ oz) butter

1. Combine 15 ml (1 tbsp) sugar with mustard and a shake of pepper.

2. Rub on to both sides of gammon steaks.

3. Transfer to a greased ovenproof dish. Surround with onions.

4. Pour in apple juice and cover tightly.

5. Bake at 200°C (400°F) Mark 6 for 30 minutes.

6. Turn gammon steaks over. Cover with apples, remaining sugar and cloves.

7. Dot with butter and cook at 180°C (350°F) Mark 4 for 20 minutes.

GRILLED GAMMON WITH PINEAPPLE Ⓕ

Preparation 5 mins **Cooking** 20 mins *Serves 4*

4 × 100 g (4 oz) gammon rashers
227 g (8 oz) can pineapple rings in juice, drained

1. Remove rinds from gammon.

2. Snip fat with scissors at 2.5 cm (1 inch) intervals to prevent gammon from curling as it cooks.

3. Stand in grill pan and grill for 5–7 minutes (or until fat becomes transparent).

4. Turn over and grill for a further 5–7 minutes, or until cooked.

5. Remove gammon and keep warm.

6. Place pineapple rings under grill and cook until heated through.

7. Serve gammon with hot pineapple rings.

SAUSAGE & LEEK SUPPER

SAUSAGE & BEAN SUPPER ⒡

Preparation 15 mins **Cooking** 30 mins *Serves 4*

15 g (½ oz) butter
1 medium onion, sliced
4 medium carrots, sliced
5 ml (1 tsp) chilli powder
450 g (1 lb) low fat sausages, sliced
25 g (1 oz) wholemeal flour
300 ml (½ pint) fresh milk
15 ml (1 tbsp) Worcestershire sauce
15 ml (1 tbsp) tomato purée
225 g (7.9 oz) can baked beans
100 g (4 oz) frozen peas
jacket potatoes to serve

1. Melt butter in a non-stick saucepan and fry onion, carrots and chilli powder for 5 mins.

2. Add sausages, cover and cook for 15 mins.

3. Stir in flour, cook for a minute, stirring.

4. Gradually add milk, heat, whisking continuously, until sauce thickens, boils and is smooth. Cook for a minute.

5. Stir in Worcestershire sauce, tomato purée, baked beans and peas.

6. Cook for 5 mins. Serve with jacket potatoes.

SAUSAGE & LEEK SUPPER ⒡

Preparation 30 mins **Cooking** 45 mins *Serves 6*

700 g (1½ lb) potatoes, sliced
25 g (1 oz) butter
450 g (1 lb) pork sausages with herbs, sliced
1 medium onion, sliced
4 medium leeks, sliced
40 g (1½ oz) flour
450 ml (¾ pint) fresh milk
100 g (4 oz) smoked Cheddar cheese, grated
25 g (1 oz) fresh breadcrumbs

1. Cook potatoes in boiling water for 5–10 minutes. Drain.

2. Melt butter in a large pan, add sausages and cook for 5 minutes.

3. Add onion and leeks and cook for a further 5 minutes.

4. Add flour, cook for 1 minute then gradually add milk.

5. Heat stirring continuously until sauce thickens, boils and is smooth. Cook for a minute.

6. Remove from heat, add 75 g (3 oz) cheese and stir until melted.

7. Transfer to an ovenproof dish, arrange potato slices on top, sprinkle over breadcrumbs and remaining cheese.

8. Bake at 200°C (400°F) Mark 6 for 30 minutes until browned.

SAUSAGES WITH DEVILLED SAUCE

Preparation 10 mins **Cooking** 20 mins   *Serves 4*

450 g (1 lb) pork sausages
15 g (½ oz) butter
1 medium onion, chopped
15 ml (1 tbsp) flour
150 ml (¼ pint) water
30 ml (2 tbsp) sweet pickle
10 ml (2 tsp) Worcestershire sauce
30 ml (2 tbsp) tomato ketchup
5 ml (1 tsp) made mustard
15 ml (1 tbsp) vinegar

1. Grill sausages until cooked.

2. Meanwhile melt butter in a non-stick saucepan and fry onion until golden.

3. Stir in flour and cook for a minute, stirring.

4. Gradually stir in water. Add remaining ingredients and bring to the boil, stirring. Cook for a minute.

5. Serve sauce with cooked sausages.

PORK 'N' CHEESE BURGERS

Preparation 15 mins **Cooking** 20 mins   *Serves 4*

450 g (1 lb) minced lean pork
15 ml (1 tbsp) Taco seasoning mix
100 g (4 oz) Lancashire cheese, grated
1 egg
salad or baps to serve

1. Place meat in a bowl and break up with a fork.

2. Add spices, most of cheese and egg. Mix until combined.

3. Using dampened hands form into 8 burgers.

4. Grill or dry fry until well browned and cooked.

5. Sprinkle with remaining cheese and grill until melted.

6. Serve with salad or baps.

PORK 'N' CHEESE BURGERS

OFFAL

FRIED LIVER

Preparation 10 mins **plus soaking**
Cooking 5 mins   Serves 4

450 g (1 lb) lambs' *or* pigs' liver, sliced
fresh milk
60 ml (4 tbsp) flour
salt and freshly ground pepper
40 g (1½ oz) butter

1. Put liver into a soup plate or shallow dish. Cover with milk.
2. Soak for 30 minutes.
3. Drain. Pat dry with absorbent kitchen paper.
4. Toss in seasoned flour.
5. Heat butter in a frying pan. Add liver, a few pieces at a time.
6. Fry until crisp and golden, allowing 2–3 minutes each side.
7. Drain on absorbent kitchen paper.

GRILLED LIVER

Preparation 5 mins **plus soaking**
Cooking 3 mins   Serves 4

450 g (1 lb) lambs' liver, sliced
fresh milk
15 g (½ oz) butter, melted

1. Put liver into a soup plate or shallow dish. Cover with milk.
2. Soak for 30 minutes.
3. Drain. Pat dry with absorbent kitchen paper.
4. Stand on grill rack. Brush with melted butter.
5. Cook under a hot grill for 1½ minutes.
6. Turn over. Brush with more butter. Grill for a further 1½ minutes.
7. Serve immediately.

BRAISED LIVER   Ⓕ

Preparation 45 mins **Cooking** 40 mins   *Serves 4*

450 g (1 lb) ox liver, sliced
60 ml (4 tbsp) flour
salt and freshly ground pepper
50 g (2 oz) butter
1 medium onion, chopped
2 medium carrots, grated
1 large potato, grated
2 celery sticks, chopped
30 ml (2 tbsp) chopped parsley
300 ml (½ pint) water
1 medium lemon, sliced
cooked rice to serve

1. Cut liver into 2.5 cm (1 inch) strips.
2. Toss in seasoned flour.
3. Melt butter in a saucepan.
4. Fry liver until crisp and well sealed, turning all the time.
5. Remove to a plate.
6. Add onion to remaining butter. Fry slowly until pale gold.
7. Stir in any left-over flour, together with carrots, potato, celery, parsley and water. Season to taste.
8. Mix well. Bring to the boil. Replace liver, and top with lemon slices.
9. Lower heat. Cover and simmer for 30 minutes or until liver is tender.
10. Serve with cooked rice.

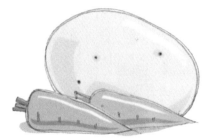

SPICY PEANUT LIVER Ⓕ

Preparation 25 mins **Cooking** 15 mins *Serves 4*

50 g (2 oz) flour
salt and freshly ground pepper
2.5 ml (½ tsp) turmeric
5 ml (1 tsp) chilli powder
450 g (1 lb) lambs' liver, cut into strips
50 g (2 oz) butter
1 medium onion, sliced
1 garlic clove, crushed
15 ml (1 tbsp) soy sauce
50 g (2 oz) dry roasted peanuts
450 ml (¾ pint) fresh milk

1. Mix flour, seasoning and spices in a large plastic bag, add liver and shake to coat with flour.

2. Melt butter in a large frying pan, add liver and fry for 3 mins or until browned.

3. Add onion and garlic and fry for 3 mins.

4. Stir in any remaining flour, soy sauce and peanuts. Cook, stirring for 2 mins.

5. Gradually add milk, cook stirring until sauce thickens, boils and is smooth.

6. Cook for a minute.

7. Cover and simmer for 5 mins.

LIVER SPECIAL Ⓕ

Preparation 30 mins **Cooking** 15 mins *Serves 4*

50 g (2 oz) flour
2.5 ml (½ tsp) curry powder
450 g (1 lb) lambs' liver, cut into strips
50 g (2 oz) butter
1 medium onion, sliced
1 green pepper, seeded and diced
400 ml (14 fl oz) fresh milk
198 g (7 oz) can sweetcorn, drained
1 eating apple, peeled, cored and sliced
boiled noodles or mashed potatoes to serve

1. Mix flour and curry powder in a large plastic bag, add liver and shake to coat with flour.

2. Melt butter in a large frying pan, add liver and fry for 3 minutes.

3. Add onion and pepper. Cook, stirring, for 3 minutes.

4. Gradually add milk. Cook, stirring until sauce thickens, boils and is smooth.

5. Cook for a minute.

6. Add sweetcorn and apple and heat through.

7. Serve with boiled noodles or mashed potatoes.

STEWED OXTAIL   Ⓕ

Preparation 20 mins **Cooking** 3¾ hrs   *Serves 4*

15 g (½ oz) butter
1 large onion, sliced
1 medium oxtail, about 1.1 kg (2 lb),
   cut into pieces
1 medium carrot, sliced
½ small swede, sliced
1 bouquet garni
450 ml (¾ pint) boiling water
30 ml (2 tbsp) flour
10 ml (2 tsp) vinegar
salt and freshly ground pepper

1. Heat butter in a large saucepan and fry onion until pale gold.
2. Add oxtail, carrot and swede. Fry briskly for 5 minutes, turning constantly.
3. Add bouquet garni and boiling water.
To microwave: Add bouquet garni and BOILING water. Transfer to a large casserole.
4. Bring to the boil, cover and simmer for 3 hours or until oxtail is tender.
To microwave: Cover and cook for 5 minutes or until boiling, then continue cooking on MEDIUM–LOW (30%) for 1½ hours or more, until oxtail is tender.
5. Remove and discard bouquet garni.
6. Refrigerate overnight. Remove fat from surface and discard.
7. Bring to the boil, cover and simmer for 30 minutes or until reheated.
To microwave: Cover and cook for 10 minutes stir occasionally or until boiling.
8. Mix flour with 45 ml (3 tbsp) cold water to make a smooth paste and stir into oxtail with vinegar.
9. Cook, stirring, until sauce thickens and boils. Simmer for 5 minutes.
To microwave: Cook for 3–5 minutes, until sauce thickens and boils.
10. Season to taste and serve.

TRIPE & ONIONS

Preparation 25 mins **Cooking** 55 mins   *Serves 4*

900 g (2 lb) dressed tripe, washed
225 g (8 oz) onions, sliced
450 ml (¾ pint) fresh milk
salt and freshly ground pepper
15 ml (1 tbsp) cornflour
15 g (½ oz) butter
chopped parsley to garnish

STEWED OXTAIL

1. Cut tripe into 5 cm (2 inch) squares.

2. Put tripe into a saucepan with onions, milk and seasoning.
To microwave: Put tripe into a casserole with onions, milk and seasoning.

3. Bring to the boil, cover and simmer gently for 35–45 mins, or until tripe is tender.
To microwave: Cover and cook for 10 mins or until boiling, then continue on MEDIUM–LOW (30%) for 20–30 mins, or until tripe is tender.

4. Mix cornflour to a smooth paste with a little cold water and stir in.

5. Cook, stirring, until sauce thickens and boils.
To microwave: Cook for about 3 mins until sauce thickens and boils.

6. Add butter, season to taste.

7. Serve sprinkled with parsley.

KIDNEY TURBIGO F

Preparation 20 mins **Cooking** 30 mins *Serves 4*

12 pickling onions or shallots
450 g (1 lb) lambs' kidneys, halved
25 g (1 oz) butter
225 g (8 oz) cocktail sausages
100 g (4 oz) button mushrooms, halved
15 ml (1 tbsp) flour
10 ml (2 tsp) tomato purée
30 ml (2 tbsp) sherry
300 ml (½ pint) stock
1 bay leaf
salt and freshly ground pepper
2 slices of bread
15 ml (1 tbsp) chopped parsley

1. Boil onions for 5 mins and drain.

2. Remove and discard skin and cores from kidneys.

3. Melt butter in a large non-stick frying pan and cook kidneys and sausages until browned. Remove and keep warm.

4. Add mushrooms, cook for 3 mins, stirring.

5. Stir in flour, tomato purée, sherry and stock. Bring to the boil, stirring.

6. Add kidneys, sausage and mushrooms to pan with bay leaf and seasoning.

7. Cover and simmer for 15 mins.

8. Cut crusts off bread and cut into triangles. Toast or fry until brown.

9. Serve with croûtons and parsley.

DEVILLED KIDNEYS

Preparation 20 mins **Cooking** 10 mins *Serves 2*

350 g (12 oz) lambs' kidneys
25 g (1 oz) butter
100 g (4 oz) mushrooms, sliced
15 ml (1 tbsp) Worcestershire sauce
30 ml (2 tbsp) tomato ketchup
5 ml (1 tsp) made English mustard
100 ml (4 fl oz) fresh whipping cream
cooked rice or toast to serve
chopped parsley to garnish

1. Remove and discard cores from kidneys and cut into bite-size pieces.

2. Melt butter in a saucepan, add kidneys and cook for 2 minutes, stirring.

3. Add mushrooms and continue cooking for 3 minutes, stirring.

4. Add sauce, ketchup, mustard and cream.

5. Mix well and heat without boiling.

6. Serve with rice or hot toast, sprinkled with chopped parsley.

CHINESE-STYLE KIDNEYS

Preparation 20 mins **Cooking** 15 mins *Serves 4*

450 g (1 lb) lambs' kidneys
25 g (1 oz) butter
175 g (6 oz) green beans,
    cut into 2.5 cm (1 inch) pieces
3 tomatoes, quartered
160 g (5.25 oz) jar black bean stir-fry sauce
75 g (3 oz) fromage frais
cooked noodles to serve

1. Remove and discard cores and skin from kidneys.

2. Cut a criss-cross design three-quarters the way through each kidney half.

3. Fry in butter until browned.

4. Add beans to kidneys. Cook, stirring for 4 minutes.

5. Add tomatoes and black bean sauce and heat until piping hot.

6. Remove from heat and stir in fromage frais.

7. Serve with cooked noodles.

CHICKEN

ROAST CHICKEN Ⓕ

Preparation 15 mins
Cooking 1 hr 40 mins   *Serves 4–6*

1.8 kg (4 lb) oven-ready chicken
streaky bacon rashers (optional)

accompany with
gravy (page 236)
bread sauce (page 237)
small cooked sausages
roast or boiled potatoes
assorted vegetables

1. If chicken is frozen, thaw completely. Check to see that there are no ice crystals in chicken cavity and legs are soft and flexible. Remove giblet pack.

2. Wash fresh or thawed bird. Dry thoroughly with absorbent kitchen paper.

3. Stand in a roasting tin. Cover breast with a few bacon rashers if used.

4. Roast at 190°C (375°F) Mark 5 allowing 20 minutes per 450 g (1 lb) plus 20 minutes. Test the deepest part of each thigh with a skewer to check that juices run clear and bird is cooked through.

5. Transfer to a board or carving dish. Leave for 5 minutes before carving.

6. Serve with accompaniments.

Variations

ROAST STUFFED CHICKEN Ⓕ

Follow recipe and method for roast chicken (above). Stuff neck end (not body cavity) with suitable stuffing (page 246). Fold neck skin under bird. Allow an extra 5 minutes per 450 g (1 lb) roasting time.

FRENCH-STYLE ROAST CHICKEN Ⓕ

Follow recipe and method for roast chicken (above). Mix 40 g (1½ oz) butter with 5 ml (1 tsp) each dried rosemary and French mustard. Place half in body cavity and smear remainder over chicken skin before roasting.

CHICKEN MARYLAND

Preparation 30 mins **Cooking** 40 mins   *Serves 4*

4×225 g (8 oz) chicken joints, skinned
fresh milk
175 g (6 oz) flour
salt and freshly ground pepper
2 eggs
50 g (2 oz) golden breadcrumbs
50 g (2 oz) butter
30 ml (2 tbsp) oil
pinch of nutmeg
1.25 ml (¼ tsp) dry mustard
150 ml (¼ pint) fresh milk
312 g (11 oz) can sweetcorn, drained
halved bananas fried in butter to serve

1. Dip chicken joints in milk. Toss in 50 g (2 oz) seasoned flour.

2. Break 1 egg in a bowl and beat. Dip in chicken, then coat with breadcrumbs. Shake off surplus crumbs.

3. Place butter and 15 ml (1 tbsp) oil in a roasting tin. Heat at 190°C (375°F) Mark 5 for 10 minutes. Add chicken and baste with hot fat.

4. Return to oven for 30 minutes or until chicken is tender.

5. Meanwhile make corn fritters. Mix together remaining flour, nutmeg and mustard.

6. Break in remaining egg and milk. Beat to form a smooth batter. Stir in sweetcorn.

7. Heat remaining oil in a non-stick frying pan.

8. Drop spoonfuls of fritter mixture into pan, turn over when underside is golden.

9. Cook for a further 3–4 minutes until cooked through.

10. Remove from pan and keep warm. Repeat with remaining mixture.

11. Serve chicken with corn fritters and fried bananas.

CHICKEN IN ORANGE CREAM

Preparation 10 mins **Cooking** 1 hr   *Serves 4*

25 g (1 oz) butter
4×100 g (4 oz) chicken breast fillets, skinned
1 medium onion, chopped
30 ml (2 tbsp) flour
300 ml (½ pint) orange juice
150 ml (5 fl oz) fresh soured cream
15 ml (1 tbsp) marmalade
2.5 ml (½ tsp) dried marjoram
wedges of orange and fresh parsley to garnish

1. Melt butter in a non-stick frying pan and brown chicken on both sides. Remove and place in an ovenproof casserole.
To microwave: Place chicken in a medium casserole.

2. Fry onion in remaining butter until soft.
To microwave: Cook butter and onion in a bowl or jug, covered, for 3 minutes.

3. Stir in flour and cook for 1 minute.
To microwave: Stir in flour.

4. Gradually blend in orange juice.

5. Bring to the boil, stirring, until thickened.
To microwave: Cook for 5 minutes, stirring once or twice, until boiling.

6. Stir in remaining ingredients and pour over chicken.

7. Cover and cook at 180°C (350°F) Mark 4 for 45 minutes, or until chicken is tender.
To microwave: Cook uncovered on MEDIUM (50%) for about 20 minutes, stirring half way, until chicken is tender.

8. Serve garnished with orange and parsley.

Variation

TURKEY IN CITRUS CREAM

Follow recipe and method for chicken in orange cream (left). Omit chicken and use 4 turkey breast steaks. Also use three fruits marmalade in place of orange marmalade.

CHICKEN IN ORANGE CREAM

FRICASSÉE OF CHICKEN Ⓕ

Preparation 30 mins **Cooking** 1¼ hrs *Serves 4*

1.6 kg (3½ lb) chicken joints,
  skinned and cut into 8 portions
300 ml (½ pint) chicken stock
300 ml (½ pint) fresh milk
100 g (4 oz) streaky bacon, chopped
4 cloves
1 large onion
1.25 ml (¼ tsp) ground nutmeg
50 g (2 oz) mushrooms, sliced
1.25 ml (¼ tsp) dried mixed herbs
salt and freshly ground pepper
25 g (1 oz) butter
25 g (1 oz) flour
4 rashers streaky bacon, halved, rolled
  and grilled to garnish
4 lemon wedges to garnish
15 ml (1 tbsp) chopped parsley to garnish

1. Put chicken into a saucepan with stock,
milk and bacon.
*To microwave: Put chicken into a large
casserole with BOILING stock, milk and
bacon.*

2. Press cloves into onion and add to chicken
with nutmeg, mushrooms, herbs and
seasoning.

3. Bring to the boil and remove any scum.
*To microwave: Cover and cook for about
12 minutes or until boiling, rearranging
chicken once or twice.*

4. Lower heat, cover and simmer gently for
1–1½ hours or until chicken is tender.
*To microwave: Continue cooking on MEDIUM
(50%) for 20 minutes, rearranging chicken
half way.*

5. Transfer chicken to plate, keep hot.

6. Strain chicken liquid and reserve.

7. Melt butter in a clean saucepan, add flour
and cook for 1 minute. Gradually blend in
chicken liquid.
*To microwave: Melt butter for 30 seconds,
add flour and gradually stir in chicken
liquid.*

8. Cook stirring until sauce boils and
thickens. Cook for 1 minute.
*To microwave: Cook for 4–5 minutes, stirring
two or three times, until sauce boils and
thickens.*

9. Pour sauce over chicken and garnish with
bacon, lemon and parsley.

CHICKEN & PARSLEY CASSEROLE Ⓕ

Preparation 40 mins **Cooking** 1¼ hrs *Serves 4*

4 × 275 g (10 oz) chicken portions, skinned
50 g (2 oz) butter
100 g (4 oz) streaky bacon, chopped
2 large onions, chopped
50 g (2 oz) flour
568 ml (1 pint) fresh milk
1 bay leaf
5 ml (1 tsp) dried mixed herbs
1 chicken stock cube
salt and freshly ground pepper
100 g (4 oz) mushrooms, sliced
30 ml (2 tbsp) chopped parsley to garnish

1. Fry chicken in 25 g (1 oz) butter until
golden. Transfer to a large casserole.
*To microwave: Arrange chicken joints in a
large casserole.*

2. Add bacon and onions to same pan and fry
gently until pale gold. Sprinkle over chicken.
*To microwave: Cook bacon uncovered for
5 mins, stirring twice until brown and crisp.
Sprinkle over chicken. Cook 25 g (1 oz) butter
and onions covered for 5 mins, then sprinkle
over chicken.*

3. Melt remaining butter, stir in flour and
cook for 1 min. Gradually blend in milk.
*To microwave: Melt remaining butter for
30 seconds, stir in flour and gradually blend
in milk.*

4. Add bay leaf, herbs and crumbled stock
cube.

5. Cook stirring until sauce boils and
thickens. Cook for 1 min.
*To microwave: Cook for about 6 mins,
stirring frequently, until sauce boils and
thickens.*

6. Season to taste and pour over chicken.

7. Cover and cook at 170°C (325°F) Mark 3
for 1 hour.
*To microwave: Cover and cook for 10 mins.
Stir sauce and rearrange chicken then
continue cooking on MEDIUM (50%) for
15 mins.*

8. Add mushrooms, cover and cook for a
further 30 mins.
*To microwave: Add mushrooms, cover and
cook on MEDIUM (50%) for a further 10 mins.*

9. Serve garnished with chopped parsley.

PIPPIN CHICKEN 🄵

Preparation 15 mins **Cooking** 25 mins *Serves 4*

15 g (½ oz) butter
1 medium onion, chopped
4×100 g (4 oz) chicken breast fillets, skinned
15 g (½ oz) cornflour
300 ml (½ pint) fresh milk
1 chicken stock cube
5 ml (1 tsp) dried mixed herbs
100 ml (4 fl oz) apple juice
100 g (4 oz) seedless black grapes

1. Melt butter in a large frying pan and fry onion and chicken for 3 minutes.
To microwave: Cook butter and onion covered for 3 minutes. Add chicken.
2. Blend cornflour with milk and add to chicken with crumbled stock cube and herbs.
3. Bring to the boil, stirring, then add apple juice. Cover and simmer for 20 minutes, stirring occasionally and turning chicken over half way.
To microwave: Add apple juice, cover and cook for 7–8 minutes, stirring once or twice, until boiling. Continue cooking on MEDIUM (50%) for 8 minutes, stirring half way, or until chicken is cooked.
4. Add grapes just before serving.

CHICKEN MYERS

Preparation 15 mins **Cooking** 55 mins *Serves 4*

225 g (8 oz) broccoli florets
4×175 g (6 oz) chicken breast portions, skinned
298 g (10.5 fl oz) can condensed cream of chicken soup
50 g (2 oz) mayonnaise
60 ml (4 tbsp) fresh double cream
2.5 ml (½ tsp) curry powder
25 g (1 oz) English Cheddar, grated

1. Cook broccoli in boiling water until almost tender. Drain well.
To microwave: Cook broccoli with 60 ml (4 tbsp) water, covered, for 5 minutes.
2. Place drained broccoli and chicken in a shallow ovenproof dish.
3. Mix together soup, mayonnaise, cream and curry powder. Spoon over chicken and broccoli, coating them well. Sprinkle with cheese.
4. Bake at 190°C (375°F) Mark 5 for 45–50 minutes or until chicken is tender.
To microwave: Cover and cook for 5 minutes, then cook on MEDIUM (50%) for 10–15 minutes, rearranging once, or until chicken is tender.

115

CHICKEN & TOMATO SUPPER

CHICKEN & TOMATO SUPPER

Preparation 45 mins **Cooking** 35 mins **Serves 4**

15 g (½ oz) butter
1 medium onion, sliced
1 green pepper, seeded and sliced
275 g (10 oz) courgettes, sliced
397 g (14 oz) can passata (sieved tomatoes)
5 ml (1 tsp) Italian herb seasoning
350 g (12 oz) chicken breast fillets, cubed
15 ml (1 tbsp) cornflour
100 g (4 oz) wholemeal bread,
    lightly toasted and cubed
100 g (4 oz) English Cheddar, cubed
parsley to garnish

1. Melt butter in a saucepan and cook onions and pepper for 3 minutes.
To microwave: Cook butter, onion and pepper covered for 3 minutes.
2. Add courgettes, tomatoes, herbs and chicken.
3. Bring to the boil, cover and simmer for 10–15 minutes until chicken is cooked.
To microwave: Cover and cook for 10–12 minutes, stirring twice, until cooked.
4. Blend cornflour with a little cold water and stir into chicken.
5. Cook until thickened.
To microwave: Cook covered for 1 minute.
6. Spoon into a flameproof dish, scatter bread and cheese over top and grill until cheese begins to melt.
7. Garnish with parsley.

CHICKEN IN TARRAGON SAUCE

Preparation 40 mins
Cooking 25 mins   *Serves 4–6*

450 g (1 lb) chicken breast fillets,
    cut into strips
25 g (1 oz) flour
25 g (1 oz) butter
1 medium onion, chopped
1 small green pepper, seeded and sliced
grated rind of 1 lemon
1 garlic clove, crushed
150 ml (¼ pint) dry white wine
15 ml (1 tbsp) finely chopped fresh tarragon
150 ml (5 fl oz) fresh double cream
10 ml (2 tsp) made wholegrain mustard
50 g (2 oz) English Cheddar, grated
cooked pasta to serve

1. Coat chicken in flour.

2. Melt butter in a non-stick frying pan. Add onion and cook for 2 mins or until soft.
To microwave: Cook onion and butter covered for 2–3 mins until soft.

3. Add chicken, pepper, lemon rind, garlic, wine and tarragon.

4. Cook for 10–15 mins.
To microwave: Cover and cook for 8 mins, stirring once or twice.

5. Stir in cream, mustard and cheese.

6. Heat through.
To microwave: Cook for 1–2 mins, heat through.

7. Serve with cooked pasta.

Coq au Vin　Ⓕ

Preparation 40 mins **Cooking** 1½ hrs　　*Serves 4*

4×275 g (10 oz) chicken portions, skinned
60 ml (4 tbsp) flour
salt and freshly ground pepper
40 g (1½ oz) butter
15 ml (1 tbsp) oil
1 large onion, chopped
1 garlic clove, crushed
100 g (4 oz) bacon, chopped
8 small onions or shallots
30 ml (2 tbsp) chopped parsley
1 bay leaf
300 ml (½ pint) dry red wine
60 ml (4 tbsp) water
100 g (4 oz) mushrooms, sliced

1. Toss chicken joints in seasoned flour.

2. Heat butter and oil in a large saucepan and fry chicken until crisp and golden on both sides. Remove to a plate.
To microwave: Heat butter and oil in a large casserole for 45 seconds.

3. Add chopped onion, garlic and bacon to remaining butter and oil in pan.
To microwave: Stir chopped onion, garlic and bacon into butter and oil.

4. Fry gently until pale gold.
To microwave: Cover and cook for 5 minutes, stirring twice.

5. Return chicken to pan.
To microwave: Add chicken to onion mixture.

6. Add small onions, parsley, bay leaf, wine and water.

7. Bring to the boil then lower heat, cover and simmer for 1 hour.
To microwave: Cover and cook for 10 minutes or until boiling. Stir well, cover and cook on MEDIUM (50%) for 15 minutes, rearranging chicken half way.

8. Add mushrooms and simmer for a further 10 minutes.
To microwave: Add mushrooms, cover and cook on MEDIUM (50%) for 5 minutes.

Chicken Cacciatore　Ⓕ

Preparation 40 mins **Cooking** 1¼ hrs　　*Serves 4*

4×275 g (10 oz) chicken portions
60 ml (4 tbsp) flour
salt and freshly ground pepper
50 g (2 oz) butter
15 ml (1 tbsp) oil
1 large onion, chopped
1 garlic clove, crushed
450 g (1 lb) tomatoes, skinned and chopped
5 ml (1 tsp) sugar
150 ml (¼ pint) chicken stock
100 g (4 oz) mushrooms, sliced
cooked pasta to serve

1. Toss chicken in seasoned flour.
To microwave: Skin chicken, if desired, before tossing in seasoned flour.

2. Heat butter and oil in large pan and fry chicken until crisp and golden on both sides. Remove to a plate.
To microwave: Arrange floured chicken in a casserole.

3. Fry onion and garlic in remaining butter and oil until pale gold.
To microwave: Cook 25 g (1 oz) butter, oil, onion and garlic covered for 5 mins.

4. Add tomatoes, sugar and stock.
To microwave: Add tomatoes, sugar and BOILING stock. Cover and cook for 5 mins.

5. Replace chicken, bring to the boil slowly, cover, lower heat and simmer for 45 mins.
To microwave: Pour sauce over chicken, cover and cook on MEDIUM (50%) for 20 mins, rearranging chicken half way.

6. Add mushrooms and simmer for a further 15 mins.
To microwave: Add mushrooms, cover and cook on MEDIUM (50%) for 5 mins.

7. Serve with pasta.

STIR-FRIED CHICKEN

Preparation 20 mins **Cooking** 10 mins *Serves 4*

25 g (1 oz) butter
2.5 ml (½ tsp) five spice powder
350 g (12 oz) chicken breast fillet,
    cut into strips
375 g (13 oz) pack fresh stir-fry vegetables
10 ml (2 tsp) soy sauce
100 g (4 oz) Double Gloucester cheese,
    cubed

1. Melt butter in a large frying pan, add spices and chicken.

2. Cook for 6 minutes until browned and cooked.

3. Add vegetables and soy sauce, stir-fry for 2 minutes.

4. Add cheese and serve immediately.

CHICKEN WITH ALMONDS

Preparation 30 mins
Cooking 30 mins   *Serves 3–4*

1 small onion, chopped
50 g (2 oz) mushrooms, sliced
25 g (1 oz) butter
10 ml (2 tsp) cornflour
300 ml (½ pint) fresh milk
350 g (12 oz) cooked chicken meat,
    chopped
1.25 ml (¼ tsp) *each* ground ginger and
    ground nutmeg
150 g (5 oz) natural yogurt
1 egg yolk
salt and freshly ground pepper
25 g (1 oz) flaked almonds, toasted

1. Fry onion and mushrooms in butter, in a saucepan, until pale gold.
To microwave: Cook onion, mushrooms and butter covered for 3 minutes.

2. Add cornflour, cook for 1 minute then gradually blend in milk.
To microwave: Add cornflour then gradually blend in 225 ml (8 fl oz) milk.

3. Cook stirring until sauce boils.
To microwave: Cook for 4–5 minutes, stirring frequently, until sauce boils.

4. Add chicken, ginger and nutmeg.

5. Simmer gently for 5–7 minutes.
To microwave: Cook for 3 minutes, stirring once or twice.

6. Beat together yogurt and egg yolk, add to chicken.

7. Cook very slowly, without boiling, until thickened.
To microwave: Cook for 1–2 minutes, stirring once or twice.

8. Season to taste and pour into a serving dish. Scatter with almonds.

CHICKEN PIE   Ⓕ

Preparation 40 mins **Cooking** 1½ hrs *Serves 4–6*

4 × 275 g (10 oz) chicken portions, skinned
2 medium carrots, halved
3 medium onions
2 medium celery sticks, sliced
1.1 litre (2 pint) water
salt and freshly ground pepper
40 g (1½ oz) butter
100 g (4 oz) mushrooms, sliced
40 g (1½ oz) flour
300 ml (½ pint) fresh milk
60 ml (4 tbsp) fresh double cream
shortcrust pastry made with
    225 g (8 oz) flour (page 364)
beaten egg to glaze

1. Place chicken, carrots, 2 onions (cut into quarters), celery and water in a large saucepan and season to taste.
To microwave: Place chicken, carrots, 2 onions (cut into quarters), celery and BOILING water into a large casserole and season to taste.

2. Bring to the boil, remove any scum then cover and simmer for 1 hour.
To microwave: Cover and cook for about 10 minutes or until boiling, then cook on MEDIUM (50%) for 20 minutes.

3. Remove chicken, discard bones and cut meat into bite-size pieces.

4. Strain chicken liquid, reserving carrots and 150 ml (¼ pint) of liquid.

5. Chop carrots and remaining onion.

6. Melt butter in a saucepan and fry onion and mushrooms until soft.
To microwave: Cook butter and onions covered for 5 minutes.

7. Add flour and cook for 1 minute. Gradually stir in milk and reserved chicken liquid.
To microwave: Add flour, then gradually stir in milk and reserved chicken liquid.

8. Cook stirring until sauce comes to the boil and thickens. Cook for a minute.
To microwave: Cook for 5–6 minutes, stirring two or three times, until sauce boils and thickens.

9. Remove from heat and stir in reserved chicken, carrots and cream. Season to taste.

10. Spoon into a 1.1 litre (2 pint) pie dish.

11. Roll out pastry on a floured work surface until 5 cm (2 inch) larger than pie dish.

12. Cut a 2.5 cm (1 inch) wide strip off pastry and place on dampened rim of dish. Brush strip with water.

13. Cover with pastry lid and press lightly to seal edges.

14. Trim off excess pastry, knock edges back to seal and crimp.

15. Brush with beaten egg to glaze.

16. Stand on a baking sheet and bake at 220°C (425°F) Mark 7 for 25–30 minutes or until pastry is cooked.

Use remaining chicken liquid to make soup.

Alternatively use 450 g (1 lb) cooked chicken, 2 sliced and cooked carrots and 150 ml (¼ pint) ready-made chicken stock. Omit steps 1–4.

Variations

CHICKEN & LEEK PIE

Follow recipe and method for chicken pie (left). Use 2 sliced leeks in place of mushrooms.

CHICKEN & HAM PIE

Follow recipe and method for chicken pie (left). Add 100 g (4 oz) cooked, diced ham at step 9.

CHICKEN PIE

TANDOORI CHICKEN

Preparation 10 mins **plus** 2 hrs **marinading**
Cooking 40 mins   *Serves 4*

3 garlic cloves, crushed
275 g (10 oz) natural yogurt
10 ml (2 tsp) garam masala
5 ml (1 tsp) *each* paprika
   and ground ginger
2.5 ml (½ tsp) *each* chilli powder,
   dry mustard and turmeric
4 × 100 g (4 oz) chicken breast fillets,
   skinned
cooked rice to serve
coriander to garnish

1. Mix garlic, yogurt and spices together in a large bowl.

2. Cut a few slashes into flesh of chicken and cover with yogurt mixture.

3. Cover and refrigerate overnight or for at least 2 hours.

4. Place on a wire roasting rack and bake at 200°C (400°F) Mark 6 for 40 minutes until brown and tender.

5. Serve with cooked rice and garnish with coriander.

TANDOORI CHICKEN

CHICKEN TIKKA

Preparation 25 mins **plus** 2 hrs **marinading**
Cooking 20 mins   *Serves 4*

275 g (10 oz) natural yogurt
juice and rind of 1 lemon
4 spring onions, finely chopped
2 garlic cloves, crushed
15 ml (1 tbsp) vinegar
5 ml (1 tsp) *each* chilli powder,
   ground coriander, turmeric and salt
15 ml (1 tbsp) grated fresh ginger
450 g (1 lb) chicken breast fillet, cubed
pitta bread, salad & lemon wedges to serve

1. Mix together all ingredients except chicken in a bowl.

2. Stir in chicken and mix well.

3. Cover and leave to marinade in refrigerator overnight or for at least 2 hours.

4. Stir occasionally.

5. Thread onto skewers.

6. Cook under a preheated medium grill or over a barbecue for about 15–20 minutes.

7. Turn regularly and baste with marinade.

8. Serve with pitta bread, salad and lemon.

TURKEY

ROAST TURKEY (F)

Preparation 20 mins
Cooking according to chart

1 oven-ready turkey
stuffing (page 246)
1 medium onion
1 eating apple, halved
50–100g (2–4oz) butter, softened, depending on size of bird
streaky bacon rashers (optional)

accompany with
gravy (page 236)
bread sauce (page 237)
cranberry sauce (page 236)
small cooked sausages
grilled bacon rolls
roast and boiled potatoes (page 171)
Brussels sprouts

1. If turkey is frozen place in its bag on a large plate in a cool place until completely thawed, see chart (right) for thawing times. Check that there are no ice crystals in turkey cavity and legs are flexible. Remove giblet pack.
2. Wash fresh or thawed bird. Dry thoroughly with absorbent kitchen paper. Cook straight away or refrigerate.
3. Stuff neck end (not body cavity) and fold neck skin under bird just before roasting.
4. Place onion and apple into body cavity.
5. Place in a roasting tin and smear butter over skin. Place bacon rashers over breast if used.
6. Roast at 190°C (375°F) Mark 5 according to recommended times in chart (right).
7. Remove bacon rashers or foil for last 30 minutes of cooking time to allow skin to brown and crisp. Test the deepest part of each thigh with a skewer to check that juices run clear and bird is cooked through.
8. Leave to stand for 15 minutes before carving. Serve with accompaniments.

TURKEY THAWING AND ROASTING CHART

Thaw below 15°C (60°F)			*Cooking Time at 190°C (375°F) Mark 5*	
Oven Ready Weight	*Number of Servings*	*Thawing Time*	*Without Foil*	*Wrapped in Foil*
3–5 lb	4–6	20 hrs	1½–1¾ hrs	1¾–2 hrs
6–7 lb	7–9	30 hrs	1¾–2 hrs	2–2¼ hrs
8–9 lb	10–14	36 hrs	2–2½ hrs	2½–2¾ hrs
10–11 lb	15–16	45 hrs	2¼–2¾ hrs	2½–3 hrs
12–13 lb	17–18	48 hrs	2¾–3 hrs	3–3¼ hrs
14–17 lb	19–25	48 hrs	3¼–3½ hrs	3½–3¾ hrs
18–22 lb	26–37	48 hrs	3½–3¾ hrs	3¾–4 hrs
23 lb plus	38 plus	48 hrs	3¾ hrs plus	4¼ hrs plus

TURKEY À LA CRÈME (F)

Preparation 15 mins **Cooking** 20 mins *Serves 4*

1 medium onion, sliced
25g (1oz) butter
350g (12oz) cooked turkey meat, cut into strips
1 red pepper, seeded and sliced
150ml (¼pint) dry white wine
salt and freshly ground pepper
150ml (5floz) fresh double cream
100g (4oz) canned sweetcorn
cooked rice to serve

1. Fry onion in butter until soft. Stir in turkey.
To microwave: Cook onion and butter, covered, for 3 minutes. Stir in turkey.
2. Add pepper, wine and seasoning. Bring to the boil, simmer for 10 minutes.
To microwave: Add pepper, wine and seasoning. Cover and cook for 3–5 minutes, until boiling. Continue cooking on MEDIUM (50%) for 5 minutes.
3. Stir in cream and sweetcorn, reheat.
To microwave: Stir in cream and sweetcorn, cover and cook for 1 minute to reheat.
4. Serve with cooked rice.

TURKEY IN PAPRIKA

TURKEY IN PAPRIKA

Preparation 20 mins **Cooking** 30 mins *Serves 4*

1 large onion, chopped
1 green pepper, seeded and chopped
25 g (1 oz) butter
10 ml (2 tsp) oil
15 ml (1 tbsp) flour
22.5 ml (1½ tbsp) paprika
15 ml (1 tbsp) tomato purée
5 ml (1 tsp) sugar
300 ml (½ pint) stock
salt and freshly ground pepper
1.25 ml (¼ tsp) caraway seeds (optional)
350 g (12 oz) cooked turkey meat,
   cut into bite-size pieces
150 g (5 oz) natural yogurt
boiled potatoes or noodles to serve
chopped parsley to garnish

1. Fry onion and pepper in butter and oil until pale gold and soft.
To microwave: Cook onion, pepper, oil and butter covered for 5 minutes, stirring once.
2. Remove from heat and stir in flour, paprika, tomato purée and sugar.
3. Gradually blend in stock, seasoning and caraway seeds if used.

4. Cook, stirring, until sauce boils & thickens.
To microwave: Cook for about 3 minutes, stir twice, until boiling.
5. Cover and simmer gently for 15 minutes.
To microwave: Cover and cook on MEDIUM (50%) for 10 minutes.
6. Add turkey to sauce with yogurt.
7. Heat through for a further 5 minutes without boiling.
To microwave: Cook for about 3 minutes, stirring once or twice.
8. Serve with potatoes or noodles, garnished with parsley.

TURKEY WITH HAM & CHEESE

Preparation 15 mins **Cooking** 25 mins *Serves 4*

4 × 100 g (4 oz) turkey breast steaks
25 g (1 oz) garlic butter, melted
2 slices cooked ham, halved
40 g (1½ oz) English Cheddar, grated
40 g (1½ oz) Double Gloucester cheese, grated
15 ml (1 tbsp) chopped parsley
15 ml (1 tbsp) fresh milk
parsley to garnish

1. Dip turkey steaks in melted butter and coat well. Place on a non-stick baking sheet.
To microwave: Brush turkey steaks well with melted butter and arrange towards outer edge of a shallow dish.

2. Bake at 200°C (400°F) Mark 6 for 20 mins.
To microwave: Cover and cook for 8 mins or until cooked.

3. Place a piece of ham on top of each piece of turkey.

4. Mix together cheeses, parsley and milk and spoon on top of ham.

5. Continue cooking for 5 mins until cheese has melted.
To microwave: Cook uncovered for about 2 mins until the cheese has melted.

6. Serve garnished with parsley.

HOT CORONATION TURKEY

Preparation 20 mins **Cooking** 25 mins   *Serves 6*

1 onion, finely chopped
15g (½oz) butter
15ml (1tbsp) curry powder
350g (12oz) jar mango chutney
450g (1lb) Greek-style yogurt
45ml (3tbsp) mayonnaise
10ml (2tsp) tomato purée
450g (1lb) cooked turkey meat, diced
cooked rice or pasta to serve

1. Cook onion in butter until soft.
To microwave: Cook onion and butter, covered, for 3 minutes.

2. Stir in curry powder and cook, stirring, for 1 minute.
To microwave: Stir in curry powder and cook for 1 minute.

3. Add chutney and heat through.
To microwave: Add chutney and cook for 1 minute.

4. Stir in yogurt, mayonnaise and tomato purée.

5. Heat until almost boiling.
To microwave: Cook for 3 minutes, stir once.

6. Add turkey and cook gently for about 15 minutes or until heated through.
To microwave: Add turkey, cover and cook for 3–5 minutes, stirring once or twice.

7. Serve with rice or pasta

TURKEY À LA KING

Preparation 20 mins **Cooking** 30 mins   *Serves 4*

1 medium green pepper, seeded and diced
25g (1oz) butter
10ml (2tsp) oil
100g (4oz) mushrooms, sliced
25g (1oz) flour
150ml (¼pint) stock
150ml (¼pint) fresh milk
350g (12oz) cooked turkey meat,
   cut into bite-size pieces
150ml (5fl oz) fresh single cream
15ml (1tbsp) dry sherry or lemon juice
salt and freshly ground pepper
cooked rice to serve

1. Fry pepper gently in butter and oil for 5 minutes.
To microwave: Cook pepper, butter and oil, covered, for 2 minutes.

2. Add mushrooms and fry gently for 5 minutes. Transfer to a plate.
To microwave: Stir in mushrooms, cover and cook for 2 minutes.

3. Stir flour into remaining butter and oil in pan and cook, stirring, for 2 minutes without browning.
To microwave: Stir flour into pepper and mushrooms.

4. Gradually blend in stock and milk.

5. Cook, stirring, until sauce thickens, boils and is smooth.
To microwave: Cook for about 5 minutes, stirring frequently, until sauce thickens, boils and is smooth.

6. Lower heat and add pepper, mushrooms and turkey. Cover and heat through gently for 10 minutes.
To microwave: Stir in turkey, cover and cook for 3 minutes or until heated through.

7. Add cream and sherry or lemon juice and season to taste.
To microwave: Add cream and sherry or lemon juice. Season to taste, cover and cook for 1–2 minutes to heat through if necessary.

8. Serve with cooked rice.

LAYERED TURKEY & BROCCOLI LOAF Ⓕ

Preparation 40 mins **Cooking** 1¾ hrs   *Serves 6*

50 g (2 oz) mushrooms, sliced
25 g (1 oz) butter
450 g (1 lb) minced turkey meat
1 medium onion, finely chopped
75 g (3 oz) fresh wholemeal breadcrumbs
2 eggs, beaten
60 ml (4 tbsp) fresh double cream
2.5 ml (½ tsp) dried tarragon
grated rind of 1 lemon
salt and freshly ground pepper
100 g (4 oz) broccoli spears, lightly cooked
cooked rice and sweetcorn to serve

1. Lightly fry mushrooms in 15 g (½ oz) butter.
*To microwave: Melt butter for 20 seconds.
Stir in mushrooms and cook covered for
1½ minutes.*

2. Use remaining butter to grease a
900 g (2 lb) loaf tin. Arrange fried mushrooms
overlapping down centre of tin.
*To microwave: Use remaining butter to
grease a 1.25 litre (2¼ pint) loaf dish. Arrange
mushrooms overlapping down centre of dish.*

3. Mix turkey, onion, breadcrumbs, eggs,
cream, tarragon, lemon rind and seasoning.

4. Spread half mixture in base of tin or dish.

5. Lay broccoli spears on top, then spread
over remaining turkey mixture.

6. Cover with foil, then place in a roasting tin
with hot water to come half way up sides of tin.
*To microwave: Cover with greaseproof paper
and place in a large shallow dish with hot
water to come half way up sides of dish.*

7. Bake at 180°C (350°F) Mark 4 for 2 hours.
*To microwave: Cook on MEDIUM (50%) for
35 minutes. Allow to stand for 5–10 minutes
in dish of water.*

8. Turn out on to a plate. Serve hot or cold.

9. Serve with rice and sweetcorn.

Alternatively arrange fried mushrooms on
top of loaf after cooking.

TURKEY PILAFF Ⓕ

Preparation 25 mins **Cooking** 30 mins   *Serves 4*

1 large onion, chopped
25 g (1 oz) butter
10 ml (2 tsp) oil
225 g (8 oz) long-grain rice

LAYERED TURKEY & BROCCOLI LOAF

568 ml (1 pint) stock
225 g (8 oz) cooked turkey meat,
  cut into bite-size pieces
50 g (2 oz) raisins
2.5 ml (½ tsp) grated orange rind
100 g (4 oz) tomatoes, skinned & chopped
25 g (1 oz) blanched, toasted and chopped
  almonds
15 ml (1 tbsp) chopped parsley

1. Fry onion in butter and oil until pale gold.
*To microwave: Cook onion, butter and oil
covered for 5 minutes.*

2. Add rice and fry for 1 minute, stirring.
To microwave: Stir in rice.

3. Pour in stock.
To microwave: Pour in BOILING stock.

4. Bring to the boil, cover, lower heat and
simmer for 15 minutes.
*To microwave: Cover, leaving a small vent
and cook for 10 minutes.*

5. Add remaining ingredients.

6. Continue simmering for a further
7–10 minutes or until the rice has absorbed
all the liquid and is tender.
*To microwave: Cover and cook for 5 minutes
or until the rice has absorbed all the liquid
and is tender.*

SPICY TURKEY STEW   Ⓕ

Preparation 35 mins **Cooking** 50 mins   *Serves 4*

225 g (8 oz) onions, chopped
1 garlic clove, crushed
50 g (2 oz) bacon, chopped
40 g (1½ oz) butter
450 g (1 lb) boneless turkey fillet, cubed
15 ml (1 tbsp) garam masala
1 large green pepper, seeded and chopped
227 g (8 oz) can chopped tomatoes
150 ml (¼ pint) stock

1. Fry onion, garlic and bacon in butter until
lightly browned.
*To microwave: Cook onion, garlic, bacon and
butter, uncovered, for 5 minutes, stir twice.*

2. Add turkey and cook until golden.
To microwave: Stir in turkey.

3. Stir in garam masala and mix well. Add
pepper, tomatoes and stock.

4. Bring to the boil, cover and simmer for
40 minutes or until turkey is tender. Uncover
for last 10 minutes of cooking time.
*To microwave: Cover and cook for
15–20 minutes, stirring frequently, or until
turkey is tender. Uncover for last 5 minutes
of cooking time.*

Turkey Marengo Ⓕ

Preparation 30 mins **Cooking** 50 mins *Serves 4*

700 g (1½ lb) boneless turkey fillet, cubed
45 ml (3 tbsp) flour
salt and freshly ground pepper
25 g (1 oz) butter
15 ml (1 tbsp) oil
1 large onion, chopped
1 garlic clove, crushed
150 ml (¼ pint) stock
150 ml (¼ pint) dry white wine
397 g (14 oz) can chopped tomatoes
225 g (8 oz) mushrooms, halved
30 ml (2 tbsp) chopped parsley
cooked rice to serve

1. Coat turkey in seasoned flour.

2. Heat butter and oil in a pan, add turkey, cook until golden. Remove to a plate.
To microwave: Cook butter and oil for 45 seconds, or until melted.

3. Add onion and garlic, cook until soft.
To microwave: Add onion and garlic, cover and cook for 5 mins.

4. Return turkey to pan, stir in stock, wine, tomatoes and mushrooms.
To microwave: Stir in turkey, stock, wine, tomatoes and mushrooms.

5. Bring to the boil, cover and simmer for 40 mins or until turkey is tender. Stir.
To microwave: Cover and cook for 15–20 mins, stirring frequently, until tender.

6. Uncover and boil rapidly to reduce sauce slightly.
To microwave: Uncover and cook for 5 mins to reduce sauce slightly.

7. Sprinkle with parsley and serve with rice.

Spiced Turkey Kebabs

Preparation 30 mins **plus** 2 hrs **marinading**
Cooking 20 mins *Serves 4*

450 g (1 lb) turkey meat, cubed
60 ml (4 tbsp) peanut butter
5 ml (1 tsp) *each* ground cumin and
   chilli powder
150 ml (¼ pint) fresh milk
175 g (6 oz) fromage frais
frisée and wedges of lime to serve

1. Thread turkey on to skewers.

2. Blend peanut butter, spices and milk.

3. Pour over kebabs, marinade for 2 hours.

4. Grill kebabs, basting with marinade.

5. Place remaining marinade in a pan, bring to the boil and cook stirring for 2 minutes.

6. Remove from heat and stir in fromage frais. Reheat without boiling.

7. Serve with sauce, frisée and lime.

Turkey & Broccoli Supper Ⓕ

Preparation 20 mins **Cooking** 30 mins *Serves 4*

175 g (6 oz) broccoli florets
25 g (1 oz) flour
25 g (1 oz) butter
300 ml (½ pint) fresh milk
salt and freshly ground pepper
100 g (4 oz) English Cheddar, grated
50 g (2 oz) flaked almonds, toasted
1 garlic clove, crushed
225 g (8 oz) cooked turkey meat, chopped

1. Cook broccoli florets in boiling water for 2–3 mins. Drain well.
To microwave: Cook broccoli florets with 45 ml (3 tbsp) water, covered for 3 mins. Allow to stand, covered, for 3 mins before draining well.

2. Place flour, butter and milk in a saucepan. Heat, whisking continuously until the sauce thickens, boils and is smooth.
To microwave: In a large jug, gradually blend milk into flour and add butter.

3. Cook for a minute. Season to taste and remove pan from heat.
To microwave: Cook, stirring frequently, for 4 mins until sauce thickens, boils and is smooth.

4. Add 75 g (3 oz) cheese, 40 g (1½ oz) almonds, garlic, turkey and broccoli.

5. Place in an ovenproof dish.

6. Mix remaining cheese and almonds together and sprinkle over turkey mixture.
To microwave: Sprinkle remaining cheese over turkey mixture.

7. Bake at 190°C (375°F) Mark 5 for 15–20 mins.
To microwave: Cook on MEDIUM (50%) for 6–8 mins. Sprinkle remaining almonds over top to serve.

DUCK & GOOSE

ROAST DUCK (F)

Preparation 10 mins
Cooking 30 mins **per 450 g (1 lb)**
Allow at least 450 g (1 lb) raw weight per person

1 oven-ready duckling
salt

accompany with
gravy (page 236)
apple sauce (page 236)
roast or boiled potatoes
green peas

1. Wash inside of bird out under running water. Dry thoroughly with absorbent kitchen paper.
2. Remove and discard any loose fat from inside cavity.
3. Weigh and calculate cooking time allowing 30 minutes per 450 g (1 lb).
4. Stand on a rack in a roasting tin, if possible so bird does not stand in fat.
5. Prick skin all over with a fork. Sprinkle well with salt.
6. Roast at 180°C (350°F) Mark 4 for calculated cooking time. Do not baste or cover.
7. Carefully drain off excess fat if it starts to reach level of rack.
8. Transfer to a board or serving dish. Leave for 5 minutes before carving.
9. Serve with accompaniments.

ROAST GOOSE (F)

Preparation 10 mins
Cooking 20 mins **per 450 g (1 lb) plus** 30 mins
Allow at least 450 g (1 lb) raw weight per person

1 oven-ready goose
salt

accompany with
gravy (page 236)
apple sauce (page 236)
roast or boiled potatoes
green peas

1. Wash inside of bird out under running water. Dry thoroughly with absorbent kitchen paper.
2. Remove and discard any loose fat from inside cavity.
3. Weigh and calculate cooking time allowing 20 mins per 450 g (1 lb) plus 30 mins.
4. Stand on a rack in a roasting tin, if possible so bird does not stand in fat.
5. Prick skin with a fork. Sprinkle with salt.
6. Roast at 200°C (400°F) Mark 6 for calculated cooking time. Do not baste or cover. Carefully drain off excess fat if it starts to reach level of rack.
7. Transfer to a board or serving dish. Leave for 20 mins before carving. Serve with accompaniments.

DUCK & ORANGE SAUCE

Preparation 20 mins **Cooking** 2¾ hrs *Serves 4*

2.3 kg (5 lb) oven ready duckling
salt
15 ml (1 tbsp) flour
grated rind and juice of 2 oranges
30 ml (2 tbsp) dry red wine
30 ml (2 tbsp) redcurrant jelly
50 ml (2 fl oz) dry sherry
sliced oranges and watercress to garnish

1. Cook duck according to recipe for roast duck (left).
2. Cut duck into 4 joints and keep hot.
3. Pour off all but 15 ml (1 tbsp) fat from roasting tin.
4. Stir in flour and cook for 2 mins on hob.
5. Add rind, juice, wine, jelly and sherry.
6. Cook gently, stirring, until jelly dissolves and sauce comes to the boil and thickens.
7. Pour a little sauce over duck. Garnish with orange and watercress.
8. Serve with remaining sauce separately.

GAME

Broadly speaking, game is in season during the autumn and winter months. There is no close season for rabbit, hare or pigeon, but the sale of hare is prohibited between March and July.

Game is generally hung to improve the flavour and make the flesh more tender. Whether or not to hang game at all is very much a matter of personal taste; there are no hard-and-fast rules. Hanging time is affected by the weather and length of time the game has been dead. It is always wise to ask the advice of the poulterer or butcher when the game is bought.

If you are given game it should be hung by the neck in a cold, dry, airy place before being plucked or drawn. A damaged or wet bird will not keep as long.

Some game is available frozen, thaw before cooking.

The table is a guide to the season and approximate hanging times.

Game	Season	Hanging time
Partridge	Sept 1–Feb 1	Up to 8 days
Pheasant	Oct 1–Feb 1	Up to 8 days
Grouse	Aug 12–Dec 10	4–5 days
Pigeon	No Close Season	2–3 days
Hare	No Close Season, but sale prohibited between March and July	7–8 days
Rabbit	No Close Season	4–5 days

ROAST RABBIT Ⓕ

Preparation 10 mins **Cooking** 15 mins per 450 g (1 lb) plus 15 mins   *Serves 4*

1 oven-ready rabbit
4 rashers streaky bacon
40 g (1½ oz) butter, melted

accompany with
gravy (page 236)
cranberry sauce (page 236)
vegetables

1. Weigh rabbit and calculate cooking time allowing 15 minutes per 450 g (1 lb) roasting time plus 15 minutes.

2. Stand in roasting tin. Top with bacon and coat with melted butter.

3. Roast at 220°C (425°F) Mark 7 for 15 minutes.

4. Reduce to 180°C (350°F) Mark 4. Continue to roast for required amount of time, basting frequently with butter.

5. Accompany with gravy, cranberry sauce and vegetables.

ROAST PHEASANT Ⓕ

Preparation 10 mins
Cooking 1–1½ hrs   *Serves 2–3*

1 oven-ready pheasant
4 rashers streaky bacon
15 g (½ oz) butter, melted
watercress to garnish

accompany with
50 g (2 oz) fresh breadcrumbs fried
    in 15 g (1 oz) butter
bread sauce (page 237)
thin gravy (page 236)
game chips
green salad (page 188)

1. Stand pheasant in roasting tin.

2. Cover pheasant breast with bacon rashers and melted butter.

3. Roast at 200°C (400°F) Mark 6 for 1–1½ hours, depending on size, basting frequently.

4. Transfer to a warm serving platter.

5. Garnish with watercress in the vent.

6. Accompany with a small dish of fried breadcrumbs (for sprinkling over each portion), bread sauce, gravy, game chips and salad.

Variation

ROAST GROUSE

Follow recipe and method for roast pheasant (left). Use 2 plucked, drawn and trussed grouse instead of pheasant. Put 25g (1oz) butter inside each bird and roast for 30–35 minutes or until tender. Garnish with watercress.

RABBIT PIE

Preparation 40 mins **Cooking** 1½ hrs *Serves 4*

6 rabbit joints, about 1.1kg (2½lb) in total
15g (½oz) butter
4 rashers bacon, chopped
2 medium potatoes, sliced
2 medium leeks, sliced
2 medium carrots, sliced
15ml (1tbsp) chopped parsley
1.25ml (¼tsp) dried mixed herbs
salt and freshly ground pepper
stock
shortcrust pastry
  made with 225g (8oz) flour (page 364)
beaten egg to glaze

1. Wash rabbit joints. Put in a pan with butter to brown. Add chopped bacon.

2. Layer rabbit, bacon and vegetables alternately in pie dish. Sprinkle each layer with parsley, herbs and seasoning.

3. Half-fill dish with stock.

4. Roll out pastry on a floured work surface and use to cover dish.

5. Make a hole in centre to allow steam to escape.

6. Decorate with pastry leaves and glaze with beaten egg.

7. Bake at 220°C (425°F) Mark 7 for 15–20 minutes, until pastry is set.

8. Reduce heat to 170°C (325°F) Mark 3 and cook for about 1¼ hours.

9. Cover with aluminium foil if pastry becomes too brown.

ROAST PHEASANT

Raised game pie

Preparation 1¼ hrs
Cooking 2½ hrs　　　　　　*Serves 6–8*

hot water crust pastry made with
　350g (12oz) flour (page 368)
225g (8oz) pork sausagemeat
450g (1.lb) raw game (pheasant, partridge,
　pigeon or a mixture)
350g (12oz) rump steak, diced
100g (4oz) lean bacon, chopped
2 pickled walnuts, chopped
1 small onion, grated
2.5ml (½tsp) dried mixed herbs
300ml (½pint) stock
beaten egg for brushing
10ml (2tsp) gelatine

1. Roll out two-thirds of pastry on a floured work surface. Use to line a raised pie mould or 18cm (7inch) loose-bottomed cake tin.

2. Cover base neatly with sausage meat.

3. Cut game into neat pieces. Discard bones, skin and gristle.

4. Put game, steak, bacon, walnuts and onion into a bowl. Add herbs and mix well.

5. Put into pie mould or cake tin. Pour in 150ml (¼pint) stock.

6. Roll out remaining pastry into a lid. Moisten edges with water and cover pie.

7. Press edges of pastry together to seal. Trim away any surplus.

8. Brush top with egg and decorate with pastry leaves (cut from trimmings). Brush with more egg.

9. Make a hole in top to allow steam to escape. Stand on a baking sheet.

10. Bake at 200°C (400°F) Mark 6 for 30 minutes.

11. Reduce to 180°C (350°F) Mark 4 for a further 1¾–2 hours.

12. Cover top with greaseproof paper during last 30 minutes to prevent pastry from browning too much.

13. Remove pie from oven. Heat remaining stock. Sprinkle in gelatine and stir until dissolved.

14. Pour into pie through hole in top and leave to cool for 12 hours.

15. Remove cake tin or mould just before serving.

Milky rabbit casserole　Ⓕ

Preparation 25 mins **Cooking** 2 hrs　　*Serves 4*

25g (1oz) butter
450g (1lb) boneless rabbit, cubed
1 bacon rasher, chopped
2 medium carrots, sliced
568ml (1pint) fresh milk
salt and freshly ground pepper
1.25ml (¼tsp) ground nutmeg
15g (½oz) cornflour
15ml (1tbsp) chopped parsley

1. Melt butter in a flameproof casserole. Add rabbit and bacon and cook until browned.
To microwave: Cook butter and bacon, uncovered, for 3 mins, stirring once. Stir in rabbit.

2. Add carrots, milk, seasoning and nutmeg.

3. Bring to the boil.
To microwave: Cover and cook for 8–10 mins until boiling.

4. Cover and bake at 180°C (350°F) Mark 4 for 1½–2 hours, or until rabbit is tender.
To microwave: Continue cooking, covered, on MEDIUM–LOW (30%) for 50mins, or until rabbit is tender.

5. Blend cornflour with a little cold water and stir into casserole.

6. On the hob, cook, stirring, until sauce thickens, boils and is smooth. Cook for 3 mins.
To microwave: Cook for 3mins, stirring once.

7. Sprinkle with parsley.

Collops of venison

Preparation 10 mins **Cooking** 20 mins　*Serves 4*

25g (1oz) butter
4×175g (6oz) venison steaks
　(or sirloin steaks)
2 small eating apples, cored and sliced
30ml (2tbsp) whisky
5ml (1tsp) honey
150ml (5fl oz) fresh double cream
5 juniper berries, crushed
sprigs of parsley to garnish

1. Melt butter in a large frying pan and cook steaks. Remove when cooked and keep warm.

2. Fry apple slices until heated through.

3. Mix together whisky, honey, cream and juniper berries.

4. Add to pan and heat until warm.

5. Pour sauce over steaks.

6. Serve garnished with parsley.

JUGGED HARE   Ⓕ

Preparation 25 mins **Cooking** 3½ hrs   *Serves 4*

75 g (3 oz) butter
1 hare, jointed
2 medium onions, sliced
2 medium carrots, sliced
1 medium celery stick, sliced
900 ml (1½ pint) water
1 bouquet garni
salt and freshly ground pepper
25 g (1 oz) flour
100 ml (4 fl oz) port
15 ml (1 tbsp) redcurrant jelly
100 g (4 oz) fresh breadcrumbs
50 g (2 oz) shredded suet
5 ml (1 tsp) dried mixed herbs
2.5 ml (½ tsp) grated lemon rind
milk to bind

1. Melt 25 g (1 oz) butter in large flameproof casserole. Add hare and fry until brown. Remove to a plate.

2. Add vegetables to pan and fry gently for 6–7 minutes.

3. Replace hare, add water, bouquet garni and seasoning.

4. Cover and bake at 180°C (350°F) Mark 4 for 2–3 hours, or until hare is tender.

5. Transfer joints of hare to a warm serving dish and keep hot.

6. Strain liquor from casserole. Pour into a clean pan.

7. Add flour, mixed to a smooth paste with 30 ml (2 tbsp) water, port and redcurrant jelly.

8. Cook, stirring, until sauce comes to the boil and thickens. Simmer for 2 minutes.

9. Remove from heat.

10. Meanwhile to make forcemeat balls mix breadcrumbs with suet, herbs, lemon rind and bind with milk.

11. Shape into 12 small balls. Fry gently in remaining butter until crisp and golden.

12. Pour sauce over hare.

13. Serve with forcemeat balls.

VEGETARIAN

VEGETABLE CASSEROLE Ⓕ

Preparation 35 mins **Cooking** 40 mins   *Serves 4*

2 medium onions, sliced
2 garlic cloves, crushed
225 g (8 oz) carrots, sliced
4 celery sticks, sliced
1 large potato, cubed
30 ml (2 tbsp) paprika
25 g (1 oz) butter
425 g (15 oz) can red kidney beans, drained
300 ml (½ pint) vegetable stock
450 ml (¾ pint) fresh milk
30 ml (2 tbsp) tomato purée
30 ml (2 tbsp) cornflour

1. Fry onions, garlic, carrots, celery, potato and paprika in butter for 5 mins.
To microwave: Cook onions, garlic, carrots, celery, potato, paprika and butter covered for 5 mins.

2. Add beans, stock, milk and tomato purée.
To microwave: Add beans, BOILING stock, milk and tomato purée.

3. Bring to the boil and simmer for 20–30 mins or until tender.
To microwave: Cover and cook for 10 mins, stirring once. Uncover and cook for 10 mins, stirring once, or until vegetables are tender.

4. Blend cornflour with a little water and add to casserole, stir until thickened.

PARSNIP ROAST Ⓕ

Preparation 40 mins **Cooking** 35 mins   *Serves 6*

700 g (1½ lb) parsnips, sliced
25 g (1 oz) butter
60 ml (4 tbsp) fresh double cream
75 g (3 oz) English Cheddar, grated
salt and freshly ground pepper
75 g (3 oz) roasted peanuts, chopped
25 g (1 oz) fresh wholemeal breadcrumbs.

1. Cook parsnips in boiling water until tender. Drain well.
To microwave: Cook parsnips with 90 ml (6 tbsp) water, covered, for about 10 mins, stirring twice, until tender. Drain.

2. Mash parsnips and stir in butter, cream and 50 g (2 oz) cheese. Season to taste.

3. Spoon half the mixture into a greased 1.1 litre (2 pint) ovenproof dish.
To microwave: Spoon half the mixture into a greased 1.1 litre (2 pint) flameproof dish.

4. Cover with half the peanuts then remaining parsnip mixture.

5. Mix remaining peanuts and cheese with breadcrumbs and sprinkle over top.

6. Bake at 220°C (425°F) Mark 7 for 15 mins or until top is golden.
To microwave: Cook for 5 mins then brown under a hot grill until golden.

VEGETABLE CURRY Ⓕ

Preparation 30 mins **Cooking** 25 mins   *Serves 4*

450 g (1 lb) carrots, sliced
450 g (1 lb) cauliflower florets
450 g (1 lb) courgettes, cut into chunks
25 g (1 oz) butter
1 medium onion, chopped
100 g (4 oz) mushrooms, halved
40 g (1½ oz) wholemeal flour
15 ml (1 tbsp) curry powder
568 ml (1 pint) fresh milk
cooked rice or chapattis to serve

1. Place carrots in a large pan of boiling water, bring back to the boil and cook for 7 minutes.
To microwave: Cook carrots with 30 ml (2 tbsp) water covered for 7 minutes, stirring once.

2. Add cauliflower, bring back to the boil and cook for 3 minutes.
To microwave: Cook cauliflower with 30 ml (2 tbsp) water covered for 7 minutes, stirring once.

3. Add courgettes, bring back to the boil and cook for 3 minutes.
To microwave: Cook courgettes covered for 4 minutes, stirring once.

4. Drain and keep warm.
To microwave: Drain the three vegetables, mix them together and keep warm.

5. Melt butter in a pan and cook onion until soft. Stir in mushrooms, flour and curry powder and cook stirring for 1 minute.
To microwave: In a large jug or bowl cook butter and onion covered for 3 minutes. Stir in flour and curry powder and cook for 30 seconds.

6. Gradually add milk, stirring continuously, until sauce thickens, boils and is smooth. Cook for a minute.
To microwave: Gradually stir in milk. Cook for 10 minutes, stirring frequently, until sauce thickens, boils and is smooth.

7. Stir in cooked vegetables and mix well.
To microwave: Stir in mushrooms and cooked vegetables.

8. Serve with cooked rice or chapattis.

PEANUT & CHEESE LOAF Ⓕ

Preparation 30 mins **Cooking** 40 mins   *Serves 6*

75 g (3 oz) peanuts, chopped
75 g (3 oz) mushrooms, chopped
100 g (4 oz) fresh wholemeal breadcrumbs
1 medium onion, chopped
1 medium carrot, grated
2.5 ml (½ tsp) dried mixed herbs
100 g (4 oz) English Cheddar, grated
1 egg, beaten
salad ingredients to garnish

1. Mix together all ingredients, except garnish.

2. Spoon into a greased 900 g (2 lb) loaf tin or a 900 ml (1½ pint) ring mould.
To microwave: Spoon into a 900 g (2 lb) loaf dish.

3. Cook at 190°C (375°F) Mark 5 for 40 minutes.
To microwave: Cover with greaseproof paper and cook on MEDIUM (50%) for 20 minutes. Allow to stand for 5 minutes before turning out.

4. Turn out on to a serving dish. Serve hot or cold garnished with salad ingredients.

CARROT & CHEESE BAKE (F)

Preparation 20 mins **Cooking** 30 mins   *Serves 4*

50 g (2 oz) butter, melted
75 g (3 oz) porridge oats
150 g (5 oz) English cheddar, grated
400 g (14 oz) carrots, grated
25 g (1 oz) wholemeal flour
45 ml (3 tbsp) fresh milk
1.25 ml (¼ tsp) dried thyme
15 ml (1 tbsp) sesame seeds
15 ml (1 tbsp) poppy seeds

1. Mix together all ingredients, except for sesame and poppy seeds.

2. Spoon into a greased ovenproof dish and press well in.
To microwave: Spoon into a greased 20.5 cm (8 inch) round dish and press well in.

3. Sprinkle sesame and poppy seeds over top.

4. Bake at 190°C (375°F) Mark 5 for 30 minutes.
To microwave: Cover with greaseproof paper and cook for 10 minutes.

VEGETABLE & NUT COBBLER (F)

Preparation 40 mins **Cooking** 50 mins   *Serves 4*

150 g (5 oz) butter
175 g (6 oz) cauliflower florets
6 baby onions
175 g (6 oz) carrots, sliced
1 medium parsnip, sliced
175 g (6 oz) green beans, sliced
397 g (14 oz) can butter beans, drained
1 vegetable stock cube
568 ml (1 pint) fresh milk
240 g (8½ oz) wholemeal self raising flour
100 g (4 oz) Red Leicester cheese, grated
freshly ground pepper
10 ml (2 tsp) baking powder
50 g (2 oz) walnuts, chopped

1. Melt 25 g (1 oz) butter in a saucepan. Add raw vegetables. Cover and cook for 10 mins, stirring occasionally.
To microwave: Cook butter, cauliflower, onions, carrots, parsnip and green beans covered for 10 mins, stirring once or twice.

2. Add butter beans, stock cube, 450 ml (¾ pint) milk, 15 g (½ oz) flour, half the cheese and seasoning.

VEGETABLE & NUT COBBLER

3. Transfer to an ovenproof casserole, cover and bake at 220°C (425°F) Mark 7 for 15 mins.
To microwave: Cover and cook for 10 mins, stir once, transfer to an ovenproof casserole.

4. Sift remaining flour and baking powder. Rub in remaining butter until mixture resembles fine breadcrumbs and add nuts. Stir in remaining milk and mix to a soft dough. Chill for 10 mins.

5. Roll out on a floured work surface to 1 cm (½ inch) thickness. Cut into 12 rounds.

6. Remove casserole from oven, uncover and place scone rounds on top. Brush with milk and sprinkle with remaining cheese.

7. Cook at 180°C (350°F) Mark 4 for 25 mins or until scones are cooked.

PEANUT MINCE Ⓕ

Preparation 30 mins **Cooking** 35 mins   *Serves 4*

1 large onion, chopped
100 g (4 oz) mushrooms, chopped
1 medium celery stick, sliced
1 large carrot, grated
25 g (1 oz) butter
2.5 ml (½ tsp) yeast extract
225 g (8 oz) peanuts, coarsely chopped
150 ml (¼ pint) fresh milk
150 ml (¼ pint) vegetable stock or water
75 g (3 oz) rolled oats
salt and freshly ground pepper
30 ml (2 tbsp) chopped parsley
mashed potato and green vegetables to serve

1. Fry vegetables in butter until pale gold.
To microwave: Cook vegetables and butter covered for 5 minutes, stirring once.

2. Stir in yeast extract, peanuts, milk and stock or water.

3. Bring to the boil, cover and simmer until vegetables are tender.
To microwave: Cover and cook for 5 minutes.

4. Add oats and continue to simmer, uncovered, until mixture is thick. Stir often.
To microwave: Cook uncovered for 4–5 minutes until mixture is thick.

5. Season to taste and stir in parsley.

6. Serve with mashed potato and green vegetables.

CHESHIRE AUBERGINE LAYER Ⓕ

Preparation 30 mins **plus** 30 mins **standing**
Cooking 55 mins   *Serves 4*

700 g (1½ lb) aubergines, sliced
salt and freshly ground pepper
90 g (3½ oz) butter
1 medium onion, chopped
1 garlic clove, crushed
397 g (14 oz) can chopped tomatoes
25 g (1 oz) flour
300 ml (½ pint) fresh milk
30 ml (2 tbsp) natural yogurt
175 g (6 oz) Cheshire cheese, grated

1. Sprinkle aubergines with salt and leave to drain in a colander for 30 minutes. Drain, rinse and pat dry.

2. Heat 15 g (½ oz) butter in a pan and fry onion until soft. Add garlic and tomatoes and simmer for 5 minutes.
To microwave: Cook 15 g (½ oz) butter and onion covered for 3 minutes. Stir in garlic and tomatoes, cover and cook for 5 minutes.

3. Put 25 g (1 oz) butter, flour and milk into a saucepan. Heat, whisking continuously until sauce thickens, boils and is smooth. Cook for a minute.
To microwave: In a large jug, gradually blend milk into flour. Add butter and cook, stirring frequently for 4 minutes until sauce thickens, boils and is smooth.

4. Stir in yogurt and 100 g (4 oz) cheese.

5. Melt remaining butter in a frying pan and fry aubergines on both sides until golden.

6. Drain aubergines on absorbent kitchen paper.

7. Arrange a third of aubergines in an ovenproof dish.
To microwave: Arrange a third of aubergines in a flameproof dish.

8. Cover with half the tomato mixture, then top with half the cheese sauce. Repeat layers, finishing with aubergines. Sprinkle with remaining cheese.

9. Bake at 180°C (350°F) Mark 4 for 40 minutes.
To microwave: Cook on MEDIUM (50%) uncovered for 15–20 minutes, then brown under a hot grill.

10. Serve immediately.

CASHEW & VEGETABLE STIR FRY

CASHEW & VEGETABLE STIR FRY

Preparation 45 mins **Cooking** 6 mins   *Serves 4*

25 g (1 oz) butter
2 garlic cloves, crushed
225 g (8 oz) carrots, thinly sliced
2 red, green or yellow peppers,
    seeded and cut into diamonds
4 celery sticks, sliced
175 g (6 oz) mushrooms, sliced
8 spring onions, sliced
100 g (4 oz) cashew nuts, toasted
30 ml (2 tbsp) chopped fresh marjoram
75 ml (3 fl oz) fresh double cream
100 g (4 oz) fromage frais

1. Melt butter in a large frying pan or wok and fry garlic and carrots for 3 minutes.
To microwave: Cook butter, garlic and carrots, covered, for 4 minutes, stirring once.

2. Add remaining vegetables and cook for 1–2 minutes, stirring continuously.
To microwave: Stir in remaining vegetables, cover and cook for 3 minutes.

3. Stir in nuts and transfer to a warm serving dish.

4. Add herbs and cream to pan and heat until hot.

To microwave: Place herbs and cream in a jug and cook for 1 minute.

5. Remove from heat and stir in fromage frais.

6. Serve sauce with vegetables.

SOUPER COURGETTES 🇫

Preparation 35 mins **Cooking** 45 mins   *Serves 4*

4 large courgettes
25 g (1 oz) butter
1 medium onion, chopped
50 g (2 oz) walnut pieces, chopped
50 g (2 oz) hazelnuts, chopped
75 g (3 oz) fresh wholemeal breadcrumbs
15 ml (1 tbsp) chopped parsley
227 g (8 oz) can chopped tomatoes with
    herbs
295 g (10.4 oz) can condensed cream of
    tomato soup
50 g (2 oz) Wensleydale cheese, grated

1. Cook whole courgettes in boiling water for 5 minutes.
To microwave: Cook whole courgettes with 60 ml (4 tbsp) water, covered, for 5 minutes, rearranging them half way.

2. Rinse under cold water, drain and cool.

3. Halve lengthways, scoop out flesh, chop and reserve.

4. Place courgette cases in a greased ovenproof dish.
To microwave: Place courgettes in a greased flameproof dish.

5. Melt butter in a saucepan, add onion and fry for 3 minutes.
To microwave: Cook butter and onion, covered for 3 minutes.

6. Add chopped courgette flesh and cook for 2 minutes.
To microwave: Stir in chopped courgette flesh, cover and cook for 2 minutes.

7. Remove from heat, stir in nuts, breadcrumbs, parsley and half of tomatoes.

8. Spoon into courgette cases. Place any remaining stuffing in dish.

9. Mix remaining tomatoes with soup and half the cheese.

10. Pour over courgettes and top with remaining cheese.

11. Cover and bake at 200°C (400°F) Mark 6 for 35 minutes.
To microwave: Cover and cook on MEDIUM (50%) for 15–18 minutes then brown under a hot grill.

LANCASHIRE MUSHROOM ROLLS

Preparation 30 mins **Cooking** 25 mins   *Serves 4*

1 medium onion, finely chopped
2 garlic cloves, crushed
40 g (1½ oz) butter
100 g (4 oz) mushrooms, chopped
75 g (3 oz) fresh wholemeal breadcrumbs
5 ml (1 tsp) dried basil
100 g (4 oz) Lancashire cheese, crumbled
8 sheets of filo pastry

1. Cook onion and garlic in a non-stick saucepan with 15 g (½ oz) butter for 1 min.

2. Add mushrooms and cook for a further 2 mins.

3. Remove from heat, stir in breadcrumbs, basil and cheese.

4. Brush half of each sheet of pastry with melted remaining butter and fold in half lengthways.

5. Divide filling between pastry. Fold over sides of pastry and roll up.

6. Place on a greased baking sheet, brush with melted butter, bake at 190°C (375°F) Mark 5 for 20 mins, until golden brown.

LANCASHIRE MUSHROOM ROLLS

Parsnip & Tomato Bake ⒡

Preparation 50 mins **Cooking** 50 mins   *Serves 4*

2 large parsnips, sliced
2 large leeks, sliced
100g (4oz) pasta, cooked
5ml (1tsp) dried mixed herbs
1 garlic clove, crushed
25g (1oz) flour
40g (1½oz) butter
300ml (½pint) fresh milk
salt and freshly ground pepper
cayenne pepper
5ml (1tsp) made mustard
175g (6oz) English Cheddar, grated
50g (2oz) fresh breadcrumbs
6 tomatoes, sliced

1. Place parsnips and leeks in a pan of boiling water, cover and simmer for 10 mins or until just tender.
To microwave: Cook parsnips and leeks covered, with 60ml (4tbsp) water, for 7 mins, stirring once.

2. Drain well and mix with cooked pasta, herbs and garlic.

3. Place flour, 25g (1oz) butter and milk in a saucepan and heat, whisking continuously, until sauce thickens, boils and is smooth. Cook for a minute then remove from heat.
To microwave: In a large jug, gradually blend milk into flour. Add 25g (1oz) butter and cook, stirring frequently, for 4 mins until sauce thickens, boils and is smooth.

4. Add seasoning and cayenne pepper to taste. Stir in mustard and 150g (5oz) cheese.

5. Melt remaining butter in a pan and fry breadcrumbs until golden brown. Set aside.
To microwave: Melt butter in a small shallow heatproof dish for 20–30 seconds and stir in breadcrumbs. Cook uncovered for about 4 mins, stirring frequently, until golden.

6. Place half the vegetables and pasta mixture in base of an ovenproof dish, cover with a layer of tomatoes, then half the sauce.

7. Repeat layers. Top with breadcrumbs and remaining cheese.

8. Bake at 190°C (375°F) Mark 5 for 30 mins.
To microwave: Cook for 5 mins or until heated through, brown under a hot grill.

Leek & Carrot Medley ⒢

Preparation 35 mins **Cooking** 25 mins   *Serves 4*

900g (2lb) leeks, thickly sliced
700g (1½lb) carrots, thickly sliced
450ml (¾pint) vegetable stock
450ml (¾pint) fresh milk
50g (2oz) cashew nuts, toasted
40g (1½oz) flour
40g (1½oz) butter
75g (3oz) English Cheddar, grated
1.25ml (¼tsp) dried sage
salt and freshly ground pepper
50g (2oz) fresh wholemeal breadcrumbs

1. Place vegetables in a saucepan with stock, bring to the boil, cover and simmer for 15 minutes.

2. Drain and reserve liquid. Make up to 900ml (1½pints) with milk.

3. Place vegetables and cashew nuts in a flameproof dish. Keep warm.

4. Place flour, butter and liquid in a saucepan and heat, whisking continuously, until sauce thickens, boils and is smooth. Cook for a minute.

5. Remove pan from heat, add cheese and sage, stir until melted. Season to taste.

6. Pour sauce over vegetables.

7. Sprinkle breadcrumbs over and grill until golden brown.

Cheese & Parsley Pudding

Preparation 1 hr **Cooking** 30 mins   *Serves 4*

2 eggs, separated
300ml (½pint) fresh milk, warmed
75g (3oz) Derby or Cheshire cheese, grated
50g (2oz) fresh breadcrumbs
2.5ml (½tsp) dry mustard
salt and freshly ground pepper
30ml (2tbsp) chopped parsley

1. Beat egg yolks with milk and cheese.

2. Mix breadcrumbs with mustard, seasoning and parsley.

3. Gradually stir in warm milk mixture and mix well.

4. Leave to stand for 30 minutes.

5. Whisk egg whites until stiff, fold into bread mixture.

6. Transfer to a 568 ml (1 pint) greased ovenproof dish. Bake at 200°C (400°F) Mark 6 for 25–30 minutes, or until golden.

CHILLI BEAN MOUSSAKA

Preparation 25 mins **plus** 30 mins **standing**
Cooking 25 mins   *Serves 4*

2 medium aubergines, sliced
salt
1 medium onion, sliced
1 garlic clove, crushed
15 ml (1 tbsp) oil
397 g (14 oz) can chopped tomatoes
5 ml (1 tsp) dried thyme
2.5 ml (½ tsp) ground cinnamon
397 g (14 oz) can kidney beans in chilli
   sauce
15 ml (1 tbsp) cornflour
150 g (5 oz) natural yogurt
150 ml (¼ pint) fresh milk
2.5 ml (½ tsp) ground nutmeg
freshly ground pepper
50 g (2 oz) Red Leicester cheese, grated

1. Sprinkle aubergines with salt and leave to drain in a colander for 30 minutes. Rinse and drain well.

2. Fry onion and garlic in oil for 5 minutes.
To microwave: Cook onion, garlic and oil covered for 3 minutes.

3. Add tomatoes, thyme, cinnamon, beans and aubergines.

4. Simmer for 15 minutes or until aubergines are soft.
To microwave: Cover and cook for 15 minutes, stirring once or twice, until aubergines are soft.

5. Blend cornflour with a little yogurt, then mix with remaining yogurt, milk, nutmeg and pepper.

6. Transfer aubergine mixture into a flameproof dish, spoon yogurt mixture over, and top with cheese.

7. Grill until cheese has melted and yogurt mixture is hot.

LEEK & CARROT MEDLEY

SPINACH & CHEESE ROULADE Ⓕ

Preparation 30 mins
Cooking 30 mins   *Serves 4–6*

25 g (1 oz) butter, melted
275 g (10 oz) spinach, fresh or frozen
3 eggs, separated
275 g (10 oz) full fat soft cheese
salt and freshly ground pepper
30 ml (2 tbsp) natural yogurt
4 spring onions, trimmed and chopped
50 g (2 oz) walnuts, roughly chopped
75 g (3 oz) Double Gloucester cheese,
   grated
2.5 ml (½ tsp) cayenne pepper
orange slices and coriander to garnish

1. Line a 31×23 cm (12×9 inch) Swiss roll tin with greaseproof paper. Brush with butter.

2. Cook spinach with a little water in a pan for 10–15 minutes until tender. Drain well. Press out as much liquid as possible.

3. Beat in egg yolks and 75 g (3 oz) soft cheese. Season to taste.

4. Whisk egg whites until softly stiff and fold into mixture.

5. Turn into prepared tin, smooth over and bake at 190°C (375°F) Mark 5 for 15 minutes until firm to the touch.

6. Turn out on to greaseproof paper. Cool slightly, then peel off baking paper.

7. Trim off outside edges and roll up with greaseproof paper.

8. Mix all remaining ingredients together.

9. Unroll roulade when cool, remove paper.

10. Spread with filling and roll up.

11. Serve chilled and garnished with orange and coriander.

FLAKY CHEESE & ONION PASTIES Ⓕ

Preparation 35 mins **Cooking** 25 mins   *Serves 4*

flaky pastry made with 225 g (8 oz) flour
   (page 366)
175 g (6 oz) Wensleydale cheese,
   finely grated
15 ml (1 tbsp) finely grated onion
beaten egg to bind
salt and freshly ground pepper
fresh milk for brushing

SPINACH & CHEESE ROULADE

1. Roll out pastry into 40.5×20.5cm (16×8inch) rectangle.

2. Cut into eight 10cm (4inch) squares.

3. Mix cheese with onion. Bind fairly stiffly with egg. Season to taste.

4. Put equal amounts of cheese mixture on to the centres of pastry squares.

5. Moisten edges of pastry with water. Fold squares in half to form triangles.

6. Press edges well together to seal. Flake by cutting with back of knife.

7. Make 2 or 3 snips across top of each pasty with scissors. Transfer to a damp baking sheet.

8. Brush with milk. Bake at 220°C (425°F) Mark 7 for 10 minutes.

9. Reduce to 200°C (400°F) Mark 6 and bake for a further 10–15 minutes or until well puffed and brown.

10. Serve hot.

GLOUCESTER PIE

Preparation 25mins **plus** 30mins **standing**
Cooking 30mins   *Serves 4*

8 slices of bread, crusts removed
butter
100g (4oz) Double Gloucester cheese, thinly sliced
225g (8oz) tomatoes, sliced
150ml (¼pint) fresh milk
1 egg
5ml (1tsp) made mustard
salt and freshly ground pepper
green vegetables or green salad to serve

1. Butter bread slices and sandwich together with cheese and tomatoes.

2. Cut each sandwich into 4 triangles.

3. Arrange in a greased shallow ovenproof dish.
To microwave: Arrange in a 20.5cm (8inch) round flameproof dish. Overlap triangles to make an even layer.

4. Beat milk with egg, mustard and season to taste. Pour over sandwiches.

5. Leave to stand for 30 minutes or until bread has absorbed liquid.

6. Bake at 190°C (375°F) Mark 5 for 25–30 minutes or until top is crisp and golden.
To microwave: Cook uncovered on MEDIUM (50%) for 7–8 minutes until set. Place under a hot grill until top is crisp and golden.

7. Serve with a green vegetable or salad.

POTATO, CHEESE & PARSLEY PIE   Ⓕ

Preparation 30mins **Cooking** 35mins   *Serves 4*

700g (1½lb) potatoes, cubed
60ml (4tbsp) fresh milk
1 egg, beaten
5ml (1tsp) dry mustard
175g (6oz) Double Gloucester cheese, grated
45ml (3tbsp) chopped parsley
2.5ml (½tsp) yeast extract
freshly ground pepper
baked tomatoes to serve

1. Cook potatoes in boiling water until tender, then drain.
To microwave: Cook potatoes with 60ml (4tbsp) water, covered, for 10 minutes, stirring once or twice, or until tender. Drain.

2. Mash with milk, egg, mustard, 100g (4oz) cheese, parsley and yeast extract. Season to taste.

3. Transfer to a greased 1.1litre (2pint) ovenproof dish.
To microwave: Transfer to a greased 1.1litre (2pint) flameproof dish.

4. Sprinkle remaining cheese over top and bake at 220°C (425°F) Mark 7 for 15 minutes or until top is light brown.
To microwave: Cook for 5 minutes. Add remaining cheese, brown under a hot grill.

5. Serve with baked tomatoes.

Variation

POTATO, CHEESE & ONION PIE   Ⓕ

Follow recipe and method for potato, cheese and parsley pie (above). Add 1 medium, chopped, boiled onion with parsley.

MEALS FOR 1&2

BACON & CHEESE POTATOES

Preparation 10 mins
Cooking 1 hr 5 mins   *Serves 2*

2×225 g (8 oz) potatoes
2 bacon rashers
175 g (6 oz) cottage cheese
2.5 ml (½ tsp) chopped parsley
50 g (2 oz) reduced fat hard cheese, grated
salad ingredients to serve

1. Wash and dry potatoes, prick skins and bake at 200°C (400°F) Mark 6 for 1 hour or until soft when pinched.
To microwave: Wash and dry potatoes, prick skins and place on absorbent kitchen paper on an ovenproof plate. Cook for 8–10 minutes, turning them over once. Check centres are cooked by inserting a skewer. Allow to stand for 5 minutes.

2. Crisply grill bacon.
To microwave: Place bacon on a roasting rack or plate and cover with absorbent kitchen paper. Cook for 3–5 minutes until bacon is crisp on edges.

3. Chop bacon and mix with cottage cheese and parsley.

4. Cut open potatoes and spoon in filling.

5. Top with grated cheese.

6. Serve with salad.

STEAKS IN RED WINE & MUSHROOM SAUCE

Preparation 5 mins **Cooking** 15 mins   *Serves 2*

25 g (1 oz) butter
2×175 g (6 oz) sirloin steaks,
   trimmed of excess fat
50 g (2 oz) mushrooms, sliced
5 ml (1 tsp) made wholegrain mustard
75 ml (3 fl oz) red wine
50 ml (2 fl oz) beef stock

1. Melt butter in a frying pan and add steaks.

2. Fry briskly for 1 minute each side.

3. Lower heat. Continue to fry for a further 3–4 minutes for rare, 4–5 minutes for medium or 7–8 minutes for well-done steak.

4. Turn steaks about every minute to ensure even cooking.

5. Transfer steaks to a plate and keep warm.

6. Add mushrooms, cook for 2 minutes.

7. Blend mustard with wine and stock.

8. Add to pan and boil for 2 minutes to reduce liquid.

9. Serve steaks with sauce.

STEAKS WITH STILTON SAUCE

Preparation 10 mins **Cooking** 15 mins   *Serves 2*

2×175 g (6 oz) sirloin steaks,
   trimmed of excess fat
15 g (½ oz) butter
1 small onion, finely chopped
30 ml (2 tbsp) sherry
100 ml (4 fl oz) fresh double cream
50 g (2 oz) Blue Stilton cheese, crumbled
15 ml (1 tbsp) chopped chives

1. Grill steaks to your liking.

2. Melt butter in a saucepan and cook onion until soft.
To microwave: Cook butter and onion, covered, for 3 minutes.

3. Add sherry and boil to reduce slightly.
To microwave: Add sherry and cook, uncovered, for 1 minute.

4. Add cream and boil for 1 minute.
To microwave: Stir in cream and cook for 30 seconds.

5. Stir in Stilton and chives.

6. Serve steaks with sauce.

DEVON CHICKEN (F)

Preparation 15 mins **Cooking** 45 mins *Serves 1*

275g (10oz) chicken piece, skinned
15g (½oz) butter
1 small onion, sliced
1 medium cooking apple, cored and sliced
1 garlic clove, crushed
75ml (3floz) cider or apple juice
140g (4.9oz) can condensed cream of
   celery soup

1. Cut chicken piece into two pieces.

2. Melt butter in a non-stick saucepan, add onion and fry for 3 minutes.
To microwave: Cook butter and onion, covered, for 3 minutes.

3. Add chicken pieces and brown on all sides.
To microwave: Add chicken pieces.

4. Add remaining ingredients and stir to mix.

5. Bring to the boil, cover and simmer gently for 40 minutes or until chicken is tender. Stir occasionally.
To microwave: Cover and cook on MEDIUM (50%) for 6–8 minutes, stirring once or twice, or until chicken is tender.

CORNED BEEF HASH (F)

Preparation 15 mins **Cooking** 20 mins *Serves 1*

225g (8oz) potato, halved
15g (½oz) butter
15ml (1tbsp) oil
1 small onion, chopped
¼ green pepper, seeded and chopped
¼ yellow pepper, seeded and chopped
100g (4oz) corned beef, cubed
freshly ground pepper

1. Boil potato for 10 minutes until just tender but firm.
To microwave: Cook potato with 60ml (4tbsp) water, covered for 5–7 minutes, stirring once, until just tender but firm.

2. Drain, cool slightly and cube.

3. Heat butter and 10ml (2tsp) oil in a non-stick frying pan.

4. Add potato and fry until golden. Remove to a plate.

5. Add remaining oil, onion and peppers and cook for 3 minutes, stirring.

6. Add corned beef and potato.

7. Cook stirring until heated through. Season to taste, and serve immediately.

CORNED BEEF HASH

TUNA BAKED AUBERGINE Ⓕ

Preparation 25 mins **plus** 30 mins **standing**
Cooking 45 mins   *Serves 2*

1 medium aubergine
salt
15g (½oz) butter
1 medium onion, finely chopped
1 garlic clove, crushed
100g (4oz) canned tuna,
    drained and flaked
100g (4oz) cooked brown rice
    (about 50g (2oz) raw)
pinch of ground bay leaves
2.5ml (½tsp) lemon juice
30ml (2tbsp) stock
2.5ml (½tsp) tomato purée
75g (3oz) Double Gloucester cheese, grated

1. Halve aubergine lengthways. Sprinkle cut surfaces with salt and stand for 30 minutes.

2. Rinse and dry with absorbent kitchen paper.

3. Scoop out flesh, leaving shell intact. Chop flesh.

4. Melt butter in a non-stick pan, add aubergine flesh, onion and garlic, cook for 4 minutes, stirring.
To microwave: Cook butter, aubergine, onion and garlic, covered, for 4 minutes.

5. Stir in tuna, rice, ground bay leaves, lemon juice, stock, tomato purée and half the cheese.

6. Fill aubergine shells with stuffing.

7. Place in an ovenproof dish and top with remaining cheese. Add 45ml (3tbsp) water.
To microwave: Place in a flameproof dish with 45ml (3tbsp) water.

8. Bake at 190°C (375°F) Mark 5 for 40 minutes. Cover with foil after 20 minutes.
To microwave: Cover and cook for 7 minutes. Top with remaining cheese and brown under a hot grill.

REDCURRANT LAMB CHOPS

Preparation 5 mins **Cooking** 25 mins   *Serves 2*

4 lamb loin chops
30ml (2tbsp) redcurrant jelly
5ml (1tsp) orange juice
pinch of ground ginger

TUNA BAKED AUBERGINE

1. Grill chops for 5–10 minutes on each side, depending on thickness.

2. Place remaining ingredients in a small pan, heat until jelly has melted.
To microwave: Place remaining ingredients in a small dish and cook, uncovered, for 30 seconds or until jelly has melted.

3. Stir to mix well.

4. Brush over chops and grill for a further minute. Turn chops over and repeat.

5. Serve at once.

RUTH'S PASTA SPECIAL

Preparation 20 mins **Cooking** 15 mins *Serves 1*

50 g (2 oz) pasta shapes
10 ml (2 tsp) cornflour
175 ml (6 fl oz) fresh milk
pinch of ground nutmeg
salt and freshly ground pepper
40 g (1½ oz) Double Gloucester cheese, grated
25 g (1 oz) mushrooms, sliced
¼ green pepper, seeded and sliced
¼ red pepper, seeded and sliced
50 g (2 oz) canned sweetcorn, drained
99 g (3.5 oz) can tuna, drained and flaked

1. Cook pasta in boiling water for 10–12 minutes. Drain well.
To microwave: Place pasta in a bowl and pour over sufficient water to cover it by 2.5 cm (1 inch). Stir well. Cook, uncovered for 6–8 minutes, stirring once. Allow to stand for 3 minutes.

2. Meanwhile, blend cornflour with a little cold milk. Stir in remaining milk.

3. Heat, whisking continuously until sauce boils, thickens and is smooth. Cook for a minute. Add nutmeg and season to taste.
To microwave: Cook for about 3 minutes, stirring frequently, until sauce boils, thickens and is smooth. Add nutmeg and season to taste.

4. Add cheese, vegetables, tuna and pasta. Mix well and heat through.
To microwave: Add cheese, vegetables, tuna and pasta. Mix well. Cook for 1 minute.

5. Pour into a serving dish and serve immediately.

145

PORK SIMLA

Preparation 10mins **Cooking** 30mins *Serves 1*

100g (4oz) pork fillet, diced
15g (½oz) flour
15g (½oz) butter
1 small onion, chopped
2.5ml (½tsp) curry powder
2.5ml (½tsp) cayenne pepper
150ml (¼pint) fresh milk
15ml (1tbsp) chutney
15g (½oz) sultanas
50ml (2fl oz) fresh soured cream
cooked rice to serve

1. Coat pork in flour.

2. Melt butter in a pan, fry onion and pork until browned.
To microwave: Cook butter and onion, covered, for 3 minutes. Stir in pork.

3. Stir in curry powder, cayenne pepper and milk.

4. Bring to the boil and simmer until pork is tender.
To microwave: Cover and cook for 3 minutes or until boiling. Stir well, cover and cook on MEDIUM-LOW (30%) for 15 minutes, stirring once.

5. Add chutney and sultanas, simmer for 5 minutes.
To microwave: Add chutney and sultanas, cover and cook on MEDIUM-LOW (30%) for 5 minutes, or until the pork is tender.

6. Remove from heat. Add cream and reheat.
To microwave: Stir in cream and cook for 30 seconds to reheat.

7. Serve with cooked rice.

SPICY PASTA

Preparation 15mins **Cooking** 12mins *Serves 2*

175g (6oz) pasta shapes
225g (8oz) fromage frais
30ml (2tbsp) chilli and garlic sauce
50g (2oz) salami or garlic sausage,
    cut into strips
½ yellow or red pepper, seeded and diced
4 spring onions, sliced
50g (2oz) pitted black olives, halved
parsley to garnish

1. Cook pasta in boiling water for 10–12 minutes.
To microwave: Place pasta in a large bowl and pour over sufficient BOILING water to cover it by 2.5cm (1inch). Stir well. Cook, uncovered, for about 7–9 minutes, stirring once or twice. Allow to stand for 5 minutes.

2. Combine fromage frais with chilli sauce.

3. Drain pasta and stir into sauce with salami, pepper, onions and olives.

4. Serve garnished with parsley.

SMOKY CAULIFLOWER SUPPER

Preparation 25mins **Cooking** 25mins *Serves 2*

1 medium cauliflower, cut into florets
4 rashers streaky bacon, cut in half
25g (1oz) butter
1 small onion, chopped
25g (1oz) flour
300ml (½pint) fresh milk
salt and freshly ground pepper
75g (3oz) smoked Cheddar cheese, grated
2.5ml (½tsp) made mustard
1 rye crispbread, crushed

1. Cook cauliflower in boiling water for 10 minutes or until tender.
To microwave: Cook cauliflower with 60ml (4tbsp) water, covered, for 8–10 minutes, stirring once, or until just tender.

2. When cooked, drain and place in a shallow flameproof dish.

3. Stretch bacon and roll up. Grill until crisp.

4. Melt butter in a pan. Fry onion until soft.
To microwave: Cook butter and onion, covered, for 3 minutes.

5. Stir in flour and milk and heat whisking continuously until sauce thickens, boils and is smooth. Cook for a minute. Season.
To microwave: Stir in flour and gradually blend in milk. Cook for about 3 minutes, stirring frequently, until sauce boils, thickens and is smooth. Season to taste.

6. Remove from heat, add 50g (2oz) cheese and mustard. Stir until melted. Pour over cauliflower.

7. Combine crispbread and remaining cheese. Sprinkle over cauliflower, grill until golden.

8. Garnish with bacon rolls to serve.

SAVOURY CRUMBLE

Preparation 15 mins **Cooking** 35 mins *Serves 2*

50 g (2 oz) wholemeal flour
50 g (2 oz) butter
2.5 ml (½ tsp) dry mustard
pinch of cayenne pepper
2.5 ml (½ tsp) paprika
15 g (½ oz) oats
225 g (8 oz) chicken breast fillet, diced
25 g (1 oz) flour
150 ml (¼ pint) fresh milk
150 g (5 oz) natural yogurt
175 g (6 oz) broccoli florets, blanched
15 g (1 oz) no-soak dried apricots, chopped
parsley to garnish

1. Place wholemeal flour in a bowl and rub in 25 g (1 oz) butter until mixture resembles fine breadcrumbs.

2. Stir in mustard, cayenne pepper, paprika and oats.

3. Place chicken and remaining butter in a saucepan. Fry gently for 10 minutes.
To microwave: Melt remaining butter for 30 seconds and stir in chicken.

4. Stir in flour and cook for a minute.
To microwave: Stir in flour.

5. Gradually add milk and yogurt. Heat, stirring continuously, until sauce boils, thickens and is smooth.
To microwave: Gradually stir in milk and yogurt. Cook, uncovered, for about 3 minutes, stirring frequently, until sauce boils, thickens and is smooth.

6. Add broccoli and apricots. Cook for 2 minutes.
To microwave: Add broccoli and apricots, cover and cook for 1 minute.

7. Pour sauce mixture into a 568 ml (1 pint) ovenproof dish and top with crumble mixture.

8. Bake at 190°C (375°F) Mark 5 for 20 minutes.

9. Serve garnished with parsley.

Variation

PORK & BROCCOLI CRUMBLE

Follow recipe and method for savoury crumble (left). Omit chicken and dried apricots. Use 225 g (8 oz) diced pork fillet.

SAVOURY CRUMBLE

CITRUS FISH KEBABS

Preparation 25 mins **Cooking** 10 mins *Serves 1*

100g (4oz) white fish fillet, cubed
4 unpeeled prawns
1 small orange,
  peeled and cut into wedges
1 ring canned pineapple, cut into chunks
1 small courgette, cut into chunks
5ml (1tsp) lemon juice
65g (2½oz) natural yogurt
2.5ml (½tsp) grated lemon rind
2.5ml (½tsp) chopped fresh dill
cooked rice to serve
lemon wedges to garnish

1. Thread fish, prawns, fruit and vegetables on to 2 skewers and brush with lemon juice.

2. Place under a moderate grill and cook for 10 minutes or until fish is cooked, turning occasionally.

3. Blend together yogurt, lemon rind and dill.

4. Serve kebabs on a bed of cooked rice with dip.

5. Garnish with lemon wedges.

CITRUS FISH KEBABS

Variation
MIXED FISH KEBABS

Follow recipe and method for citrus fish kebabs (left). Omit prawns, orange and pineapple. Use 75g (3oz) white fish fillet and 75g (3oz) smoked fish fillet, cubed. Thread onto 2 skewers with courgette, 4 cherry tomatoes and 4 button mushrooms.

GINGERED FISH

Preparation 20 mins **Cooking** 15 mins *Serves 2*

15g (½oz) butter
1 medium onion, sliced
1cm (½inch) piece fresh root ginger,
  peeled and chopped
1 garlic clove, crushed
1 small red pepper, seeded and chopped
175g (6oz) cauliflower florets
225g (8oz) boned monkfish or huss, cubed
1.25ml (¼tsp) turmeric
150ml (¼pint) fresh milk
100g (4oz) skimmed milk soft cheese
chopped chives to garnish

1. Melt butter in a non-stick saucepan and add onion, ginger and garlic. Cook until soft.
To microwave: Cook butter, onion, ginger and garlic, covered for 3 minutes.

2. Add pepper, cauliflower, fish and turmeric.

3. Cook stirring for 2 minutes.
To microwave: Cover and cook for 2 minutes.

4. Add milk, bring to the boil, cover and simmer for 5 minutes.
To microwave: Add milk, cover and cook for 5 minutes, stirring once. Allow to stand for a few minutes.

5. Mix soft cheese with a little of the hot milk and stir into vegetables and fish.

6. Heat gently without boiling.
To microwave: Cook on MEDIUM (50%) for 1–2 minutes to heat through if necessary – do not boil.

7. Serve sprinkled with chopped chives.

CHICKEN CASSEROLE 🅕

Preparation 10 mins **Cooking** 1½ hrs   *Serves 1*

1 chicken stock cube
50 ml (2 fl oz) hot water
275 g (10 oz) chicken portion, skinned
227 g (8 oz) can chopped tomatoes
150 g (5 oz) frozen casserole vegetables
1 bay leaf
2.5 ml (½ tsp) dried mixed herbs
5 ml (2 tsp) mushroom ketchup (optional)
1 large potato, unpeeled

1. Dissolve stock cube in hot water.

2. Place chicken in a small ovenproof casserole dish with stock, tomatoes, vegetables, herbs and mushroom ketchup.

3. Cover and bake casserole and potato separately at 190°C (375°F) Mark 5 for 1½ hours, or until chicken is tender.
To microwave: Prick potato and cook for 6–8 minutes, turning over half way. Check centre is cooked by inserting a skewer. Wrap potato in foil and allow to stand. Meanwhile, cover casserole and cook for 10 minutes. Stir sauce and vegetables spooning them over chicken. Cover and continue cooking on MEDIUM–LOW (30%) for 10 minutes, until chicken is tender.

LEICESTER CHEESE PUDDING

Preparation 20 mins **plus** 30 mins **standing**
Cooking 30 mins   *Serves 2*

4 slices wholemeal bread, crusts removed
15 g (½ oz) butter, softened
25 g (1 oz) crunchy peanut butter
100 g (4 oz) Red Leicester cheese, grated
15 ml (1 tbsp) chopped parsley
2 eggs
300 ml (½ pint) fresh milk
2.5 ml (½ tsp) made mustard
salt and freshly ground pepper

1. Make sandwiches using bread, butter, peanut butter and 50 g (2 oz) cheese.

2. Cut into triangles and arrange in a shallow, greased 568 ml (1 pint) ovenproof dish.
To microwave: Cut into triangles and arrange in a shallow, greased 20.5 cm (8 inch) round flameproof dish.

3. Mix parsley and remaining cheese together and sprinkle over sandwiches.

4. Whisk together eggs, milk, mustard and seasoning.

5. Pour over sandwiches and leave to stand for 30 minutes.

6. Bake at 180°C (350°F) Mark 4 for 30 minutes until set and golden.
To microwave: Cook, uncovered, on MEDIUM (50%) for about 10 minutes until just set. Brown lightly under a hot grill.

7. Serve immediately.

BUTTER BEAN BAKE

Preparation 15 mins **Cooking** 30 mins   *Serves 1*

15 g (½ oz) butter
1 small onion, chopped
½ green pepper, seeded and diced
227 g (8 oz) can chopped tomatoes with herbs
220 g (7.7 oz) can butter beans, rinsed and drained
10 ml (2 tsp) tomato purée
1 egg
100 g (4 oz) cottage cheese
25 g (1 oz) Double Gloucester cheese with onion and chives, grated

QUICK KIDNEYS

1. Melt butter in a small non-stick frying pan. Fry onion and pepper for 3 minutes.
To microwave: Cook butter, onion and pepper, covered, for 3 minutes.

2. Add tomatoes, bring to the boil and simmer for 5 minutes.
To microwave: Add tomatoes, cover and cook for 4 minutes.

3. Stir in butter beans and tomato purée.

4. Spoon into a 568 ml (1 pint) ovenproof dish.
To microwave: Spoon into a 568 ml (1 pint) flameproof dish.

5. Beat egg into cottage cheese and stir in half the grated cheese.

6. Spoon over tomato mixture and top with remaining cheese.

7. Bake at 180°C (350°F) Mark 4 for 30 minutes.
To microwave: Cover and cook on MEDIUM (50%) for 5 minutes, then brown lightly under a hot grill.

PIPPA'S PIZZA Ⓕ

Preparation 25 mins **Cooking** 25 mins   *Serves 2*

227 g (8 oz) can chopped tomatoes
1 medium onion, sliced
2.5 ml (½ tsp) dried basil
75 g (3 oz) wholemeal self raising flour
75 g (3 oz) self raising flour
40 g (1½ oz) butter
75 ml (3 fl oz) fresh milk
50 g (2 oz) frozen mixed vegetables
100 g (4 oz) English Cheddar, grated
dried basil to garnish

1. Place tomatoes, onion and basil in a non-stick pan and cook until most of the liquid has evaporated, stir frequently.
To microwave: Place tomatoes, onion and basil in a dish and cook, uncovered, for about 10 mins, stirring occasionally, until most of the liquid has evaporated.

2. Place flours in a bowl.

3. Rub butter into flour until mixture resembles fine breadcrumbs.

4. Add milk and mix to a soft dough.

5. Roll out on a floured work surface to a 20.5 cm (8 inch) circle.

6. Place on a greased baking sheet and pinch edge of dough to form a rim.

7. Stir mixed vegetables into tomato mixture, spoon over pizza base.

8. Top with cheese and a pinch of basil.

9. Bake at 200°C (400°F) Mark 6 for 20 mins.

QUICK KIDNEYS Ⓕ

Preparation 10 mins **Cooking** 20 mins   *Serves 1*

150 g (5 oz) lambs' kidneys, halved
15 g (½ oz) butter
227 g (8 oz) can tomatoes
50 ml (2 fl oz) stock
50 g (2 oz) mushrooms, sliced
50 g (2 oz) frozen sweetcorn
50 g (2 oz) frozen peas
cooked rice or toast to serve

1. Remove and discard skin and core from kidneys and cut into bite-size pieces.

2. Melt butter in a non-stick pan, add kidneys and cook until lightly brown.

3. Add tomatoes, stock and mushrooms. Bring to the boil and simmer for 10 minutes.

4. Add frozen vegetables, bring back to the boil and cook for a further 5 minutes. Stir occasionally.

5. Serve with cooked rice or toast.

CHICKEN LIVER STIR-FRY

Preparation 10 mins **Cooking** 5 mins   *Serves 2*

225 g (8 oz) chicken livers
25 g (1 oz) butter
1 garlic clove, crushed
2 spring onions, sliced
175 g (6 oz) cabbage, shredded
225 g (8 oz) bean sprouts
100 g (4 oz) frozen sweetcorn
½ red pepper, seeded and sliced
45 ml (3 tbsp) orange juice
45 ml (3 tbsp) soy sauce

1. Remove and discard stringy parts of livers. Roughly chop remainder.

2. Melt butter and fry garlic, onions and liver for 3 minutes.

3. Add cabbage, bean sprouts, sweetcorn and red pepper, cook stirring for 2 minutes.

4. Stir in orange juice and soy sauce. Remove from heat and serve immediately.

RICE
AND
PASTA

LASAGNE PAGE 161 · NUTTY BEAN PILAFF PAGE 158
CRAB & RICE RING PAGE 156

RICE

BOILED RICE   F

Method One   **Cooking** 20 mins   *Serves 4*

225 g (8 oz) long grain rice
568 ml (1 pint) water

1. Rinse rice under running cold water. Place in a large pan with water.
To microwave: Rinse rice under running cold water. Place in a large bowl with BOILING water.

2. Bring quickly to the boil, stir to loosen grains.
To microwave: Stir well.

3. Cover with a well fitting lid. Reduce heat and simmer for about 15–20 minutes or until rice is tender and water has been absorbed.
To microwave: Cover, leaving a small vent, and cook for 10 minutes. Allow to stand, covered, for 3 minutes until all the water has been absorbed.

4. Stir with a fork to separate grains.

This volume method of cooking rice depends on having twice the amount of liquid to rice. This can be used for any quantity of rice. Cook brown rice in 750 ml (1¼ pint) water for 25–30 minutes.
To microwave: Cook brown rice in 750 ml (1¼ pint) BOILING water for about 20 minutes.

Variations
The water can be replaced with stock, tomato or orange juice or use half and half with water.

ONION RICE   F

Follow the recipe and method for boiled rice (above). After cooking add 1 medium chopped onion, fried in butter.

LEMON & BUTTER RICE   F

Add a thick slice of lemon to the rice before cooking. Follow recipe and method for boiled rice (above). Remove lemon and stir in 40 g (1½ oz) butter before serving.

BOILED RICE   F

Method Two   **Cooking** 20 mins   *Serves 4*

225 g (8 oz) long grain rice.

1. Place rice in a large pan of boiling water.
To microwave: Place rice in a large bowl and pour over sufficient BOILING water to cover it by 5 cm (2 inch).

2. Bring back to the boil and stir.
To microwave: Stir well.

3. Cover and simmer for about 15–20 minutes or until rice is tender. Drain.
To microwave: Cook, uncovered, for 12 minutes. Allow to stand for 3 minutes before draining.

Cook brown rice for about 25–30 minutes.
To microwave: Cook brown rice for about 20 minutes.

FRIED RICE

Preparation 15 mins **Cooking** 20 mins   *Serves 6*

40 g (1½ oz) butter
6 spring onions, sliced
1 garlic clove, crushed
50 g (2 oz) mushrooms, sliced
2 eggs, beaten
350 g (12 oz) cooked long grain rice
75 g (3 oz) cooked ham, diced
100 g (4 oz) frozen peas
100 g (4 oz) frozen sweetcorn
soy sauce to serve

1. Melt butter in a wok or frying pan.

2. Add onions, garlic and mushrooms. Cook stirring for 5 minutes. Remove to a plate.

3. Add eggs to pan and cook until lightly scrambled.

4. Return onion mixture to pan, add rice, ham and remaining vegetables.

5. Cook stirring for 5–10 minutes, or until rice is heated and peas and sweetcorn are cooked.

6. Serve accompanied with soy sauce.

PILAU RICE Ⓕ

Preparation 5 mins **plus** 30 mins **soaking**
Cooking 25 mins   *Serves 4–6*

275g (10oz) basmati rice
15ml (1 tbsp) oil
2.5ml (½ tsp) cumin seeds
4 green cardamoms
4 cloves
2.5ml (1 inch) stick of cinnamon
1 bay leaf

1. Place rice in a sieve and wash under cold running water.

2. Leave to soak in cold water for 30 minutes. Drain well.

3. Heat oil in a saucepan, add spices and fry for 1 minute.
To microwave: Place oil and spices in a large bowl and cook for 45 seconds.

4. Stir in rice. Add sufficient cold water to come to 2.5cm (1 inch) above top of rice.
To microwave: Stir in rice. Add 750ml (1¼ pint) BOILING water and stir well.

5. Bring to the boil, cover, reduce heat and simmer for 20 minutes or until rice is tender and water absorbed.
To microwave: Cover, leaving a small vent and cook for 10 minutes. Allow to stand for 3 minutes until all the liquid has been absorbed.

6. Gently stir with a fork to separate grains and serve.

Alternatively add 5ml (1 tsp) turmeric to rice before cooking for yellow pilau rice.

RISOTTO MILANESE Ⓕ

Preparation 10 mins **Cooking** 30 mins *Serves 4*

few saffron strands
45ml (3 tbsp) hot water
25g (1oz) butter
1 small onion, finely chopped
350g (12oz) arborio or risotto rice
900ml (1½ pint) hot chicken stock
salt and freshly ground pepper
50g (2oz) mature English Cheddar, grated

1. Place saffron and hot water in a cup and leave to stand.

2. Melt butter in a large saucepan. Add onion and fry for 5 minutes.
To microwave: Place butter and onion in a large bowl and cook, covered, for 3 minutes.

3. Add rice and stir to coat with butter.

4. Add 100ml (4 fl oz) hot stock to rice, cook gently stirring frequently until absorbed. Add a little more stock, when it is absorbed, add a little more. Stir frequently. Continue until all the stock has been added. This should take about 25 minutes until rice is thick, creamy and tender.
To microwave: Add BOILING stock and stir well. Cover, leaving a small vent. Cook for about 15 minutes, stirring occasionally, until rice is thick, creamy and tender, and all the stock has been absorbed. Allow to stand, covered, for 3 minutes.

5. Add saffron, water and season to taste.

6. Stir in most of the cheese.

7. Serve with remaining cheese.

PAELLA

Preparation 25 mins
Cooking 35 mins   *Serves 4–6*

25g (1oz) butter
15ml (1 tbsp) oil
8 chicken thighs, skinned
1 medium onion, chopped
2 garlic cloves, crushed
225g (8oz) long grain rice
5ml (1 tsp) saffron strands
568ml (1 pint) warm chicken stock
1 bay leaf
225g (8oz) frozen peas
1 red pepper, seeded and diced
2 tomatoes, quartered
100g (4oz) peeled prawns
100g (4oz) cooked, shelled mussels
8 unpeeled prawns and lemon wedges to garnish

1. Heat butter and oil in a large frying pan.

2. Add chicken and fry until lightly brown. Remove and keep warm.

3. Add onion and garlic to pan and fry until golden.

4. Add rice and cook for a minute, stirring.

5. Return chicken to pan with saffron, stock and bay leaf.

6. Bring to the boil, cover and simmer slowly for 15 minutes.

7. Stir occasionally and add more stock if necessary.

8. Uncover and stir in vegetables.

9. Cover and cook for 5 minutes, or until peas are cooked.

10. Add prawns, mussels and heat through.

11. Serve garnished with whole prawns and lemon wedges.

STUFFED PEPPERS WITH RICE & CHEESE

Preparation 15 mins **Cooking** 25 mins *Serves 4*

4 medium red or green peppers
225g (8oz) freshly cooked rice
  (about 100g (4oz) raw)
75g (3oz) cooked sliced mushrooms
50g (2oz) cooked peas
100g (4oz) Lancashire cheese, grated
2.5ml (½tsp) made mustard
150ml (5floz) fresh single cream
salt and freshly ground pepper
25g (1oz) butter

1. Cut tops off peppers. Remove inside seeds and fibres.

2. Put peppers into a large saucepan of boiling water and simmer for 2 minutes.
To microwave: Stand peppers in a dish with 45ml (3tbsp) water, cover and cook for 5 minutes.

3. Carefully lift out peppers. Stand upside down to drain on absorbent kitchen paper.
To microwave: Drain carefully.

4. Mix together rice, mushrooms, peas, cheese, mustard and cream. Season to taste.

5. Stand peppers in a shallow ovenproof dish. Fill with cheese and rice mixture.

6. Put a knob of butter on top of each pepper. Cover with aluminium foil.
To microwave: Put a knob of butter on top of each pepper.

7. Bake at 180°C (350°F) Mark 4 for 20 minutes.
To microwave: Cover and cook for about 15 minutes until peppers are tender.

PAELLA

STUFFED PEPPERS WITH RICE & MEAT Ⓕ

Preparation 15 mins **Cooking** 25 mins *Serves 4*

4 medium red or green peppers
225g (8oz) lean minced beef
1 medium onion, finely chopped
75g (3oz) mushrooms, sliced
225g (8oz) freshly cooked rice
   (about 100g (4oz) raw)
2 medium tomatoes, skinned and chopped
10ml (2tsp) Worcestershire sauce
salt and freshly ground pepper
65ml (2½fl oz) water
25g (1oz) butter

1. Cut tops off peppers. Remove inside seeds and fibres.

2. Put peppers into a large saucepan of boiling water and simmer for 2 minutes.
To microwave: Stand peppers in a dish with 45ml (3tbsp) water, cover and cook for 5 minutes.

3. Carefully lift out peppers. Stand upside down to drain on absorbent kitchen paper.
To microwave: Drain carefully.

4. Dry fry beef in a non-stick pan until browned. Add onion and mushrooms and cook for 3 minutes.
To microwave: Cook onion, covered, for 3 minutes. Stir in beef, breaking it up with a fork. Cover and cook for 5 minutes, stirring once. Stir in mushrooms, cover and cook for 3 minutes.

5. Stir in rice, tomatoes and Worcestershire sauce. Season to taste.

6. Stand peppers in a shallow ovenproof dish. Fill with meat and rice mixture.

7. Pour water into dish. Put a knob of butter on top of each pepper.

8. Bake at 180°C (350°F) Mark 4 for 20 minutes.
To microwave: Cover and cook for about 15 minutes until peppers are tender.

CRAB & RICE RING

Preparation 15 mins **Cooking** 20 mins *Serves 6*

100g (4oz) long grain rice
350g (12oz) cottage cheese
195g (6.8oz) can sweetcorn with peppers, drained
45ml (3tbsp) mayonnaise
5ml (1tsp) Worcestershire sauce
few drops of hot pepper sauce
salt and freshly ground pepper
10ml (2tsp) chopped fresh dill
170g (6oz) can crabmeat, drained
fresh dill, frisée and cherry tomatoes to garnish

1. Cook rice in boiling water for 15–20 minutes, or until tender.
To microwave: Place rice in a large bowl with 300ml (½pint) BOILING water and stir well. Cover, leaving a vent and cook for 10 minutes. Allow to stand for 3 minutes until all the water has been absorbed.

2. Rinse in cold water and drain well.

3. Place in a bowl with cottage cheese, sweetcorn, mayonnaise, sauces and mix.

4. Season to taste and gently stir in dill and crabmeat.

5. Spoon into an oiled 1.1 litre (2pint) ring mould, pressing firmly in.

6. Cover and chill.

7. Invert rice ring onto a serving plate.

8. Garnish with dill, frisée and tomatoes.

KOULIBIAC Ⓕ

Preparation 35 mins **Cooking** 1 hr *Serves 4*

100g (4oz) long grain rice
418g (14.75oz) can red salmon, drained
25g (1oz) butter
1 small onion, chopped
50g (2oz) mushrooms, sliced
2 eggs, hard-boiled, shelled and chopped
30ml (2tbsp) chopped parsley
60ml (4tbsp) fresh double cream
30ml (2tbsp) sherry
salt and freshly ground pepper
375g (13oz) puff pastry
beaten egg to glaze

1. Cook rice in boiling water for 20 minutes, or until tender. Drain well.

To microwave: Place rice in a large bowl with 300ml (½pint) BOILING water and stir well. Cover, leaving a small vent and cook for 10 minutes. Allow to stand for 3 minutes until all the water has been absorbed.

2. Remove and discard skin and bones from salmon. Flake the flesh.

3. Melt butter in a saucepan and fry onion and mushrooms for 3 minutes.

To microwave: Cook butter, onion and mushrooms, covered, for 3 minutes.

4. Add to rice with salmon, eggs, parsley, cream and sherry. Season to taste.

5. Roll out pastry on a floured work surface to 30.5cm (12inch) square.

6. Spoon filling down centre of pastry.

7. Brush edges of pastry with beaten egg.

8. Bring together edges of pastry and seal at ends and down the centre.

9. Invert onto a baking sheet and brush with beaten egg.

10. Score pastry with a knife in a diamond pattern.

11. Bake at 200°C (400°F) Mark 6 for 40 minutes or until golden brown.

STANDBY RICE SALAD

Preparation 5 mins **Cooking** 30 mins *Serves 4–6*

225g (8oz) long grain brown rice
175g (6oz) frozen peas
175g (6oz) frozen sweetcorn
French dressing
    made with 60ml (4tbsp) oil (page 196)
50g (2oz) roasted peanuts

1. Place rice in a large pan of boiling water.

To microwave: Place rice in a large bowl and pour over sufficient BOILING water to cover it by 5cm (2inch).

2. Bring back to the boil and stir to loosen grains.

To microwave: Stir well.

3. Cover and simmer for 25–30 minutes.

To microwave: Cook, uncovered, for 20 minutes or until just tender.

4. Add peas and sweetcorn for last 5 minutes of cooking time.

To microwave: Stir in peas and sweetcorn. Cook uncovered for 5 minutes.

5. Drain and rinse under cold water.

6. Stir dressing and peanuts into rice.

7. Spoon into a serving bowl and chill until ready to serve.

NUTTY BEAN PILAFF

Preparation 20mins plus soaking
Cooking 1¼hrs   *Serves 4–6*

175g (6oz) dried red kidney beans
225g (8oz) brown basmati rice
25g (1oz) butter
1 medium onion, chopped
3 celery sticks, sliced
100g (4oz) chestnut mushrooms, sliced
30ml (2tbsp) pesto sauce
100g (4oz) cashew nuts, toasted

1. Place beans in a large bowl and cover with at least four times the same amount of cold water.

2. Leave to soak for at least 8 hours or overnight.

3. Drain beans and rinse under cold water.

4. Place in a large saucepan and cover with at least four times the same amount of cold water (do not add salt as this will toughen pulses).

5. Bring to the boil and boil rapidly for 10 minutes (this will destroy any potential toxins that may be present).

6. Reduce heat, cover and simmer for about 1 hour or until beans are tender. Older beans will take longer to cook.

7. Top up with boiling water if necessary.

8. Meanwhile, cook rice in boiling water for about 25 minutes or until tender. Drain.
To microwave: Place rice in a large bowl with 750ml (1¼pint) BOILING water and stir well. Cover, leaving a small vent, and cook for about 20 minutes or until tender. Allow to stand for 3 minutes until all the water has been absorbed.

9. Melt butter in a pan. Add onion, celery and mushrooms and cook stirring for 5 minutes.
To microwave: Cook onion, celery and mushrooms, covered, for 5 minutes.

10. Add drained, cooked beans, onion mixture, pesto and nuts to rice.

11. Stir well to mix and serve immediately.

Alternatively use drained contents of a 425g (15oz) can red kidney beans. Omit steps 1–7.

SMOKED CHEESE & RICE SALAD

Preparation 25mins **Cooking** 30mins *Serves 4*

100g (4oz) brown rice
175g (6oz) frozen peas
312g (11oz) can mandarin segments in natural juice
150g (5oz) natural yogurt
7.5ml (1½tsp) mint sauce
150g (5oz) smoked Cheddar cheese, cubed
150g (5oz) reduced fat hard cheese, cubed
½ medium onion, chopped
½ medium red pepper, seeded and diced
chopped parsley to garnish

1. Cook rice in boiling water for approximately 30 minutes.
To microwave: Place rice in a large bowl with 450ml (¾pint) BOILING water and stir well. Cover, leaving a vent, and cook for about 20 minutes or until tender. Allow to stand.

2. Add peas for last 5 minutes of cooking time. Drain and rinse under cold water.
To microwave: Cook peas with 15ml (1tbsp) water, covered, for 5 minutes, stirring once. Drain and rinse rice and peas under cold water.

3. Drain mandarins, reserving 45ml (3tbsp) of juice.

4. Mix juice, yogurt and mint sauce together and stir into rice.

5. Stir in mandarins, cheese, onions and pepper.

6. Spoon into a serving bowl and garnish with chopped parsley.

Variation

SMOKED CHEESE & PASTA SALAD

Follow recipe and method for smoked cheese and rice salad (above). Omit rice and use 100g (4oz) pasta shapes.

PASTA

SPAGHETTI BOLOGNESE Ⓕ

Preparation 20 mins **Cooking** 1 hr   *Serves 4*

15 ml (1 tbsp) oil
15 g (½ oz) butter
50 g (2 oz) streaky bacon, chopped
1 medium onion, finely chopped
2 celery sticks, finely chopped
1 medium carrot, finely chopped
100 g (4 oz) mushrooms, sliced
1 garlic clove, crushed
450 g (1 lb) lean minced beef
350 ml (12 floz) stock
30 ml (2 tbsp) tomato purée
1 bay leaf
2.5 ml (½ tsp) dried oregano
350 g (12 oz) spaghetti

1. Heat oil and butter in a saucepan and cook bacon until it starts to brown.
To microwave: Cook oil, butter and bacon, uncovered, for 3 mins, stirring once.

2. Add vegetables and garlic, cook stirring until golden.
To microwave: Stir in vegetables and garlic. Cover and cook for 5 mins.

3. Add beef and cook until brown.
To microwave: Stir in beef, breaking it up.

4. Add stock, tomato purée, herbs and bring to the boil. Cover and cook for 45–50 mins on a low heat. Stir occasionally.
To microwave: Stir in BOILING stock, tomato purée, and herbs. Cook for 10 mins, stirring twice, or until boiling. Cover, cook on MEDIUM (50%) for 20 mins, stir occasionally.

5. Meanwhile cook spaghetti in boiling water until tender, about 10–12 mins. Stir occasionally. Drain.
To microwave: Break spaghetti into a large bowl and pour over sufficient BOILING water to cover it by 2.5 cm (1 inch). Stir. Cook, uncovered, for 7 mins, stirring frequently. Allow to stand for 3 mins. Drain.

6. Serve pasta with bolognese sauce.

SPAGHETTI BOLOGNESE

SPAGHETTI MARINARA

SPAGHETTI NEAPOLITAN Ⓕ

Preparation 2 mins **Cooking** 12 mins · *Serves 4*

350g (12oz) spaghetti
freshly made tomato sauce made with
   397g (14oz) tomatoes (page 238)
accompany with
100g (4oz) English Cheddar, grated

1. Cook spaghetti in boiling water for
10–12 minutes or until tender, stirring often
to prevent sticking.
*To microwave: Break spaghetti in a large
bowl and pour over sufficient BOILING water
to cover it by 2.5cm (1 inch). Stir. Cook,
uncovered, for 7 minutes, stirring frequently.
Allow to stand for 3 minutes.*

2. Drain well. Transfer equal amounts to 4
warm serving plates.

3. Pour tomato sauce over each one.

4. Serve hot with cheese.

Variation

SPAGHETTI MARINARA

Follow recipe and method for spaghetti
Neapolitan (above). Add 175g (6oz) peeled
prawns and 100g (4oz) cooked, shelled
mussels and heat through before serving.

SEAFOOD LASAGNE

Preparation 20 mins **Cooking** 40 mins · *Serves 6*

50g (2oz) flour
50g (2oz) butter
568ml (1 pint) fresh milk
225g (8oz) smoked haddock,
   skinned and cubed
100g (4oz) peeled prawns
100g (4oz) peas
grated rind of ½ lemon
100g (4oz) ready-to-cook lasagne verdi
1 egg, beaten
150g (5oz) natural yogurt
100g (4oz) English Cheddar, grated

1. Place flour, butter and milk in a pan, heat
whisking until sauce thickens, boils and is
smooth. Cook for a minute.
*To microwave: Place flour in a bowl or jug
and gradually blend in milk. Add butter and
cook for 5–6 minutes, stirring frequently,
until sauce thickens, boils and is smooth.*

2. Add fish, prawns, peas and lemon rind.

3. Place half the mixture in a
25.5×20.5cm (10×8 inch) ovenproof dish.
*To microwave: Place half the mixture in a
25.5×20.5cm (10×8 inch) flameproof dish –
use a deep one to prevent bubbling over.*

4. Cover with half the lasagne and repeat the layers.

5. Whisk together egg and yogurt, stir in half the cheese and pour over lasagne.

6. Sprinkle over remaining cheese and bake at 200°C (400°F) Mark 6 for 35 minutes until golden brown.

To microwave: Cook, uncovered, on MEDIUM (50%) for about 30 minutes until pasta is tender. Sprinkle remaining cheese over top and brown under a hot grill.

LASAGNE Ⓕ

Preparation 10 mins **Cooking** 40 mins   *Serves 4*

25 g (1 oz) flour
25 g (1 oz) butter
450 ml (¾ pint) fresh milk
pinch of ground nutmeg
2.5 ml (½ tsp) made mustard
75 g (3 oz) English Cheddar, grated
salt and freshly ground pepper
75 ml (3 fl oz) stock
bolognese sauce made with
   450 g (1 lb) beef (page 159)
100 g (4 oz) ready-to-cook lasagne

1. Place flour, butter and milk in a pan, heat, whisking until sauce thickens, boils and is smooth. Cook for a minute.

To microwave: Place flour in a bowl or jug and gradually blend in milk. Add butter and cook for 4–5 minutes, stirring frequently, until sauce thickens, boils and is smooth.

2. Remove from heat. Add nutmeg, mustard and half the cheese and stir until melted. Season to taste.

3. Add stock to bolognese sauce and place half the mixture in a 25.5×20.5 cm (10×8 inch) ovenproof dish.

To microwave: Add stock to bolognese sauce and place half the mixture in a 25.5×20.5 cm (10×8 inch) flameproof dish – use a deep one to prevent bubbling over.

4. Cover with half the lasagne, repeat layers.

5. Pour cheese sauce over lasagne and sprinkle remaining cheese on top.

To microwave: Pour cheese sauce over lasagne, covering it completely.

6. Bake at 180°C (350°F) Mark 6 for 35 minutes until golden and pasta is tender.

To microwave: Cook, uncovered, on MEDIUM (50%) for about 30 minutes until pasta is tender. Sprinkle remaining cheese over top and brown under a hot grill.

SEAFOOD LASAGNE

LENTIL LASAGNE

Preparation 25 mins **Cooking** 1 hr   *Serves 4*

15 g (½ oz) butter
1 medium onion, chopped
1 green pepper, seeded and chopped
175 g (6 oz) split red lentils
397 g (14 oz) can tomatoes
300 ml (½ pint) stock
300 ml (½ pint) fresh milk
30 ml (2 tbsp) tomato purée
5 ml (1 tsp) dried mixed herbs
freshly ground pepper
100 g (4 oz) ready-to-cook lasagne
2 eggs
225 g (8 oz) natural yogurt
100 g (4 oz) English Cheddar, grated

1. Melt butter in a saucepan, add onion and cook until soft.
To microwave: Cook butter and onion, covered, for 3 minutes.

2. Add pepper, lentils, tomatoes, stock, 150 ml (¼ pint) milk, tomato purée, herbs and pepper. (It may look curdled to begin with.)
To microwave: Stir in pepper, lentils, tomatoes, BOILING stock, 150 ml (¼ pint) milk, tomato purée, herbs and pepper.

3. Bring to the boil, cover and simmer for 15–20 minutes until lentils are tender.
To microwave: Cover and cook for 20 minutes, stirring occasionally, or until lentils are tender.

4. Place half the lentil mixture in a 25.5×20.5 cm (10×8 inch) ovenproof dish.
To microwave: Place half the lentil mixture in a 25.5×20.5 cm (10×8 inch) flameproof dish – use a deep one to prevent bubbling over.

5. Cover with half the lasagne, repeat layers.

6. Whisk together eggs, remaining milk and yogurt. Stir in half the cheese and pour over lasagne.

7. Sprinkle remaining cheese over lasagne and bake at 200°C (400°F) Mark 6 for 35 minutes or until golden brown.
To microwave: Cook, uncovered, on MEDIUM (50%) for about 30 minutes until pasta is tender. Sprinkle remaining cheese over top and brown under a hot grill.

VEGETABLE LASAGNE

VEGETABLE LASAGNE Ⓕ

Preparation 45 mins **Cooking** 50 mins *Serves 4*

350g (12oz) carrots, thinly sliced
350g (12oz) courgettes, thinly sliced
100g (4oz) mushrooms, sliced
1 medium onion, thinly sliced
1 green pepper, seeded and thinly sliced
100g (4oz) celery, thinly sliced
1 vegetable stock cube
200ml (7fl oz) water
60ml (4tbsp) flour
50g (2oz) butter
568ml (1pint) fresh milk
salt and freshly ground pepper
100g (4oz) ready-to-cook lasagne
175g (6oz) English Cheddar, grated

1. Place vegetables in a saucepan with stock cube and water. Bring to the boil, cover and simmer for 10–15 minutes.
To microwave: Place vegetables in a large casserole with crumbled stock cube and BOILING water. Cover and cook for 15 minutes, stirring occasionally.

2. Place flour, butter and milk in a pan, heat whisking continuously until sauce thickens, boils and is smooth. Cook for a minute and season to taste.
To microwave: Place flour in a bowl or jug and graudally blend in milk. Add butter and cook for 5–6 minutes, stirring frequently, until sauce thickens, boils and is smooth. Season to taste.

3. Place half the vegetable mixture in base of a 25.5×20.5cm (10×8inch) ovenproof dish.
To microwave: Place half the vegetable mixture in a base of a 25.5×20.5cm (10×8inch) flameproof dish – use a deep one to prevent bubbling over.

4. Cover with half of the lasagne, some sauce and cheese. Repeat layers.

5. Top with remaining sauce and cheese.
To microwave: Cover lasagne completely with remaining sauce.

6. Bake at 190°C (375°F) Mark 5 for 35 minutes.
To microwave: Cook on MEDIUM (50%) for about 30 minutes until pasta is tender. Sprinkle remaining cheese over top and brown under a hot grill.

TUNA & SWEETCORN LASAGNE Ⓕ

Preparation 30 mins **Cooking** 50 mins *Serves 4*

397g (14oz) can chopped tomatoes
    with herbs
1 medium onion, chopped
50g (2oz) mushrooms, sliced
1 medium green pepper,
    seeded and sliced
1 garlic clove, crushed
400g (14oz) can tuna in brine,
    drained and flaked
100g (4oz) canned sweetcorn, drained
100g (4oz) ready-to-cook lasagne
30ml (2tbsp) cornflour
2.5ml (½tsp) dry mustard
450ml (¾pint) fresh milk
50g (2oz) mature English Cheddar, grated

1. Place vegetables and garlic in a pan, bring to the boil and cook for 3 minutes.
To microwave: Cook onion and garlic, covered, for 3 minutes. Stir in tomatoes, mushrooms and pepper. Cover and cook for 5 minutes.

2. Stir in tuna and sweetcorn.

3. Layer in a 25.5×20.5cm (10×8inch) ovenproof dish with lasagne.
To microwave: Layer sauce and pasta in a 25.5×20.5cm (10×8inch) flameproof dish – use a deep one to prevent bubbling over.

4. Blend together cornflour, mustard and a little milk.

5. Heat remaining milk to boiling point, pour onto cornflour and stir well.
To microwave: Heat remaining milk for about 4 minutes until boiling. Pour onto cornflour and stir well.

6. Return to heat, cook stirring until sauce thickens, boils and is smooth.
To microwave: Cook for about 2 minutes, stirring once, until sauce thickens, boils and is smooth.

7. Stir in half the cheese, pour over lasagne.

8. Sprinkle remaining cheese over lasagne.

9. Bake at 200°C (400°F) Mark 6 for 35–40 minutes.
To microwave: Cook, uncovered, on MEDIUM (50%) for about 30 minutes until pasta is tender, then brown under a hot grill.

MACARONI CHEESE WITH BACON

VEGETABLE CANNELLONI ⓕ

Preparation 35 mins **Cooking** 45 mins *Serves 4*

15g (½oz) butter
1 small onion, finely chopped
100g (4oz) aubergines, diced
100g (4oz) courgettes, diced
2 tomatoes, skinned and chopped
1 garlic clove, crushed
100ml (4floz) tomato juice
40g (1½oz) flour
40g (1½oz) butter
450ml (¾pint) fresh milk
salt and freshly ground pepper
75g (3oz) English Cheddar, grated
60ml (4tbsp) natural yogurt
12 ready-to-cook cannelloni tubes

1. Melt butter in a saucepan, add vegetables, garlic and tomato juice. Cook for 10 minutes.
To microwave: Melt butter for 30 seconds and stir in vegetables, garlic and tomato juice. Cook, uncovered, for 10 minutes, stirring once.

2. Place flour, butter and milk in a pan.
To microwave: Place flour in a bowl or jug and gradually blend in milk. Add butter.

3. Heat, stirring continuously until sauce thickens, boils and is smooth. Cook for a minute. Season to taste.
To microwave: Cook for 4–5 minutes, stirring frequently, until sauce thickens, boils and is smooth. Season to taste.

4. Add 50g (2oz) cheese and yogurt, stir until melted.

5. Spoon vegetable mixture into cannelloni tubes.

6. Place in an ovenproof dish and pour over sauce.
To microwave: Place in a flameproof dish and pour sauce over to cover pasta completely.

7. Sprinkle over remaining cheese.

8. Bake at 180°C (350°F) Mark 4 for 30 minutes.
To microwave: Cover and cook on MEDIUM (50%) for about 25 minutes until pasta is tender, then brown under a hot grill.

MACARONI CHEESE Ⓕ

Preparation 10 mins **Cooking** 15 mins *Serves 4*

225g (8oz) macaroni
40g (1½oz) butter
40g (1½oz) flour
2.5ml (½tsp) dry mustard
568ml (1pint) fresh milk
175g (6oz) Lancashire or English Cheddar
  cheese, grated
salt and freshly ground pepper
parsley to garnish

1. Cook macaroni in boiling water until tender, about 7–10 minutes.
To microwave: Place macaroni in a large bowl and pour over sufficient BOILING water to cover 2.5cm (1inch). Stir well. Cook, uncovered, for 7 minutes, stirring occasionally. Allow to stand.

2. Meanwhile melt butter in a saucepan, add flour and mustard and cook slowly for 2 minutes. Stir often and do not allow mixture to brown.
To microwave: Melt butter for 1 minute. Stir in flour and mustard and cook for 1 minute.

3. Gradually blend in milk. Cook, stirring until sauce thickens, boils and is smooth. Simmer for 2 minutes and remove from heat.
To microwave: Gradually blend in milk. Cook for 5–6 minutes, stirring frequently, until sauce thickens, boils and is smooth.

4. Stir in 100g (4oz) cheese. Season to taste.

5. Drain macaroni, add to sauce and mix.

6. Transfer to a 1.1litre (2pint) greased flameproof dish.

7. Sprinkle remaining cheese on top and brown under a hot grill.

8. Garnish with parsley.

If macaroni cheese is prepared in advance, re-heat at 200°C (400°F) Mark 6 for 25 minutes.
To microwave: Cook on MEDIUM (50%) for about 15 minutes.

Variations

MACARONI CHEESE WITH BACON Ⓕ

Follow recipe and method for macaroni cheese (above). Add 100g (4oz) chopped and lightly fried bacon to sauce with macaroni.

MACARONI BROCCOLI CHEESE Ⓕ

Follow recipe and method for macaroni cheese (left). Add 225g (8oz) lightly cooked and drained broccoli florets to sauce with macaroni.

SALMON MACARONI Ⓕ

Preparation 20 mins **Cooking** 25 mins *Serves 4*

100g (4oz) pasta shapes
15g (½oz) butter
1 medium onion, chopped
25g (1oz) wholemeal flour
300ml (½pint) fresh milk
75g (3oz) English Cheddar, grated
213g (7.5oz) can pink salmon,
  drained and flaked
15ml (1tbsp) chopped parsley
freshly ground pepper
1 medium tomato, sliced
25g (1oz) fresh wholemeal breadcrumbs

1. Cook pasta in boiling water for 10–12 minutes.
To microwave: Place pasta in a large bowl with sufficient BOILING water to cover it by 2.5cm (1inch). Stir well. Cook, uncovered, for 7 minutes, stirring occasionally. Allow to stand.

2. Melt butter in a saucepan and cook onion until soft.
To microwave: Cook butter and onion for 3 minutes.

3. Stir in flour, gradually stir in milk, cook stirring until sauce thickens, boils and is smooth. Cook for a minute.
To microwave: Stir in flour and gradually blend in milk. Cook for 3–4 minutes, stirring frequently, until sauce thickens, boils and is smooth.

4. Remove from heat, stir in half the cheese, flaked salmon, drained pasta, parsley and pepper.

5. Spoon into a flameproof dish, arrange tomato on top.

6. Mix breadcrumbs and remaining cheese, sprinkle over tomato.

7. Either grill until toasted or bake at 200°C (400°F) Mark 6 for 15 minutes.
To microwave: Brown under a hot grill.

PASTICCIO   Ⓕ

Preparation 30 mins
Cooking 1 hr 20 mins   *Serves 4*

225g (8oz) macaroni
225g (8oz) lean minced beef
50g (2oz) bacon, chopped
1 medium onion, chopped
1 medium carrot, chopped
1 celery stick, sliced
1 garlic clove, crushed
30ml (2tbsp) tomato purée
225ml (8floz) stock
225g (8oz) frozen peas
50g (2oz) flour
50g (2oz) butter
568ml (1pint) fresh milk
50g (2oz) Double Gloucester cheese, grated

1. Cook macaroni in boiling water for 7–10 mins.
To microwave: Place macaroni in a large bowl and pour over sufficient BOILING water to cover it by 2.5cm (1inch). Stir well. Cook, uncovered, for 7 mins, stirring occasionally. Allow to stand.

2. Dry fry beef in a non-stick pan until brown.
To microwave: Break up beef into a large casserole.

3. Add bacon, onion, carrot, celery, garlic, tomato purée and stock.
To microwave: Stir in bacon, onion, carrot, celery, garlic, tomato purée and BOILING stock.

4. Bring to the boil, cover and simmer gently for 40 mins.
To microwave: Cover and cook for 15 mins, stirring occasionally.

5. Mix meat, drained macaroni and peas.

6. Place in an ovenproof dish.
To microwave: Place in a large flameproof dish.

7. Place flour, butter and milk in a saucepan, heat stirring until sauce thickens, boils and is smooth. Cook for a minute.
To microwave: Place flour in a bowl or jug and gradually blend in milk. Add butter and cook for 5–6 mins, stirring frequently, until sauce thickens, boils and is smooth.

8. Remove from heat, add half the cheese and stir until melted. Season to taste.

9. Pour over beef and sprinkle with remaining cheese.
To microwave: Pour over beef.

10. Bake at 180°C (350°F) Mark 4 for 30 mins.
To microwave: Cook, uncovered, on MEDIUM (50%) for 10 mins. Sprinkle remaining cheese over top and brown under a hot grill.

PASTA SUPPER

Preparation 15 mins **Cooking** 10 mins *Serves 4*

275 g (10 oz) tagliatelle
15 g (½ oz) butter
1 medium onion, chopped
175 g (6 oz) frozen peas
175 g (6 oz) frozen sweetcorn
150 ml (¼ pint) stock
15 ml (1 tbsp) cornflour
300 ml (10 fl oz) fresh single cream
175 g (6 oz) cooked smoked ham,
   cut into strips
freshly ground pepper
50 g (2 oz) Caerphilly cheese, grated

1. Cook pasta in boiling water for
8–10 minutes.
*To microwave: Place pasta in a large bowl
and pour over sufficient BOILING water to
cover it by 2.5 cm (1 inch). Stir well. Cook,
uncovered, for 8 minutes, stirring
occasionally. Allow to stand.*

2. Meanwhile melt butter in a saucepan and
cook onion until soft.
*To microwave: Cook butter and onion,
covered, for 3 minutes.*

3. Add peas, sweetcorn and stock, cook for
2 minutes.
*To microwave: Stir in peas, sweetcorn and
stock. Cover and cook for 2 minutes.*

4. Blend cornflour with a little cold water.

5. Stir into vegetables with cream and ham.
Cook gently until thickened. Season to taste.
*To microwave: Stir into vegetables with
cream and ham. Cover and cook for about
8 minutes, stirring frequently, until
thickened. Season to taste.*

6. Drain pasta and stir into sauce.

7. Serve sprinkled with cheese.

Variation

TUNA PASTA SUPPER

Follow recipe and method for pasta supper
(left). Omit smoked ham and Caerphilly
cheese. Use a 198 g (7 oz) can of tuna,
drained and flaked and 50 g (2 oz) grated
Double Gloucester cheese.

PASTA SUPPER

TASTY PASTA

Preparation 20 mins **Cooking** 20 mins *Serves 4*

275g (10oz) tagliatelle
175g (6oz) broccoli florets
25g (1oz) butter
75g (3oz) mushrooms, sliced
100g (4oz) smoked bacon, chopped
2 garlic cloves, crushed
2.5ml (½tsp) dried basil
40g (1½oz) flour
568ml (1 pint) fresh milk
50g (2oz) Red Cheshire cheese, grated

1. Cook pasta in boiling water for 5 mins.
To microwave: Place pasta in a large bowl and pour over sufficient water to cover it by 2.5cm (1inch). Stir well. Cook, uncovered, for 8 mins, stirring occasionally. Allow to stand.

2. Add broccoli, return to the boil and cook for a further 5 mins or until tender.
To microwave: Cook broccoli in 60ml (4tbsp) water, covered, for 5 mins, stirring once, or until tender.

3. Melt butter in a pan, add mushrooms, bacon, garlic and basil. Cook for 5 mins.
To microwave: Cook butter, mushrooms, bacon, garlic and basil, covered, for 5 mins.

4. Add flour and milk, heat stirring continuously until sauce thickens, boils and is smooth. Cook for 1 min.
To microwave: Stir in flour then gradually blend in milk. Cook for 5–6 mins, stirring frequently, until sauce thickens, boils and is smooth.

5. Remove from heat, add most of the cheese and stir until melted. Season to taste.

6. Stir drained pasta into sauce.

7. Serve sprinkled with remaining cheese.

BEEF & NOODLE BAKE

Preparation 20 mins
Cooking 1 hr 5 mins   *Serves 4–6*

450g (1lb) lean minced beef
1 medium onion, chopped
2 garlic cloves, chopped
1 green pepper, seeded and chopped
227g (7oz) can tomatoes
1 vegetable stock cube
175g (6oz) medium egg noodles
275g (10oz) fresh soured cream
225g (8oz) cottage cheese
50g (2oz) Double Gloucester cheese, grated

BEEF & NOODLE BAKE

PETE'S PASTA SALAD

1. Dry fry mince in a non-stick pan until browned.
To microwave: Break up mince into a large casserole.

2. Add vegetables and stock cube, bring to the boil, cover and simmer for 15 minutes, stir occasionally.
To microwave: Stir in vegetables and crumbled stock cube, cover and cook for 15 minutes, stirring occasionally.

3. Spoon into an ovenproof dish.
To microwave: Spoon into a flameproof dish.

4. Meanwhile cook noodles as label directs and drain.
To microwave: Put noodles into a large bowl and pour over sufficient BOILING water to cover them by 2.5cm (1inch). Stir well. Cook, uncovered, for 3 minutes, stirring once. Allow to stand for 3 minutes before draining.

5. Mix soured cream and cottage cheese together, then stir in noodles.

6. Arrange noodles over meat and sprinkle cheese over the top.
To microwave: Arrange noodles over meat.

7. Cook at 180°C (350°F) Mark 4 for 45 minutes.
To microwave: Cook, uncovered, on MEDIUM (50%) for 15 minutes. Sprinkle cheese over top and brown under a hot grill.

PETE'S PASTA SALAD

Preparation 25 mins **Cooking** 12 mins *Serves 6*

225g (8oz) pasta spirals
225g (8oz) broccoli florets
225g (8oz) Double Gloucester cheese
1 medium eating apple, cored and sliced
15ml (1tbsp) lemon juice
425g (15oz) can red kidney beans, rinsed and drained
150ml (5floz) fresh soured cream
30ml (2tbsp) apple juice
30ml (2tbsp) chopped parsley

1. Cook pasta in boiling water for 10 mins.
To microwave: Put pasta into a large casserole and pour over sufficient BOILING water to cover it well. Cook, uncovered, for 8 mins, stirring occasionally.

2. Add broccoli. Boil for 2 mins.
To microwave: In a separate casserole, cook broccoli with 60ml (4tbsp) water, covered, for 5 mins, stirring once.

3. Rinse pasta and broccoli under cold water and drain well. Cut cheese into cubes.

4. Sprinkle apple with lemon juice and mix with pasta, broccoli, cheese and beans.

5. Mix together cream, apple juice and parsley. Serve dressing with salad.

ACCOMPANYING VEGETABLES & SALADS

FRUITY BEAN SALAD PAGE 190 · BROCCOLI HOLLANDAISE PAGE 182
POTATOES ANNA PAGE 172

VEGETABLES

ROAST POTATOES

Preparation 20 mins **Cooking** 55 mins   *Serves 4*

700 g (1½ lb) potatoes
50 g (2 oz) butter
15 ml (1 tbsp) oil

1. Cut potatoes into quarters or leave whole if new.

2. Cook in boiling water for 5–7 minutes. Drain.
To microwave: Cook with 90 ml (6 tbsp) water, covered, for 8 minutes, stirring once. Drain.

3. Heat butter and oil in a roasting tin.

4. Add potatoes and turn in tin until well coated with butter and oil.

5. Roast at 200°C (400°F) Mark 6 for 45 minutes or until crisp and golden, basting at least twice.

MASHED POTATOES 🄵

Preparation 20 mins **Cooking** 20 mins   *Serves 4*

700 g (1½ lb) potatoes, halved
15 g (½ oz) butter
45 ml (3 tbsp) fresh cream or milk
chopped parsley to garnish (optional)

1. Cook potatoes in boiling water until tender. Drain.
To microwave: Cut potatoes into small cubes. Cook with 90 ml (6 tbsp) water covered, for 8–12 minutes, stirring twice, until tender. Drain.

2. Mash finely with a potato masher (or rub through a sieve).

3. Add butter, fresh cream or milk and stir until well mixed.

4. Pile into a warm dish and sprinkle with parsley if used.

MINTED NEW POTATOES 🄵

Preparation 5 mins
Cooking 15–20 mins   *Serves 4*

700 g (1½ lb) unpeeled new potatoes
15 g (½ oz) butter
3 fresh mint leaves

1. Cook potatoes in boiling water until tender. Drain.
To microwave: Cook potatoes with 90 ml (6 tbsp) water, covered, for 8–12 minutes, stirring twice, until tender. Drain.

2. Stand saucepan of potatoes over a low heat. Add butter and mint.
To microwave: Add butter and mint.

3. Cover and leave over a low heat for 2 minutes, shaking pan frequently.
To microwave: Cover and cook for 1–2 minutes, shaking dish once.

4. Remove mint and serve.

SAUTÉ POTATOES

Preparation 15 mins **Cooking** 20 mins   *Serves 4*

700 g (1½ lb) potatoes, halved
50 g (2 oz) butter
30 ml (2 tbsp) oil

1. Cook potatoes in boiling water for 5–7 minutes. Drain and cool.

2. Cut into 0.5 cm (¼ inch) thick slices.

3. Heat butter and oil in a large heavy frying pan. Add potato slices.

4. Fry until golden-brown on both sides, turning occasionally.

Variation

POTATOES LYONNAISE

Follow recipe and method for sauté potatoes (above). When potatoes in pan are golden brown, add 225 g (8 oz) sliced onions, fried in butter or oil until golden. Mix well and serve.

JACKET POTATOES

Preparation 5 mins **Cooking** 1 hr   *Serves 4*

4 large potatoes, about 175g (6oz) each
oil
50g (2oz) butter

1. Wash, scrub and dry potatoes.
2. Prick well all over with fork or make small slits in each with a sharp knife (to prevent potatoes from bursting in oven).
3. Brush with oil. Stand on a baking sheet.
To microwave: Omit oil. Stand potatoes in a circle on absorbent kitchen paper on an ovenproof plate.
4. Bake at 200°C (400°F) Mark 6 for 1 hour or until potatoes feel tender when gently pressed.
To microwave: Cook for 10–13 minutes, turning them over half way. Check centres are cooked by inserting a skewer.
5. Remove from oven. Cut a large cross on top of each one.
6. Holding potato in a clean tea towel, squeeze base firmly to enlarge cut.
7. Put a piece of butter on to each one.
8. Serve immediately.

Alternatively serve with fresh soured cream and chives instead of butter.

POTATOES ANNA

Preparation 40 mins **Cooking** 2 hrs   *Serves 4*

700g (1½lb) potatoes
40g (1½oz) butter, melted
salt and freshly ground pepper

1. Slice potatoes very thinly.
2. Dry well on absorbent kitchen paper.
3. Brush a 1.1 litre (2 pint) ovenproof dish with butter. Fill with layers of potato slices arranged in overlapping circles.
To microwave: Brush a 1.1 litre (2 pint) flameproof dish with butter. Fill with layers of potato slices arranged in overlapping circles.

4. Brush each layer with butter and season.
5. Brush top layer with butter.
6. Cover with greased aluminium foil.
To microwave: Cover dish.
7. Bake at 190°C (375°F) Mark 5 for 1¼–1½ hours.
To microwave: Cook on MEDIUM (50%) for 20–25 minutes until tender.
8. Turn out onto a warm ovenproof plate (potatoes should stay moulded in dish shape).
To microwave: Brown top under a hot grill. Run a knife round edge of dish and turn potatoes out onto a flameproof plate.
9. Return to oven for a further 20–30 minutes, or until outside is golden brown.
To microwave: Cook second side under a hot grill until golden brown.
10. Serve immediately.

CASSEROLED POTATOES

Preparation 30 mins **Cooking** 1 hr   *Serves 4*

700g (1½lb) potatoes
salt and freshly ground pepper
25g (1oz) butter
300ml (½pint) fresh milk

1. Cut potatoes into thin slices.
2. Dry on absorbent kitchen paper.
3. Fill a 1.1 litre (2 pint) greased ovenproof dish with layers of potato slices, seasoning between layers.
To microwave: Fill a 1.1 litre (2 pint) greased flameproof dish with layers of potato slices, seasoning between layers.
4. Melt 15g (½oz) butter and mix with milk.
To microwave: Melt 15g (½oz) butter for 30 seconds and mix with milk.
5. Pour into dish.
6. Cover top with remaining butter, cut into thin flakes.
7. Cook at 190°C (375°F) Mark 5 for 1 hour, or until potatoes are tender.
To microwave: Cook uncovered for 5 minutes, then continue cooking on MEDIUM (50%) for 15–20 minutes until tender. Brown under a hot grill.
8. Serve immediately.

DUCHESSE POTATOES

Preparation 35 mins **Cooking** 35 mins *Serves 4*

450 g (1 lb) potatoes, halved
25 g (1 oz) butter
2 egg yolks
10 ml (2 tsp) hot milk
a little egg white

1. Cook potatoes in boiling water until tender. Drain.
To microwave: Cut potatoes into small cubes. Cook with 60 ml (4 tbsp) water, covered, for 6–9 minutes, stir twice, until tender. Drain.

2. Mash then rub through a fine sieve and return to saucepan.

3. Stand over a low heat.
To microwave: Cook for 1 minute.

4. Add butter, egg yolks, milk. Beat until smooth.

5. Transfer to a piping bag fitted with a large star-shaped nozzle.

6. Pipe fairly small mounds or whirls onto a greased baking sheet.

7. Leave until cold. Brush with egg white.

8. Bake at 220°C (425°F) Mark 7 for 15 minutes or until golden.

9. Serve hot.

POTATOES DAUPHINOIS

Preparation 25 mins **Cooking** 1¾ hrs *Serves 4*

700 g (1½ lb) potatoes, thinly sliced
salt and freshly ground pepper
1 garlic clove, crushed
ground nutmeg
50 g (2 oz) mature English Cheddar, grated
150 ml (5 fl oz) fresh double cream
150 ml (¼ pint) fresh milk
7 g (¼ oz) butter

1. Arrange layer of potato slices in a greased 1.1 litre (2 pint) ovenproof dish. Season lightly add a little garlic, nutmeg and cheese.
To microwave: Arrange a layer of potato slices in the base of a 1.1 litre (2 pint) greased flameproof dish. Season lightly and add a little of the garlic, nutmeg and cheese.

2. Repeat until all potatoes are used.

3. Mix cream and milk, pour over potatoes. Dot with butter.

4. Bake at 170°C (325°F) Mark 3 for 1¾ hours or until potatoes are cooked.
To microwave: Cook for 5 minutes, then continue cooking on MEDIUM (50%) for 20–25 minutes until tender. Brown under a hot grill.

POTATOES DAUPHINOIS

SWEET-SOUR RED CABBAGE

CRISP BOILED CABBAGE

Preparation 15 mins **Cooking** 10 mins *Serves 4*

700g (1½lb) young cabbage
15g (½oz) butter

1. Shred cabbage finely, discarding hard stalks.

2. Plunge into 5cm (2inch) of rapidly boiling water, in a saucepan.
To microwave: Put into a large casserole with 60ml (4tbsp) water.

3. Cover and simmer for 6–8 minutes.
To microwave: Cover and cook for 10–12 minutes, stirring twice.

4. Tip into colander and drain well.

5. Return to pan and add butter.
To microwave: Return to casserole and add butter.

6. Cover. Stand over a low heat for a further 2 minutes, shaking pan frequently.
To microwave: Cover and cook for 1 minute. Stir well.

7. Serve immediately.

SWEET-SOUR WHITE CABBAGE

Preparation 10 mins **Cooking** 10 mins *Serves 4*

700g (1½lb) white cabbage, shredded
25g (1oz) butter
30ml (2tbsp) water
30ml (2tbsp) vinegar
pinch of mixed spice
10ml (2tsp) soft brown sugar
salt and freshly ground pepper

1. Put cabbage in a saucepan with all remaining ingredients.
To microwave: Put cabbage in a large casserole with remaining ingredients.

2. Cover. Cook over a low heat for 7–10 minutes, or until cabbage is just tender but still slightly crisp. Shake pan frequently while cabbage is cooking.
To microwave: Cover and cook for 10–12 minutes, stirring twice, or until the cabbage is just tender but still slightly crisp.

3. Uncover and cook fairly briskly until no liquid remains (about 5 minutes).
To microwave: Uncover and cook for about 5 minutes, stirring once or twice, until no liquid remains.

SWEET-SOUR RED CABBAGE

Preparation 20 mins
Cooking 25 mins   *Serves 4–6*

25 g (1 oz) butter
900 g (2 lb) red cabbage, shredded
30 ml (2 tbsp) soft brown sugar
5 ml (1 tsp) caraway seeds
3 cloves
450 g (1 lb) cooking apples,
   peeled, cored and chopped
15 ml (1 tbsp) cornflour
60 ml (4 tbsp) vinegar
300 ml (½ pint) water
salt and freshly ground pepper

1. Melt butter in a large saucepan. Add cabbage and fry briskly for 5 minutes, shaking pan frequently.

2. Stir in sugar, caraway seeds, cloves and apples.

3. Mix cornflour to a thin paste with vinegar. Add water and pour over cabbage.

4. Cook, stirring, until mixture comes to the boil and thickens. Season to taste.

5. Reduce heat. Cover pan and simmer very slowly for 20 minutes.

6. Stir occasionally. Serve hot.

SAVOURY CABBAGE

Preparation 15 mins **Cooking** 10 mins   *Serves 4*

700 g (1½ lb) young cabbage
25 g (1 oz) butter
2 rashers streaky bacon, chopped
1 medium onion, finely chopped
pinch of ground nutmeg

1. Shred cabbage finely, discard hard stalks.

2. Heat butter in a large saucepan.
To microwave: Cook butter and bacon, uncovered, for 1½ minutes. Stir in onion and cook, uncovered for 3 minutes.

3. Add bacon, then all remaining ingredients. Cover and cook very gently for 7–10 minutes, shaking pan frequently, or until cabbage is just tender.
To microwave: Add remaining ingredients and stir well. Cover and cook for 10–12 minutes, stirring twice, or until cabbage is just tender.

COLCANNON

Preparation 30 mins **Cooking** 20 mins   *Serves 4*

450 g (1 lb) cabbage, shredded
450 g (1 lb) potatoes, halved
2 leeks, finely chopped
150 ml (¼ pint) fresh milk
salt and freshly ground pepper
pinch of ground mace
25 g (1 oz) butter, melted

1. Boil cabbage in water until cooked, drain well and keep warm.
To microwave: Cook cabbage with 60 ml (4 tbsp) water, covered, for 7–9 minutes, stirring twice.

2. Meanwhile, place potatoes and leeks in a pan with milk. Bring to the boil, cover and simmer until cooked.
To microwave: Cook potatoes, leeks and milk, covered, for 9–11 minutes until tender.

3. Mash potatoes with leeks and season. Add cabbage to potatoes and mix well.
To microwave: Mash potatoes with leeks and season. Cook cabbage 1–2 minutes to reheat, drain and mix well with potatoes.

4. Spoon into a serving dish, make a hollow in the centre and pour in melted butter.

BUTTERED CORN ON THE COB

Preparation 10 mins **Cooking** 5 mins   *Serves 4*

4 corn on the cob
50 g (2 oz) butter
salt and freshly ground pepper

1. Remove husks and silk from corn.

2. Put into a large frying pan, half full of gently boiling water.
To microwave: Wrap the cobs individually in greased greaseproof paper and place two on a plate.

3. Boil for 4–5 minutes only, turning corn over once if water is insufficiently deep to cover them.
To microwave: Cook for 3 minutes, then turn them over. Continue cooking for 2–4 minutes until tender. Cook the remaining cobs in the same way.

4. Drain and serve with butter and seasoning.

MARROW PROVENÇALE Ⓕ

Preparation 50 mins **Cooking** 45 mins   *Serves 4*

1 medium marrow, peeled
25 g (1 oz) butter
1 medium onion, grated
1 garlic clove, crushed
1 green pepper, seeded and chopped
225 g (8 oz) tomatoes, chopped
100 g (4 oz) Lancashire cheese
    or English Cheddar, grated

1. Cut marrow into 2.5 cm (1 inch) rings and remove seeds from centres. Cut rings into 2.5 cm (1 inch) cubes.

2. Melt butter in a large saucepan and fry marrow for 6–7 minutes or until golden. Transfer to a plate.
To microwave: Melt butter in a large casserole for 30 seconds.

3. Place onion, garlic and green pepper in remaining butter in pan. Fry until pale gold.
To microwave: Stir in onion, garlic and green pepper. Cover and cook for 3 minutes.

4. Add tomatoes and marrow and mix well.
To microwave: Add tomatoes and marrow, cover and cook for 15 minutes, stirring two or three times, or until the marrow is tender.

5. Place half mixture in an ovenproof dish.
To microwave: Arrange half the mixture in a flameproof dish.

6. Cover with 50 g (2 oz) cheese, then the remaining marrow mixture. Sprinkle with remaining cheese.

7. Bake at 190°C (375°F) Mark 5 for 30 minutes.
To microwave: Cook for 3 minutes then brown lightly under a hot grill.

BUTTER-BAKED TOMATOES

Preparation 5 mins **Cooking** 15 mins   *Serves 4*

4 large tomatoes
15 g (½ oz) butter, melted
salt and freshly ground pepper

1. Stand tomatoes, stem sides down, in an ovenproof dish.
To microwave: Stand tomatoes in a circle, stem sides down, in a small shallow dish.

2. Cut a shallow cross on top of each one.

3. Brush with butter and season.

4. Bake at 200°C (400°F) Mark 6 for 15 minutes.
To microwave: Cook uncovered for 2 minutes, then continue cooking on MEDIUM (50%) for 3–4 minutes.

ROAST PARSNIPS

Preparation 5 mins **Cooking** 55 mins   *Serves 4*

4 medium parsnips
25 g (1 oz) butter
15 ml (1 tbsp) oil

1. Cut parsnips in half lengthways then into chunks and cook in boiling water for 5 minutes. Drain well.
To microwave: Cut parsnips in half lengthways, then into chunks. Cook with 90 ml (6 tbsp) water, covered, for 5 minutes, stirring once.

2. Meanwhile, place the butter and oil in an ovenproof dish, bake at 190°C (375°F) Mark 5 for 5 minutes.

3. Add parsnips to dish and turn until well coated with butter and oil.

4. Roast for 50 minutes or until crisp and golden. Basting at least twice.

FRENCH-STYLE PEAS

Preparation 5 mins **Cooking** 10 mins   *Serves 4*

450 g (1 lb) frozen peas
6 large lettuce leaves, shredded
25 g (1 oz) butter
3 spring onions, finely sliced
2.5 ml (½ tsp) sugar
75 ml (3 fl oz) stock

1. Put all ingredients into a saucepan.
To microwave: Put all ingredients in a casserole.

2. Slowly bring to the boil, cover and simmer very gently for 5–10 minutes, or until peas are tender.
To microwave: Cover and cook for 7–9 minutes, stirring twice, until peas are tender.

3. Add a little extra water if necessary.

SWISS PEAS WITH RICE

Preparation 5 mins **Cooking** 15 mins *Serves 4*

350 g (12 oz) frozen peas
1 small onion, chopped
1 garlic clove, crushed
25 g (1 oz) butter
175 g (6 oz) freshly cooked rice
(about 75 g (3 oz) raw)
30 ml (2 tbsp) chopped parsley

1. Cook peas in boiling water for 5 minutes or until tender.
To microwave: Cook peas with 30 ml (2 tbsp) water, covered, for 5–7 minutes or until tender.

2. Meanwhile fry onion and garlic in butter until pale gold.
To microwave: In a separate dish, cook onion, garlic and butter, covered, for 3 minutes.

3. Drain peas and stir into onions with rice and parsley.

4. Heat through, gently, for about 5 minutes. Stir frequently.
To microwave: Cover and cook for 1–2 minutes. Stir well before serving.

5. Serve hot or cold.

PEASE PUDDING

Preparation Soaking overnight
Cooking 2¾ hrs *Serves 4–6*

450 g (1 lb) split peas, soaked overnight
15 g (½ oz) butter
1 egg yolk
salt and freshly ground pepper

1. Drain split peas and place in a saucepan. Cover with boiling water and bring slowly to the boil. Boil rapidly for 10 minutes.
To microwave: Drain split peas and put into a casserole. Cover well with BOILING water and cook for 12 minutes.

2. Cover pan and simmer gently for 1¾–2 hours, stirring occasionally. Add extra boiling water if peas become dry.
To microwave: Cover and cook on MEDIUM–LOW (30%) for 1–1½ hours, stirring occasionally.

3. Process in a food processor or push through a sieve.

4. Add butter and egg yolk. Mix and season.

5. Place in a greased ovenproof dish, bake at 180°C (350°F) Mark 4 for 30 minutes.
To microwave: Spoon into a greased 15 cm (6 inch) round dish. Cook on MEDIUM–LOW (30%) for about 10 minutes.

GLAZED & SUGARED ONIONS

FRIED ONIONS

Preparation 10 mins **Cooking** 10 mins *Serves 4*

40 g (1½ oz) butter
3 medium onions, thinly sliced

1. Heat butter in a frying pan.
To microwave: Melt butter for 45 seconds.

2. Add onion slices and fry until golden brown, stirring frequently to prevent burning.
To microwave: Add onions, cover and cook for 8–10 minutes, stirring once.

GLAZED & SUGARED ONIONS

Preparation 10 mins **Cooking** 20 mins *Serves 4*

12 small onions
50 g (2 oz) butter
pinch of salt
15 ml (1 tbsp) soft brown sugar

1. Cook onions in boiling water for 15 minutes, or until tender.
To microwave: Cook onions with 60 ml (4 tbsp) water, covered, for 6–8 minutes, stirring once, until tender.

2. Drain, dry on absorbent kitchen paper.

3. Melt butter in a frying pan, add salt and sugar. Heat for 1 minute.
To microwave: Cook butter, salt and sugar for 1 minute.

4. Add onions. Toss in butter mixture until well coated.

5. Cook over a very low heat until glazed and golden.
To microwave: Cook, uncovered for 2–3 minutes, stirring once.

FRENCH-FRIED ONION RINGS

Preparation 15 mins **Cooking** 10 mins *Serves 4*

4 medium onions, thinly sliced
fresh milk
self raising flour
salt and freshly ground pepper
deep fat or oil for frying

1. Separate onions into rings.

2. Dip in milk, then toss in seasoned flour.

3. Fry in hot fat or oil until crisp and golden.

4. Drain on absorbent kitchen paper and serve immediately.

BACON-STUFFED ONIONS

Preparation 30 mins **Cooking** 1¼ hrs   *Serves 4*

4 large onions
50 g (2 oz) fresh breadcrumbs
100 g (4 oz) lean bacon, chopped
fresh single cream
freshly ground pepper
25 g (1 oz) butter

1. Cook onions in boiling water for 30 minutes. Drain and reserve 75 ml (5 tbsp) onion water.

2. Cut the top off of each onion.

3. Carefully remove centres, leaving 1 cm (½ inch) thick onion shells.

4. Chop onion centres finely. Mix with breadcrumbs and bacon.

5. Add sufficient cream to bind mixture together. Season to taste.

6. Spoon mixture back into onion shells.

7. Stand filled onions in a shallow ovenproof dish. Pour in onion water.

8. Top each with a knob of butter.

9. Bake at 190°C (375°F) Mark 5 until tender, about 45 minutes.

Variation

CHEESE & PARSLEY-STUFFED ONIONS

Follow recipe and method for bacon-stuffed onions (left). Use 100 g (4 oz) grated Wensleydale or Derby cheese instead of bacon and 15 ml (1 tbsp) chopped parsley.

ONIONS IN CHEESE SAUCE

Preparation 5 mins **Cooking** 15 mins   *Serves 4*

8 small onions
300 ml (½ pint) cheese coating sauce
(page 232)
15 ml (1 tbsp) toasted breadcrumbs
to garnish

1. Cook onions in boiling water for 15 minutes, or until tender.
To microwave: Cook onions with 60 ml (4 tbsp) water, covered, for 5–7 minutes, stirring once, or until tender.

2. Drain. Transfer to a serving dish.

3. Coat with hot sauce and sprinkle with breadcrumbs.

BACON-STUFFED ONIONS

CHINESE-STYLE GREEN BEANS

CHINESE-STYLE GREEN BEANS

Preparation 25 mins **Cooking** 15 mins *Serves 4*

450g (1lb) runner beans
4 rashers lean bacon, chopped
1 small onion, chopped
1 small garlic clove, crushed
15g (½oz) butter
30ml (2tbsp) soy sauce

1. Top and tail beans and remove stringy sides.

2. Slice beans diagonally into thin strips.

3. Cook in boiling water for 10–15 minutes, or until tender.
To microwave: Cook with 60ml (4tbsp) water, covered, for 10–12 minutes, stirring at least twice.

4. Fry bacon, onion and garlic in butter until pale gold.
To microwave: Cook bacon and butter, uncovered for 2 minutes. Stir in onion and garlic, cover and cook for 3 minutes or until soft.

5. Drain beans and return to pan.
To microwave: Drain beans and return to dish.

6. Stir in bacon mixture and soy sauce.

7. Heat through gently, shaking pan frequently.
To microwave: Cover and cook for 1–2 minutes to heat through.

VICHY CARROTS

Preparation 15 mins **Cooking** 20 mins *Serves 4*

450g (1lb) carrots, thinly sliced
25g (1oz) butter
5ml (1tsp) sugar
5ml (1tsp) lemon juice
15ml (1tbsp) chopped parsley to garnish

1. Put carrots into a saucepan with water to cover, half the butter, sugar and lemon juice.
To microwave: Put carrots into a casserole with 15ml (1tbsp) water, half the butter, sugar and lemon juice.

2. Cover. Simmer gently for 15–20 minutes, or until tender and liquid has evaporated.
To microwave: Cover and cook for 8–10 minutes, stirring twice, until tender.

3. Stir in remaining butter and sprinkle with parsley to serve.

CARROTS IN PARSLEY SAUCE

Preparation 10 mins **Cooking** 15 mins *Serves 4*

450 g (1 lb) small new carrots
300 ml (½ pint) parsley coating sauce
(page 232)

1. Cook whole carrots in boiling water until just tender. Drain.
To microwave: Cook whole carrots with 60 ml (4 tbsp) water, covered, for 7–9 minutes, stirring twice, until tender.

2. Transfer to a serving dish and coat with hot sauce.

SPINACH WITH CREAM SAUCE

Preparation 10 mins **Cooking** 15 mins *Serves 4*

700 g (1½ lb) fresh spinach
25 g (1 oz) butter
10 ml (2 tsp) flour
150 ml (5 fl oz) fresh single cream
salt and freshly ground pepper

1. Cut away any tough stems from spinach.

2. Wash leaves thoroughly under cold running water to remove grit.

3. Tear into small pieces. Put into a saucepan with 30 ml (2 tbsp) water.
To microwave: Tear into small pieces. Put into a casserole.

4. Cover. Cook for 5–10 minutes, or until tender. Drain well, press water out by pressing with the back of a wooden spoon.
To microwave: Cover and cook for 8–10 minutes, stirring twice, until tender. Drain well, pressing water out with the back of a wooden spoon.

5. Melt butter in a pan. Stir in flour. Cook for 2 minutes without browning.
To microwave: Melt butter for 45 seconds and stir in flour.

6. Gradually blend in cream.

7. Cook, stirring, until sauce comes to the boil, thickens and is smooth.
To microwave: Cook for 2–3 minutes, stirring frequently, until the sauce thickens, boils and is smooth.

8. Add spinach and season to taste.

9. Heat through gently.
To microwave: Cook for 1 minute to heat.

CARROTS IN PARSLEY SAUCE

BRUSSELS SPROUTS & CHESTNUTS

Preparation 25 mins **Cooking** 20 mins *Serves 4*

275g (10oz) chestnuts
450g (1lb) Brussels sprouts
15g (½oz) butter

1. Slit shells of chestnuts with a sharp knife.

2. Place in a pan of cold water and bring to the boil. Cook for 5 minutes. Drain and leave to cool.
To microwave: Arrange in one layer in a shallow dish. Cook uncovered for 3 minutes, then remove any that are cooked. Continue cooking for 1 minute and remove any that are cooked. Repeat until all the chestnuts are cooked.

3. Peel, removing shell and brown skin.

4. Remove outer leaves from sprouts and cut a cross in the stem end of each sprout.

5. Cook sprouts in boiling water for 10 minutes.
To microwave: Cook with 90ml (6tbsp) water, covered, for 7–10 minutes, stirring at least twice, or until tender.

6. Drain sprouts and return to pan. Add chestnuts and butter and stand over a low heat for 2 minutes, shaking pan frequently.
To microwave: Drain sprouts and return to dish. Add chestnuts and butter, cover and cook for 1–2 minutes, shaking once.

Alternatively use dried chestnuts. Soak overnight before cooking until tender.

BROCCOLI HOLLANDAISE

Preparation 10 mins **Cooking** 12 mins *Serves 4*

700g (1½lb) fresh broccoli
hollandaise sauce (page 234)

1. Remove large leaves and cut away tough parts of stalks from broccoli.

2. Cook in boiling water for 10–12 minutes or until stalks are tender.
To microwave: Cook with 90ml (6tbsp) water, covered, for 8–12 minutes, stirring at least twice, until stalks are tender.

3. Drain thoroughly and transfer to a serving dish.

4. Coat with hollandaise sauce.

CAULIFLOWER WITH CHEESE SAUCE

Preparation 10 mins **Cooking** 15 mins *Serves 4*

1 medium cauliflower, cut into florets
300ml (½pint) cheese coating sauce (page 232)
25g (1oz) English Cheddar, grated

1. Cook cauliflower in boiling water until tender, about 12–15 minutes.
To microwave: Cook cauliflower with 60ml (4tbsp) water, covered, for 8–10 minutes, stirring twice, until just tender.

2. Drain and transfer to a flameproof dish.

3. Coat with hot sauce. Sprinkle with cheese.

4. Brown under a hot grill.

LEEKS WITH WHITE OR HOLLANDAISE SAUCE

Preparation 10 mins **Cooking** 15 mins *Serves 4*

4 medium leeks
basic white coating sauce (page 231) or hollandaise sauce (page 234)

1. Trim leeks. Remove all but 5cm (2inch) of green leaves.

2. Cut each leek in half lengthways. Wash very thoroughly under cold running water to remove any grit.

3. Put into a saucepan containing 5cm (2inch) boiling water.
To microwave: Put into a dish with 60ml (4tbsp) water.

4. Cover. Simmer for 10–15 minutes, or until tender.
To microwave: Cover and cook for 6–8 minutes, rearranging once, or until tender.

5. Drain. Transfer to a serving dish. Coat with hot sauce.

BRUSSELS SPROUTS AND CHESTNUTS

CREAMED BROAD BEANS

Preparation 15 mins **Cooking** 20 mins *Serves 4*

450g (1lb) shelled broad beans
50g (2oz) mushrooms, sliced
25g (1oz) butter
150ml (5floz) fresh double cream

1. Cook beans in boiling water for
15–20 minutes, or until tender.
*To microwave: Cook beans with 60ml (4tbsp)
water, covered, for 5–7 minutes, stirring
once or twice.*

2. Meanwhile, fry mushrooms in butter and
keep warm.
*To microwave: Cook mushrooms and butter,
covered, for 2 minutes.*

3. Drain beans and return to pan.
*To microwave: Drain beans and return to
dish.*

4. Add mushrooms and pan juices with
cream. Mix well.
*To microwave: Add mushrooms with their
juices and cream. Mix well.*

5. Reheat gently.
To microwave: Cook for 1 minute to reheat.

Alternatively use 300ml (½pint) basic white
coating sauce (page 231) instead of cream.

CREAMED SWEDE

Preparation 20 mins **Cooking** 20 mins *Serves 4*

450g (1lb) swede, diced
15g (½oz) butter
30ml (2tbsp) fresh single cream or milk
large pinch of ground nutmeg
salt and freshly ground pepper

1. Cook swede in boiling water for about
20 minutes, or until tender.
*To microwave: Cook swede with
90ml (6tbsp) water, covered, for
8–10 minutes stirring twice, until tender.*

2. Drain and mash finely.

3. Stand pan over low heat. Add butter,
cream and nutmeg.
*To microwave: Cook for 1 minute then stir in
butter, cream and nutmeg.*

4. Beat until smooth and creamy.

5. Season to taste.

6. Serve hot.

Variation

CREAMED TURNIPS

Follow recipe and method for creamed
swede (above). Use 450g (1lb) young turnips
instead of swede.

FRIED AUBERGINE

Preparation 35 mins **Cooking** 7 mins *Serves 4*

1 medium aubergine
salt
fresh milk
flour
40 g (1½ oz) butter
15 ml (1 tbsp) oil

1. Cut aubergine into 0.5 cm (¼ inch) thick slices.
2. Sprinkle with salt and leave for 30 minutes.
3. Rinse and drain thoroughly. Dry on absorbent kitchen paper.
4. Dip in milk then coat in flour.
5. Fry gently in hot butter and oil until crisp, golden and tender about 5–7 minutes.
6. Drain on absorbent kitchen paper.

STUFFED AUBERGINES

Preparation 40 mins **Cooking** 30 mins *Serves 4*

2 medium aubergines
1 large onion, finely chopped
4 rashers streaky bacon, chopped
1 small green pepper,
    seeded and chopped
450 g (1 lb) tomatoes, skinned and chopped
25 g (1 oz) butter
100 g (4 oz) mushrooms, sliced
50 g (2 oz) fresh breadcrumbs
salt and freshly ground pepper
75 g (3 oz) Lancashire cheese, grated

1. Halve aubergines lengthways.
2. Scoop out flesh, leaving 0.5 cm (¼ inch) thick shells.
3. Chop flesh and put into saucepan with onion, bacon, green pepper, tomatoes and butter.
4. Simmer gently until aubergine is tender.
5. Remove from heat. Stir in mushrooms and breadcrumbs. Season to taste.
6. Spoon mixture into aubergine shells. Sprinkle with cheese.
7. Bake at 200°C (400°F) Mark 6 for 20 minutes.

RATATOUILLE

Preparation 25 mins **Cooking** 1 hr *Serves 4*

1 large onion, thinly sliced
1 garlic clove, crushed
25 g (1 oz) butter
30 ml (2 tbsp) oil
2 medium aubergines, sliced
225 g (8 oz) courgettes or young marrow, sliced
1 medium green pepper, seeded and chopped
397 g (14 oz) can tomatoes
salt and freshly ground pepper
30 ml (2 tbsp) chopped parsley

1. Fry onion and garlic gently in butter and oil for 3–4 minutes.
To microwave: Cook onion, garlic and butter, covered, for 3 minutes.
2. Add remaining vegetables to pan with seasoning and parsley.
To microwave: Add remaining vegetables, seasoning and parsley.
3. Cover pan. Simmer gently for 1 hour.
To microwave: Cover and cook for 15–20 minutes, stirring gently two or three times.
4. Serve hot or cold.

BRAISED CELERY

Preparation 10 mins **Cooking** 25 mins *Serves 4*

1 medium head of celery
juice of ½ medium lemon
150 ml (¼ pint) stock
25 g (1 oz) butter

1. Remove leaves from celery.
2. Cut sticks into 7.5 cm (3 inch) lengths. Wash thoroughly.
3. Put in a saucepan with lemon juice, stock and butter.
To microwave: Put in a casserole with lemon juice, stock and butter.
4. Cover and simmer for 20 minutes, or until tender.
To microwave: Cover and cook for about 10 minutes, stirring twice, or until tender.

5. Lift out celery and place in a serving dish. Keep hot.

6. Boil briskly any liquid left in pan, until reduced to about 75 ml (3 fl oz).
To microwave: Cook any liquid left in dish, uncovered, until reduced to about 75 ml (3 fl oz).

7. Pour over celery.

FRIED MUSHROOMS

Preparation 5 mins **Cooking** 5 mins   *Serves 2*

25 g (1 oz) butter
225 g (8 oz) mushrooms, halved

1. Melt butter in a saucepan. Add mushrooms and stir until well coated with butter.
To microwave: Melt butter in a shallow dish for 30 seconds. Stir in mushrooms, coating them well.

2. Fry briskly, uncovered, for 5 minutes. Shake pan often.
To microwave: Cook, uncovered, for about 2 minutes, stirring once.

3. Serve immediately.

GRILLED MUSHROOMS

Preparation 5 mins **Cooking** 5 mins   *Serves 2–4*

225 g (8 oz) large open mushrooms
25 g (1 oz) butter
salt and freshly ground pepper

1. Wipe mushrooms with a dry cloth. Remove stalks.

2. Stand mushrooms, brown sides down in a grill pan. Place a little butter on each mushroom.

3. Grill for 2–2½ minutes, depending on size.

4. Turn over. Put a knob of remaining butter on each.

5. Season and grill for a further 2–2½ minutes.

6. Serve immediately.

RATATOUILLE

TASTY COURGETTE BAKE

Preparation 30 mins **Cooking** 1 hr   *Serves 4*

700 g (1½ lb) courgettes, sliced
75 g (3 oz) smoked streaky bacon, chopped
1 medium onion, sliced
3 eggs
300 ml (½ pint) fresh milk
2.5 ml (½ tsp) dried marjoram
100 g (4 oz) English Cheddar, grated

1. Blanch courgettes in boiling water for 2 minutes, drain well and cool.
To microwave: Cook courgettes with 60 ml (4 tbsp) water, covered, for 5 minutes, stirring once. Drain well and cool.

2. Place bacon and onion in a non-stick pan, cook, stirring, for 5 minutes.
To microwave: Cook bacon and onion, uncovered, for 5 minutes, stirring occasionally.

3. Lightly grease a large ovenproof dish. Place courgettes, bacon and onion in dish.

4. Beat together eggs, milk and herbs. Stir in 75 g (3 oz) cheese and pour over courgettes.

5. Sprinkle with remaining cheese.

6. Bake at 180°C (350°F) Mark 4 for 55 minutes or until set.

ROOT VEGETABLE BAKE

Preparation 30 mins
Cooking 1¼ hrs   *Serves 4–6*

225 g (8 oz) potatoes
225 g (8 oz) carrots
225 g (8 oz) parsnips
15 g (½ oz) butter
½ onion, sliced
2 eggs, beaten
450 ml (¾ pint) fresh milk
freshly ground pepper
paprika

1. Cut potatoes, carrots and parsnips into "chips".

2. Grease an ovenproof dish with a little of the butter.

3. Mix together all vegetables and place in dish.

4. Whisk together eggs and milk, season and pour over vegetables.

5. Dot with remaining butter and dust with paprika.

6. Bake at 190°C (375°F) Mark 5 for 1¼ hours until vegetables are tender and egg mixture has set.

TASTY COURGETTE BAKE

COLD GLOBE ARTICHOKES

POACHED ASPARAGUS

Preparation 5 mins **Cooking** 15 mins   *Serves 4*

24 asparagus spears
hollandaise sauce (page 234)
  or clarified butter (page 240)

1. Trim off 2.5 cm (1 inch) from base of asparagus.

2. Put into a large, fairly shallow saucepan or frying pan and half-fill with water.
To microwave: Arrange in a dish with the stalks towards the outside. Add 60 ml (4 tbsp) water.

3. Bring slowly to the boil, lower heat. Cover and simmer for 12–15 minutes, or until tender.
To microwave: Cover and cook for 7–8 minutes, rearranging them once.

4. Drain and serve with sauce.

COLD GLOBE ARTICHOKES

Preparation 20 mins **Cooking** 45 mins   *Serves 4*

4 medium globe artichokes
French dressing (page 196)

1. To clean artichokes, hold by stem end (at base) and plunge heads in and out of a large deep bowl of cold water.

2. Cut off stems.

3. Pull away bottom row of leaves from each, these are tough.

4. With kitchen scissors, trim off any browned edges of leaves.

5. Place artichokes in a pan of boiling water and cook gently for 45 minutes.
To microwave: Place upright in a dish with 60 ml (4 tbsp) water, cover and cook for 10–12 minutes.

6. Drain upside down then chill.

7. Serve with dressing.

To eat artichokes, pull off leaves with fingers one at a time. Dip base of each leaf (the edible part) in dressing and tease through the teeth to remove the flesh. Discard rest of leaf. Continue until you come to a pale cone of leaves. Lift these off and discard. Discard also the fuzzy centre underneath. Eat remaining heart with dressing.

Artichokes may be served hot, immediately after draining. Accompany with either melted butter or hollandaise sauce (page 234).

187

SALADS

DRESSED GREEN SALAD

Preparation 15 mins   *Serves 4*

1 Webb, Cos or round lettuce
1 garlic clove, peeled (optional)
French dressing made with
    60 ml (4 tbsp) oil (page 196)

1. Wash lettuce well and shake dry.

2. Halve garlic clove. Press cut sides against base and sides of salad bowl.

3. Tear lettuce into bite-size pieces and put into bowl.

4. Just before serving, pour over dressing.

5. With wooden spoon and fork, toss lettuce in dressing until every piece is coated.

Variations

MIXED SALAD

Follow recipe and method for dressed green salad (above). Add torn-up watercress and/or frisée.

SUMMER SALAD

Follow recipe and method for dressed green salad (above). Add slices of cucumber, tomatoes, radishes, strips of red or green pepper and spring onions.

TOMATO & ONION SALAD

Preparation 15 mins   *Serves 4*

450 g (1 lb) tomatoes, sliced
French dressing made with
    60 ml (4 tbsp) oil (page 196)
½ onion, finely chopped
30 ml (2 tbsp) chopped parsley

1. Arrange tomatoes in a large shallow serving dish.

2. Pour over dressing and sprinkle with onion and parsley.

3. Serve chilled.

CUCUMBER SALAD

Preparation 15 mins   *Serves 4*

½ Cos or Webb lettuce
1 small cucumber, diced
150 g (5 oz) natural yogurt
30 ml (2 tbsp) mayonnaise
15 ml (1 tbsp) lemon juice
salt and freshly ground pepper

1. Wash lettuce and shake dry.

2. Tear leaves into bite-size pieces and put into a serving dish.

3. Add cucumber and mix well.

4. Combine yogurt with mayonnaise and lemon juice. Season to taste.

5. Pour over lettuce and cucumber and toss well.

COLESLAW

Preparation 25 mins   *Serves 4*

2 medium eating apples, cored
15 ml (1 tbsp) lemon juice
½ medium white cabbage,
    about 225 g (8 oz), finely shredded
1 medium carrot, grated
1 small onion, chopped
50 g (2 oz) Red Leicester cheese, grated
30 ml (2 tbsp) chopped parsley
150 ml (5 fl oz) fresh soured cream
30 ml (2 tbsp) fresh milk
2.5 ml (½ tsp) Worcestershire sauce
salt and freshly ground pepper

1. Grate apples coarsely and sprinkle with lemon juice.

2. Place in a large bowl with cabbage, carrot, onion, cheese and parsley. Mix well.

3. Mix soured cream with milk, Worcestershire sauce, and seasoning.

4. Pour over cabbage mixture and mix well.

5. Transfer to a serving dish.

GREEN BEAN SALAD

Preparation 15 mins **plus** 2 hrs **standing**
Cooking 10 mins   *Serves 4*

450 g (1 lb) green beans
60 ml (4 tbsp) oil
1.25 ml (¼ tsp) dry mustard
salt and freshly ground pepper
1 garlic clove, crushed
30 ml (2 tbsp) wine vinegar
30 ml (2 tbsp) chopped parsley
30 ml (2 tbsp) chopped chives
60 ml (4 tbsp) fresh double cream

1. Trim beans and cut into 2.5 cm (1 inch) lengths.
2. Cook in boiling water until tender.
To microwave: Cook with 60 ml (4 tbsp) water, covered for 9–12 minutes, stirring twice, until tender.
3. Meanwhile, beat oil with mustard, seasoning to taste and garlic.
4. Gradually beat in vinegar and continue beating until dressing is thick.
5. Stir in 15 ml (1 tbsp) each parsley and chives.
6. Drain beans. While still hot, stir in dressing.

7. Cool then refrigerate for 2 hours. Just before serving stir in cream and sprinkle with remaining herbs.

BEAN POT SALAD

Preparation 20 mins   *Serves 4*

425 g (15 oz) can red kidney beans, rinsed and drained
425 g (15 oz) can cannellini beans, rinsed and drained
425 g (15 oz) can chickpeas, rinsed and drained
50 g (2 oz) radishes, sliced
100 g (4 oz) cooked peas
175 g (6 oz) Red Leicester cheese, cubed
150 g (5 oz) natural yogurt
5 ml (1 tsp) chopped fresh chervil (optional)
10 ml (2 tsp) creamed horseradish sauce
30 ml (2 tbsp) fresh milk

1. Mix together beans, chickpeas, vegetables and cheese.
2. Mix all remaining ingredients together.
3. Serve salad with dressing drizzled over.

BEAN POT SALAD

CURRIED RICE & BEAN SALAD

Preparation 35 mins **Cooking** 30 mins   *Serves 6*

175g (6oz) long grain brown rice
15ml (1tbsp) curry paste
60ml (4tbsp) mayonnaise
30ml (2tbsp) chopped fresh coriander or
   parsley
425g (15oz) can red kidney beans,
   rinsed and drained
100g (4oz) mushrooms, sliced
½ green pepper, seeded and chopped
½ orange pepper, seeded and chopped
50g (2oz) currants
50g (2oz) roasted peanuts

1. Cook rice in boiling water for
25–30 minutes, until tender.
*To microwave: Put rice in a medium
casserole and pour over 1 litre (1¾ pint)
BOILING water. Stir well. Cook, uncovered,
for 20–25 minutes, stir once, until tender.*

2. Rinse in cold water and drain well.

3. Blend curry paste and mayonnaise.

4. Add dressing to rice with remaining
ingredients and mix well.

FIESTA SALAD

Preparation 25 mins **Cooking** 30 mins   *Serves 4*

100g (4oz) long grain brown rice
175g (6oz) frozen broad beans
½ red pepper, seeded and diced
½ orange pepper, seeded and diced
225g (8oz) reduced fat hard cheese, cubed
100g (4oz) black grapes,
   halved and seeded
45ml (3tbsp) reduced calorie vinaigrette
   dressing
chopped parsley to garnish

1. Cook rice in boiling water for 30 minutes.
*To microwave: Put rice into a medium
casserole and pour over 750ml (1¼ pint)
BOILING water. Cook, uncovered, for
20–25 minutes, stirring once, until tender.*

2. Add broad beans 5 minutes before end of
cooking time.
*To microwave: In a separate casserole, cook
broad beans with 30ml (2tbsp) water,
covered, for about 6 minutes, stirring once,
until tender.*

3. Drain rice and beans, rinse in cold water.

4. Leave until cold then add vegetables,
cheese, grapes and dressing, mix well.

5. Sprinkle with chopped parsley and serve.

FRUITY BEAN SALAD

Preparation 45 mins **plus chilling**   *Serves 4*

425g (15oz) can chickpeas,
   rinsed and drained
220g (7.75oz) can red kidney beans,
   rinsed and drained
100g (4oz) bean sprouts
100g (4oz) radishes, sliced
2 medium carrots, chopped
1 green pepper, seeded and chopped
2 medium oranges, peeled,
   segmented and chopped
100g (4oz) green grapes,
   halved and seeded
1 medium eating apple, cored,
   chopped and dipped in lemon juice
275g (10oz) natural yogurt
1.25ml (¼tsp) ground ginger
30ml (2tbsp) chopped fresh mint
2.5ml (½tsp) sugar

1. Mix together chickpeas, beans, vegetables
and fruit. Chill.

2. Mix a spoonful of yogurt with ground
ginger then stir into remaining yogurt with
mint and sugar. Chill.

3. Serve salad with sauce drizzled over.

POTATO SALAD

Preparation 30 mins   *Serves 4*

450g (1lb) cold cooked potatoes
2 spring onions, finely chopped
150g (5oz) mayonnaise
75ml (5tbsp) fresh double cream
snipped chives or paprika to garnish

1. Cut potatoes into small cubes.
2. Put into a large bowl and mix with onions.
3. Add mayonnaise and cream and stir gently with spoon until potato cubes are thickly coated.
4. Pile into a serving dish and sprinkle with chives or paprika.

RUSSIAN SALAD

Preparation 25 mins   *Serves 4*

1 lettuce heart
225 g (8 oz) cooked potatoes, cubed
225 g (8 oz) cooked carrots, cubed
100 g (4 oz) cooked peas
100 g (4 oz) cooked green beans
mayonnaise
1 egg, hard-boiled, shelled to garnish
4 gherkins, sliced to garnish

1. Wash lettuce and shake leaves dry.
2. Arrange in salad bowl.
3. Put cooked vegetables into large bowl.
4. Mix gently with mayonnaise, adding enough to coat vegetables fairly thickly.
5. Pile on to lettuce. Garnish with wedges of hard-boiled egg and slices of gherkin.

BULGHUR WHEAT SALAD

Preparation 30 mins **plus soaking**   *Serves 4*

225 g (8 oz) bulghur wheat
4 spring onions, sliced
½ red pepper, seeded and diced
¼ cucumber, diced
25 g (1 oz) chopped parsley
30 ml (2 tbsp) chopped fresh mint
30 ml (2 tbsp) chopped fresh coriander
1 garlic clove, crushed
45 ml (3 tbsp) oil
45 ml (3 tbsp) lemon juice
salt and freshly ground pepper
lemon slices and fresh mint to garnish

1. Place bulghur wheat in a bowl and cover with water. Leave to soak for 30 minutes.
2. Line a sieve with a piece of absorbent kitchen paper and drain bulghur wheat through it. Use a wooden spoon to press out as much water as possible.
3. Place bulghur wheat in a bowl. Add vegetables and herbs, mix well.
4. Add garlic, oil, lemon juice and seasoning. Stir to mix.
5. Serve garnished with lemon slices and a sprig of fresh mint.

CHEDDAR CHEESE & APPLE SALAD

Preparation 25 mins   *Serves 4*

½ round lettuce
150 ml (5 fl oz) fresh soured cream
45 ml (3 tbsp) fresh milk
5 ml (1 tsp) lemon juice
salt and freshly ground pepper
2 medium eating apples, cored and diced
225 g (8 oz) English Cheddar, diced
2 canned pineapple rings,
    drained and chopped
parsley to garnish

1. Wash lettuce and shake leaves dry.

2. Tear into bite-size pieces and use to cover base of a serving dish.

3. Combine soured cream with milk, lemon juice and seasoning.

4. Add apples, cheese and pineapple to soured cream mixture and mix together.

5. Pile on to lettuce.

6. Garnish with parsley.

Alternatively use pears in place of apples.

COTTAGE CHEESE & PEACH SALAD

Preparation 20 mins   *Serves 4*

½ Cos lettuce
French dressing made with
    30 ml (2 tbsp) oil (page 196)
350 g (12 oz) cottage cheese
75 ml (5 tbsp) mayonnaise or fresh soured
    cream
100 g (4 oz) salted cashew nuts
410 g (14.4 oz) can peach slices, drained
50 g (2 oz) black grapes

1. Wash lettuce and shake leaves dry.

2. Tear into bite-size pieces and toss with French dressing

3. Use to cover base of 4 individual serving plates.

4. Put cottage cheese into a bowl. Combine with mayonnaise or soured cream and nuts.

5. Pile equal amounts on to plates.

6. Arrange peach slices and grapes around cheese.

Alternatively use 2 fresh peaches when in season.

SPINACH AND COTTAGE CHEESE SALAD.

SPINACH & COTTAGE CHEESE SALAD

Preparation 20 mins **Cooking** 5 mins   *Serves 4*

225 g (8 oz) back bacon, chopped
450 g (1 lb) fresh spinach
1 Webb or Cos lettuce
150 ml (¼ pint) oil
5 ml (1 tsp) dry mustard
5 ml (1 tsp) sugar
15 ml (1 tbsp) very finely grated onion
salt and freshly ground pepper
60 ml (4 tbsp) wine or cider vinegar
225 g (8 oz) cottage cheese

1. Fry bacon in its own fat until crisp. Drain on absorbent kitchen paper.
To microwave: Cook bacon, uncovered, for 6–8 minutes, stirring frequently, until beginning to brown. Drain on absorbent kitchen paper.

2. Thoroughly wash and drain spinach. Repeat with lettuce.

3. Tear spinach and lettuce leaves into bite-size pieces (discarding stems) and put into a large salad bowl. Add bacon and mix well.

4. Mix oil with mustard, sugar, onion and seasoning to taste. Beat in vinegar.

5. Pour half over salad greens and bacon and toss well.

6. Mix cottage cheese with remaining dressing and spoon into centre of salad greens.

SANDRINGHAM SALAD

Preparation 25 mins   *Serves 4*

175 g (6 oz) red cabbage, shredded
1 green pepper, seeded and sliced
175 g (6 oz) beansprouts
350 g (12 oz) cooked duck meat, shredded
2 large oranges, peeled and segmented
45 ml (3 tbsp) raisins
French dressing made with
  60 ml (4 tbsp) oil (page 196)
15 ml (1 tbsp) soy sauce

1. Place vegetables, duck and fruit in a bowl.

2. Add French dressing and soy sauce. Mix well to coat with dressing.

LUNCHTIME SALAD

Preparation 30 mins   *Serves 2*

1 medium pear, cored and chopped
30 ml (2 tbsp) lemon juice
175 g (6 oz) cucumber, chopped
2 medium carrots, grated
100 g (4 oz) white cabbage, shredded
175 g (6 oz) Red Leicester cheese, cubed
75 g (3 oz) natural yogurt
30 ml (2 tbsp) salad cream
2.5 ml (½ tsp) dried mixed herbs
2 tomatoes, cut into wedges
wholemeal bread rolls

1. Dip chopped pear into lemon juice and mix with vegetables and cheese.

2. Mix together yogurt, salad cream and herbs.

3. Pour over salad and arrange tomato wedges around the edge.

4. Serve with wholemeal bread rolls.

APPLE & WALNUT SALAD

Preparation 25 mins   *Serves 4*

½ Cos or Webb lettuce
3 large eating apples
juice of 1 medium lemon
6 celery sticks, sliced
75 g (3 oz) walnut pieces, coarsely chopped
150 g (5 oz) mayonnaise
75 ml (5 tbsp) fresh double cream
  or soured cream
15 ml (1 tbsp) vinegar

1. Wash lettuce leaves and shake dry.

2. Tear into bite-size pieces and use to cover base of serving dish.

3. Core 2 apples and chop. Dip in lemon juice. Add to celery, together with nuts and mix well.

4. Combine mayonnaise with cream and vinegar.

5. Pour over apple mixture and toss until ingredients are thickly coated.

6. Arrange over lettuce.

7. Cut remaining apple into thin slices.

8. Dip into lemon juice to prevent browning then arrange on top of salad.

TROPICAL PRAWN SALAD

TROPICAL PRAWN SALAD

Preparation 35 mins **Cooking** 20 mins   *Serves 4*

175 g (6 oz) long grain rice
225 g (8 oz) skimmed milk soft cheese
15 ml (1 tbsp) curry powder
juice of ½ lemon
90 ml (6 tbsp) fresh milk
2 medium eating apples,
    cored and chopped
1 banana, peeled and sliced
450 g (1 lb) peeled prawns
1 green pepper, seeded and diced
227 g (8 oz) can pineapple in natural juice,
    drained and chopped
chopped parsley to garnish

1. Cook rice in boiling water, rinse under cold water and drain well.
To microwave: Put rice into a medium casserole and pour over 568 ml (1 pint) BOILING water. Cook, uncovered, for 10 minutes. Rinse under cold water and drain well.

2. Mix together soft cheese, curry powder, 15 ml (1 tbsp) lemon juice and milk.

3. Dip apples and banana in remaining lemon juice.

4. Mix half the apples with prawns and soft cheese dressing.

5. Stir remaining apples into rice with banana, green pepper and pineapple.

6. Place rice in a serving dish and spoon prawn mixture over.

7. Garnish with chopped parsley.

TROPICANA SALAD

Preparation 25 mins   *Serves 4*

2 large bananas, peeled and sliced
2 medium eating apples, cored and diced
30 ml (2 tbsp) lemon juice
2 large oranges, peeled and sliced
150 ml (5 fl oz) fresh soured cream
5 ml (1 tsp) creamed horseradish sauce

1. Dip banana and apple in lemon juice. Place in a bowl.

2. Cut orange slices into quarters. Add to fruit.

3. Mix any remaining lemon juice, soured cream and horseradish.

4. Add to fruit and stir gently to coat fruit with dressing.

TUNA & BACON SALAD

Preparation 25 mins **Cooking** 5 mins   *Serves 4*

225g (8oz) bacon, chopped
½ Cos lettuce
2 spring onions, chopped
198g (7oz) can tuna, drained and flaked
2 eggs, hard-boiled, shelled and chopped
cucumber and soured cream mayonnaise
   made with 60ml (4tbsp) fresh soured
   cream (page 197)

1. Fry bacon in its own fat until crisp. Drain
on absorbent kitchen paper.
*To microwave: Cook bacon, uncovered, for
6–8 minutes, stirring frequently, until
beginning to brown. Drain on absorbent
kitchen paper.*
2. Wash lettuce and shake leaves dry.
3. Tear into bite-size pieces and put into a
large bowl.
4. Add bacon, onions, tuna and eggs. Toss
well and transfer to a serving dish.
5. Pour a little dressing over salad. Serve
remainder separately.

HERRING SALAD

Preparation 30 mins   *Serves 4*

½ Cos lettuce
3 rollmop herrings
150ml (5floz) fresh soured cream
30ml (2tbsp) fresh milk
2.5ml (½tsp) paprika
2.5ml (½tsp) grated lemon rind
2 eggs, hard-boiled, shelled and chopped
1 small pickled cucumber, sliced

1. Wash lettuce and shake leaves dry.
2. Tear into bite-size pieces and use to cover
base of serving dish.
3. Drain rollmops well, unroll and cut into
strips. Place in a bowl and add soured
cream, milk, paprika, lemon rind and
chopped eggs.
4. Mix well then pile onto lettuce.
5. Garnish with slices of pickled cucumber.
6. Serve chilled.

SWEETCORN & CHICKEN SALAD

Preparation 20 mins   *Serves 4*

1 head of chicory
330g (11.6oz) can sweetcorn, drained
225g (8oz) cooked chicken meat,
   cut into bite-size pieces
½ red pepper, seeded and chopped
60ml (4tbsp) garlic mayonnaise (page 197)
30ml (2tbsp) natural yogurt
100g (4oz) Red Cheshire cheese, cubed

1. Separate leaves of chicory, wash and
drain. Arrange on a round platter, radiating
from centre.
2. Mix together sweetcorn, chicken and red
pepper.
3. Add mayonnaise and yogurt. Stir to mix.
4. Gently stir in cheese and pile into centre
of chicory leaves.

SWEDISH SAUSAGE SALAD

Preparation 25 mins   *Serves 4*

½ round lettuce
1 medium eating apple, cored and diced
15ml (1tbsp) lemon juice
350g (12oz) cooked sausages, sliced
225g (8oz) cooked potatoes, diced
1 green pepper, seeded and sliced
100g (4oz) cooked red kidney beans
Swedish mayonnaise made with
   65g (2½oz) apple purée (page 197)

1. Wash lettuce, shake leaves dry and use to
cover base of a serving dish.
2. Sprinkle apple with lemon juice.
3. Place apple, sausage, potato, green
pepper, beans and Swedish mayonnaise in a
large bowl and mix well.
4. Spoon sausage mixture on to lettuce and
serve.

SALAD DRESSINGS

Many dressings in this section are ideal to serve with meat fondues or as dips.

All quantities of dressings are sufficient for 4–6 servings.

FRENCH DRESSING

Preparation 10 mins

2.5 ml (½ tsp) *each* of salt,
   sugar and dry mustard
1.25 ml (¼ tsp) Worcestershire sauce
60 ml (4 tbsp) oil
30 ml (2 tbsp) vinegar (wine for preference)
   or lemon juice

1. Put salt, sugar, mustard and Worcestershire sauce into a basin.
2. Gradually add oil and beat until smooth.
3. Gradually beat in vinegar or lemon juice. Continue beating until dressing thickens.

Variations

BLUE STILTON DRESSING

Follow recipe and method for French dressing (above). Gradually beat dressing into 25–50 g (1–2 oz) finely mashed Blue Stilton cheese.

CREAMED ONION DRESSING

Follow recipe and method for French dressing (above). Gradually beat dressing into 75 g (3 oz) cream cheese. Add 5 ml (1 tsp) finely grated onion and 15 ml (1 tbsp) chopped parsley

MAYONNAISE

Preparation 20 mins *Makes about 300 ml (½ pint)*

2 egg yolks
2.5 ml (½ tsp) *each* of dry mustard,
   salt and sugar
1.25 ml (¼ tsp) Worcestershire sauce
   (optional)
freshly ground pepper
300 ml (½ pint) oil
30 ml (2 tbsp) vinegar or lemon juice
15 ml (1 tbsp) hot water

1. Place yolks, mustard, salt, sugar, Worcestershire sauce (if used) and pepper in a bowl. Beat until smooth.
2. Beating more quickly, add 150 ml (¼ pint) oil, **slowly, a drop at a time** and continue beating until mayonnaise is very thick.
3. Stir in 15 ml (1 tbsp) vinegar or lemon juice.
4. Beat in remaining oil gradually, about 10 ml (2 tsp) at a time.
5. When all the oil has been added, stir in remaining vinegar or lemon juice and hot water. (The water helps prevent separation.)
6. Adjust seasoning to taste. Transfer to a covered container. Will keep in a refrigerator for up to 2 weeks.

All ingredients for mayonnaise should be at room temperature.

Variations

THOUSAND ISLAND MAYONNAISE

Follow recipe and method for mayonnaise (above). Stir 60 ml (4 tbsp) fresh double cream, 20 ml (4 tsp) tomato ketchup, 2.5 ml (½ tsp) chilli sauce, 30 ml (2 tbsp) finely chopped stuffed olives, 10 ml (2 tsp) finely chopped onion, 15 ml (1 tbsp) finely chopped green pepper, 1 hard-boiled egg, shelled and finely chopped and 45 ml (3 tbsp) chopped parsley into the mayonnaise after adding the hot water.

MAYONNAISE, THOUSAND ISLAND MAYONNAISE, TARTARE SAUCE

GARLIC MAYONNAISE

Follow recipe and method for mayonnaise (left). Stir 1 crushed garlic clove into mayonnaise after adding the hot water. Chill before using.

CURRY MAYONNAISE

Follow recipe and method for mayonnaise (left). Stir 10 ml (2 tsp) curry powder, 5 ml (1 tsp) finely chopped onion, a pinch of cayenne pepper and 15 ml (1 tbsp) sweet pickle into the mayonnaise after adding the hot water.

SWEDISH MAYONNAISE

Follow recipe and method for mayonnaise (left). Stir 150 g (5 oz) thick, unsweetened apple purée, 15 ml (1 tbsp) creamed horseradish sauce and 75 ml (5 tbsp) fresh soured cream into mayonnaise after adding the hot water.

TARTARE SAUCE

Follow recipe and method for mayonnaise (left). Stir 15 ml (1 tbsp) each finely chopped capers and parsley and 30 ml (2 tbsp) finely chopped gherkins to mayonnaise after adding the hot water.

CUCUMBER & SOURED CREAM MAYONNAISE

Preparation 15 mins

½ recipe mayonnaise (page 196)
60 ml (4 tbsp) fresh soured cream
½ small cucumber, finely diced
5 ml (1 tsp) lemon juice
15 ml (1 tbsp) chopped chives
salt and freshly ground pepper

1. Place all ingredients in a bowl, mix well.

SOURED CREAM WITH STILTON DRESSING

Preparation 10 mins **plus** 15 mins **standing**

50 g (2 oz) Blue Stilton cheese
150 ml (5 fl oz) fresh soured cream
30 ml (2 tbsp) fresh milk
salt and freshly ground pepper

1. Mash Stilton finely in a bowl.
2. Gradually blend in cream and milk.
3. Season. Stand for 15 mins before using.
4. Add more milk for a thinner dressing.

SOURED CREAM DRESSING, WHOLEGRAIN MUSTARD, TOMATO AND PARSLEY VARIATIONS

SOURED CREAM DRESSING

Preparation 5 mins **plus** 15 mins **standing**

150 ml (5 fl oz) fresh soured cream
15 ml (1 tbsp) fresh milk
15 ml (1 tbsp) lemon juice or vinegar
5 ml (1 tsp) sugar
salt and freshly ground pepper
coriander to garnish

1. Beat soured cream together with milk and lemon juice or vinegar.

2. Stir in sugar. Season to taste.

3. If a thinner dressing is preferred, add a little extra milk.

4. Leave to stand for 15 minutes before using to allow the flavour to develop.

Alternatively any one of the following can be added to the dressing before standing for 15 minutes.

45 ml (3 tbsp) chopped parsley
5 ml (1 tsp) made wholegrain mustard
15 ml (1 tbsp) creamed horseradish sauce
30 ml (2 tbsp) tomato ketchup
10 ml (2 tsp) paprika
    blended with 10 ml (2 tsp) fresh milk

MUSTARD DRESSING

Preparation 5 mins **Cooking** 10 mins

15 ml (1 tbsp) flour
pinch of cayenne pepper
20 ml (4 tsp) sugar
5 ml (1 tsp) dry mustard
2.5 ml (½ tsp) salt
150 ml (¼ pint) fresh milk
2 egg yolks, beaten
60 ml (4 tbsp) vinegar

1. Mix dry ingredients with a little cold milk until smooth.

2. Heat remaining milk and when boiling stir into the blended ingredients. Return mixture to pan and bring to the boil, stirring continuously.
To microwave: Cook remaining milk for about 1 minute until boiling, then stir into blended ingredients. Cook for 1–1½ minutes, stirring once.

3. Cool slightly, stir in egg yolks and return pan to heat.

4. Cook gently until mixture thickens, but do not allow to boil.
To microwave: Cook for 10 seconds then stir.

5. When cool, stir in vinegar.

YOGURT DRESSING

Preparation 5 mins **plus** 15 mins **standing**

150 g (5 oz) natural yogurt
30 ml (2 tbsp) fresh single cream
15 ml (1 tbsp) lemon juice
5 ml (1 tsp) sugar
salt and freshly ground pepper

1. Pour yogurt into a bowl. Beat in cream, lemon juice and sugar.

2. Season to taste and leave to stand for 15 minutes before using to allow the flavour to develop.

Variations

PIQUANT YOGURT DRESSING

Follow recipe and method for yogurt dressing (above). Add 5 ml (1 tsp) Worcestershire sauce, 1.25 ml (¼ tsp) cayenne pepper, 5 ml (1 tsp) paprika and ½ crushed garlic clove, before standing.

CURRY YOGURT DRESSING

Follow recipe and method for yogurt dressing (left). Add 10 ml (2 tsp) curry powder and 15 ml (1 tbsp) sweet pickle before standing.

TOMATO YOGURT DRESSING

Follow recipe and method for yogurt dressing (left). Add 15 ml (1 tbsp) each tomato ketchup, creamed horseradish sauce and 3 finely chopped spring onions before standing.

MIXED CHEESE DRESSING

Preparation 10 mins

50 g (2 oz) Blue Stilton cheese
100 g (4 oz) cream cheese
25 g (1 oz) English Cheddar, finely grated
½ garlic clove, crushed (optional)
150 ml (¼ pint) fresh milk
salt and freshly ground pepper

1. Mash Stilton and cream cheese together.
2. Add Cheddar and garlic (if used).
3. Gradually beat in milk. Season to taste.

MIXED CHEESE DRESSING

EGGS
AND
EGG RECIPES

PEAR & HAZELNUT MERINGUE PAGE 216 · SEAFOOD PANCAKES PAGE 206
HOT CHOCOLATE SOUFFLÉ PAGE 212 · BOILED EGG PAGE 201

EGGS

FRIED EGG

Cooking 3 mins   *Serves 1*

fat or oil for frying
1 egg

1. Heat a little fat or oil in a frying pan over a medium heat.

2. Break egg into pan. Baste with hot fat, tipping pan if necessary to pool fat.

3. Cook until white is firm and yolk is cooked to your liking.

4. Remove from pan with a fish slice.

5. Serve immediately.

POACHED EGG

Preparation 2 mins **Cooking** 5 mins   *Serves 1*

15 ml (1 tbsp) vinegar
1 egg
hot buttered toast to serve

1. Half fill a saucepan with water. Add vinegar to water and bring to the boil.
To microwave: Put 150 ml (¼ pint) water into a small bowl or jug with 5 ml (1 tsp) vinegar. Cook for 1½–2 minutes until boiling.

2. Crack egg into a cup and slide into water.

3. Cook gently for 3–5 minutes until lightly set, then lift out with a slotted spoon.
To microwave: Pierce yolk and cook for 20–30 seconds. Allow to stand for 1–2 minutes, then lift out with a slotted spoon.

4. Serve immediately with hot buttered toast.

EGGS BÉNÉDICT   Ⓕ

Preparation 10 mins **Cooking** 10 mins **Serves 4**

4 small slices of bread
4 eggs
4 thin slices of lean ham
freshly made hollandaise sauce (page 234)

1. Toast bread on both sides.

2. Poach eggs (as left).

3. Top each slice of toast with a slice of ham. Place drained poached eggs on top.

4. Spoon over sauce and serve.

BOILED EGGS – HOT WATER METHOD

Cooking 5½–7 mins   *Serves 1–2*

2 eggs

1. Place eggs in a saucepan of enough boiling water to completely cover them.

2. Bring back to the boil and simmer gently for 5½–7 minutes depending on how set you like your eggs.

BOILED EGGS – COLD WATER METHOD

Cooking 5–6 mins   *Serves 1–2*

2 eggs

1. Place eggs in a saucepan and cover with cold water.

2. Bring to the boil and simmer gently for 4–5 minutes depending on how set you like your egg. Time from when the water comes to the boil.

HARD-BOILED EGGS

Cooking 12 mins   *Serves 1–2*

2 eggs

1. Place eggs in a saucepan of enough boiling water to completely cover them.

2. Bring back to the boil and simmer gently for 10–12 minutes.

3. Drain and place under running cold water to prevent them from cooking further.

4. Leave to cool then crack shells and peel.

5. Rinse if any shell remains on the white and dry on absorbent kitchen paper.

CREAMED CORN & HAM SCRAMBLE

SCRAMBLED EGGS

Preparation 1 min **Cooking** 1½ mins   *Serves 1*

2 eggs
15 ml (1 tbsp) fresh milk
salt and freshly ground pepper
7 g (¼ oz) butter
hot buttered toast to serve

1. Break eggs into a bowl, add milk and seasoning and beat with a fork until mixed.

2. Melt butter in a small saucepan.
To microwave: Add butter, to eggs.

3. Pour in eggs and stir over a gentle heat moving cooked eggs from bottom and sides of pan.
To microwave: Cook for about 1½ minutes, stirring frequently, particularly when eggs begin to set around edge of bowl.

4. Remove from heat when lightly set as eggs continue cooking slightly.

5. Spoon on to toast and serve immediately.

EGG & MUSHROOM SAVOURY

Preparation 25 mins **Cooking** 15 mins   *Serves 4*

25 g (1 oz) butter
225 g (8 oz) mushrooms, halved
6 eggs
30 ml (2 tbsp) fresh milk
30 ml (2 tbsp) chopped parsley
2 large tomatoes, sliced
75 g (3 oz) Lancashire cheese, grated

1. Melt butter in a non-stick saucepan, add mushrooms and cook for 3–5 minutes until soft and golden.
To microwave: Melt butter in a bowl for 45 seconds. Stir in mushrooms, cover and cook for 3 minutes, stirring once.

2. Transfer mushrooms to a 568 ml (1 pint) greased flameproof dish.

3. Beat eggs with milk and parsley.

4. Pour into pan, scramble lightly until set.
To microwave: Pour into bowl and cook for 3–4 minutes, stirring frequently, or until lightly set.

5. Spoon over mushrooms, top with slices of tomato and sprinkle with cheese.

6. Brown under a hot grill.

CREAMED CORN & HAM SCRAMBLE

Preparation 7 mins **Cooking** 5 mins   *Serves 4*

6 eggs
60 ml (4 tbsp) fresh single cream
15 g (½ oz) butter
198 g (7 oz) can sweetcorn
100 g (4 oz) lean ham, finely chopped
large pinch of ground nutmeg
salt and freshly ground pepper
4 slices hot buttered toast
fresh parsley to garnish

1. Beat eggs and cream well together.

2. Pour into frying pan. Add butter, drained sweetcorn, ham, grated nutmeg and season. *To microwave: Pour into a bowl. Add butter, sweetcorn, ham, nutmeg and season to taste.*

3. Scramble over a low heat until creamy. *To microwave: Cook for 6–7 minutes, stirring frequently when eggs begin to set around edge of bowl, until lightly set.*

4. Pile equal amounts on to buttered toast.

5. Garnish with parsley.

PIPÉRADE

Preparation 35 mins **Cooking** 45 mins   *Serves 4*

350 g (12 oz) onions, chopped
50 g (2 oz) butter
10 ml (2 tsp) oil
3 medium green peppers,
    seeded and cut into strips
450 g (1 lb) tomatoes,
    skinned and chopped
1.25 ml (¼ tsp) dried marjoram or basil
salt and freshly ground pepper
6 eggs
60 ml (4 tbsp) fresh double cream

1. Fry onion gently in butter and oil until soft but not brown.

2. Add peppers to pan. Cook slowly with onion until soft.

3. Add tomatoes to pan with herbs and season to taste. Cover and simmer for 20 minutes or until most of liquid has evaporated.

4. Beat eggs lightly with cream. Pour over vegetable mixture.

5. Cook, stirring, until eggs are lightly scrambled.

PIPÉRADE

OMELETTES

Ideally, omelettes should be made in a special omelette pan (kept only for omelette-making), or in a non-stick frying pan. If you have neither of these and want to make omelettes in your ordinary frying pan, you can achieve better results by 'proving' the pan first. This will prevent the egg mixture from sticking and can be done very simply.

To 'prove' a pan quickly, first melt a knob of butter in the pan, then sprinkle the base liberally with cooking salt. Heat together slowly for a few minutes until hot, then rub clean with absorbent kitchen paper. Do *not* attempt to 'prove' non-stick pans.

If you are considering buying a special omelette pan, make sure it has a heavy base, curved sides, and is fairly shallow. It is important to 'prove' this pan well before use. After use just wipe the inside clean with absorbent kitchen paper. *Don't* wash, or it will need reproving.

A 15–18cm (6–7inch) pan takes a 2–3 egg omelette.

PLAIN OR FRENCH OMELETTE (UNFILLED)

Preparation 2 mins **Cooking** 3–5 mins   *Serves 1*

2 eggs
10 ml (2 tsp) water
salt and freshly ground pepper
15 g (½ oz) butter
parsley to garnish

1. Beat eggs and water lightly together. Season to taste.

2. Put butter into omelette pan. Heat until sizzling but not brown.

3. Swirl round to coat base and sides of pan.

4. Pour in beaten eggs.

5. After about 5 seconds, move edges of setting omelette to centre of pan with a fork, knife or spatula.

6. At same time tilt pan quickly in all directions with other hand so that uncooked egg flows to edges.

7. Continue until mixture is lightly set and top is slightly moist.

8. Remove from heat. Fold in half in pan and slide out on to a warm plate.

9. Garnish with parsley and serve immediately.

Variations

BACON, MUSHROOM & ONION OMELETTE

Fry in a little butter 15 ml (1 tbsp) *each* finely chopped bacon, mushrooms and onion. Add to beaten eggs just before making plain omelette.

HERB OMELETTE

Add 15 ml (1 tbsp) finely chopped fresh herbs to egg mixture before cooking. Parsley, chives or chervil can be used.

OMELETTE FILLINGS

Add before folding the omelette – step 8.

CHEDDAR CHEESE
40 g (1½ oz) grated English Cheddar.

PRAWN – 50 g (2 oz) peeled prawns.

MUSHROOM
50 g (2 oz) sliced mushrooms fried lightly in butter

HAM – 50 g (2 oz) lean chopped ham

STILTON AND ONION
40 g (1½ oz) crumbled Blue Stilton cheese mixed with 2 sliced spring onions

CHEESE WITH CHIVE AND ONION
40 g (1½ oz) grated Double Gloucester cheese with chives and onions

SAGE DERBY
40 g (1½ oz) grated Sage Derby cheese.

SOFT CHEESE AND GARLIC
100 g (4 oz) curd cheese mixed with ½ crushed garlic clove and 5 ml (1 tsp) chopped parsley

SPANISH OMELETTE

Preparation 25 mins **Cooking** 15 mins *Serves 2*

25 g (1 oz) butter
10 ml (2 tsp) oil
1 large onion, thinly sliced
1 large boiled potato, diced
100 g (4 oz) tomatoes, chopped
50 g (2 oz) red or green pepper, chopped
4 eggs
10 ml (2 tsp) water
salt and freshly ground pepper

1. Put butter and oil into a 23 cm (9 inch) frying pan.
2. When hot and sizzling, add onion and potato.
3. Fry gently until both are pale gold, turning fairly often.
4. Add tomatoes and pepper. Fry for a further 2–3 minutes.
5. Beat eggs lightly with water. Season to taste then pour into pan over vegetables.
6. Cook gently until base is firm.
7. Stand below a pre-heated hot grill.
8. Leave for 1–2 minutes, until top is just set.
9. Slide flat, unfolded omelette on to a plate. Cut into 2 portions. Serve immediately.

SWEET SOUFFLÉ OMELETTE

Preparation 10 mins **Cooking** 10 mins *Serves 4*

2 eggs, separated
15 g (½ oz) sugar
1.25 ml (¼ tsp) vanilla essence
15 g (½ oz) butter
30 ml (2 tbsp) jam, warmed
icing sugar to serve

1. Beat egg yolks with sugar and vanilla until very thick and pale in colour.
2. Beat egg whites to a stiff snow.
3. Gently fold into egg yolk mixture.
4. Melt butter in omelette pan. Swirl round to coat sides and base of pan.
5. When hot and sizzling, pour in egg mixture.
6. Cook without moving for 2–2½ minutes or until base is set and underside is golden.
7. Stand below a pre-heated hot grill.
8. Leave 2–3 minutes or until top is well puffed and golden.
9. Remove from grill and run a spatula around edge to loosen it.
10. Score a line down centre, spread with jam, fold in half, dust with icing sugar and serve immediately.

BATTERS

It has for many years been accepted that batter is improved by standing; but research has shown that this is not so. Long beating of batter is unnecessary. The batter will rise satisfactorily if the egg and the first half of the milk are beaten in briskly for a short time.

To keep pancakes warm as they are being made, stack one on top of the other on a large plate. Stand over a pan of gently simmering water. Cover with a large lid or second plate.

To store cooked pancakes, stack in an airtight container with greaseproof paper between each. They can be refrigerated for a 1 or 2 days. To re-heat, fry about 30 seconds per side in pan lightly brushed with butter. Alternatively, heat in the microwave oven on MEDIUM (50%).

PANCAKES

Preparation 5 mins **Cooking** 20 mins   *Makes 8*

100g (4oz) flour
pinch of salt
1 egg
300ml (½pint) fresh milk
15ml (1tbsp) melted butter (optional)
melted butter or oil for frying

1. Sift flour and salt into a bowl. Break in egg.

2. Gradually add half the milk, beating to form a smooth batter.

3. Pour in remaining milk and beat until quite smooth. Stir in melted butter.

4. Lightly brush base of a 20.5cm (8 inch) frying pan with melted butter. Stand over a medium heat.

5. When pan and butter are hot, pour in 45ml (3 tbsp) of batter tilting pan to cover base.

6. Cook until pancake moves freely, turn, cook until golden.

7. Repeat with remaining batter.

Variations

LEMON OR ORANGE PANCAKES Ⓕ

Follow recipe and method for pancakes (left). Sprinkle with sugar and lemon or orange juice. Roll up by sliding nearest edge of pancake between prongs of a fork and turning fork over and over. Accompany with lemon or orange wedges.

SEAFOOD PANCAKES

Preparation 15 mins **Cooking** 15 mins   *Serves 4*

25g (1oz) flour
450ml (¾pint) fresh milk
25g (1oz) butter
350g (12oz) white fish fillet,
    cut into 2.5cm (1inch) cubes
75g (3oz) frozen peas
100g (4oz) peeled prawns or chopped
    seafood sticks
10ml (2tsp) made wholegrain mustard
50g (2oz) Cheddar cheese with garlic and
    herbs, grated
8 freshly cooked pancakes (left)

1. Place flour, milk and butter in a pan, heat, whisking continuously until sauce thickens, boils and is smooth.
To microwave: Place flour in a jug. Gradually blend in 300ml (½pint) milk only. Add butter and cook for 3–4 minutes, stir frequently, until sauce thickens, boils and is smooth.

2. Add fish and peas, cook for 5 minutes, stir occasionally.
To microwave: Stir in fish and peas. Cook for 3–4 minutes, stirring twice.

3. Add prawns and heat through.
To microwave: Add prawns and cook for 1–2 minutes to heat through.

4. Remove from heat, add mustard and cheese, stir until melted.

5. Divide filling between pancakes and roll up or fold into triangles

6. Serve immediately.

206

CHICKEN PANCAKES Ⓕ

Preparation 15 mins **Cooking** 10 mins   *Serves 4*

15 g (½ oz) flour
15 g (½ oz) butter
300 ml (½ pint) fresh milk
pinch of dried basil
350 g (12 oz) cooked chicken meat, diced
225 g (8 oz) broccoli, cooked in small florets
225 g (8 oz) carrots, diced and cooked
8 freshly cooked pancakes (page 206)
50 g (2 oz) English Cheddar, grated

1. Place flour, butter and milk in a saucepan, heat whisking until sauce thickens, boils and is smooth. Cook for a minute.
To microwave: Gradually blend milk into flour. Add butter and cook for 3–4 minutes, stirring frequently, until sauce thickens, boils and is smooth.

2. Stir in basil, chicken and vegetables and cook until heated through.

3. Divide between pancakes and roll up or fold into triangles.

4. Place in an ovenproof dish, sprinkle with cheese and grill until melted or bake at 200°C (400°F) Mark 6 for 20 minutes.

CHILLI PANCAKES Ⓕ

Preparation 20 mins **Cooking** 25 mins   *Serves 4*

1 medium onion, chopped
1 garlic clove, crushed
425 g (15 oz) can red kidney beans, rinsed and drained
425 g (15 oz) can baked beans
397 g (14 oz) can tomatoes
10 ml (2 tsp) chilli powder
225 g (8 oz) frozen green beans
1 yellow pepper, seeded and chopped
8 freshly cooked pancakes (page 206)
50 g (2 oz) Red Leicester cheese, grated

1. Place onion, garlic, beans, tomatoes and chilli in a pan and simmer for 15 minutes.
To microwave: Cook onion, garlic, beans, tomatoes and chilli powder, uncovered, for 10 minutes, stirring once.

2. Add green beans and pepper, cook for a further 5 minutes or until mixture is thick.
To microwave: Stir in green beans and pepper. Cover and cook for 5 minutes.

3. Divide filling between pancakes and fold into triangles.

4. Place in a baking dish in one layer.

5. Sprinkle with cheese, grill until melted.

CHILLI PANCAKES

AMERICAN PANCAKES Ⓕ

Preparation 5 mins **Cooking** 15 mins   *Makes 8*

225 g (8 oz) flour
20 ml (4 tsp) baking powder
10 ml (2 tsp) caster sugar
5 ml (1 tsp) salt
2 eggs
350 ml (12 fl oz) fresh milk
25 g (1 oz) butter, melted
butter for frying
maple syrup and whipped cream to serve

1. Sift flour, baking powder, sugar and salt into a bowl.

2. Whisk eggs, milk and melted butter together. Stir into dry ingredients and mix until evenly blended.

3. Heat a little butter in a frying pan and when hot pour in sufficient batter to give a 12.5 cm (5 inch) pancake, 0.5 cm (¼ inch) thick.

4. Cook until top of pancake looks bubbly, turn and cook until golden.

5. Repeat making 8 pancakes.

6. Serve with maple syrup and cream.

YORKSHIRE PUDDING

Preparation 5 mins
Cooking 40–45 mins   *Serves 6–8*

100 g (4 oz) flour
pinch of salt
1 egg
300 ml (½ pint) fresh milk
40 g (1½ oz) butter

1. Sift flour and salt into a bowl. Break in egg.

2. Gradually add half the milk, beating to form a smooth batter.

3. Pour in remaining milk and beat until quite smooth.

4. Pre-heat oven to 220°C (425°F) Mark 7. Put butter into a 25.5×30.5 cm (10×12 inch) baking tin. Heat for 10 minutes or until a faint haze just appears.

5. Pour in batter.

6. Bake just above centre of oven for 40–45 minutes.

Variation

SMALL YORKSHIRE PUDDINGS

Follow recipe and method for Yorkshire pudding (left). Place butter in a 12 section bun tin and heat as step 4. Pour in batter and cook for 15–20 minutes.

TOAD IN THE HOLE

Preparation 5 mins **Cooking** 55 mins *Serves 4–6*

25 g (1 oz) butter
450 g (1 lb) sausages
100 g (4 oz) flour
pinch of salt
1 egg
300 ml (½ pint) fresh milk

1. Place butter and sausages in a 25.5×30.5 cm (10×12 inch) roasting tin.

2. Cook at 220°C (425°F) Mark 7 for 10 minutes.

3. Meanwhile, sift flour and salt into a bowl. Break in egg.

4. Gradually add half the milk, beating to form a smooth batter.

5. Pour in remaining milk and beat until quite smooth.

6. Pour batter into roasting tin and bake for 40–45 minutes, until batter is well risen and golden.

Variations

MEATBALL BATTER PUDDING

Follow recipe and method for toad in the hole (above) but omit sausages. After pouring batter into roasting tin add 450 g (1 lb) lean minced beef, seasoned and shaped into 12 meat balls.

APPLE BATTER PUDDING

Follow recipe and method for toad in the hole (above) but omit sausages. Add 450 g (1 lb) peeled, cored and thickly sliced apples to butter and 50 g (2 oz) sugar, 5 ml (1 tsp) ground cinnamon to batter.

COATING BATTER

Preparation 5 mins

For coating fish, meat and vegetables

100 g (4 oz) plain or self-raising flour
1.25 ml (¼ tsp) salt
1 egg
15 ml (1 tbsp) butter, melted
150 ml (¼ pint) fresh milk

1. Sift flour and salt into a bowl.
2. Beat to a smooth batter with unbeaten egg, butter and milk.
3. Use as required.

SAVOURY FRITTER BATTER

Preparation 10 mins

For coating fish, meat, poultry and vegetables

100 g (4 oz) flour
2.5 ml (½ tsp) salt
freshly ground pepper
150 ml (¼ pint) lukewarm water
15 ml (1 tbsp) butter, melted
2 egg whites

1. Sift flour and salt into a bowl. Add pepper.
2. Gradually mix to a thick, smooth batter with water and butter.
3. Whisk egg whites to a stiff snow.
4. Fold into flour mixture.
5. Use as required.

SWEET FRITTER BATTER

Preparation 10 mins

For coating fruit such as apples, bananas and pineapple

50 g (2 oz) flour
pinch of salt
5 ml (1 tsp) icing sugar, sifted
60 ml (4 tbsp) lukewarm water
10 ml (2 tsp) butter, melted
1 egg white

1. Sift flour and salt into a bowl. Add sugar.
2. Gradually mix to a thick, smooth batter with water and butter.
3. Whisk egg white to a stiff snow.
4. Fold into flour mixture.
5. Use as required.

APPLE FRITTERS

APPLE FRITTERS

Preparation 10 mins **Cooking** 5 mins   *Serves 4*

3 medium cooking apples,
  peeled and cored
sweet fritter batter made with 50 g (2 oz)
  flour (page 209)
deep fat or oil for frying
sifted icing sugar
fresh cream or natural yogurt to serve

1. Cut apples into 0.5 cm (¼ inch) thick rings.

2. Coat with fritter batter. Fry in deep hot fat
or oil for 2–3 minutes or until golden.

3. Remove from pan and drain on absorbent
kitchen paper.

4. Dredge thickly with sifted icing sugar.

5. Accompany with fresh single cream,
soured cream or natural yogurt.

Variation

BANANA FRITTERS

Follow recipe and method for apple fritters
(above). Omit apples and use small
bananas, peeled and cut in half lengthways.

SWEET CHEESE BLINTZES

Preparation 25 mins **Cooking** 25 mins   *Serves 4*

pancake batter made with 100 g (4 oz) flour
  (page 206)
350 g (12 oz) curd cheese
1 egg yolk
60 ml (4 tbsp) sugar
5 ml (1 tsp) vanilla essence
about 50 g (2 oz) butter
5 ml (1 tsp) ground cinnamon
150 ml (5 fl oz) fresh soured cream
  or natural yogurt

1. Cook 8 pancakes on **one side only**. Turn
out on to a clean tea-towel.

2. Mix cheese with egg yolk, 30 ml (2 tbsp)
sugar and vanilla.

3. Put equal amounts onto centres of **cooked**
sides of pancakes.

4. Fold edges of pancakes over filling,
envelope style.

5. Melt butter in a frying pan. Leave until
hot and sizzling.

6. Put in 4 blintzes, with joins underneath.
Fry on both sides until golden.

7. Remove from pan. Drain on absorbent
kitchen paper. Keep warm.

8. Add more butter to pan if necessary. Fry remaining blintzes until golden.

9. Sprinkle with sugar and cinnamon.

10. Serve hot with soured cream or yogurt.

CRÊPES SUZETTES

Preparation 5 mins **Cooking** 10 mins   *Serves 4*

8 cooked pancakes (page 206)
50g (2oz) butter
25g (1oz) caster sugar
2.5ml (½tsp) grated lemon rind
2.5ml (½tsp) grated orange rind
60ml (4tbsp) Cointreau, Curaçao
  or Grand Marnier
30ml (2tbsp) brandy

1. Fold pancakes into fan shapes.

2. Melt butter in a frying pan. Add sugar, lemon and orange rind and liqueur.

3. Bring to the boil. Add pancakes.

4. Heat through, turning twice.

5. Warm brandy and pour into pan. Set brandy alight and allow it to flame.

6. Serve pancakes as soon as flames have subsided.

MOCK CRÊPES SUZETTES

Preparation 5 mins **Cooking** 10 mins   *Serves 4*

8 cooked pancakes (page 206)
50g (2oz) butter
50g (2oz) caster sugar
finely grated rind & juice of 1 large orange
45ml (3tbsp) sweet sherry or white wine

1. Fold pancakes into fan shapes.

2. Melt butter in a frying pan. Add sugar, orange rind and juice and sherry or wine.
To microwave: Melt butter in a shallow dish for 45 seconds. Stir in orange rind and juice, and sherry or wine.

3. Bring to the boil. Add pancakes.
To microwave: Cook, uncovered, for 2–3 minutes, stirring twice, until boiling. Add pancakes.

4. Heat through, turning twice.
To microwave: Cook, uncovered, for 1–2 minutes, turning once.

5. Serve immediately

CRÊPES SUZETTES

SOUFFLÉS

CHEESE SOUFFLÉ

Preparation 15 mins **Cooking** 1 hr   *Serves 4*

50g (2oz) butter
50g (2oz) flour
300ml (½pint) fresh milk, warmed
100g (4oz) English Cheddar, grated
5ml (1tsp) made mustard
salt and freshly ground pepper
1.25ml (¼tsp) Worcestershire sauce
3 egg yolks
4 egg whites

1. Melt butter in a saucepan and add flour. Cook for 2 minutes without browning, stirring all the time.

2. Gradually whisk in warm milk (with a whisk, not a spoon). Continue whisking gently until sauce thickens, boils and is smooth.

3. Simmer for about 2 minutes. Sauce should be quite thick and leave sides of pan clean.

4. Remove from heat and cool slightly. Beat in cheese, mustard, seasoning, Worcestershire sauce and egg yolks.

5. Beat egg whites to a stiff snow. Gently fold into sauce mixture with a large metal spoon.

6. Transfer to a greased 1.4litre (2½pint) soufflé dish (or similar straight-sided, heatproof dish).

7. Bake at 190°C (375°F) Mark 5 for 50 minutes. The soufflé should be well-risen with a high, golden crown.

8. Remove from oven and serve immediately.

It is *vital* not to open the oven door while the soufflé is baking or it will fall.

Variations

HAM SOUFFLÉ

Follow recipe and method for cheese soufflé (above) but omit cheese. Before beating in egg yolks add 100g (4oz) finely chopped ham.

SMOKED MACKEREL SOUFFLÉ

Follow recipe and method for cheese soufflé (left). Add half the cheese. Before beating in egg yolks add 100g (4oz) finely flaked, smoked mackerel.

COTSWOLD SOUFFLÉ

Follow recipe and method for cheese soufflé (left). Use Double Gloucester with onion and chives in place of Cheddar.

MUSHROOM SOUFFLÉ

Follow recipe and method for cheese soufflé (left) but omit cheese and Worcestershire sauce. Before beating in egg yolks add 100g (4oz) finely chopped, fried mushrooms.

BACON SOUFFLÉ

Follow recipe and method for cheese soufflé (left) but omit cheese. Before beating in egg yolks add 100g (4oz) finely chopped, fried bacon.

HOT CHOCOLATE SOUFFLÉ

Preparation 15 mins **Cooking** 45 mins   *Serves 4*

50g (2oz) plain chocolate dots
60ml (4tbsp) flour
150ml (¼pint) fresh milk
50g (2oz) caster sugar
15g (½oz) butter
3 egg yolks
4 egg whites
icing sugar to serve

CHEESE SOUFFLÉ

1. Place chocolate in a bowl with 30ml (2tbsp) water and melt over a saucepan of hot water.
To microwave: Place chocolate in a bowl with 30ml (2tbsp) water and cook on MEDIUM (50%) for about 2 minutes, stirring occasionally, until melted.

2. Blend flour with a little cold milk to make a smooth paste.

3. Heat remaining milk with sugar.
To microwave: Heat remaining milk with sugar for 1½ minutes.

4. Mix hot milk with melted chocolate then pour onto flour paste, stirring to mix.

5. Return to pan and bring to the boil, stirring.
To microwave: Cook for 2–2½ minutes, stirring frequently, until sauce boils and is very thick. Stir well.

6. Cook for 2 minutes, stirring occasionally.
To microwave: Cook for 30 seconds.

7. Remove from heat, stir in butter and cool slightly.

8. Stir in egg yolks.

9. Whisk egg whites to a stiff snow and gently fold in to chocolate mixture.

10. Transfer to a well greased 1.1 litre (2 pint) soufflé dish.

11. Bake at 200°C (400°F) Mark 6 for 35 minutes until well risen with a high crown.

12. Dust with icing sugar and serve immediately.

Variations

HAZELNUT OR WALNUT SOUFFLÉ

Follow recipe and method for chocolate soufflé (left) but omit chocolate. Add 75g (3oz) finely chopped hazelnuts or walnuts before beating in egg yolks.

COFFEE SOUFFLÉ

Follow recipe and method for chocolate soufflé (left) but omit chocolate. Add 15ml (1 tbsp) instant coffee granules to hot milk.

BANANA SOUFFLÉ

Follow recipe and method for chocolate soufflé (left) but omit chocolate. Add 2 small bananas, mashed with 10ml (2tsp) lemon juice before beating in egg yolks.

COLD SOUFFLÉS

To prepare a soufflé dish for a cold soufflé

Cut a strip of greaseproof paper long enough to go around the soufflé dish. It should be deep enough to stand about 5 cm (2 inch) above the top of the dish. Secure paper with string or adhesive tape around outside of dish. It should fit closely around the rim to prevent mixture escaping down sides of dish.

Brush inside of greaseproof paper with a little oil and stand prepared dish on a small tray.

LEMON SOUFFLÉ **Ⓕ**

Preparation 30 mins **Cooking** 2 mins   *Serves 4*

15 ml (1 tbsp) gelatine
45 ml (3 tbsp) water
4 eggs, separated
100 g (4 oz) caster sugar
grated rind and juice of 2 medium lemons
300 ml (10 fl oz) fresh double cream,
    softly whipped
40 g (1½ oz) chopped, toasted almonds
whipped cream and crystallised lemon
    slices to decorate

1. Prepare dish as left.

2. Sprinkle gelatine over water in a basin. Stand for 10 minutes.

3. Dissolve gelatine over a pan of boiling water. Leave to cool.
To microwave: Cook for about 30 seconds, stirring every 10 seconds, until dissolved.

4. Whisk egg yolks and sugar together in a bowl over a pan of hot water until very thick and pale.

5. Remove bowl from hot water and continue whisking until mixture is cool.

6. Gently whisk in dissolved gelatine, lemon rind and juice.

7. Leave until just beginning to thicken and set.

8. Beat egg whites to a stiff snow.

9. Gently fold cream into lemon mixture. Fold in beaten egg whites.

10. Pour into prepared soufflé dish. Chill until firm and set.

11. Just before serving, ease paper away from mixture with a knife dipped into hot water. Gently press chopped nuts against sides of soufflé.

12. Decorate top with whipped cream and crystallised lemon slices.

LEMON SOUFFLÉ

MERINGUES

MERINGUES (F)

Preparation 20 mins
Cooking 2½ hrs   *Makes 16 Meringue Halves*

2 egg whites
pinch of cream of tartar (optional)
100g (4oz) caster sugar
25g (1oz) granulated sugar

1. Brush a large baking sheet with oil. Cover with a double thickness of greaseproof or non-stick baking paper. Do *not* brush paper with more oil.

2. Put egg whites into a clean dry bowl. Add cream of tartar, if used. Beat until stiff and peaky.

3. Add half the caster sugar.

4. Continue beating until meringue is shiny and stands in firm peaks.

5. Add remaining caster sugar. Beat until meringue is very stiff and silky-looking and texture is fairly close. Gently fold in granulated sugar.

6. Pipe or spoon 16 rounds or ovals on to prepared sheet.

7. Bake at 110°C (225°F) Mark ¼ for 2½ hours or until crisp and firm.

8. Transfer to a wire cooling rack and leave until cold.

Variations

COFFEE MERINGUES (F)

Follow recipe and method for meringues (above). Add 10ml (2tsp) instant coffee powder with granulated sugar. Sandwich together with whipped cream or coffee butter cream (page 329).

BROWN SUGAR MERINGUES (F)

Follow recipe and method for meringues (above). Use 100g (4oz) soft brown sugar in place of caster sugar. Sandwich together with whipped cream.

WALNUT CHOCOLATE FINGERS (F)

Follow recipe and method for meringues (left). Add 50g (2oz) very finely chopped walnuts with granulated sugar. Pipe 20 7.5cm (3inch) lengths of mixture on to a prepared baking sheet. When cold dip ends in melted chocolate. Sandwich together with whipped cream.

MERINGUE TOPPING (F)

Preparation 15 mins

2 egg whites
75g (3oz) caster sugar
15ml (1tbsp) granulated sugar (optional)

1. Put egg whites into a clean dry bowl. Beat until stiff and peaky (when bowl is turned upside down the whites should stay where they are).

2. Gently fold in caster sugar with a large metal spoon.

3. Pile meringue over pie or pudding, etc., and sprinkle with granulated sugar, if used.

Baking
Quick cooking is essential if meringue is used as decoration on frozen or chilled desserts; therefore **flash bake** dish towards top of a hot oven 230°C (450°F) Mark 8 until meringue just starts turning gold. About 1–3 minutes but no longer.

If meringue is on a **pudding** or pie that is made to be served cold later, it is important to dry out the meringue thoroughly, otherwise it will sag on standing and become wet and syrupy; therefore put dish into centre of a very slow oven 110°C (225°F) Mark ¼ and bake for 1½–2 hours, or until meringue is firm, crisp and golden.

For a **hot pudding** topped with meringue, bake in centre of a slow oven 150°C (300°F) Mark 2 for 20–30 minutes, or until pale gold.

SNOW EGGS

Preparation 30 mins **plus chilling**
Cooking 20 mins   *Serves 4*

3 eggs, separated
100 g (4 oz) caster sugar
450 ml (¾ pint) fresh milk
5 ml (1 tsp) vanilla essence
or 2.5 ml (½ tsp) grated lemon rind

1. Beat egg whites to a stiff snow.

2. Add 50 g (2 oz) sugar and continue beating until mixture is shiny and stands in firm peaks.

3. Put milk into a saucepan. Heat slowly until bubbles start appearing (it must never boil). Reduce heat.

4. Shape meringue into ovals between two tablespoons dipped in warm water and float shapes on simmering milk.

5. Poach gently for 2 minutes, turning once.

6. Carefully lift out meringues and place onto absorbent kitchen paper.

7. Pour warm milk onto egg yolks and whisk lightly.

8. Pour into a heavy based saucepan (or basin standing over a pan of simmering water). Add remaining sugar and cook, stirring all the time until custard thickens. Do not boil.

9. Remove from heat, add vanilla or lemon rind and cool.

10. Pour into a serving dish, arrange poached meringues on top and chill.

PEAR & HAZELNUT MERINGUE

Preparation 50 mins
Cooking 45 mins   *Serves 6–8*

4 egg whites
275 g (10 oz) caster sugar
few drops of vanilla essence
5 ml (1 tsp) vinegar
100 g (4 oz) ground hazelnuts, toasted
450 g (1 lb) pears, peeled, cored & chopped
300 ml (10 fl oz) fresh double cream, whipped
whole hazelnuts to decorate

1. Whisk egg whites until stiff, then whisk in 250 g (9 oz) of sugar a spoonful at a time.

2. Continue whisking until meringue is very stiff and holds its shape.

3. Fold in vanilla essence, vinegar and nuts.

4. Divide mixture between two lined and greased 20.5 cm (8 inch) sandwich tins and spread evenly.

5. Bake at 180°C (350°F) Mark 4 for 45 minutes.

6. Place pears, remaining sugar and 50 ml (2 fl oz) water in a saucepan. Cover and cook for 10–15 minutes until tender.

7. Strain off any liquid and leave until cold. Fold into ¾ of the cream.

8. Sandwich meringue rounds together with filling.

9. Decorate with remaining cream and nuts.

LEMON MERINGUE TOPS

Preparation 30 mins **Cooking** 40 mins *Serves 4*

25 g (1 oz) cornflour
300 ml (½ pint) fresh milk
100 g (4 oz) caster sugar
25 g (1 oz) butter, diced
grated rind and juice of 1 lemon
2 eggs, separated

1. Blend cornflour with milk.

2. Pour into a small saucepan and heat, stirring, until sauce thickens, boils and is smooth.
To microwave: Pour into a jug or bowl and cook for about 3 minutes, stirring frequently, until sauce thickens, boils and is smooth.

3. Add 50 g (2 oz) sugar, butter and lemon rind. Stir in lemon juice.

4. Cool slightly. Stir in egg yolks.

5. Turn mixture into 4 ramekin dishes.

6. Whisk egg whites stiffly. Fold in all but a spoonful of remaining sugar.

7. Pile meringue over lemon filling in each dish.

8. Sprinkle with remaining sugar.

9. Bake at 150°C (300°F) Mark 2 for 20–30 minutes until golden brown.
To microwave: Cook on MEDIUM (50%) for about 4 minutes until set. Brown lightly under a grill if wished.

ALMOND & APRICOT MERINGUE DESSERT

Preparation 45 mins **Cooking** 1 hr   *Serves 6–8*

4 egg whites
225 g (8 oz) caster sugar
pinch of cream of tartar
75 g (3 oz) ground almonds
100 g (4 oz) canned apricots, drained
450 ml (15 fl oz) fresh double cream
grated chocolate to decorate

1. Line two baking sheets with greased greaseproof or non-stick baking paper.
2. Draw a 20.5 cm (8 inch) circle on the under side of each piece of paper.
3. Whisk egg whites until stiff, add 15 ml (1 tbsp) caster sugar and cream of tartar, continue whisking for 1 minute.
4. Fold in remaining sugar and almonds.
5. Spread mixture between marked circles.
6. Bake at 140°C (275°F) Mark 1 for 1¼ hours or until bottom of meringues are firm.
7. Remove paper and leave to cool.
8. Purée apricots in a blender until smooth.
9. Whip cream until softly stiff. Fold apricot purée into two thirds of cream.
10. Put one meringue disc on serving plate.
11. Cover with cream and apricot mixture, top with remaining meringue disc.
12. Decorate with remaining cream and grated chocolate.

STRAWBERRY PAVLOVA

Preparation 20 mins **Cooking** 1 hr   *Serves 6*

3 egg whites
5 ml (1 tsp) cornflour
5 ml (1 tsp) vinegar
175 g (6 oz) caster sugar
300 ml (10 fl oz) fresh double cream
225 g (8 oz) strawberries

1. Whisk egg whites until stiff.
2. Mix cornflour and vinegar together and whisk into egg whites with half the sugar.
3. Fold in remaining sugar.
4. Spoon mixture into a round on to a baking sheet covered with greaseproof or non-stick baking paper.
5. Bake at 170°C (325°F) Mark 3 for 1 hour or until crisp and dry.
6. Whip cream until softly stiff.
7. Pile cream into centre of pavlova and decorate with strawberries.

LIGHT MEALS AND SNACKS

A SELECTION OF OPEN SANDWICHES
CHEESY AVOCADO TOASTS PAGE 223 · WENSLEYDALE PIZZAS PAGE 229

SANDWICHES

Use fresh bread. Make sure that the slices are not too thick.

Allow 175 g (6 oz) softened and well-creamed butter for every 24 large bread slices.

Make sure that the butter completely covers the bread slices. It acts as a waterproof barrier, preventing moisture from fillings seeping through into the bread and making it soggy.

Prepare all fillings beforehand and check to see that they are well seasoned. If using soft fillings, such as chopped hard-boiled eggs combined with natural yogurt, have something crisp – lettuce or chopped celery for example – to go with it. Contrast of texture adds interest.

Allow 225 g (8 oz) sliced meat, cheese or smoked fish to fill about 8 sandwiches. The number of sandwiches to allow per person will depend on appetite and type of fillings used. As a general guide, allow 1½ to 2 full rounds or 6 to 8 small sandwiches for each person. A round is two slices of bread.

If sandwiches are made in advance at night for a packed lunch the next day, wrap them in aluminium foil or in a polythene bag and keep in a refrigerator overnight.

Crust removal is a matter of choice. Large sandwiches keep better if the crusts are left on. Dainty afternoon sandwiches, made from very thin bread, look more attractive and less clumsy if the crusts are removed.

Although many recipes use slices of bread, rolls or French bread can be used instead.

DANISH-STYLE OPEN SANDWICHES

Whether you are using white, brown, rye bread or pumpernickel, make sure the slices are covered thickly with butter.

See that the butter comes right to the edges of every slice. Cover bread and butter with lettuce or frisée if desired.

Be generous with toppings and garnishes. Provide knives and forks.

IDEAS FOR TOPPINGS

Peeled prawns and mayonnaise garnished with paprika and lemon slices.

Sliced egg and tomato garnished with mayonnaise and chopped chives.

Salami and cottage cheese garnished with chopped parsley.

Sliced Double Gloucester cheese garnished with black grapes and apple slices.

Sliced cooked sausage and coleslaw garnished with parsley.

Cooked salmon and mayonnaise garnished with sliced cucumber and lemon.

Cooked sliced chicken garnished with mayonnaise, chopped tomato and asparagus tips.

Cottage cheese garnished with a selection of fresh fruit.

Cooked sliced pork loin and mayonnaise garnished with sliced apple and orange.

Smoked mackerel with cucumber and tomato, garnished with lemon slices.

Sliced Blue Stilton cheese garnished with rolled cooked ham and watercress.

Bean salad and grated carrot garnished with cherry tomatoes.

Sliced Cambridge Blue cheese and grapes.

CHEESY EGG SANDWICH

Preparation 10 mins   *Serves 4*

3 eggs, hard boiled and shelled
225 g (8 oz) cottage cheese
45 ml (3 tbsp) salad cream
25 g (1 oz) Red Leicester cheese, grated
mustard and cress
8 slices of bread
butter

1. Mash eggs with cottage cheese and salad cream.

2. Stir in grated cheese, mustard and cress.

3. Spread bread with butter.

4. Make into sandwiches with filling.

CHEESE & CELERY SANDWICH

Preparation 10 mins   *Serves 6*

12 large slices of brown bread
butter
175 g (6 oz) Cheshire cheese, thinly sliced
45 ml (3 tbsp) chopped celery
60 ml (4 tbsp) fresh double cream

1. Spread bread with butter.
2. Sandwich slices together, in pairs, with cheese followed by celery well mixed with double cream.
3. Cut each sandwich into 2 or 4 pieces.

CHEESE, APPLE & CELERY SANDWICH

Preparation 20 mins   *Serves 2*

25 g (1 oz) smoked Cheddar cheese, grated
50 g (2 oz) reduced fat hard cheese, grated
2 celery sticks, finely chopped
1 medium eating apple, cored and grated
cress
30 ml (2 tbsp) mayonnaise
4 slices of wholemeal bread
butter

1. Mix together cheeses, celery, apple, cress and mayonnaise.
2. Spread bread with butter.
3. Make into sandwiches with filling.

CRESS, CHEESE & CARROT SANDWICH

Preparation 10 mins   *Serves 4*

12 large slices of brown bread
butter
mustard and cress
175 g (6 oz) Double Gloucester cheese, thinly sliced
90 ml (6 tbsp) grated carrot
60 ml (4 tbsp) fresh soured cream
or natural yogurt

1. Spread bread with butter.
2. Sandwich slices together, in pairs, with mustard and cress and cheese, followed by grated carrot mixed with cream or yogurt.
3. Cut each sandwich into 2 or 4 pieces.

CHEESE & PEANUT SANDWICH

Preparation 20 mins   *Serves 2*

25 g (1 oz) butter
100 g (4 oz) English Cheddar, grated
50 g (2 oz) roasted peanuts, chopped
4 slices of wholemeal bread
2 tomatoes, sliced

1. Cream together butter and cheese, stir in peanuts.
2. Spread mixture on to two slices of bread.
3. Top with sliced tomato and remaining slices of bread.

PEANUT & SWEETCORN SANDWICH

Preparation 5 mins   *Serves 1*

butter for spreading
2 slices of wholemeal bread
50 g (2 oz) peanut butter
25 g (1 oz) canned sweetcorn, drained
alfalfa sprouts or bean sprouts

1. Butter bread and spread 1 slice with peanut butter.
2. Cover with a layer of sweetcorn, then a layer of alfalfa sprouts and remaining bread.

MALT BREAD & CHEESE SANDWICH

Preparation 10 mins   *Serves 2*

8 slices of malt bread
100 g (4 oz) full fat soft cheese
fresh fruit to garnish

1. Make malt bread and soft cheese into sandwiches.
2. Serve garnished with fresh fruit.

PASTRAMI & CHEESE SANDWICH

Preparation 10 mins   *Serves 1*

1 wholemeal roll
butter
25 g (1 oz) pastrami
25 g (1 oz) reduced fat hard cheese, sliced
1 tomato, sliced

1. Split roll and spread with butter.

2. Sandwich together with pastrami, cheese and tomato.

SMOKED MACKEREL & CHEESE SANDWICH

Preparation 15 mins   *Serves 4*

175 g (6 oz) smoked mackerel fillets, flaked
100 g (4 oz) cottage cheese
75 g (3 oz) canned sweetcorn, drained
15 ml (1 tbsp) chopped parsley
8 slices of brown bread
butter

1. Mix mackerel, cottage cheese, sweetcorn and parsley together.

2. Spread bread with butter.

3. Divide filling between 4 slices.

4. Cover with remaining slices of bread.

ORANGE & MACKEREL SANDWICH

Preparation 20 mins   *Serves 2*

½ orange, peeled and segmented
45 ml (3 tbsp) natural yogurt
75 g (3 oz) green grapes,
    halved and seeded
2 poppy seed rolls
butter
100 g (4 oz) smoked mackerel fillets, flaked

1. Chop orange segments and stir into yogurt with grapes.

2. Split rolls in half lengthways and spread with butter.

3. Place smoked mackerel on base of rolls and spoon yogurt on top.

4. Replace tops on rolls, to serve.

ORANGE & MACKEREL SANDWICH

BACON, LETTUCE & CHEESE SANDWICH

Preparation 10 mins   *Serves 2*

4 slices of granary bread
butter
15 ml (1 tbsp) mayonnaise
lettuce
2 tomatoes, sliced
4 rashers streaky bacon, well grilled
75 g (3 oz) Somerset Brie, sliced

1. Spread bread with butter.
2. Spread 2 slices with mayonnaise.
3. Arrange lettuce, tomato, bacon and cheese on top.
4. Cover with remaining bread.

BACON & BANANA SANDWICH

Preparation 10 mins   *Serves 4*

12 large slices of bread
butter
3 medium bananas, peeled and mashed
12 rashers bacon, grilled

1. Spread bread with butter.
2. Sandwich slices together, in pairs, with mashed bananas and bacon rashers.
3. Cut each sandwich into 2 or 4 pieces.

STILTON & BANANA SANDWICH

Preparation 20 mins   *Serves 2*

4 slices of granary bread
butter
1 banana, peeled and sliced
lemon juice
50 g (2 oz) Blue Stilton cheese, crumbled
2 spring onions, sliced

1. Spread bread with butter.
2. Dip banana in lemon juice.
3. Arrange filling ingredients on two slices of bread.
4. Cover with remaining bread.

STILTON, LETTUCE & HAM SANDWICH

Preparation 10 mins   *Serves 4*

12 large slices of bread
butter
175 g (6 oz) Blue Stilton cheese, sliced
6 slices lean cooked ham
lettuce, shredded

1. Spread bread with butter.
2. Sandwich slices together, in pairs, with cheese, ham and lettuce.
3. Cut each sandwich into 2 or 4 pieces.

BERRY BRIE SANDWICH

Preparation 15 mins   *Serves 2*

4 slices of wholemeal bread
butter
30 ml (2 tbsp) cranberry jelly
50 g (2 oz) Somerset Brie, sliced
lettuce

1. Spread bread with butter.
2. Spread jelly on to two slices of bread.
3. Arrange cheese on top and cover with lettuce and remaining bread.

MANGO CHICKEN SANDWICH

Preparation 20 mins   *Serves 2*

100 g (4 oz) cooked chicken meat, chopped
45 ml (3 tbsp) natural yogurt
5 ml (1 tsp) curry powder
30 ml (2 tbsp) mango chutney
4 slices of granary bread
butter
lettuce

1. Mix together chicken, yogurt, curry powder and mango chutney.
2. Spread bread with butter.
3. Divide filling between 2 slices.
4. Top with lettuce and remaining 2 slices of bread.

CHEESE & BEAN PITTAS

PITTA POCKETS

Preparation 20 mins   *Serves 4*

50 g (2 oz) cooked brown rice
225 g (8 oz) cottage cheese with onions and
    chives
198 g (7 oz) can sweetcorn, drained
1 red or green pepper, seeded and diced
4 pitta breads
shredded lettuce

1. Mix together rice, cottage cheese,
sweetcorn and pepper.
2. Halve pitta breads and open to form
pockets.
3. Place a little lettuce in each one.
4. Fill with cottage cheese mixture.

CHEESE & BEAN PITTAS

Preparation 20 mins   *Serves 4*

425 g (15 oz) can mixed bean salad
½ red pepper, seeded and diced
225 g (8 oz) Sage Derby cheese, cubed
4 pitta breads
frisée or lettuce, shredded

1. Drain beans, reserving 60 ml (4 tbsp) of
liquid.
2. Stir in pepper, cheese and reserved liquid.
3. Halve pitta breads and open to form
pockets.
4. Place a little frisée or lettuce in each one
then fill with bean mixture.

CHEESY AVOCADO TOASTS

Preparation 15 mins **Cooking** 10 mins   *Serves 2*

2 slices of wholemeal bread
½ ripe avocado
lemon juice
100 g (4 oz) cottage cheese
50 g (2 oz) English Cheddar, grated

1. Toast bread on one side only.
2. Peel and stone avocado, slice flesh and
dip in lemon juice.
3. Mix with cottage cheese and half of
Cheddar.
4. Spoon on to untoasted side of bread and
cover with remaining Cheddar.
5. Grill until warm and cheese has melted.

WELSH RAREBIT

Preparation 5 mins **Cooking** 10 mins   *Serves 4*

4 large slices of bread
25g (1oz) butter, softened
5ml (1tsp) made mustard
1.25ml (¼tsp) salt
shake of cayenne pepper
1.25ml (¼tsp) Worcestershire sauce
175g (6oz) Lancashire cheese or
   English Cheddar, grated
30ml (2tbsp) fresh milk

1. Toast bread on one side only.

2. Cream butter well. Stir in mustard, salt, cayenne pepper, Worcestershire sauce, cheese and milk.

3. Spread equal amounts thickly over untoasted sides of bread.

4. Brown under a hot grill.

Variation

BUCK RAREBIT

Follow recipe and method for Welsh rarebit (above). Serve each slice with a poached egg on top.

FRUITY CHEESE TOAST

Preparation 5 mins **Cooking** 5 mins   *Serves 1*

1 slice of soft grain bread
15ml (1tbsp) apricot chutney
1 small banana
40g (1½oz) Double Gloucester cheese, grated

1. Toast bread on one side only.
2. Spread untoasted side with chutney.
3. Peel and slice banana, arrange on top of chutney.
4. Cover with cheese and grill.
5. Serve hot.

PRAWN TOASTIES

Preparation 10 mins **Cooking** 7 mins   *Serves 2*

2 slices of wholemeal bread
100g (4oz) peeled prawns
100g (4oz) cottage cheese
1 garlic clove, crushed
50g (2oz) Cheshire cheese, grated
5ml (1tsp) sesame seeds (optional)

PRAWN TOASTIES

1. Toast bread on one side only.

2. Mix together prawns, cottage cheese, garlic and half of the cheese.

3. Spoon on to untoasted sides of bread.

4. Sprinkle with remaining cheese and sesame seeds.

5. Grill until heated through and serve.

DERBY GRILLS

Preparation 20 mins **Cooking** 10 mins   *Serves 2*

1 medium eating apple
lemon juice
2 slices of hot, buttered toast
2 sausages, cooked and sliced
apple chutney
75 g (3 oz) Sage Derby cheese, grated
paprika to garnish

1. Core apple, slice and dip into lemon juice.

2. Arrange on toast and place sausage on top.

3. Spread a little chutney over sausage and sprinkle over cheese.

4. Grill until cheese is bubbling.

5. Sprinkle with a little paprika to garnish.

6. Serve hot.

TASTY TOASTED SANDWICHES

Preparation 15 mins **Cooking** 2 mins   *Serves 4*

8 slices of wholemeal bread
50 g (2 oz) butter, softened
90 ml (6 tbsp) peach chutney
4 slices lean cooked ham
100 g (4 oz) Double Gloucester cheese with onions and chives, grated

1. Butter one side of each slice of bread.

2. Turn over and spread other side with chutney.

3. Place ham on chutney side of 4 slices of bread. Cover with grated cheese.

4. Top with remaining slices of bread, butter side up.

5. Press together and place in a preheated sandwich toaster.

6. Cook for about 2 minutes until crisp and browned. Alternatively grill until crisp.

7. Serve hot.

TOASTED LANCASHIRE CHEESE WITH APPLE SANDWICH

Preparation 10 mins **Cooking** 10 mins *Serves 4*

8 large slices of bread
butter
175g (6oz) Lancashire cheese, crumbled
2 eating apples, peeled, cored and sliced
watercress or parsley to garnish

1. Spread bread thickly with butter.
2. Sandwich together in pairs with filling.
3. Toast each sandwich lightly on both sides.
4. Press down firmly and cut into 2 triangles.
5. Garnish with watercress or parsley.
6. Serve immediately.

If cooking in a toasted sandwich maker, butter both sides of bread.

Variations

TOASTED CHEESE & PICKLE SANDWICH

Follow recipe and method for toasted Lancashire cheese and apple sandwich (above). Omit Lancashire cheese and apples. Fill with 175g (6oz) sliced English Cheddar and mustard pickle.

TOASTED BACON & MUSHROOM SANDWICH

Follow recipe and method for toasted Lancashire cheese and apple sandwich (above). Omit Lancashire cheese and apples. Fill with 225g (8oz) grilled bacon rashers and 100g (4oz) sliced and fried or grilled mushrooms.

TOASTED BEEF & TOMATO SANDWICH

Follow recipe and method for toasted Lancashire cheese with apple sandwich (above). Omit Lancashire cheese and apples. Fill with 175g (6oz) cold, sliced roast beef, made mustard and 4 sliced tomatoes.

HAWAIIAN CLUB SANDWICH

Preparation 15 mins **Cooking** 5 mins *Serves 1*

3 large slices of freshly made toast
butter
4 small crisp lettuce leaves
1 canned pineapple ring, well drained
50g (2oz) Derby cheese, sliced
mild mustard
2 stuffed olives or gherkins to garnish

1. Spread first slice of toast with butter and cover with lettuce leaves and pineapple ring.
2. Top with second slice of toast and spread with more butter.
3. Cover with cheese. Spread cheese with a little mild mustard.
4. Butter third slice of toast. Put on top of cheese, buttered side down.
5. Cut into 2 triangles and garnish with olives or gherkins speared on to cocktail sticks.

Variation

SAUSAGE & CHUTNEY CLUB SANDWICH

Follow recipe and method for Hawaiian club sandwich (above). For first layer, use crisp lettuce leaves topped with slices of cold cooked pork sausages. For second layer, use sliced Wensleydale cheese covered with sweet pickle or chutney.

PEPPERAMI MUFFINS

Preparation 20 mins **Cooking** 10 mins *Serves 2*

2 muffins
60ml (4 tbsp) tomato chutney
40g (1½oz) mushrooms, sliced
40g (1½oz) Red Leicester cheese, grated
40g (1½oz) Wensleydale cheese, grated
25g (1oz) stick of snack salami, sliced

1. Split muffins and toast one side of each.
2. Spread chutney over untoasted side of each one.
3. Arrange mushrooms on top of chutney.

4. Mix together cheeses and salami, divide between muffins.

5. Grill until cheese is bubbling.

6. Serve hot.

NUTTY STILTON CRUMPETS

Preparation 15 mins **Cooking** 10 mins *Makes 8*

175 g (6 oz) Blue Stilton cheese, crumbled
25 g (1 oz) butter, softened
15 ml (1 tbsp) port
15 ml (1 tbsp) natural yogurt
25 g (1 oz) chopped mixed nuts
8 crumpets
8 walnut halves, stuffed olives and
    chopped parsley to garnish

1. Combine cheese, butter, port and yogurt. Stir in nuts.

2. Toast one side of each crumpet.

3. Spread cheese mixture on to untoasted side of crumpets.

4. Grill until bubbling.

5. Garnish with walnuts, olives and parsley.

6. Serve hot.

HAM & PINEAPPLE TOPNOTS

Preparation 10 mins **Cooking** 15 mins *Serves 4*

4 ham steaks
4 crumpets
100 g (4 oz) English Cheddar, grated
2.5 ml (½ tsp) dry mustard
30 ml (2 tbsp) fresh milk
4 pineapple rings
watercress to garnish

1. Slowly grill ham steaks.

2. Toast crumpets at same time.

3. Mix cheese, mustard and milk together.

4. Spread on top of each toasted crumpet and grill until golden brown.

5. Place grilled ham steaks on top of toasted cheese and crown with rings of pineapple.

6. Heat through under grill.

7. Garnish with sprigs of watercress.

HAM & PINEAPPLE TOPNOTS

PIZZAS

PIZZA NEAPOLITAN ⓕ

Preparation 30 mins Cooking 35 mins *Serves 2*

1 small onion, finely chopped
1 garlic clove, crushed
30 ml (2 tbsp) oil
227 g (8 oz) can chopped tomatoes
10 ml (2 tsp) tomato purée
10 ml (2 tsp) dried mixed herbs
25 g (1 oz) mushrooms, sliced
salt and freshly ground pepper
150 g (5 oz) packet pizza base
 or bread mix
½ green pepper, seeded and sliced
50 g (2 oz) mozzarella cheese, grated
50 g (2 oz) English Cheddar, grated

1. Fry onion and garlic in oil until soft.
To microwave: Cook onion, garlic and oil, covered, for 3 minutes.

2. Add tomatoes, tomato purée and herbs. Bring to the boil and simmer for 5–10 minutes.
To microwave: Stir in tomatoes, tomato purée and herbs. Cook, uncovered, for 5 minutes.

3. Add mushrooms and continue cooking for 5–10 minutes or until most of the liquid has evaporated. Season to taste.
To microwave: Stir in mushrooms and cook, uncovered, for 5 minutes. Season to taste.

4. Make up pizza base mix as directed on packet. (To obtain hand hot water to make up dough, mix ⅓ boiling water with ⅔ cold water.)

5. Lightly grease a pizza tin or baking sheet.

6. Roll out dough on a floured work surface to approx. 20.5 cm (8 inch) and place in tin.

7. Spoon tomato mixture on to dough, arrange pepper on top.

8. Sprinkle with cheeses and bake in a pre-heated oven at 240°C (475°F) Mark 9 for 8–10 minutes.

For a thicker base allow dough to stand for 15 minutes before adding tomato topping.

Variations

PEPPERONI PIZZA ⓕ

Follow recipe and method for pizza Neapolitan (left), add an extra 50 g (2 oz) mushrooms to sauce and top with 50 g (2 oz) sliced pepperoni.

BEEF & TOMATO PIZZA ⓕ

Follow recipe and method for pizza Neapolitan (left), adding 225 g (8 oz) minced beef with onion and garlic. Also add 30 ml (2 tbsp) Worcestershire sauce to sauce, and cook for 20 minutes.

SEAFOOD PIZZA

Follow recipe and method for pizza Neapolitan (left), adding 50 g (2 oz) peeled prawns to sauce and topping with 50 g (1.8 oz) can drained anchovy fillets.

FRUIT & NUT PIZZA

Follow recipe and method for pizza Neapolitan (left), adding 25 g (1 oz) sultanas, 25 g (1 oz) capers and 25 g (1 oz) pine nuts to tomato sauce and topping with 50 g (2 oz) black olives and 2 rings of canned pineapple, chopped.

RATATOUILLE PIZZA

Follow recipe and method for pizza Neapolitan (left), and use 390 g (13.7 oz) can ratatouille instead of tomato sauce and omit steps 1–3. Top with 75 g (3 oz) sliced mushrooms and cheese.

HOT 'N' SPICY PIZZA Ⓕ

Preparation 25 mins
Cooking 12–15 mins   *Serves 4*

225 g (8 oz) self raising flour
50 g (2 oz) butter
100 ml (4 fl oz) fresh milk
397 g (14 oz) can chopped tomatoes, drained
198 g (7 oz) can sweetcorn, drained
99 g (3.5 oz) can tuna in brine, drained and flaked
2 fresh green chillis, seeded and sliced
100 g (4 oz) Double Gloucester cheese, sliced
50 g (1.8 oz) tin anchovies, drained

1. Place flour in a bowl, rub in butter until mixture resembles breadcrumbs.

2. Add milk and mix to a dough.

3. Roll out to 28×18 cm (11×7 inches).

4. Place on a greased baking sheet and spread with tomatoes.

5. Arrange remaining ingredients on top.

6. Bake at 220°C (425°F) Mark 7 for 12–15 minutes until golden brown.

FRENCH BREAD PIZZAS Ⓕ

Preparation 25 mins **Cooking** 5 mins   *Makes 2*

15 cm (6 inch) length French bread
60 ml (4 tbsp) tomato ketchup
5 ml (1 tsp) dried mixed herbs
½ small onion, thinly sliced
½ green pepper, seeded and chopped
50 g (2 oz) mushrooms, sliced
75 g (3 oz) Double Gloucester cheese with chives and onion, grated
4 black grapes, halved, to garnish

1. Cut bread in half lengthways.

2. Toast crust side.

3. Mix together tomato ketchup and herbs and spread on to cut side of bread.

4. Add onion, pepper and mushrooms.

5. Top with cheese and grill. Serve hot garnished with grapes.

Variation

WENSLEYDALE PIZZAS

Follow recipe and method for French bread pizzas (above). Omit Double Gloucester cheese and grapes. Use crumbled Wensleydale cheese and garnish with anchovy fillets and black olives.

PIZZA NEAPOLITAN

SAUCES
STUFFINGS
MARINADES

BRANDY SAUCE PAGE 241 · CRANBERRY SAUCE PAGE 236
BRANDY BUTTER (HARD SAUCE) PAGE 245 · CHESTNUT STUFFING PAGE 247

SAVOURY SAUCES

SAUCES

A **pouring sauce** will glaze the back of a wooden spoon and pours easily. Use for vegetables, pasta, or serving separately, or if you prefer a thin sauce.

A **coating sauce** will coat the back of a wooden spoon and will only just settle to its own level in the saucepan. Use for coating eggs, chicken, fish and vegetables.

If you use wholemeal flour for a sauce you will need to add a little extra liquid and cook slightly longer to fully cook the flour.

BASIC WHITE POURING SAUCE Ⓕ

Preparation 2 mins **Cooking** 15 mins   *Serves 4*

15g (½oz) butter
15g (½oz) flour
300ml (½pint) fresh milk
salt and freshly ground pepper

1. Melt butter in a saucepan. Add flour and cook over a low heat, stirring, for 2 minutes. Do not allow mixture (roux) to brown.
To microwave: Melt butter in a bowl or jug for 30 seconds and stir in flour. Cook, uncovered, for ½–1 minute.
2. Gradually blend in milk.
3. Cook, stirring, until sauce thickens, boils and is smooth.
To microwave: Cook for 3–4 minutes, stirring frequently, until sauce thickens, boils and is smooth.
4. Simmer gently for 3 minutes.
To microwave: Cook for ½–1 minute.
5. Season to taste.

Variation

BASIC WHITE COATING SAUCE Ⓕ

Follow recipe and method for basic white pouring sauce (above). Increase butter and flour to 25g (1oz) each.

ONE STAGE WHITE SAUCE Ⓕ

Follow recipe for basic white pouring sauce (left). Put butter, flour and milk into a saucepan. Heat, whisking continuously, until sauce thickens, boils and is smooth. Season.
To microwave: Put flour in a bowl or jug and gradually blend in milk. Add butter and cook for 3–4 minutes, stirring frequently, until sauce thickens, boils and is smooth.

SIMPLE WHITE POURING SAUCE Ⓕ

Preparation 5 mins **Cooking** 15 mins   *Serves 4–6*

15g (½oz) cornflour
300ml (½pint) fresh milk
small knob of butter (optional)
salt and freshly ground pepper

1. Mix cornflour to a smooth paste with a little cold milk.
2. Warm remainder of milk. Pour on to paste and mix well.
To microwave: Heat remaining milk for 2 minutes. Pour on to paste and mix well.
3. Return to pan.
To microwave: Return to bowl or jug.
4. Cook, stirring, until sauce thickens, boils and is smooth.
To microwave: Cook for 1–2 minutes, stirring frequently, until sauce thickens, boils and is smooth.
5. Simmer for 2 minutes.
To microwave: Cook for ½–1 minute.
6. Remove from heat and stir in butter, if used. Season to taste.

Variation

SIMPLE WHITE COATING SAUCE Ⓕ

Follow recipe and method for simple white pouring sauce (above). Increase cornflour to 20g (¾oz).

PARSLEY SAUCE   Ⓕ

For bacon, ham and fish dishes.

Follow recipe and method for either basic white pouring sauce or basic white coating sauce (page 231). After seasoning, stir in 30 ml (2 tbsp) chopped parsley.

CHEESE SAUCE   Ⓕ

For fish, poultry, ham, bacon, egg and vegetable dishes.

Follow recipe and method for either basic white pouring sauce or basic white coating sauce (page 231). Before seasoning, stir in 50 g (2 oz) finely grated English Cheddar or 50 g (2 oz) crumbled Lancashire cheese, 2.5–5 ml (½–1 tsp) made mustard and a pinch of cayenne pepper.

MUSTARD SAUCE   Ⓕ

For herring, mackerel, cheese, ham and bacon dishes.

Follow recipe and method for either basic white pouring sauce or basic white coating sauce (page 231). Before seasoning, stir in 10 ml (2 tsp) dry mustard mixed with 10 ml (2 tsp) vinegar. Reheat gently before using.

MUSHROOM SAUCE   Ⓕ

For fish, poultry, veal, egg and cheese dishes.

Follow recipe and method for either basic white pouring sauce or basic white coating sauce (page 231). Before seasoning stir in 50–75 g (2–3 oz) mushrooms – finely chopped and lightly fried in butter. Reheat gently before using.

PRAWN SAUCE

For fish dishes.

Follow recipe and method for either basic white pouring sauce or basic white coating sauce (page 231). Before seasoning, stir in 50 g (2 oz) finely chopped, peeled prawns, 2.5 ml (½ tsp) dry mustard mixed with 10 ml (2 tsp) lemon juice and 2.5 ml (½ tsp) anchovy essence. Reheat gently before using.

ONION SAUCE   Ⓕ

For tripe, grilled and roast lamb.

Follow recipe and method for either basic white pouring sauce or basic white coating sauce (page 231). Before seasoning stir in 1 large onion, boiled and finely chopped. Reheat gently before using.

LEMON SAUCE   Ⓕ

For fish, poultry, egg and veal dishes

Follow recipe and method for either basic white pouring sauce or basic white coating sauce (page 231) Before seasoning stir in the grated rind of 1 small lemon and 15 ml (1 tbsp) lemon juice. Reheat gently before using.

RICH WHITE SAUCE (BÉCHAMEL)   Ⓕ

Preparation 15 mins **plus** 30 mins **standing**
Cooking 25 mins   *Serves 4*

For fish, poultry, egg and vegetable dishes

300 ml (½ pint) fresh milk
1 small onion, quartered
1 small carrot, sliced
½ small celery stick, sliced
2 cloves
6 white peppercorns
1 blade of mace
1 sprig of parsley
25 g (1 oz) butter
25 g (1 oz) flour
salt and freshly ground pepper
30 ml (2 tbsp) fresh double cream

1. Put milk into a saucepan.
To microwave: Put milk in a large bowl or jug.

2. Add onion, carrot, celery, cloves, peppercorns, mace and parsley.

3. Slowly bring just to the boil.
To microwave: Cook, uncovered, for 4–5 mins until just boiling.

4. Remove from heat and cover. Leave to stand for 30 mins.

5. Strain and reserve flavoured milk.

RICH WHITE SAUCE (BÉCHAMEL)

6. Melt butter in pan, add flour and cook over a low heat, stirring, for 2 mins. Do not allow mixture (or roux) to brown.
To microwave: Melt butter in a bowl for 30 secs, stir in flour and cook, uncovered, for 1 min.

7. Gradually blend in flavoured milk.

8. Cook, stirring, until sauce thickens, boils and is smooth. Simmer gently for 3 mins.
To microwave: Cook for 3–4 mins, stirring frequently, until sauce thickens, boils and is smooth. Cook for a further 1 min.

9. Remove from heat, season, stir in cream.

Variations

MOCK HOLLANDAISE

For poultry and fish dishes.

Follow recipe and method for Béchamel sauce (left). Before seasoning, stir in 1 egg yolk mixed with 30 ml (2 tbsp) fresh double cream and 10 ml (2 tsp) lemon juice. Reheat gently. Do not allow to boil.

AURORE SAUCE 

For fish and egg dishes.

Follow recipe and method for Béchamel sauce (left). Before seasoning, stir in 30 ml (2 tbsp) tomato purée and 2.5 ml (½ tsp) sugar. Reheat gently. Do not boil.

MORNAY SAUCE

For poultry, fish, shellfish and egg dishes.

Follow recipe and method for Béchamel sauce (left). Before seasoning, stir in an extra 30 ml (2 tbsp) fresh double cream and 50 g (2 oz) grated English Cheddar. Stand over a low heat. Whisk until sauce is smooth. Do not allow to boil.

BLENDER HOLLANDAISE

Preparation 10 mins **Cooking** 5 mins   *Serves 4*

3 egg yolks
15 ml (1 tbsp) lemon juice
salt and freshly ground pepper
100 g (4 oz) butter, melted

1. Place egg yolks, lemon juice and seasoning in a blender or food processor.

2. Cover and blend for a few secs to mix.

3. Gradually pour hot, melted butter into blender while processing at high speed.

4. Blend until thick and light.

5. Serve immediately.

HOLLANDAISE SAUCE

Preparation 5 mins **Cooking** 15 mins   *Serves 6*

For asparagus, broccoli, poached fish, egg and chicken dishes

5 ml (1 tsp) lemon juice
5 ml (1 tsp) wine vinegar
15 ml (1 tbsp) cold water
3 white peppercorns
½ small bay leaf
4 egg yolks
225 g (8 oz) butter, softened
salt and freshly ground pepper

1. Put lemon juice, vinegar, water, peppercorns and bay leaf into a saucepan. Boil gently until liquor is reduced by half.

2. Leave until cold and strain.

3. Put egg yolks and reduced vinegar liquor into a double saucepan (or basin standing over a pan of gently simmering water).

4. Whisk until thick and foamy.

5. Gradually add butter, a tiny piece at a time. Continue whisking until each piece has been absorbed by the sauce.

6. Season to taste.

7. Serve immediately.

Variation

MOUSSELINE SAUCE

For same dishes as hollandaise sauce.

Follow recipe and method for hollandaise sauce (left). Stir in 45 ml (3 tbsp) lightly whipped fresh double cream just before serving.

VELOUTÉ SAUCE   🅕

Preparation 5 mins **Cooking** 50 mins *Serves 4–6*

For poultry and veal, or poached, grilled and steamed fish dishes

25 g (1 oz) butter
25 g (1 oz) mushrooms, finely chopped
2 or 3 parsley sprigs
25 g (1 oz) flour
300 ml (½ pint) poultry, veal or fish stock (depending on dish)
2 peppercorns
10 ml (2 tsp) lemon juice
60 ml (4 tbsp) fresh double cream
    or soured cream
salt and freshly ground pepper

1. Melt butter in a saucepan. Add mushrooms and parsley and fry gently for 5 minutes.
To microwave: Cook butter and mushrooms in a bowl or jug, covered, for 2 minutes.

2. Stir in flour. Gradually blend in stock. Add peppercorns.

3. Cook, stirring, until sauce comes to the boil and thickens.
To microwave: Cook for 3–4 minutes, stirring frequently until sauce thickens, boils and is smooth.

4. Reduce heat, cover pan. Simmer very gently for 30 minutes.
To microwave: Cover loosely and cook on MEDIUM–LOW (30%) for 10 minutes, stirring occasionally.

5. Strain, stir in lemon juice and cream. Season to taste.

6. Reheat gently before using. Do not allow to boil.
To microwave: Cook for 30 seconds to heat through.

BÉARNAISE SAUCE

Preparation 5 mins **Cooking** 20 mins   *Serves 4*

For meat grills and roasts or grilled fish

30 ml (2 tbsp) tarragon wine vinegar
45 ml (3 tbsp) wine vinegar
15 ml (1 tbsp) finely chopped onion
2 egg yolks
10 ml (2 tsp) cold water
100 g (4 oz) butter, softened
salt and freshly ground pepper
15 ml (1 tbsp) chopped parsley

1. Put both vinegars and onion into a saucepan. Boil gently until liquid is reduced by about one-third.

2. Leave until cold and strain.

3. Put egg yolks, reduced vinegar liquor and water into a double saucepan (or basin standing over a pan of simmering water). Whisk until thick and fluffy.

4. Gradually add butter, a tiny piece at a time. Continue whisking until each piece has been absorbed by the sauce and it has thickened.

5. Season to taste and stir in parsley.

BÉARNAISE SAUCE

MEAT OR POULTRY GRAVY Ⓕ

Preparation 5 mins **Cooking** 15 mins *Serves 4–6*

fat and sediment from roasting tin
15 ml (1 tbsp) cornflour
300 ml (½ pint) stock or vegetable water

1. Pour off all but 15 ml (1 tbsp) fat from roasting tin.
To microwave: Pour 15 ml (1 tbsp) meat fat and sediment from roasting tin into a bowl or jug.

2. Add cornflour, mix with fat and sediment.

3. Stand tin over a low heat. Gradually blend in stock or vegetable water.
To microwave: Gradually blend in stock or cooking water from vegetables.

4. Cook, stirring, until gravy comes to the boil and thickens.
To microwave: Cook for 3–4 minutes, stirring frequently until gravy thickens, boils and is smooth.

5. Lower heat. Simmer for 3 minutes.
To microwave: Cook for ½–1 minute.

CUMBERLAND SAUCE Ⓕ

Preparation 10 mins **plus** 10 mins **standing**
Cooking 10 mins *Serves 4*

For ham and game dishes

150 ml (¼ pint) red wine or port
60 ml (4 tbsp) redcurrant jelly
grated rind and juice of 1 medium lemon
    and orange
10 ml (2 tsp) finely grated onion
5 ml (1 tsp) made mustard
1.25 ml (¼ tsp) ground ginger
salt and freshly ground pepper

1. Put all ingredients into a pan. Slowly bring just up to the boil, stirring occasionally.
To microwave: Put all ingredients in a bowl or jug and cook for about 4 minutes, stirring occasionally, until boiling.

2. Remove from heat. Cover and leave for 10 minutes.

3. Leave unstrained and serve hot or strain and serve cold.

CRANBERRY SAUCE Ⓕ

Preparation 3 mins **Cooking** 25 mins *Serves 6*

For poultry, duck, goose, game, turkey and lamb.

300 ml (½ pint) water
175 g (6 oz) granulated sugar
225 g (8 oz) cranberries

1. Put water and sugar into a saucepan. Heat slowly until sugar dissolves.
To microwave: Put water and sugar into a large bowl and cook for 3 minutes, stirring frequently, until sugar dissolves.

2. Add cranberries. Cook fairly quickly for 2–3 minutes or until skins pop open.
To microwave: Stir in cranberries, cover loosely and cook for 4–5 minutes, stirring twice, until skins pop open.

3. Reduce heat. Simmer gently for 10 minutes.
To microwave: Uncover and cook on MEDIUM (50%) for 10 minutes, stirring once.

4. Serve hot or cold.

APPLE SAUCE Ⓕ

Preparation 10 mins **Cooking** 15 mins *Serves 6*

For grilled or roast pork, duck and goose dishes

450 g (1 lb) cooking apples,
    peeled, cored and sliced
45 ml (3 tbsp) water
10 ml (2 tsp) caster sugar (optional)

1. Put apples into a saucepan with water and cook until soft and pulpy.
To microwave: Put apples into a large bowl with 30 ml (2 tbsp) water. Cover and cook for 5 minutes, stirring twice.

2. Either beat to a purée or rub through a sieve or liquidise.

3. Return to pan, add sugar, if used.
To microwave: Return to bowl and add sugar, if used

4. Reheat gently.
To microwave: Cook for 1–2 minutes to heat through.

5. Serve hot or cold.

BREAD SAUCE Ⓕ

Preparation 5 mins **Cooking** 30 mins *Serves 4–6*

For roast poultry

4 cloves
1 small onion
6 peppercorns
1 blade of mace or
    large pinch of ground nutmeg
½ small bay leaf
300 ml (½ pint) fresh milk
50 g (2 oz) fresh white breadcrumbs
salt and freshly ground pepper
25 g (1 oz) butter
30 ml (2 tbsp) fresh single cream

1. Press cloves into onion and put into a saucepan.
To microwave: Press cloves into onion and put in a bowl.

2. Add peppercorns, mace or nutmeg, bay leaf and milk.

3. Slowly bring to the boil. Reduce heat, cover pan and simmer for 15 minutes.
To microwave: Cover loosely and cook for about 5 minutes until boiling. Continue cooking on MEDIUM–LOW (30%) for 10 minutes.

4. Strain. Combine hot milk with breadcrumbs. Simmer gently for 10–15 minutes. Stir occasionally.
To microwave: Strain. Combine hot milk with breadcrumbs. Cook on MEDIUM (50%) for 5 minutes, stirring occasionally.

5. Season to taste, stir in butter and cream.

6. Reheat gently.
To microwave: Cook, uncovered, for 1 minute. Stir well.

MINT SAUCE Ⓕ

Preparation 10 mins   *Serves 4–6*

For roast lamb

60 ml (4 tbsp) finely chopped fresh mint
45 ml (3 tbsp) boiling water
15 ml (1 tbsp) caster sugar
1.25 ml (¼ tsp) salt
45 ml (3 tbsp) vinegar

1. Stir mint into boiling water. Add sugar and salt.

2. Leave until cold.

3. Add vinegar and mix well.

TOMATO SAUCE 🌀

Preparation 10 mins
Cooking 25 mins   *Serves 4–6*

For meat, fish, eggs and pasta dishes

25 g (1 oz) butter
5 ml (1 tsp) oil
1 medium onion, chopped
1 garlic clove, crushed
397 g (14 oz) can chopped tomatoes
15 ml (1 tbsp) tomato purée
300 ml (½ pint) vegetable stock
pinch of ground mace
10 ml (2 tsp) dried mixed herbs
freshly ground pepper

1. Heat butter and oil in a saucepan. Add onion and garlic and fry until golden.
To microwave: Cook butter, oil, onion and garlic, covered, for 3 minutes.

2. Stir in tomatoes, tomato purée, stock, mace and herbs.

3. Season to taste.

4. Bring to the boil, stirring. Reduce heat and cover.
To microwave: Cook, uncovered, for 5 minutes until boiling. Stir well.

5. Simmer gently for 20 minutes.
To microwave: Cook, uncovered, for 10 minutes, stirring occasionally.

BARBECUE SAUCE 🌀

Preparation 3 mins **Cooking** 25 mins *Serves 4–6*

For meat, poultry or fish

300 ml (½ pint) tomato ketchup
25 g (1 oz) butter
45 ml (3 tbsp) vinegar
1.25 ml (¼ tsp) chilli powder
5 ml (1 tsp) brown sugar
2.5 ml (½ tsp) celery salt
2.5 ml (½ tsp) dried mixed herbs

1. Put all ingredients into a saucepan.
To microwave: Put all ingredients into a bowl or jug and stir well.

2. Bring slowly to the boil, stirring.
To microwave: Cover and cook for 4–5 minutes, stirring frequently, until boiling.

3. Cover pan and simmer gently for 15 minutes.
To microwave: Cook, covered, on MEDIUM–LOW (30%) for 8–10 minutes.

BROWN (OR ESPAGNOLE) SAUCE 🅕

Preparation 20 mins **Cooking** 1 hr   *Serves 4*

25 g (1 oz) butter
5 ml (1 tsp) oil
25 g (1 oz) lean ham or bacon, chopped
½ small onion, chopped
½ small celery stick, chopped
25 g (1 oz) mushrooms, chopped
½ small carrot, sliced
25 g (1 oz) flour
450 ml (¾ pint) beef stock
10 ml (2 tsp) tomato purée or 1 small
   chopped tomato
1 small bay leaf
2 sprigs of parsley
salt and freshly ground pepper

1. Put butter and oil into pan. Heat until both are sizzling.
2. Add ham or bacon, onion, celery, mushrooms and carrot.
3. Fry gently for 7–10 minutes or until golden.
4. Add flour and cook, stirring, until it turns light brown.
5. Gradually blend in stock. Cook, stirring, until sauce comes to the boil and thickens.
6. Add purée or chopped tomato, bay leaf and parsley. Cover pan.
7. Simmer gently for 30 minutes.
8. Strain, season to taste.
9. Reheat before using.
If a darker colour is desired add a few drops of gravy browning.

LEMON BUTTER SAUCE

Preparation 5 mins **Cooking** 5 mins   *Serves 4*

For poached and steamed fish dishes

75 g (3 oz) clarified butter (page 240)
15 ml (1 tbsp) chopped parsley
5 ml (1 tsp) lemon juice

1. Place butter in a saucepan. Heat gently until it turns light brown.
2. Stir in remaining ingredients.
3. Serve immediately.

BARBECUE SAUCE

CLARIFIED BUTTER   Ⓕ

Clarifying butter raises the temperature at which butter browns and burns and also allows you to store it for a longer period of time.

It can be used for cooking, melted as a sauce or for sealing such foods as pâtés.

1. Place butter in a pan and melt over a low heat.
To microwave: Place butter in a bowl and cook on MEDIUM–LOW (30%) until melted.

2. Leave to stand for a few minutes then strain through muslin into a clean bowl.

3. Discard milky sediment in base of pan.

4. Store in refrigerator.

5. Melt required amount of clarified butter when ready to use.

SWEET & SOUR SAUCE

Preparation 5 mins
Cooking 30 mins   *Serves 4–6*

For meat fondues, meats or poultry

50 g (2 oz) butter
2 medium onions, finely chopped
30 ml (2 tbsp) tomato purée
300 ml (½ pint) cider
150 ml (¼ pint) water
15 ml (1 tbsp) demerara sugar
salt and freshly ground pepper
30 ml (2 tbsp) Worcestershire sauce
30 ml (2 tbsp) mango chutney
15 ml (1 tbsp) arrowroot

1. Melt butter in a saucepan and fry onions until soft but not brown.
To microwave: Cook butter and onions, covered, for 5 minutes, stirring once.

2. Add all remaining ingredients except arrowroot.

3. Bring to the boil, stirring and simmer for 15–20 minutes uncovered.
To microwave: Cook, uncovered, for 10 minutes, stirring occasionally.

4. Blend arrowroot with 30 ml (2 tbsp) water, add to pan and cook, stirring, for 1 minute.
To microwave: Blend arrowroot with 30 ml (2 tbsp) water, add to sauce and cook for 1 minute. Stir well.

5. Serve hot or cold.

CURRY SAUCE   Ⓕ

Preparation 10 mins
Cooking 1 hr 15 mins   *Serves 4*

For pouring over hard-boiled eggs or mixing with cooked fish, chicken, meat or vegetables

50 g (2 oz) butter
10 ml (2 tsp) oil
2 large onions, finely chopped
1 garlic clove, crushed
30 ml (2 tbsp) curry powder
15 ml (1 tbsp) flour
2 cloves
15 ml (1 tbsp) tomato purée
1.25 ml (¼ tsp) *each*, ground ginger and cinnamon
30 ml (2 tbsp) sweet pickle or chutney
15 ml (1 tbsp) lemon juice
450 ml (¾ pint) stock or water

1. Put butter and oil into a pan. Heat until both are sizzling.
To microwave: Put butter and oil into a large bowl or jug and melt for 45 seconds.

2. Add onions and garlic. Fry gently until pale gold.
To microwave: Stir in onions and garlic, cover and cook for 5 minutes, stirring once.

3. Stir in curry powder and flour. Add cloves, tomato purée, ginger and cinnamon, sweet pickle or chutney and lemon juice.

4. Gradually blend in stock or water. Slowly bring to the boil, stirring.
To microwave: Gradually blend in BOILING stock or water and cook for about 4 minutes until boiling. Stir well.

5. Lower heat and cover pan. Simmer slowly for 45 minutes–1 hour.
To microwave: Cover and cook on MEDIUM (50%) for about 15 minutes, stirring occasionally.

6. The sauce may be strained and reheated before using.

SWEET SAUCES

SWEET WHITE SAUCE

Preparation 5 mins
Cooking 15 mins   *Serves 4–6*

For steamed and baked puddings

15 g (½ oz) cornflour
300 ml (½ pint) fresh milk
knob of butter
15 ml (1 tbsp) caster sugar

1. Mix cornflour to a smooth paste with a little of the cold milk.

2. Warm remaining milk in a pan. Pour on to paste and mix well. Return to pan.
To microwave: Cook remaining milk for 2 minutes, pour on to paste and mix well.

3. Cook, stirring until sauce thickens, boils and is smooth. Simmer for 2 minutes.
To microwave: Cook for about 2 minutes, stirring frequently, until sauce thickens, boils and is smooth.

4. Remove from heat. Stir in butter and sugar.

Variations

BRANDY SAUCE

For Christmas puddings, baked and steamed fruit puddings.

Follow recipe and method for sweet white sauce (above). Add 30 ml (2 tbsp) brandy with butter and sugar.

VANILLA SAUCE

For steamed and baked puddings

Follow recipe and method for sweet white sauce (above). Add 5 ml (1 tsp) vanilla essence with butter and sugar.

COCOA SAUCE

Follow recipe and method for sweet white sauce (above). Add 15 g (½ oz) cocoa powder with the cornflour.

RUBY RED SAUCE

Preparation 10 mins **Cooking** 7 mins   *Serves 6*

For ice-cream or steamed puddings

225 g (8 oz) frozen summer fruits, thawed
175 g (6 oz) redcurrant jelly
50 ml (2 fl oz) port
10 ml (2 tsp) arrowroot

1. Place fruit in a blender or food processor and purée.

2. Pass through a sieve to remove seeds.

3. Place purée in a saucepan with jelly and port.
To microwave: Place purée in a bowl or jug with jelly and port.

4. Heat until jelly has melted.
To microwave: Cook for about 4 minutes, stirring frequently, or until jelly has melted.

5. Blend arrowroot with a little water, add a little warm sauce then stir into pan.
To microwave: Blend arrowroot with a little water, add a little warm sauce, then stir into bowl.

6. Cook, stirring until sauce thickens.
To microwave: Cook for 1 minute or until sauce thickens.

RASPBERRY SAUCE

Preparation 10 mins   *Serves 6*

For fresh fruit, ice cream and mousses

225 g (8 oz) raspberries
icing sugar, sifted

1. Place raspberries in a blender or food processor and purée.

2. Pass through a sieve to remove seeds.

3. Stir sufficient icing sugar into fruit purée to sweeten to taste.

4. Serve, or store in refrigerator.

JAM OR MARMALADE SAUCE · SPONGE PUDDING (PAGE 266)

JAM OR MARMALADE SAUCE

Preparation 5 mins
Cooking 15 mins   *Serves 4–6*

For steamed and baked puddings

10 ml (2 tsp) arrowroot or cornflour
150 ml (¼ pint) cold water
60 ml (4 tbsp) jam or marmalade
10 ml (2 tsp) lemon juice

1. Mix arrowroot or cornflour to a smooth paste with a little of the cold water.

2. Put remaining water into a pan. Add jam or marmalade and lemon juice.
To microwave: Put remaining water into a bowl or jug and add jam or marmalade and lemon juice.

3. Heat gently, stir until jam has dissolved. Blend with arrowroot or cornflour paste.
To microwave: Cook for 2 minutes, stirring twice, until jam has dissolved. Pour on to arrowroot or cornflour paste.

4. Return to pan. Cook, stirring, until sauce boils, thickens and clears.
To microwave: Return to bowl or jug and cook for 1–2 minutes, stirring once, until sauce boils, thickens and clears.

5. Simmer for 2 minutes.
To microwave: Cook for a further 30 seconds.

BUTTERSCOTCH SAUCE

Preparation 2 mins
Cooking 15 mins   *Serves 4–6*

For steamed and baked puddings, sliced bananas, or ice cream

150 ml (5 fl oz) fresh double cream
50 g (2 oz) unsalted butter
75 g (3 oz) soft light brown sugar
2.5 ml (½ tsp) vanilla essence

1. Place cream, butter and sugar in a saucepan.
To microwave: Place cream, diced butter and sugar in a bowl.

2. Heat gently, stirring until sugar has dissolved.
To microwave: Cook for 1½ minutes. Stir well until sugar has dissolved.

3. Boil for 2 minutes until syrupy.
To microwave: Cook for 2 minutes, stirring once or twice, until syrupy.

4. Stir in vanilla and serve warm.

242

CHOCOLATE SAUCE

Preparation 10 mins
Cooking 15 mins   *Serves 4–6*

For steamed and baked puddings

15 ml (1 tbsp) cornflour
300 ml (½ pint) fresh milk
50 g (2 oz) plain chocolate, grated
2.5 ml (½ tsp) vanilla essence
15 g (½ oz) butter
15 ml (1 tbsp) caster sugar

1. Mix cornflour to a smooth paste with a little of the cold milk.

2. Put remaining milk into a saucepan and add chocolate. Heat very slowly until chocolate melts.
To microwave: Pour remaining milk into a bowl or jug and add chocolate. Cook for 2 minutes, stir once, until chocolate melts.

3. Pour on to cornflour paste and mix well. Return to pan.
To microwave: Pour on to cornflour paste and mix well. Return to bowl or jug.

4. Cook, stirring, until sauce comes to the boil and thickens.
To microwave: Cook for 2 minutes, stirring once until sauce boils and thickens.

5. Add vanilla, butter and sugar. Simmer for 3 minutes.
To microwave: Add vanilla, butter and sugar and cook for 1 minute.

LUXURY CHOCOLATE SAUCE

Preparation 5 mins **Cooking** 5 mins   *Serves 4–6*

For ice cream or profiteroles

175 g (6 oz) plain chocolate
20 g (¾ oz) butter
45 ml (3 tbsp) water
45 ml (3 tbsp) golden syrup
5 ml (1 tsp) vanilla essence

1. Break chocolate into small pieces.

2. Place in a small pan with butter, water and golden syrup.
To microwave: Place in a bowl or jug with butter, water and golden syrup.

3. Heat gently until chocolate has melted.
To microwave: Cook on MEDIUM (50%) for 2–3 minutes, stirring twice.

4. Remove from heat. Add vanilla essence and stir to mix. Serve warm.

BUTTERSCOTCH SAUCE

REAL CUSTARD SAUCE

Preparation 5 mins **plus** 15 mins **standing**
Cooking 15 mins
Serves 4–6

For steamed and baked puddings, fruit and mince pies, stewed fruit

300 ml (½ pint) fresh milk
1 vanilla pod
4 egg yolks
25 g (1 oz) sugar

1. Reserve 45 ml (3 tbsp) milk. Place remaining milk and vanilla pod in a saucepan. Bring almost to the boil.
To microwave: Reserve 45 ml (3 tbsp) milk. Put remaining milk and vanilla pod into a bowl or jug and cook for 2 minutes, until almost boiling.

2. Remove from heat and leave to stand for 15 minutes.

3. Place egg yolks, sugar and reserved milk in a bowl. Beat until thick and creamy.

4. Remove vanilla pod from milk and pour milk on to egg mixture.

5. Strain mixture into a heavy based saucepan and cook, stirring, until custard thinly coats the back of a spoon (about the thickness of single cream).
To microwave: Strain mixture into a bowl or jug and cook for 1 minute. Continue cooking on MEDIUM–LOW (30%) for 4–5 minutes, stirring frequently, or until custard thinly coats the back of a spoon – about the thickness of single cream.

6. Pour into a cold jug.

7. Serve hot or cold. The sauce thickens on cooling.

Variations

COFFEE CUSTARD SAUCE

Follow recipe and method for real custard sauce (left). Omit vanilla and add 5 ml (1 tsp) instant coffee granules to warm milk.

ORANGE CUSTARD SAUCE

Follow recipe and method for real custard sauce (left). Omit vanilla and add 5 ml (1 tsp) grated orange rind before heating milk.

REAL CUSTARD SAUCE

FRUIT SAUCE

Preparation 2 mins **Cooking** 5 mins   *Serves 4*

For ice cream, baked or steamed puddings

30 ml (2 tbsp) cornflour
300 ml (½ pint) fruit juice

1. Blend cornflour with a little of the juice.
2. Heat remaining juice in a pan until almost boiling.
To microwave: Pour remaining juice into a bowl or jug and cook for about 3 minutes or until almost boiling.
3. Stir hot juice on to cornflour mixture, stirring.
4. Pour back into pan and bring to the boil stirring.
To microwave: Cook for 1–2 minutes, stirring once, until boiling.
5. Cook for 1 minute.
To microwave: Cook for 30 seconds.
6. Serve immediately.

FUDGE SAUCE

Preparation 10 mins **Cooking** 15 mins   *Serves 4*

For ice cream, steamed and baked puddings

25 g (1 oz) plain chocolate
15 g (½ oz) butter
30 ml (2 tbsp) fresh milk, warmed
100 g (4 oz) soft brown sugar
15 ml (1 tbsp) golden syrup
2.5 ml (½ tsp) vanilla essence

1. Break up chocolate. Put into a basin standing over a saucepan of hot water. Add butter.
To microwave: Break chocolate into a bowl or jug. Add butter.
2. Leave until chocolate and butter have melted, stirring once or twice.
To microwave: Cook on MEDIUM (50%) for 1–2 minutes, stirring once, until melted.
3. Blend in milk. Transfer to a pan. Add sugar and golden syrup.
To microwave: Blend in milk and add sugar and golden syrup.

4. Stand over a low heat. Stir until sugar has dissolved.
To microwave: Stir well until sugar has dissolved.
5. Bring to the boil. Boil steadily without stirring for 5 minutes.
To microwave: Cook for about 1 minute until boiling, then cook for a further 1 minute without stirring.
6. Remove from heat. Add vanilla and mix well.
7. Serve hot.

For a sauce that hardens quickly over ice cream, boil for an extra 2–3 minutes. If there is any sauce left over, it can be reheated in a basin over a pan of simmering water.

BRANDY BUTTER (HARD SAUCE) Ⓕ

Preparation 20 mins   *Serves 6–8*

For Christmas puddings, mince pies, baked and steamed fruit puddings

100 g (4 oz) butter, softened
100 g (4 oz) icing sugar, sifted
100 g (4 oz) caster sugar
15 ml (1 tbsp) fresh milk
15 ml (1 tbsp) brandy
50 g (2 oz) ground almonds
ground cinnamon

1. Beat butter until creamy.
2. Gradually beat in icing and caster sugars alternately with milk and brandy. Cream until light and fluffy.
3. Add almonds and mix well.
4. Pile into small dish. Sprinkle lightly with cinnamon.

Variation

RUM BUTTER Ⓕ

Follow recipe and method for brandy butter (above) but use rum in place of brandy.

STUFFINGS

Stuffings should not be made over-wet by the addition of too much milk, egg, water or stock, etc. For best results, the stuffing should be fairly loose and crumbly but at the same time be firm enough to hold its shape when gathered together either with a fork, spoon or fingertips. When stuffing a bird only place stuffing in the neck end, not in the body cavity unless it is boned. Do not stuff poultry, meat, fish, etc, until just before it is to be cooked.

Do not pack stuffing too tightly as it will expand on cooking. Cook any surplus stuffing in an ovenproof dish.

SAUSAGEMEAT STUFFING   Ⓕ

Preparation 15 mins

For chicken, turkey, veal and beef

225 g (8 oz) pork sausagemeat
100 g (4 oz) fresh breadcrumbs
2.5 ml (½ tsp) dried thyme
1.25 ml (¼ tsp) ground nutmeg
10 ml (2 tsp) chopped parsley
salt and freshly ground pepper
45 ml (3 tbsp) fresh milk

1. Put all ingredients into a bowl.
2. Knead well together.
3. Use as required.

SAGE & ONION STUFFING   Ⓕ

Preparation 20 mins **Cooking** 20 mins

For pork, duck and goose

225 g (8 oz) onions, quartered
100 g (4 oz) fresh breadcrumbs
2.5 ml (½ tsp) dried sage
salt and freshly ground pepper
25 g (1 oz) butter, melted
fresh milk

1. Cook onions in boiling water until tender.
To microwave: Chop onions roughly, cover and cook for 5 minutes, stirring once.
2. Drain and chop finely.
3. Mix with breadcrumbs, sage and seasoning.
4. Bind loosely with melted butter and milk.
5. Use as required.

LEMON, PARSLEY & THYME STUFFING   Ⓕ

Preparation 25 mins

For veal, poultry and fish

100 g (4 oz) fresh breadcrumbs
15 ml (1 tbsp) chopped parsley
2.5 ml (½ tsp) grated lemon rind
2.5 ml (½ tsp) dried thyme
salt and freshly ground pepper
25 g (1 oz) butter, melted
fresh milk

1. Mix breadcrumbs with parsley, lemon rind, thyme and seasoning.
2. Bind loosely with melted butter and milk.
3. Use as required.

PRAWN STUFFING

Preparation 25 mins

For fish and tomatoes

100 g (4 oz) fresh breadcrumbs
10 ml (2 tsp) chopped parsley
2.5 ml (½ tsp) grated lemon rind
50 g (2 oz) peeled prawns, chopped
salt and freshly ground pepper
25 g (1 oz) butter, melted
fresh milk

1. Mix breadcrumbs with parsley, lemon rind, prawns and seasoning.
2. Bind loosely with melted butter and milk.
3. Use as required.

LEMON, PARSLEY & THYME STUFFING

CHESTNUT STUFFING Ⓕ

Preparation 15 mins **plus soaking overnight**
Cooking 30 mins

For chicken and turkey

100 g (4 oz) dried chestnuts,
   soaked overnight
100 g (4 oz) fresh breadcrumbs
10 ml (2 tsp) finely grated onion
1.25 ml (¼ tsp) ground nutmeg
30 ml (2 tbsp) chopped parsley (optional)
salt and freshly ground pepper
50 g (2 oz) butter, melted
fresh single cream

1. Drain chestnuts. Cook in boiling water
until tender, about 20–30 minutes.
*To microwave: Drain chestnuts and put into
a small casserole. Pour over sufficient
BOILING water to just cover them. Cover and
cook for 10–15 minutes until tender.*

2. Drain and mince or chop chestnuts finely.
Mix with breadcrumbs, onion, nutmeg,
parsley and seasoning.

3. Bind with melted butter, fresh single cream.

4. Use as required.

Alternatively use 225 g (8 oz) shelled, fresh
chestnuts, instead of dried.

APPLE & WALNUT STUFFING Ⓕ

Preparation 35 mins

For pork, lamb, duck, goose, bacon joints
and rabbit

450 g (1 lb) cooking apples, peeled, cored
   and chopped
15 ml (1 tbsp) sugar
100 g (4 oz) fresh breadcrumbs
25 g (1 oz) walnut halves, chopped
10 ml (2 tsp) finely grated onion (optional)
salt and freshly ground pepper
50 g (2 oz) butter, melted
beaten egg

1. Mix apples with sugar, breadcrumbs,
walnuts and onion, if used.

2. Season to taste. Mix loosely with melted
butter and beaten egg if necessary.

3. Use as required.

FONDUES

MEAT FONDUES

Hints and tips for Meat Fondues

Meat fondue pans are usually made from stainless steel or copper.

The pan should be only half full of oil to avoid danger at the table.

It is best to heat the oil on the cooker to 182°C (360°F) or until a small cube of bread turns golden in less than a minute when dropped in the oil.

The fondue burner should be securely placed on a protected table.

The pan should be placed on the burner so that the handle cannot be knocked.

Take care not to place too much food in the oil at one time as it can cause the oil to bubble up and rapidly cool.

Fondue forks are used only to spear the food for cooking in the oil, not for eating from, as this could burn the mouth.

FONDUE BOURGUIGNONNE

Preparation 15 mins **plus** 3 hrs **marinading**
Cooking 10 mins **plus at table**   *Serves 4*

450g (1 lb) fillet or rump steak, cubed
wine marinade made with 90 ml (6 tbsp)
   wine (page 252) (optional)
cooking oil

accompany with
onion dip (page 55)
curry mayonnaise (page 197)
cucumber and soured cream mayonnaise
   (page 197)
jacket potatoes with butter (page 172)
side salad (see salad section, page 188)
gherkins or stuffed olives

1. Marinate beef for 1–3 hours or overnight.
2. Drain and dry thoroughly on absorbent kitchen paper to prevent oil from spitting when meat is cooked.

3. Half fill meat fondue pan with oil. Heat gently to 182°C (360°F) or until a small cube of bread, dropped into the oil, turns golden within 1 minute. Keep oil hot over fondue burner on the table.

4. Serve thoroughly drained meat on individual plates and allow each person to spear the meat on their fondue fork and cook to their requirements.

5. Serve with accompaniments.

CHEESE FONDUES

Hints and tips for Cheese Fondues

Cheese fondue pans are usually thick-based, flameproof, and generally metal or pottery.

Cheese may tend to burn over the fondue flame so stir from time to time.

Always use a dry wine, cider or apple juice in the fondue. A little lemon juice helps to make the wine drier.

Lemon juice also helps to prevent the fondue from curdling.

A little more cheese or blended cornflour will help to thicken a thin fondue.

Alternatively, carefully blend in a little wine to a thick fondue.

CHEDDAR CHEESE FONDUE

Preparation 5 mins **Cooking** 10 mins *Serves 4–6*

1 garlic clove
300 ml (½ pint) dry white wine or dry cider
5 ml (1 tsp) lemon juice
450g (1 lb) English Cheddar, grated
15 ml (1 tbsp) cornflour
25g (1 oz) butter
freshly ground pepper
pinch of ground nutmeg
30 ml (2 tbsp) Kirsch

accompany with
1 crusty French loaf, cubed and celery

1. Rub inside of cheese fondue pan with cut garlic clove.
To microwave: Rub inside of a large bowl with cut garlic clove.

2. Pour in wine or cider and lemon juice, heat gently. Gradually add cheese and cornflour mixed together. Add butter.
To microwave: Add cheese and cornflour and stir together. Stir in wine or cider, lemon juice and butter.

3. Heat, stirring continuously, until cheese has melted and the mixture is thick and creamy.
To microwave: Cook, uncovered, for 6–8 minutes, stirring frequently, until cheese has melted and mixture is thick and creamy.

4. Stir in remaining ingredients.

5. Serve hot with cubes of French bread and celery.

STILTON CHEESE FONDUE

Preparation 15 mins
Cooking 10 mins   *Serves 4–6*

1 garlic clove
300 ml (½ pint) apple juice
225 g (8 oz) Blue Stilton cheese, crumbled
225 g (8 oz) Red Leicester cheese, grated
15 ml (1 tbsp) cornflour

accompany with
1 crusty French loaf, cubed
4 medium apples, cored & cut into wedges

1. Rub inside of cheese fondue pan with cut garlic clove.
To microwave: Rub inside of a large bowl with cut garlic clove.

2. Pour in apple juice and heat gently. Gradually add cheeses and cornflour together.
To microwave: Add cheeses and cornflour and stir together. Stir in apple juice.

3. Heat, stirring continuously, until cheese has melted and mixture is thick and creamy.
To microwave: Cook, uncovered, for 6–8 minutes, stirring frequently, until cheese has melted and mixture is thick and creamy.

4. Serve hot with French bread and apples.

CHEDDAR CHEESE FONDUE

CHEESE & TOMATO FONDUE

Preparation 5 mins **Cooking** 5–10 mins *Serves 4*

225 g (8 oz) Cheshire cheese, grated
50 g (2 oz) Blue Stilton cheese, grated
295 g (10.4 oz) can condensed tomato soup
5 ml (1 tsp) Worcestershire sauce
45 ml (3 tbsp) sherry

accompany with
1 crusty French loaf, cubed

1. Place all ingredients except sherry in cheese fondue pan.
To microwave: Place all ingredients, except sherry, in a large bowl.
2. Heat, stirring continuously, until cheese melts and mixture is thick and creamy. Do not boil. Stir in sherry.
To microwave: Cook, uncovered, for 6–7 minutes, stir often until cheese melts and mixture is thick and creamy. Add sherry.
3. Serve hot, with cubes of French bread.

MICROWAVE FONDUE

Preparation 10 mins **Cooking** 8 mins *Serves 4*

225 g (8 oz) Double Gloucester cheese with chives and onions, grated
225 g (8 oz) English Cheddar, grated
30 ml (2 tbsp) cornflour
300 ml (½ pint) apple juice
2.5 ml (½ tsp) made mustard
chopped parsley to garnish

accompany with
wedges of apple, celery, bread and mushrooms

1. Put cheese and cornflour into a large bowl and stir together. Stir in apple juice and mustard.
2. To microwave: Cook, uncovered, for 6–8 minutes, stirring frequently, until cheese melts and mixture is thick and smooth.
3. Sprinkle with parsley.
4. Serve with wedges of apple, celery, bread and mushrooms.

AVOCADO FONDUE

Preparation 10 mins **Cooking** 20 mins *Serves 4*

1 garlic clove
25 g (1 oz) butter
1 medium onion, finely chopped
25 g (1 oz) flour
1 ripe avocado
60 ml (4 tbsp) lemon juice
225 ml (8 fl oz) fresh milk
salt and freshly ground pepper
50 g (2 oz) English Cheddar, grated
150 ml (5 fl oz) fresh single cream
few drops of Tabasco sauce

accompany with
peeled prawns
selection of bite-size pieces of raw vegetables

1. Rub inside of cheese fondue pan with cut garlic clove.
To microwave: Rub inside of a large bowl with cut garlic clove.
2. Melt butter in pan, add onion and fry until soft but not brown.
To microwave: Add butter and onion, cover and cook for 5 minutes, stirring once.
3. Stir in flour and cook for 2 minutes. Remove from heat.
To microwave: Stir in flour and cook, uncovered, for 1 minute.
4. Remove and discard stone and skin from avocado. Mash or liquidise flesh and add to pan together with lemon juice, milk and seasoning.
5. Heat gently, stirring continuously, for 5 minutes but do not boil.
To microwave: Cook, uncovered, for 5–6 minutes, stirring frequently.
6. Add cheese and stir until melted. Then stir in cream and Tabasco sauce.
To microwave: Add cheese and stir until melted. Stir in cream and Tabasco sauce. Cook, uncovered, for 1 minute.
7. Serve immediately with accompaniments.

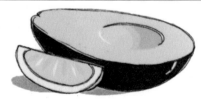

SWEET FONDUES

'Dippers and dunkers' for sweet fondues may be a selection of biscuits, plain cake, sponge fingers, macaroons, marshmallows or pieces of fruit.

CHOCOLATE FONDUE

Preparation 5 mins **Cooking** 10 mins   *Serves 4*

225 g (8 oz) plain chocolate
150 ml (5 fl oz) fresh double cream
30 ml (2 tbsp) Kirsch

accompany with
fresh fruit and cubed plain cake

1. Grate chocolate and place in fondue pan with cream.
To microwave: Grate chocolate and place in a bowl with cream.

2. Heat gently, stirring continuously, until chocolate has melted. Do not boil.
To microwave: Cook for about 3 minutes, stirring frequently, until chocolate has melted. Do not boil.

3. Stir in Kirsch.

4. Serve hot with accompaniments.

MOCHA FONDUE

Preparation 5 mins **Cooking** 10 mins   *Serves 4*

225 g (8 oz) milk chocolate
15 ml (1 tbsp) instant coffee granules
150 ml (5 fl oz) fresh double cream
30 ml (2 tbsp) Crème de Caçao or Tia Maria liqueur

accompany with
fresh fruit and marshmallows

1. Grate chocolate and mix with instant coffee.

2. Place cream in fondue pan with chocolate and coffee.
To microwave: Place cream in a bowl, add chocolate and coffee.

3. Heat gently, stirring continuously, until chocolate has melted.
To microwave: Cook for about 3 minutes, stirring frequently, until chocolate has melted.

4. Add liqueur.

5. Serve hot with accompaniments.

Alternatively for a non-alcoholic sweet fondue, omit liqueur and add 30 ml (2 tbsp) fresh milk.

MARINADES

Marinades are used to tenderise uncooked foods and to improve their flavour and preserve their colour before cooking.

Once raw foods have been coated with the chosen marinade they should be covered, put into a refrigerator and left for the required amount of time.

As a general rule, cubed meat and fish should be marinated for 1–3 hours; large joints of meat and whole fish, overnight.

As most marinades contain an acid they, together with the food to be marinated, should be put into a glass, stainless steel or enamel dish or tray.

YOGURT MARINADE AND CHICKEN MARINADE

WINE MARINADE 🅕

Preparation 10 mins **plus** 8–12 hrs **marinading**

For large legs and shoulders of lamb and game

90 ml (6 tbsp) dry red wine
45 ml (3 tbsp) wine vinegar
45 ml (3 tbsp) oil
1 sprig each fresh parsley and thyme
2 small bay leaves, crumbled
1 garlic clove, crushed
1 small onion, sliced
1.25 ml (¼ tsp) ground nutmeg
15 ml (1 tbsp) caster sugar
shake of cayenne pepper

1. Combine ingredients well together.

2. Pour over meat.

3. Cover and refrigerate 8–12 hours, turning at least twice.

Yogurt Marinade

Preparation 10 mins **plus** 3 hrs **marinading**

For cubes of lamb

275 g (10 oz) natural yogurt
30 ml (2 tbsp) lemon juice
30 ml (2 tbsp) grated onion
5 ml (1 tsp) salt
2 garlic cloves, crushed

1. Combine ingredients well together.
2. Add cubes of lamb. Toss until well coated.
3. Cover and chill for at least 3 hours, turning frequently.

Spice Marinade Ⓕ

Preparation 5 mins **plus** 5 hrs **marinading**

For cubes or small fillets of fish; cubes or cutlets of lamb

10 ml (2 tsp) grated lemon rind
10 ml (2 tsp) turmeric
10 ml (2 tsp) ground ginger
2 garlic cloves, crushed
60 ml (4 tbsp) lemon juice
5 ml (1 tsp) salt

1. Combine ingredients well together.
2. Add fish or meat. Coat with marinade mixture.
3. Cover and chill for 5 hours, turning frequently.

Fiery Marinade

Preparation 10 mins **plus** 2–3 hrs **marinading**

For pork fillet and chops

10 ml (2 tsp) cayenne pepper
60 ml (4 tbsp) lemon juice
1 small onion, finely grated
2.5 ml (½ tsp) dry mustard
20 ml (4 tsp) Worcestershire sauce
5 ml (1 tsp) salt

1. Combine ingredients well together.
2. Add meat. Coat all over with marinade mixture.
3. Cover and chill for 2–3 hours, turning frequently.

Lemon Marinade Ⓕ

Preparation 10 mins **plus** 3 hrs **marinading**

For cubes or small fillets of fish; cubes or cutlets of lamb

30 ml (2 tbsp) lemon juice
45 ml (3 tbsp) oil
salt and freshly ground pepper

1. Combine ingredients well together.
2. Add fish or meat. Coat all over with marinade mixture.
3. Cover and chill for at least 3 hours, turning frequently.

Chicken Marinade Ⓕ

Preparation 15 mins **plus** 2–3 hrs **marinading**

For portions of chicken or turkey

45 ml (3 tbsp) oil
90 ml (6 tbsp) dry white wine or cider
1 garlic clove, crushed
1 small onion, finely chopped
2.5 ml (½ tsp) celery salt
freshly ground pepper
2.5 ml (½ tsp) dried thyme or rosemary

1. Gradually beat oil into wine or cider. Stir in remaining ingredients.
2. Add chicken portions. Coat all over with marinade mixture.
3. Cover and chill for 2–3 hours, turning at least twice.

Beer Marinade Ⓕ

Preparation 10 mins **plus** 4–5 hrs **marinading**

For joints of beef and thick steaks

90 ml (6 tbsp) oil
300 ml (½ pint) beer
1 garlic clove, crushed
30 ml (2 tbsp) lemon juice
15 ml (1 tbsp) caster sugar
2.5 ml (½ tsp) salt

1. Gradually beat oil into beer then stir in remaining ingredients. Pour over meat.
2. Cover and refrigerate 4–5 hours, turning at least twice.

BUTTERS

These are highly-seasoned butters which add piquancy and flavour to grilled or fried meat and fish.

After making, they should be well chilled and can be cut into small round pats or shapes of 0.5 cm (¼ inch) thickness and put on to the hot food immediately before serving.

All quantities are for 4

LEMON BUTTER Ⓕ

Preparation 10 mins **plus chilling**

For fish, veal and chicken

50 g (2 oz) butter
5 ml (1 tsp) grated lemon rind
5 ml (1 tsp) lemon juice

1. Cream butter until soft.
2. Gradually beat in lemon rind and juice.
3. Chill and use as required.

GARLIC BUTTER Ⓕ

Preparation 10 mins **plus chilling**

For steaks or bread

50 g (2 oz) butter
2 garlic cloves, crushed

1. Cream butter until soft. Beat in garlic.
2. Chill and use as required.

TOMATO BUTTER Ⓕ

Preparation 5 mins **plus chilling**

For veal, lamb, bacon, ham and shellfish

50 g (2 oz) butter
10 ml (2 tsp) tomato purée
1.25 ml (¼ tsp) sugar
1.25 ml (¼ tsp) Worcestershire sauce

1. Cream butter until soft.
2. Beat in remaining ingredients. Chill.

GARLIC BUTTER · DEVILLED BUTTER · MUSTARD BUTTER

MUSTARD BUTTER Ⓕ

Preparation 10 mins **plus chilling**

For beef, lamb, bacon, ham, shellfish, herrings and mackerel

50 g (2 oz) butter
5 ml (1 tsp) made mustard *or* **10 ml (2 tsp) French** *or* **wholegrain mustard**

1. Cream butter until soft.
2. Gradually beat in mustard.
3. Chill and use as required.

DEVILLED BUTTER Ⓕ

Preparation 10 mins **plus chilling**

For shellfish, ham, bacon and pork

50 g (2 oz) butter
2.5 ml (½ tsp) dry mustard
5 ml (1 tsp) Worcestershire sauce
5 ml (1 tsp) lemon juice
pinch of cayenne pepper

1. Cream butter until soft.
2. Beat in remaining ingredients.
3. Chill and use as required.

HERB BUTTER Ⓕ

Preparation 15 mins **plus chilling**

For fish

15 ml (1 tbsp) fresh tarragon
15 ml (1 tbsp) fresh chervil
15 ml (1 tbsp) fresh parsley
50 g (2 oz) butter
1 spring onion, finely chopped

1. Put tarragon, chervil and parsley into a bowl and chop finely.
2. Cream butter until soft.
3. Gradually beat in herbs and onion.
4. Chill and use as required.

HORSERADISH BUTTER Ⓕ

Preparation 5 mins **plus chilling**

For beef, herrings and mackerel

50 g (2 oz) butter
15 ml (1 tbsp) creamed horseradish sauce

1. Cream butter until soft.
2. Gradually beat in horseradish sauce.
3. Chill and use as required.

PUDDINGS
AND
DESSERTS

OATIE FRUIT CRUMBLE PAGE 269 · CHOCOLATE ORANGE CHARLOTTE PAGE 289
APPLE ICE PAGE 296 · PINA COLADA CHEESECAKE PAGE 286

HOT PUDDINGS

FRUIT PIE 🄵

Preparation 30 mins
Cooking 1 hr 5 mins   *Serves 4–6*

900 g (2 lb) apples, rhubarb, gooseberries,
  plums, damsons, fresh apricots, cooking
  cherries, blackberries or mixture of fruits
50–100 g (2–4 oz) sugar, depending on
  sharpness of fruit
short crust (page 364)
  or flaky pastry (page 366)
  made with 225 g (8 oz) flour
beaten egg or milk for brushing
caster sugar
fresh cream, yogurt *or* custard to serve

1. Prepare fruit according to type.

2. Fill a 1.1 litre (2 pint) pie dish with
alternate layers of fruit and sugar. Begin and
end with fruit. Dome fruit in centre so that it
supports pastry.

3. Roll out pastry on a floured work surface.
Cut into an oval or round 4 cm (1½ inch)
wider than top of dish.

4. Moisten edges of dish with water. Line
with a strip of pastry cut from trimmings.

5. Moisten strip with water then cover with
pastry lid, pressing edges well together to
seal. Trim away surplus pastry.

6. Flake edges by cutting lightly with back
of a knife then 'ridge' with a fork all the way
round.

7. Brush with beaten egg or milk. Make
2 slits in top to allow steam to escape.

8. Bake at 220°C (425°F) Mark 7 for
15 minutes.

9. Reduce to 180°C (350°F) Mark 4 and bake
for a further 30–45 minutes.

10. Remove from oven. Sprinkle lightly with
caster sugar.

11. Serve with fresh single or double cream,
soured cream, natural yogurt or custard.

DOUBLE CRUST FRUIT PIE 🄵

Preparation 20 mins
Cooking 30 mins   *Serves 4–6*

short crust pastry
  made with 275 g (10 oz) flour
  (page 364)
450 g (1 lb) stewed, cooked fruit, i.e.
  apples, rhubarb,
  gooseberries, plums,
  damsons, fresh apricots,
  cooking cherries, blackberries
  or mixture of fruits
beaten egg or milk for brushing
caster sugar
fresh cream, ice-cream
  or custard to serve

1. Cut pastry into 2 equal pieces.

2. Roll out half on a floured work surface
and use to line a 20.5 cm (8 inch) flat
ovenproof plate (or shallow ovenproof pie
plate).

3. Cover pastry – to within 2.5 cm (1 inch) of
edges – with fruit.

4. Moisten edges of pastry with water. Cover
with lid, rolled and shaped from remaining
pastry.

5. Press edges well together to seal. Trim
away surplus pastry.

6. Flake edges by cutting lightly with back
of a knife then 'ridge' with a fork all the way
round.

7. Brush with beaten egg or milk. Make
2 slits in top to allow steam to escape then
stand pie on a baking sheet.

8. Bake at 200°C (400°F) Mark 6 for
30 minutes.

9. Remove from oven. Sprinkle lightly with
caster sugar.

10. Serve with fresh single or double cream,
soured cream, ice cream or custard.

SEMOLINA PUDDING

Preparation 5 mins **Cooking** 15 mins   *Serves 4*

568 ml (1 pint) fresh milk
40 g (1½ oz) semolina
25 g (1 oz) caster sugar
15 g (½ oz) butter

1. Put milk into a saucepan and heat until lukewarm.
To microwave: Put milk in a large bowl and cook for 3 minutes until lukewarm.

2. Sprinkle in semolina. Cook slowly, stirring, until mixture comes to the boil and thickens.
To microwave: Sprinkle in semolina and stir well. Cook for about 5 minutes, stirring frequently, until mixture boils and thickens.

3. Add sugar and butter. Cook very gently for a further 5–7 minutes, stirring often.
To microwave: Add sugar and butter. Cook on MEDIUM (50%) for about 5 minutes, stirring often.

Alternatively turn the pudding into a 568 ml (1 pint) greased ovenproof dish as soon as it has come to the boil and thickened. Sprinkle with ground nutmeg and bake at 170°C (325°F) Mark 3 for 30 minutes.
To microwave: Alternatively, pour cooked pudding into a flameproof dish, sprinkle with ground nutmeg and brown lightly under a hot grill.

Variation

SAGO PUDDING

Follow recipe and method for semolina pudding (above). Use sago instead of semolina.

RICE PUDDING (or BARLEY or TAPIOCA)

Preparation 10 mins **plus** 30 mins **standing**
Cooking 2–2½ hrs   *Serves 4*

50 g (2 oz) pudding rice
   (or flaked rice, barley or tapioca)
568 ml (1 pint) fresh milk
25 g (1 oz) caster sugar
1 strip of lemon rind
ground nutmeg
15 g (½ oz) butter

1. Wash rice and drain well. Put into a 900 ml (1½ pint) greased ovenproof dish and stir in milk, sugar and lemon rind.
To microwave: Wash rice and drain well. Put into a large bowl and stir in milk, sugar and lemon rind.

2. Sprinkle top with nutmeg. Dot with butter.

3. Bake at 150°C (300°F) Mark 2 and bake for 2–2½ hours.
To microwave: Cook for about 7 mins or until boiling. Stir, cover and cook on MEDIUM–LOW (30%) for 30–45 mins, stir occasionally, until thick and creamy. Pour into a flameproof dish and brown lightly under a hot grill.

TAPIOCA ORANGE PUDDING

Preparation 15 mins **plus** 30 mins **standing**
Cooking 25 mins   *Serves 4*

2 large oranges
568 ml (1 pint) fresh milk
50 g (2 oz) tapioca
75 g (3 oz) desiccated coconut
pinch of ground allspice
25 g (1 oz) caster sugar
30 ml (2 tbsp) orange liqueur (optional)
150 ml (5 fl oz) fresh single cream

1. Pare zest from oranges and place in a saucepan with milk. Bring to the boil, remove from the heat, stand for 30 mins.
To microwave: Pare zest from oranges and place in a large bowl with milk. Cook for about 5 mins, stir occasionally, until boiling.

2. Remove and discard zest; add tapioca, 50 g (2 oz) coconut and allspice.

3. Bring to the boil and simmer for 15 mins, until thick and creamy, stir occasionally.
To microwave: Cook for 3–4 mins, stir occasionally, until boiling, continue cooking on MEDIUM (50%) for about 10 mins, stir occasionally, until thick and creamy.

4. Remove pith from oranges and cut into segments, reserve some whole for decoration, chop remainder.

5. Toast remaining coconut and reserve for decoration.

6. Stir oranges into tapioca with sugar, liqueur and cream.

7. Pour into serving dishes and top with toasted coconut and orange segments.

MACARONI PUDDING

Preparation 15 mins **Cooking** 15 mins   *Serves 4*

22.5 ml (1½ tbsp) custard powder
900 ml (1½ pint) fresh milk
40 g (1½ oz) butter
115 g (4½ oz) macaroni
25 g (1 oz) sultanas
25 g (1 oz) sugar
ground nutmeg
30 ml (2 tbsp) demerara sugar

1. Blend custard powder with a little milk.
2. Place remaining milk in a saucepan with 25 g (1 oz) butter and bring to the boil.
To microwave: Place remaining milk in a large bowl with 25 g (1 oz) butter. Cook for about 7 mins or until boiling.
3. Add macaroni and sultanas. Simmer for 7 mins, stir occasionally.
To microwave: Stir in macaroni and sultanas. Cook, uncovered, for 7 mins, stir occasionally.
4. Remove from heat and stir in blended custard powder and sugar.
5. Bring to the boil, cook stirring for 2 mins.
To microwave: Cook for about 2 mins, then allow to stand for 5 mins.

6. Pour into a flameproof dish. Sprinkle with nutmeg and demerara. Dot with remaining butter.
7. Grill until sugar has melted.

EASTERN RICE PUDDING

Preparation 5 mins **Cooking** 35 mins   *Serves 4*

900 ml (1½ pint) fresh milk
40 g (1½ oz) creamed coconut
2.5 ml (½ tsp) ground cinnamon
pinch of ground cloves
75 g (3 oz) pudding rice
25 g (1 oz) brown sugar
chopped pistachio nuts and fruit to serve

1. Place milk, coconut and spices in a saucepan, heat until coconut has dissolved.
To microwave: Place milk, coconut and spices into a large bowl, heat for 6 mins, stir often, until coconut has dissolved.
2. Stir in rice and sugar.
3. Bring to the boil, then simmer for 30 mins or until rice is tender. Stir.
To microwave: Cook 5 mins or until boiling. Stir, cook on MEDIUM–LOW (30%) for about 30 mins, stir often, until rice is tender.
4. Serve hot with nuts and fruit.

EASTERN RICE PUDDING

EVE'S OR APPLE PUDDING (F)

Preparation 20 mins **Cooking** 1¼ hrs *Serves 4–5*

450 g (1 lb) cooking apples, peeled, cored
    and sliced
75 g (3 oz) caster sugar
sponge pudding
    made with 100 g (4 oz) flour (page 266)
fresh double cream to serve

1. Arrange apples in layers, in a
1.4 litre (2½ pint) greased, ovenproof dish,
sprinkling sugar between layers.

2. Cover with sponge pudding mixture.

3. Bake at 180°C (350°F) Mark 4 for
1–1¼ hours or until wooden cocktail stick,
inserted into centre of sponge mixture,
comes out clean.
*To microwave: Cook, uncovered, for
5–7 minutes until surface is still slightly
moist and a wooden cocktail stick, inserted
into centre of sponge, comes out clean.*

4. Serve with fresh double cream.

Alternatively gooseberries, rhubarb, apple
mixed with blackberries, plums or damsons
may be used instead of apples.

APRICOT AND GINGER PUDDING (F)

Preparation 30 mins
Cooking 55 mins   *Serves 4–6*

410 g (14.4 oz) can apricot halves in
    natural juice, drained
100 g (4 oz) butter
100 g (4 oz) sugar
1 egg, beaten
75 g (3 oz) self raising flour
75 g (3 oz) wholemeal self raising flour
10 ml (2 tsp) ground ginger
150 ml (¼ pint) fresh milk

1. Place drained apricots in base of a
greased ovenproof dish.
*To microwave: Grease and base-line a
1.4 litre (2½ pint) ring mould. Arrange
drained apricots in base.*

2. Melt butter and sugar in a small pan over
a low heat, cool for 4 minutes.
*To microwave: Place butter and sugar in a
large bowl and cook for 2 minutes until
melted. Cool for 4 minutes.*

3. Add egg and beat well. Stir in flours and
ginger, gradually add milk.

EVE'S PUDDING

4. Pour over apricots and bake at 180°C (350°F) Mark 4 for 50 minutes.

To microwave: Pour over apricots and cook, uncovered, for 8–9 minutes or until surface is still slightly moist and a wooden cocktail stick, inserted into sponge, comes out clean. Allow to stand for 5 minutes then turn out.

BAKED EGG CUSTARD

Preparation 15 mins **Cooking** 1 hr   *Serves 4*

3 eggs or 4 egg yolks
568 ml (1 pint) fresh milk
25 g (1 oz) caster sugar
ground nutmeg

1. Beat whole eggs or egg yolks with milk. Strain into a 900 ml (1½ pint) greased, ovenproof dish, then stir in sugar.

2. Sprinkle with nutmeg. Stand in a roasting tin containing enough water to come about half way up sides of dish.

To microwave: Sprinkle with nutmeg. Stand dish in a larger container with enough BOILING water to come half way up dish.

3. Bake at 170°C (325°F) Mark 3 for 45 minutes–1 hour or until firm.

To microwave: Cook on MEDIUM (50%) for 15–20 minutes until just set. Allow to stand for 5 minutes before serving.

CUSTARD TART

Preparation 15 mins **Cooking** 1 hr   *Serves 4–6*

short crust pastry made with 175 g (6 oz) flour (page 364)
300 ml (½ pint) fresh milk
2 eggs plus 1 egg yolk
25 g (1 oz) caster sugar
ground nutmeg

1. Roll out pastry on a floured work surface. Use to line a 20.5 cm (8 inch) greased flan tin or pie plate.

2. Heat milk until warm.

3. Beat milk with eggs, egg yolk and sugar. Strain into pastry case.

4. Sprinkle top with nutmeg. Bake at 200°C (400°F) Mark 6 for 15 minutes.

5. Reduce temperature to 170°C (325°F) Mark 3 and bake for a further 30–45 minutes or until custard has set.

BAKED RICE CUSTARD

Preparation 20 mins **Cooking** 1½ hrs   *Serves 6*

50 g (2 oz) pudding rice
3 eggs, beaten
50 g (2 oz) sugar
2.5 ml (½ tsp) vanilla essence
568 ml (1 pint) fresh milk
40 g (1½ oz) sultanas
pinch of ground nutmeg

1. Cook rice in boiling water for 10 minutes, drain well.

2. Beat eggs, sugar, vanilla essence and milk together.

3. Stir in sultanas and rice.

4. Pour into an ovenproof dish and sprinkle with nutmeg. Stand in a roasting tin containing enough hot water to come halfway up sides of dish.

5. Bake at 170°C (325°F) Mark 3 for 1½ hours or until just set.

LEMON LAYER PUDDING

Preparation 20 mins **Cooking** 45 mins   *Serves 4*

grated rind and juice of 1 lemon
50 g (2 oz) butter
100 g (4 oz) sugar
2 eggs, separated
50 g (2 oz) self raising flour
300 ml (½ pint) fresh milk

1. Add lemon rind to butter and sugar and whisk until pale and fluffy.

2. Add egg yolks and flour and beat well.

3. Stir in milk and 45 ml (3 tbsp) lemon juice.

4. Whisk egg whites until stiff, fold into lemon mixture.

5. Pour into a greased ovenproof dish.

6. Stand in a shallow tin of water and bake at 200°C (400°F) Mark 6 for about 45 minutes, until top is set and spongy to touch.

This pudding will separate into a custard layer with a sponge topping.

LUXURY BREAD & BUTTER PUDDING

Bread & Butter Pudding

Preparation 30 mins **plus** 30 mins **standing**
Cooking 1 hr   *Serves 4*

8 slices of bread, crusts removed
50 g (2 oz) butter
50 g (2 oz) currants or sultanas (or mixture)
40 g (1½ oz) caster sugar
2 eggs
568 ml (1 pint) fresh milk

1. Spread bread thickly with butter. Cut into fingers, small squares or triangles.

2. Place half into a 1.1 litre (2 pint) greased, ovenproof dish.
To microwave: Place half into a 1.1 litre (2 pint) flameproof dish.

3. Sprinkle with fruit and half the sugar.

4. Top with remaining bread, buttered sides uppermost. Sprinkle with remaining sugar.

5. Beat eggs and milk well together. Strain into dish over bread.

6. Leave to stand for 30 mins so that bread absorbs some of the liquid.

7. Bake at 170°C (325°F) Mark 3 for 45 mins– 1 hour until pudding is set and top is crisp.
To microwave: Cook on MEDIUM (50%) for 15–20 mins or until just set. Brown lightly under a hot grill.

Luxury Bread & Butter Pudding

Preparation 30 mins **plus** 30 mins **standing**
Cooking 1 hr   *Serves 4*

300 ml (½ pint) fresh milk
1 vanilla pod
40 g (1½ oz) sugar
8 slices of fruit bread (about 225 g (8 oz))
50 g (2 oz) butter
3 eggs
150 ml (5 fl oz) fresh double cream
apricot jam to glaze
toasted almonds to decorate

1. Gently heat milk with vanilla pod and sugar until almost boiling.
To microwave: Cook milk, vanilla pod and sugar for 2–3 minutes until almost boiling.

2. Leave to stand for 15 minutes to cool.

3. Butter bread, cut into triangles and arrange in a flameproof dish.

4. Beat together eggs and cream.

5. Remove vanilla pod from milk and gradually stir milk into cream mixture.

6. Pour over bread and leave to stand for 30 minutes.

7. Place dish in a roasting tin containing enough hot water to come half way up dish.
To microwave: Stand dish in a larger container with enough BOILING water to come half way up the dish.

8. Bake at 170°C (325°F) Mark 3 for 1 hour, until custard has set.
To microwave: Cook, uncovered, on MEDIUM (50%) for 15–20 minutes or until just set.

9. Toast lightly under a grill for a crisp top.

10. Glaze with sieved, warm jam and sprinkle with toasted almonds.

BREAD PUDDING   Ⓕ

Preparation 25 mins **plus** 30 mins **standing**
Cooking 1½ hrs   *Serves 10*

1 small loaf of bread, about 400g (14oz)
100g (4oz) sugar
175g (6oz) shredded suet or butter, cut into small pieces
75ml (5tbsp) ground mixed spice
350g (12oz) dried mixed fruit
juice and rind of 1 lemon
juice and rind of 1 orange
2 eggs, beaten
fresh milk to mix if required
caster sugar to serve
custard or fresh cream to serve

1. Break bread up and place in a bowl.

2. Cover with cold water and leave to stand for 30 minutes.

3. Squeeze all water out of bread and crumble into a bowl.

4. Add sugar, suet, spice, fruit, juice, rind and eggs.

5. Stir well to mix. It should be like the dropping consistency of a fruit cake. Add a little milk if necessary.

6. Pour into a greased roasting tin.

7. Bake at 180°C (350°F) Mark 4 for 1½ hours or until firm to the touch. Cover with greaseproof paper if it starts to go too brown. Sprinkle with caster sugar.

8. Serve cut into squares, either hot with custard or cold with fresh cream.

APRICOT BREAD PUDDING

Preparation 25 mins **plus** 15 mins **standing**
Cooking 40 mins   *Serves 4*

8 slices of wholemeal bread
75g (3oz) no-soak dried apricots, chopped
50g (2oz) sultanas
30ml (2tbsp) clear honey
2 eggs
568ml (1pint) fresh milk
grated rind of ½ lemon
5ml (1tsp) mixed spice
custard to serve

1. Cut bread into triangles and place half in base of an ovenproof dish.

2. Mix apricots and sultanas, sprinkle half over bread and drizzle with half of the honey. Repeat layers.

3. Beat eggs with milk, lemon rind and spice.

4. Pour over bread and leave to stand for 15 minutes.

5. Bake at 180°C (350°F) Mark 4 for 40 minutes or until set.

6. Serve with custard.

CABINET PUDDING

Preparation 20 mins **plus** 30 mins **standing**
Cooking 1 hr   *Serves 4*

6 trifle sponges
50g (2oz) glacé cherries, chopped
25g (1oz) caster sugar
2 eggs
568ml (1pint) fresh milk
5ml (1tsp) vanilla essence
fresh double cream to serve

1. Cut each trifle sponge into 6 cubes.

2. Put cake cubes and cherries into a basin. Add sugar and toss lightly together to mix.

3. Beat eggs, milk and vanilla well together. Gently stir into cake cube mixture.

4. Leave to stand for 30 minutes. Turn into a 900ml (1½pint) well-greased pudding basin. Cover securely with buttered greaseproof paper or aluminium foil.

5. Steam very gently for 1 hour.

6. Turn out carefully on to a warm plate.

7. Serve with fresh double cream.

APPLE AMBER

Preparation 30 mins **Cooking** 40 mins *Serves 4*

450 g (1 lb) cooking apples, peeled, cored
    and sliced
15 ml (1 tbsp) water
25 g (1 oz) butter
50 g (2 oz) caster sugar
45 ml (3 tbsp) stale cake crumbs
    (plain cake is best)
5 ml (1 tsp) ground cinnamon
2 egg yolks
meringue topping made with 2 egg whites
    (page 215)
fresh double cream to serve

1. Put apples into a saucepan with water
and butter.
*To microwave: Put apples into a bowl with
water and butter.*

2. Cook until soft and pulpy. Beat until
smooth.
*To microwave: Cook and cover for about
5 minutes until soft and pulpy. Beat until
smooth.*

3. Add sugar, cake crumbs, cinnamon and
egg yolks. Mix well.

4. Transfer to a 900 ml (1½ pint) ovenproof
dish and top with meringue.
*To microwave: Transfer to a 900 ml (1½ pint)
flameproof dish and top with meringue.*

5. Bake at 150°C (300°F) Mark 2 for
30 minutes or until meringue is light gold.
*To microwave: Cook, uncovered, on MEDIUM
(50%) for about 5 minutes until meringue is
firm and set. Brown lightly under a hot grill.
Allow to stand for 5 minutes before serving.*

6. Serve with fresh double cream.

BAKED APPLES WITH SYRUP & LEMON

Preparation 25 mins **Cooking** 1 hr *Serves 4*

4 cooking apples
15 ml (1 tbsp) golden syrup
2.5 ml (½ tsp) grated lemon rind
25 g (1 oz) butter
45 ml (3 tbsp) warm water
fresh cream, yogurt or custard to serve

APPLE AMBER

1. Wash apples and wipe dry. Remove cores two-thirds of the way down each one.

2. With a sharp knife, score a line round each apple, about a third of the way down from top.

3. Stand apples in an ovenproof dish.
To microwave: Stand apples on a plate, leaving a space in the centre.

4. Mix syrup and lemon rind well together. Spoon equal amounts into apple cavities.

5. Top each with a knob of butter. Pour water into dish.
To microwave: Top each with a knob of butter. Omit water.

6. Bake at 180°C (350°F) Mark 4 for 45 minutes–1 hour or until apples puff up and are tender.
To microwave: Cook, uncovered, for 4–7 minutes or until apples are tender. Allow to stand for 3 minutes before serving.

7. Serve with fresh single or double cream, soured cream, natural yogurt or custard.

Variation

BAKED APPLES WITH MINCEMEAT

Follow recipe and method for baked apples (left). Omit golden syrup and lemon rind. Stuff centre of the apples with mincemeat.

TREACLE TART   Ⓕ

Preparation 25 mins **Cooking** 30 mins   *Serves 4*

short crust pastry
   made with 175g (6oz) flour (page 364)
50g (2oz) fresh white breadcrumbs
225g (8oz) golden syrup
2.5ml (½tsp) grated lemon rind
10ml (2tsp) lemon juice
fresh cream, yogurt or custard to serve

1. Roll out pastry on a floured work surface. Use to line a 20.5cm (8inch) pie plate.

2. Trim surplus pastry from edges.

3. Mix breadcrumbs with syrup, lemon rind and juice. Spread over pastry to within 2.5cm (1inch) of edges. Moisten edges with cold water.

4. Cut remaining pastry into thin strips. Arrange in a criss-cross design over treacle filling.

5. Press strips well on to pastry edges and put plate on to a baking sheet.

6. Bake at 200°C (400°F) Mark 6 for 30 minutes or until pastry is golden.

7. Serve with fresh single or double cream, soured cream, natural yogurt or custard.

JAM ROLY-POLY PUDDING

SPONGE PUDDING Ⓕ

Preparation 25 mins **Cooking** 2 hrs   *Serves 4*

100g (4oz) self raising flour
pinch of salt
100g (4oz) butter
100g (4oz) caster sugar
2 eggs, beaten
30ml (2 tbsp) fresh milk
fresh cream or sweet sauce to serve

1. Sift flour and salt into a bowl.

2. Cream butter and sugar until light and fluffy.

3. Add eggs a little at a time with a spoonful of flour, beating well after each addition.

4. Fold in remaining flour alternately with milk.

5. Transfer to a greased and base-lined 900ml (1½ pint) pudding basin.

6. Cover with buttered greaseproof paper or foil. Pleat once to allow pudding to rise.
To microwave: Cover with buttered greaseproof paper.

7. Secure with string. Using extra string to make a handle for ease of removal.
To microwave: Crease paper down sides of bowl to make a close fitting cap.

8. Place in a steamer over a pan of boiling water and cover. Alternatively place on a metal trivet in a large saucepan and add boiling water to come half way up sides of basin. Add pudding and cover.
To microwave: Stand basin on a low microwave rack.

9. Steam steadily 1½–2 hours or until well risen and firm.
To microwave: Cook for 4–5 minutes until surface is still slightly moist and a wooden cocktail stick, inserted in centre, comes out clean. Allow to stand for 3 minutes before turning out.

10. Turn out on to a warm plate and decorate.

11. Serve with fresh cream or a sweet sauce (see sauce section, page 241).

Variations

CHOCOLATE SPONGE PUDDING Ⓕ

Follow recipe and method for sponge pudding (left) but use 75g (3oz) self raising flour only. Sift into bowl with salt plus 25g (1oz) cocoa powder. Cream butter and sugar with 2.5ml (½tsp) vanilla essence.

FRUIT SPONGE PUDDING ⓕ

Follow recipe and method for sponge pudding (left). Stir in 50g (2oz) currants, sultanas or raisins after beating in eggs.

JAM, MARMALADE OR SYRUP SPONGE PUDDING ⓕ

Follow recipe and method for sponge pudding (left). Put 45ml (3tbsp) jam, marmalade or syrup into bottom of a greased and base-lined basin before adding pudding mixture.

ROLY-POLY PUDDING ⓕ

Preparation 25mins **Cooking** 1½hrs *Serves 4*

suet crust pastry
   made with 175g (6oz) flour (page 367)
75ml (5tbsp) golden syrup, treacle,
   marmalade or jam
5ml (1tsp) grated lemon rind
sweet sauce to serve

1. Roll out pastry into a 25.5×20.5cm (10×8inch) rectangle.

2. Spread with syrup, treacle, marmalade or jam to within 2.5cm (1inch) of edges. Sprinkle with lemon rind.

3. Moisten edges of pastry with cold water. Roll up loosely like a Swiss roll, starting from one of the shorter sides.

4. Press edges together and join well to seal. Wrap loosely in greased greaseproof paper then in aluminium foil.
To microwave: Wrap loosely in non-stick baking parchment or buttered greaseproof paper.

5. Twist ends of foil so that they stay closed. Steam pudding for 1½ hours or bake uncovered at 180°C (350°F) Mark 4 for 30 minutes.
To microwave: Twist ends of paper so that they stay closed. Place on a flat plate and cook on MEDIUM (50%) for about 10 minutes until cooked through. Allow to stand for 3 minutes.

6. Unwrap and serve with a sweet sauce to taste (see sauce section, page 241).

STEAMED SUET PUDDING ⓕ

Preparation 20mins **Cooking** 3hrs   *Serves 4*

100g (4oz) flour
1.25ml (¼tsp) salt
7.5ml (1½tsp) baking powder
100g (4oz) fresh breadcrumbs
75g (3oz) caster sugar
75g (3oz) shredded suet
1 egg, beaten
90–120ml (6–8tbsp) fresh milk to mix
sweet sauce to serve

1. Sift flour, salt and baking powder into a bowl.

2. Add breadcrumbs, sugar and suet. Mix to a soft batter with beaten egg and milk.

3. Turn into a greased 1.1litre (2pint) pudding basin and cover securely with buttered greaseproof paper or aluminium foil.
To microwave: Turn into a greased 1.1litre (2pint) pudding basin and cover with greaseproof paper.

4. Steam for 2½–3 hours.
To microwave: Cook for 6–7 minutes or until cooked through. Allow to stand for 2–3 minutes.

5. Turn out on to a warm plate.

6. Serve with a sweet sauce to taste (see sauce section, page 241).

Variations

FAIR LADY PUDDING ⓕ

Follow recipe and method for steamed suet pudding (above). Add grated rind of 1 medium orange or lemon with sugar.

FOUR-FRUIT PUDDING ⓕ

Follow recipe and method for steamed suet pudding (above). Add 25g (1oz) *each* dates, figs and prunes – all chopped – and 25g (1oz) mixed chopped peel with sugar.

COLLEGE PUDDING ⓕ

Follow recipe and method for steamed suet pudding (above). Sift 5ml (1tsp) mixed spice with flour. Add 100g (4oz) mixed dried fruit with sugar (use ½ caster sugar and ½ soft brown sugar).

PINEAPPLE UPSIDE DOWN PUDDING Ⓕ

Preparation 30 mins **Cooking** 1 hr   *Serves 4–6*

150 g (5 oz) butter
25 g (1 oz) soft brown sugar
227 g (8 oz) can pineapple rings in natural juice, drained
4 glacé cherries, halved
100 g (4 oz) sugar
2 eggs, beaten
175 g (6 oz) self raising flour
angelica to decorate
custard or fresh cream to serve

1. Melt 25 g (1 oz) butter and stir in brown sugar. Pour into a greased and base-lined 20.5 cm (8 inch) round cake tin.
To microwave: Melt 25 g (1 oz) butter for 30 seconds and stir in brown sugar. Pour into a greased and base-lined 20.5 cm (8 inch) round cake dish.

2. Place pineapple rings and glacé cherries on top of butter and sugar.

3. Cream remaining butter and sugar until pale and fluffy. Gradually beat in eggs.

4. Fold in flour. Spread over pineapple rings.
To microwave: Fold in flour and 60 ml (4 tbsp) pineapple juice. Spread over pineapple rings.

5. Bake at 180°C (350°F) Mark 4 for 1 hour, or until centre springs back when lightly pressed with a finger.
To microwave: Stand dish on a low microwave rack and cook for 6–7 minutes until surface is still slightly moist and a wooden cocktail stick, inserted into centre, comes out clean.

6. Leave to stand for 5 minutes.

7. Turn out on to a plate and decorate.

8. Serve with custard or fresh cream.

Variation

CHOCOLATE & PEAR UPSIDE DOWN PUDDING Ⓕ

Follow recipe and method for pineapple upside down pudding (left). Use canned pear halves instead of pineapple and 25 g (1 oz) cocoa powder in place of 25 g (1 oz) flour in sponge mixture.

PINEAPPLE UPSIDE DOWN PUDDING

FRUIT CRUMBLE Ⓕ

Preparation 25 mins **Cooking** 1 hr *Serves 4*

450g (1 lb) cooking apples, rhubarb,
 gooseberries, damsons, plums,
 blackberries or red or blackcurrants
75–100g (3–4 oz) granulated sugar,
 depending on sharpness of fruit
175g (6 oz) flour
75g (3 oz) butter
50g (2 oz) caster sugar
 (or demerara sugar if microwaving)
fresh cream or custard to serve

1. Prepare fruit according to type. Put into a
1.1 litre (2 pint) ovenproof dish in layers with
granulated sugar.
*To microwave: Prepare fruit according to
type. Put into a 20.5 cm (8 inch) round
flameproof dish in layers with granulated
sugar.*

2. Sift flour into a bowl. Rub butter into flour
until mixture resembles fine breadcrumbs.
Stir in sugar.

3. Sprinkle crumble thickly and evenly over
fruit.

4. Press down lightly with palm of hand then
smooth top with a knife.

5. Bake at 190°C (375°F) Mark 5 for
15 minutes. Reduce to 180°C (350°F) Mark 4
for a further 45 minutes or until top is lightly
brown.
*To microwave: Cook, uncovered, for
5–6 minutes. Brown lightly under a hot grill
if wished.*

6. Serve with fresh double cream, soured
cream or custard.

Variations

OATIE FRUIT CRUMBLE Ⓕ

Follow recipe and method for fruit crumble
(above). For the crumble topping use
wholemeal flour, brown sugar and 25g (1 oz)
porridge oats.

GINGER FRUIT CRUMBLE Ⓕ

Follow recipe and method for fruit crumble
(above). For the crumble topping use
demerara sugar instead of caster sugar and
5 ml (1 tsp) ground ginger.

CRISPY LEMON CRUMBLE Ⓕ

Follow recipe and method for fruit crumble
(left). Add grated rind of 1 lemon and
30 ml (2 tbsp) crushed cornflakes to crumble
topping.

APPLE CHARLOTTE

Preparation 25 mins **Cooking** 1 hr *Serves 4*

100g (4 oz) caster sugar
100g (4 oz) fresh breadcrumbs
grated rind of 1 medium lemon
450g (1 lb) cooking apples, peeled, cored
 and sliced
75g (3 oz) butter, melted
fresh cream or custard to serve

1. Combine sugar, breadcrumbs and lemon
rind.

2. Fill a 1.1 litre (2 pint) greased, ovenproof
dish with alternate layers of breadcrumb
mixture and apples. Begin and end with
breadcrumb mixture, sprinkling melted
butter between layers.

3. Bake at 190°C (375°F) Mark 5 for
45 minutes–1 hour or until apples are tender
and top is golden brown.

4. Serve with fresh double cream, soured
cream or custard.

HONEY & SPICE PUDDING Ⓕ

Preparation 20 mins **Cooking** 40 mins *Serves 4*

410g (14.4 oz) can pears in natural juice,
 drained
2 eggs
25g (1 oz) brown sugar
25g (1 oz) clear honey
50g (2 oz) flour
2.5 ml (½ tsp) mixed spice
custard to serve

1. Place pears in an ovenproof dish.

2. Whisk together eggs, sugar and honey
until thick and creamy.

3. Fold in flour and spice, pour over pears.

4. Bake at 180°C (350°F) Mark 4 for
40 minutes or until risen and firm to touch.

5. Serve hot with custard.

CHRISTMAS PUDDING Ⓕ

Preparation 40 mins
Cooking 6 hours **plus** 2 hours **before serving**
Makes 2, each pudding serves 8

100g (4oz) flour
2.5ml (½tsp) mixed spice
1.25ml (¼tsp) ground nutmeg
225g (8oz) fresh breadcrumbs
275g (10oz) shredded suet
225g (8oz) soft brown sugar
350g (12oz) *each* raisins and sultanas
50g (2oz) chopped mixed peel
50g (2oz) walnut halves
    or blanched almonds, chopped
grated rind of 1 small orange
4 eggs, beaten
50ml (2floz) brandy or dry sherry
2.5ml (½tsp) almond essence
150ml (¼pint) fresh milk
sweet sauce or fresh double cream to serve

To microwave use:
    chilled, grated butter in place of suet;
    dark brown sugar;
    30ml (2tbsp) only of brandy or sherry;
    plus 60ml (4tbsp) milk

1. Sift flour, spice and nutmeg into a large bowl.

2. Add breadcrumbs, suet, sugar, raisins, sultanas, peel, nuts, orange rind and mix.

3. Combine with eggs, brandy or sherry, almond essence and milk. Mix well.

4. Divide between two greased and base-lined 1.1 litre (2 pint) pudding basins.

5. Cover with buttered greaseproof paper or foil. Pleat once to allow pudding to rise.
To microwave: Cover with buttered greaseproof paper.

6. Secure with string. Use extra string to make a handle for ease of removal.
To microwave: Crease paper down sides of bowls to make close fitting caps.

7. Place in a steamer over a pan of boiling water and cover. Alternatively place a metal trivet in a large saucepan and add boiling water to come halfway up the sides of basin. Add pudding and cover.
To microwave: Stand one bowl on a low microwave rack.

8. Steam steadily for 6 hours, replenishing water as it boils away.
To microwave: Cook on MEDIUM–LOW (30%) for about 25–30 minutes until top is still slightly moist.

CHRISTMAS PUDDING

9. Remove from steamer, leave until cold.
To microwave: Cool completely. Cook second pudding as above.

10. Cover with foil. Store in a cool place.
To microwave: Cover with foil and store in refrigerator for up to 2–3 weeks.

11. To serve, cover and steam for 2 hours.
To microwave: To serve, remove foil, cover with greaseproof paper and stand bowl on a serving plate. Cook on MEDIUM (50%) for 7–10 minutes.

12. Turn out on to a warm dish.

13. Serve with sweet sauce to taste or fresh double cream.

QUEEN OF PUDDINGS

Preparation 25 mins **plus** 30 mins **standing**
Cooking 1¼ hrs   *Serves 4*

100g (4oz) fresh white breadcrumbs
25g (1oz) caster sugar
5ml (1tsp) grated lemon rind
450ml (¾pint) fresh milk
25g (1oz) butter
2 egg yolks
30ml (2tbsp) raspberry jam, warmed
meringue topping made with 2 egg whites
(page 215)

1. Put breadcrumbs, sugar and lemon rind into a basin.

2. Toss lightly together to mix.

3. Pour milk into a saucepan. Add butter and heat gently until butter melts.
To microwave: Pour milk into a jug, add butter and cook for 2–3 minutes until butter melts.

4. Pour on to breadcrumb mixture. Stir well and leave to stand for 30 minutes.

5. Beat in egg yolks.

6. Spread in a 900ml (1½pint) greased ovenproof dish.
To microwave: Spread in a 900ml (1½pint) greased flameproof dish.

7. Bake at 170°C (325°F) Mark 3 for 30 minutes or until firm and set.
To microwave: Cook, uncovered, on MEDIUM (50%) for 8–10 minutes until firm and set.

8. Remove from oven and spread with jam. Cover with whirls of meringue.

9. Return to oven and bake for a further 30–40 minutes or until meringue is pale gold.
To microwave: Cook, uncovered, on MEDIUM (50%) for about 4 minutes until risen and set. Brown lightly under a hot grill. Allow to stand for 5 minutes before serving.

COLD DESSERTS

BLANCMANGE

Preparation 15 mins **plus chilling**
Cooking 5 mins   *Serves 4*

45 ml (3 tbsp) cornflour
568 ml (1 pint) fresh milk
40 g (1½ oz) sugar
5 ml (1 tsp) vanilla essence
15 g (½ oz) butter

1. Blend cornflour to a smooth paste with a little milk.

2. Warm remaining milk and combine with cornflour paste, then return to pan.
To microwave: Heat remaining milk for 2 minutes and combine with cornflour paste.

3. Cook, stirring, until mixture comes to the boil and thickens. Reduce heat to low and simmer for 3 minutes.
To microwave: Cook for about 3 minutes, stirring frequently, until mixture thickens and boils.

4. Remove from heat and stir in remaining ingredients.

5. Pour into a 568 ml (1 pint) mould, first rinsed with cold water, then cool.

6. Refrigerate until cold and firm. Turn out on to a plate.

Variations

CHOCOLATE BLANCMANGE

Follow recipe and method for blancmange (above) but add 50 g (2 oz) melted chocolate to cooked mixture.

HONEY BLANCMANGE

Follow recipe and method for blancmange (above) but use 30 ml (2 tbsp) honey in place of sugar.

COFFEE BLANCMANGE

Follow recipe and method for blancmange (above) but add 10 ml (2 tsp) instant coffee granules to milk while it is warming.

LEMON MILK JELLY

Preparation 10 mins **plus chilling**
Cooking 10 mins   *Serves 4*

20 ml (4 tsp) gelatine
45 ml (3 tbsp) water
50 g (2 oz) caster sugar
5 ml (1 tsp) grated lemon rind
568 ml (1 pint) fresh milk
yellow food colouring (optional)

1. Sprinkle gelatine over water in a small bowl.

2. Leave to stand for 10 minutes.

3. Dissolve gelatine over a pan of hot water and cool slightly.
To microwave: Cook for about 30 seconds, stirring every 10 seconds, until dissolved. Cool slightly.

4. Put sugar, lemon rind and milk into a saucepan.

5. Stand over a very low heat until sugar dissolves.

6. When gelatine and milk are both lukewarm, combine by pouring milk gently on to gelatine.

7. Stir well and tint pale yellow with colouring, if used.

8. Pour into a 900 ml (1½ pint) mould, first rinsed with cold water.

9. Refrigerate until set.

10. Turn out on to a plate to serve.

Variations

ORANGE MILK JELLY

Follow recipe and method for lemon milk jelly (above) but use grated orange rind instead of lemon rind and colour pale orange with orange food colouring.

COFFEE MILK JELLY

Follow recipe and method for lemon milk jelly (above) but omit lemon rind and colouring. Instead, add 10 ml (2 tsp) instant coffee granules to milk.

FROSTED FRUIT MOULD

Preparation 30 mins **plus** 2 hrs **chilling** *Serves 4*

135g (4¾oz) packet lemon jelly
75ml (5 tbsp) boiling water
150ml (¼ pint) fairly thick apricot purée,
   made from stewed or canned fruit
10ml (2 tsp) grated lemon rind
150g (5oz) natural yogurt
16 black grapes, in pairs
1 egg white, lightly beaten
45ml (3 tbsp) caster sugar

1. Put jelly and boiling water into a saucepan and stand over a very low heat until jelly dissolves.
To microwave: Put jelly and BOILING water in a bowl and cook for about 1 minute, stirring once or twice, or until jelly dissolves.

2. Pour into a measuring jug and make up to 300ml (½ pint) with cold water. Stir in fruit purée and lemon rind.

3. Leave until cold but still liquid, then gradually beat into yogurt.

4. When evenly combined, transfer to a 568ml (1 pint) jelly mould, rinsed first with cold water.

5. Chill for at least 2 hours.

6. Before serving, frost grapes by dipping in beaten egg white then tossing in caster sugar.

7. Turn mould out on to a plate and surround with grapes.

STRAWBERRY JELLY FLUFF

Preparation 20 mins **plus chilling**   *Serves 4*

135g (4¾oz) packet strawberry jelly
150ml (¼ pint) boiling water
275g (10oz) strawberry yogurt
100g (4oz) fresh strawberries, sliced

1. Dissolve jelly in boiling water. Make up to 300ml (½ pint) with cold water.
To microwave: Place jelly cubes in a bowl with 150ml (¼ pint) cold water. Cook for 2 minutes, stir until completely dissolved. Make up to 300ml (½ pint) with cold water.

2. Chill until almost set (about 1 hour).

3. Whisk yogurt into setting jelly and continue whisking until light and fluffy.

4. Reserve 4 slices of strawberry and divide remainder between 4 glasses.

5. Pour jelly over strawberries and chill.

6. Decorate with reserved strawberries.

FROSTED FRUIT MOULD

VANILLA HONEYCOMB MOULD

Preparation 30 mins **plus chilling**
Cooking 15 mins   *Serves 4–6*

20 ml (4 tsp) gelatine
60 ml (4 tbsp) hot water
2 eggs, separated
50 g (2 oz) caster sugar
568 ml (1 pint) fresh milk
5 ml (1 tsp) vanilla essence

1. Sprinkle gelatine over water in a small bowl. Leave to stand for 10 minutes.

2. Dissolve gelatine over a pan of hot water and cool slightly.
To microwave: Cook for about 30 seconds, stirring every 10 seconds, until dissolved. Cool slightly.

3. Beat egg yolks and sugar together until thick. Transfer to a double saucepan (or basin standing over a saucepan of simmering water). Alternatively use a thick based saucepan.

4. Add milk. Cook, stirring, until custard thickens and coats back of a spoon thinly. (Do not boil or mixture will curdle.)

5. Remove from heat and add vanilla and dissolved gelatine.

6. Whisk egg whites to a stiff snow and fold into custard mixture.

7. Pour into a 1.1 litre (2 pint) mould, first rinsed with cold water.

8. Chill until firm and set. Turn out on to a plate.

GRAPE & BUTTERSCOTCH POTS

Preparation 15 mins **plus chilling**   *Serves 4*

225 g (8 oz) seedless grapes
150 ml (5 fl oz) fresh soured cream
150 ml (¼ pint) fresh milk
49 g (1.7 oz) sachet butterscotch instant dessert mix
grated rind and juice of ½ lemon

1. Reserve 8 grapes, halve remainder and place in 4 individual dishes.

2. Combine soured cream with milk in a bowl.

3. Sprinkle dessert mix on top of cream and milk, whisk until light and creamy.

4. Stir in lemon rind and juice.

5. Spoon over grapes and chill well.

6. Decorate with reserved grapes and serve.

EASY FRUIT BRÛLÉE

Preparation 10 mins **plus** 2 hrs **chilling**
Cooking 5 mins   *Serves 4*

350 g (12 oz) mixed summer fruits
200 ml (7 fl oz) fresh double cream
200 g (7 oz) natural yogurt
65 g (2½ oz) demerara sugar

1. Reserve some fruit for decoration. Place remainder in base of a flameproof dish.

2. Whip cream until softly stiff, fold in yogurt. Spread over fruit and chill for 2 hours.

3. Sprinkle sugar over cream and place under a hot grill for a few minutes until sugar melts and caramelizes.

4. Serve decorated with reserved fruit.

STRAWBERRY CRISPY LAYER

Preparation 20 mins   *Serves 6*

350 g (12 oz) curd cheese, softened
275 g (10 oz) strawberry yogurt
1 round chocolate cornflake crisp
100 g (4 oz) strawberries, sliced
3 strawberries, halved for decoration

1. Mix together curd cheese and yogurt.

2. Place cornflake crisp in a large plastic bag and crush into small pieces.

3. Place a layer of cornflake crisp in the base of 6 serving glasses, then a layer of fruit topped with a layer of yogurt mixture. Repeat layers.

4. Decorate with a little cornflake crisp and halved strawberries.

RASPBERRY & WALNUT SWIRL

Preparation 20 mins   *Serves 4*

225 g (8 oz) raspberries
30 ml (2 tbsp) clear honey
150 g (5 oz) natural yogurt
225 g (8 oz) fromage frais
50 g (2 oz) walnuts, roughly chopped
mint and raspberries for decoration

1. Lightly mash raspberries with a fork and mix with half the quantities of honey, yogurt and fromage frais.

2. In a separate bowl mix remaining honey, yogurt, fromage frais and walnuts.

3. Place half of raspberry mixture into 4 individual dishes.

4. Spoon over most of walnut mixture and then remaining raspberry mixture.

5. Top with remaining walnut mixture and swirl mixtures together with a cocktail stick.

6. Decorate with whole raspberries and sprigs of mint.

APPLE & HAZELNUT CRUNCH

Preparation 20 mins **plus chilling**
Cooking 10 mins   *Serves 4*

450 g (1 lb) apples,
    peeled, cored and sliced
sugar
150 g (5 oz) hazelnut yogurt
2 fruit and nut crunchy bars
slices of apple, dipped in lemon juice

1. Place apples in a saucepan with 45 ml (3 tbsp) water. Simmer until tender.
To microwave: Place apples in a bowl with 45 ml (3 tbsp) water. Cover and cook for 3–4 minutes until tender.

2. Add sufficient sugar to sweeten to taste. Leave until cold.

3. Stir yogurt into stewed apple.

4. Spoon into 4 glasses or individual dishes.

5. Crush fruit and nut bars and sprinkle over apple.

6. Decorate with apple slices.

FRUITY YOGURT POTS

FRUITY YOGURT POTS

Preparation 20 mins **plus chilling**
Cooking 3 mins   *Serves 4*

7.5 ml (1½ tsp) gelatine
45 ml (3 tbsp) orange juice
15 ml (1 tbsp) clear honey
425 g (15 oz) natural yogurt
50 g (2 oz) no-soak dried apricots, chopped
175 g (6 oz) grapes, seeded and quartered

1. Sprinkle gelatine over orange juice in a small bowl. Leave to stand for 10 minutes.

2. Dissolve gelatine over a pan of hot water. Leave to cool.
To microwave: Cook for 20–30 seconds, stirring every 10 seconds, until dissolved. Leave to cool.

3. Blend together honey and yogurt.

4. Reserve some fruit to decorate, stir remainder into yogurt with gelatine.

5. Divide between 4 individual dishes and decorate with reserved fruit.

6. Chill until set.

PASHKA   Ⓕ

Preparation 25 mins **plus chilling overnight**
                         Serves 8

450 g (1 lb) curd cheese
75 g (3 oz) caster sugar
2.5 ml (½ tsp) vanilla essence
75 ml (3 fl oz) fresh double cream
50 g (2 oz) blanched almonds, chopped
50 g (2 oz) raisins
50 g (2 oz) glacé fruits, chopped
1 piece preserved stem ginger, chopped
glacé fruit, angelica, almonds to decorate

1. Line a 900 ml (1½ pint) basin with a double thickness of scalded muslin (or use a *clean* J-cloth).

2. Beat cheese, sugar and vanilla essence together until smooth.

3. Lightly whip cream and fold into cheese mixture with almonds, fruit and ginger.

4. Spoon into prepared bowl and fold cloth over. Cover with a saucer and place a weight on top. Chill overnight.

5. Remove weight and plate, unfold cloth and invert pudding on to a serving plate. Peel off muslin.

6. Decorate with glacé fruit and nuts.

YOGURT CRUNCH CUPS

Preparation 10 mins   *Serves 4*

4 peach halves, fresh or canned
275 g (10 oz) Greek-style natural yogurt
50 g (2 oz) crunchy oat cereal
4 chocolate shells
4 chocolate leaves, to decorate

1. Chop peaches and stir into yogurt with cereal.

2. Spoon mixture into chocolate shells and decorate with chocolate leaves.

3. Serve immediately.

YUMMY CHOCOLATE PUDDING

Preparation 15 mins **plus chilling**
Cooking 10 mins   *Serves 4*

30 ml (2 tbsp) cornflour
25 g (1 oz) sugar
300 ml (½ pint) fresh milk
100 g (4 oz) plain chocolate
150 ml (5 fl oz) fresh whipping cream
grated white chocolate and cocoa powder
    to decorate

1. Mix cornflour and sugar to a paste with a little milk.

2. Heat remaining milk in a small pan until almost boiling, stir into cornflour mixture and return to pan.

3. Heat stirring until mixture thickens and boils. Cook stirring for 2 minutes. Remove from the heat.

4. Break up chocolate and add to sauce, stir until melted.

5. Cover with dampened greaseproof paper and leave to cool, but not cold and set.

6. Whip cream until softly stiff. Fold into chocolate mixture.

7. Spoon into four individual dishes and chill.

8. Decorate with white chocolate and dust with cocoa powder.

GOOSEBERRY WHIP

Preparation 25 mins **plus chilling**
Cooking 10 mins   *Serves 4*

225 g (8 oz) gooseberries
45 ml (3 tbsp) cold water
25–50 g (1–2 oz) granulated sugar
10 ml (2 tsp) gelatine
60 ml (4 tbsp) hot water
2.5 ml (½ tsp) grated lemon rind
100 ml (4 fl oz) fresh double cream
10 ml (2 tsp) fresh milk
1 egg white
green food colouring (optional)
angelica leaves to decorate

1. Top and tail gooseberries. Put into a saucepan with cold water.
To microwave: Top and tail gooseberries. Put into a bowl with cold water.

2. Bring slowly to the boil. Cover pan with a lid and simmer until fruit is soft.
To microwave: Cover and cook for 3–4 minutes, stirring occasionally, until soft.

3. Remove from heat. Sweeten to taste with sugar. Either rub through a sieve or liquidise.

4. Sprinkle gelatine over water in a small basin. Leave to stand for 10 minutes.

5. Dissolve gelatine over a pan of hot water. Leave to cool.
To microwave: Cook for about 30 seconds, stirring every 10 seconds, until dissolved. Leave to cool.

6. Add cooled gelatine to gooseberry mixture with lemon rind. Leave until just beginning to thicken.

7. Whip 50 ml (2 fl oz) cream and milk together until softly stiff. Gradually stir in fruit mixture.

8. Beat egg white to a stiff snow and fold in.

9. Tint pale green with colouring, if used. Turn into a large serving bowl and chill until firm and set.

10. Just before serving, whip remaining cream until softly stiff and use with angelica to decorate.

CRÈME CARAMEL

Preparation 15 mins **Cooking** 1¼ hrs   *Serves 4*

115 g (4½ oz) sugar
150 ml (¼ pint) cold water
568 ml (1 pint) fresh milk
4 eggs, lightly whisked
2.5 ml (½ tsp) vanilla essence
150 ml (5 fl oz) fresh single cream

1. Put 100 g (4 oz) sugar and cold water into a small heavy based saucepan. Stand over a low heat and stir until sugar dissolves.
To microwave: Put 100 g (4 oz) sugar and water into a large heatproof dish.

2. Bring to the boil, then boil more briskly – without stirring – until syrup turns a deep gold. Remove from heat and pour into a greased 900 ml (1½ pint) ovenproof dish.
To microwave: Cook for 2 minutes. Stir until sugar dissolves, then cook for 4–5 minutes until golden brown.

3. Tilt dish quickly so that base is completely covered with caramel.

4. Warm milk and pour on to lightly whisked eggs, remaining sugar and vanilla.
To microwave: Heat milk for 3 minutes and pour on to lightly whisked eggs, remaining sugar and vanilla.

5. Strain into dish and stand in a roasting tin containing enough hot water to come half way up sides of dish.
To microwave: Strain into dish and stand in a larger container with enough BOILING water to come half way up the dish.

6. Bake at 170°C (325°F) Mark 3 and cook for 1 hour or until set.
To microwave: Cook on MEDIUM (50%) for 10–15 minutes until just set.

7. Remove from oven and cool.

8. Turn out onto a serving dish when completely cold, preferably next day.

9. Serve chilled with single cream.

Variation

SMALL CRÈMES CARAMEL

Follow recipe and method for crème caramel (above). Very carefully spoon equal amounts of hot caramel into 6 individual, well greased metal moulds or ramekin dishes. Strain in custard mixture, bake for 45 min, or until set. Leave until completely cold before unmoulding.

CRÈME BRÛLÉE ('BURNT' CREAM)

Preparation 15 mins **plus chilling**
Cooking 15 mins   *Serves 4*

4 egg yolks
300 ml (10 fl oz) fresh double cream
45 ml (3 tbsp) icing sugar, sifted
5 ml (1 tsp) vanilla essence
caster sugar

1. Beat egg yolks thoroughly.

2. Heat cream until hot in a double saucepan (or basin standing over a saucepan of simmering water).

3. Pour hot cream on to yolks, beating all the time.

4. Return mixture to saucepan or basin. Add icing sugar and vanilla.

5. Cook without boiling, stirring all the time, until mixture thickens and coats back of a spoon heavily.

6. Remove from heat, pour into 568 ml (1 pint) greased, flameproof dish and chill overnight.

7. About 1 hour before serving, sprinkle a 0.5 cm (¼ inch) thick layer of caster sugar over the top.

8. Stand under a hot grill and leave until sugar starts to turn deep gold and caramelise.

9. Remove from heat and chill again.

CRÈME MONTE CARLO

Preparation 20 mins **plus chilling**   *Serves 4*

312 g (11 oz) can mandarin oranges in natural juice
300 ml (10 fl oz) fresh double cream
30 ml (2 tbsp) fresh milk
30 ml (2 tbsp) icing sugar, sifted
5 ml (1 tsp) grated tangerine rind (optional)
6 meringue halves, bought or home made

1. Reserve 8 mandarin segments for decoration.

2. Divide remainder, with some juice, between 4 sundae glasses.

3. Whip cream and milk together until mixture stands in soft peaks then stir in sugar and tangerine rind if used.

4. Break up meringues into small pieces and fold into cream mixture.

5. Pile over fruit in glasses. Decorate each with 2 mandarin segments.

6. Chill well before serving.

SYLLABUB

Preparation 15 mins
plus 3 hrs **standing and chilling**   *Serves 6*

150 ml (¼ pint) white wine
30 ml (2 tbsp) lemon juice
10 ml (2 tsp) grated lemon rind
75 g (3 oz) caster sugar
300 ml (10 fl oz) fresh double cream
grated lemon rind to decorate

1. Put wine, lemon juice, rind and sugar into a bowl. Leave for a minimum of 3 hours.

2. Add cream and whip until mixture stands in soft peaks.

3. Transfer to 6 wine or sundae glasses and decorate with grated lemon rind.

4. Chill for several hours before serving.

ORANGE SYLLABUB

Preparation 15 mins **plus chilling**   *Serves 4*

rind and juice of 1 medium orange
30 ml (2 tbsp) orange liqueur
50 g (2 oz) caster sugar
100 g (4 oz) fromage frais
150 ml (5 fl oz) fresh double cream
orange rind to decorate
crisp biscuits to serve

1. Stir orange rind, juice, liqueur and sugar into fromage frais.

2. Whip cream until softly stiff and fold into orange mixture.

3. Spoon into 4 wine glasses and chill.

4. Decorate with orange rind and serve with crisp biscuits.

This dessert separates into two layers when chilled.

RICH FRUIT FOOL

RICH FRUIT FOOL

Preparation 30 mins **plus cooling**
Cooking 15 mins   *Serves 4*

450 g (1 lb) gooseberries, apples, black or
    redcurrants, rhubarb, blackberries or
    raspberries
45 ml (3 tbsp) water
75–175 g (3–6 oz) caster sugar, to sweeten
    depending on sharpness of fruit
350 ml (12 fl oz) fresh double cream
30 ml (2 tbsp) fresh milk
red or green food colouring (optional)
chopped walnuts or chopped toasted
    almonds and fruit for decoration

1. Prepare fruit according to type. Put into a
saucepan with water.
*To microwave: Prepare fruit according to
type. Put into a bowl with water.*

2. Bring slowly to the boil, cover with lid and
simmer until fruit is soft.
*To microwave: Cover and cook for
2–5 minutes, stirring occasionally, or until
fruit is soft.*

3. Remove from heat. Add sugar to taste.
Either rub through a sieve or liquidise. Leave
until completely cold.

4. Whip 300 ml (½ pint) cream and milk
together until lightly stiff then gradually fold
in fruit purée.

5. If fool is pale in colour tint with food
colouring, if used.

6. Transfer to 4 sundae glasses and chill.

7. Before serving, whip remaining cream
until thick, pipe whirls on top of each fool,
then decorate with nuts and fruit.

Variations

CUSTARD FRUIT FOOL

Follow recipe and method for rich fruit fool
(left) but instead of cream and milk,
combine 300 ml (½ pint) fairly thick cold
custard with fruit purée.

CUSTARD CREAM
FRUIT FOOL

Follow recipe and method for rich fruit fool
(left) but use half the cream and milk and
150 ml (¼ pint) cold custard. Mix custard with
fruit purée then fold in whipped cream and
milk.

SUMMER PUDDING   Ⓕ

Preparation 25 mins **plus chilling overnight**
Cooking 10 mins   *Serves 4–6*

6 large slices of bread, crusts removed
100g (4oz) sugar
75ml (5tbsp) water
700g (1½lb) soft summer fruits (either
     rhubarb, raspberries, strawberries,
     gooseberries, stoned cherries, black or
     redcurrants, or a mixture of fruits)
fruits and a sprig of mint to decorate
150ml (5floz) fresh double cream
15ml (1tbsp) fresh milk

1. Cut bread into neat fingers.
2. Put sugar and water into a saucepan and
heat slowly until sugar melts, stirring.
To microwave: Put sugar and water into a
bowl and cook for about 2 minutes, stirring
frequently, until dissolved.
3. Add fruit and simmer gently for about
7–10 minutes (gooseberries and
blackcurrants may take a few minutes
longer).
To microwave: Add fruit, cover and cook for
3–7 minutes, stirring occasionally, until soft.
4. Reserve a few spoonfuls of the juice.

5. Line base and sides of a 1.1litre (2pint)
pudding basin with bread fingers.
6. Add half the hot fruit mixture. Cover with
more bread fingers.
7. Pour in remaining fruit mixture and top
with remaining bread fingers.
8. Cover with a saucer or plate. Place a
heavy weight on top.
9. Refrigerate overnight.
10. Turn out on to a plate. If there are any
white patches spoon reserved juice over
them. Decorate with fruit and mint.
11. Serve with cream, whipped with milk
until lightly stiff.

Variation

AUTUMN PUDDING   Ⓕ

Follow recipe and method for summer
pudding (left). In place of soft summer fruits
use 700g (1½lb) prepared mixed autumn
fruit such as blackberries, apples, pears and
plums.

SUMMER PUDDING

GINGER PEAR TRIFLE

GINGER PEAR TRIFLE

Preparation 30 mins **Cooking** 5 mins · *Serves 6*

15 g (½ oz) custard powder
15 ml (1 tbsp) sugar
300 ml (½ pint) fresh milk
150 g (5 oz) ginger cake, sliced
410 g (14.4 oz) can pears in natural juice,
 drained and sliced
150 ml (¼ pint) cider
150 ml (5 fl oz) fresh whipping cream
25 g (1 oz) flaked almonds, toasted

1. Blend custard powder and sugar with a little of the milk.

2. Bring remaining milk to the boil and pour on to custard mixture, stirring well.
To microwave: Heat milk for 2–3 minutes or until boiling. Pour on to custard mixture, stirring well.

3. Return to pan, bring to the boil, stirring. Cook for 1 minute. Leave to cool.
To microwave: Cook for 1 minute. Cool.

4. Arrange ginger cake in a glass serving dish. Cover with pears and pour over cider.

5. Pour cooled custard over trifle and leave to set.

6. Whip cream until softly stiff.

7. Pipe over custard and decorate with almonds.

8. Serve chilled.

CHOCOLATE APRICOT TRIFLE

Preparation 20 mins plus chilling *Serves 4–6*

1 cream-filled chocolate Swiss roll
410 g (14.4 oz) can apricot halves
30 ml (2 tbsp) orange juice or brandy
150 ml (5 fl oz) fresh double cream
15 ml (1 tbsp) fresh milk
30 ml (2 tbsp) icing sugar, sifted
50 g (2 oz) plain chocolate,
 grated for decoration

1. Cut Swiss roll into about 10 slices. Arrange over base of a shallow serving dish, overlapping if necessary.

2. Moisten with 60 ml (4 tbsp) syrup from apricots mixed with juice or brandy. Arrange drained apricots on top.

3. Whip cream and milk together until softly stiff. Stir in sugar.

4. Pile over apricots and chill.

5. Just before serving, sprinkle with chocolate.

RASPBERRY AMARETTO TRIFLE

Preparation 30 mins **Cooking** 5 mins   *Serves 8*

4 trifle sponges
60 ml (4 tbsp) raspberry jam
150 ml (¼ pint) sherry
45 ml (3 tbsp) almond liqueur (optional)
50 g (2 oz) ground almonds
50 g (2 oz) ratafia biscuits, crumbled
225 g (8 oz) frozen raspberries, thawed
4 egg yolks
50 g (2 oz) caster sugar
15 g (½ oz) cornflour
450 ml (¾ pint) fresh milk
300 ml (10 fl oz) fresh double cream
toasted almonds to decorate

1. Halve trifle sponges and sandwich together with jam.

2. Cut each into 4 and arrange in a trifle dish.

3. Pour over sherry and 15 ml (1 tbsp) almond liqueur. Sprinkle with 25 g (1 oz) ground almonds and crumbled ratafia biscuits.

4. Reserve a few raspberries for decoration and place remainder in dish.

5. Blend egg yolks, sugar and cornflour with 15 ml (1 tbsp) milk.

6. Heat remaining milk in a saucepan.
To microwave: Heat milk for 2–3 minutes.

7. When hot, blend in cornflour mixture and heat gently until thickened, stirring continuously.
To microwave: Blend in cornflour mixture and cook for about 2 minutes, stirring frequently, until thickened.

8. Remove from heat and stir in remaining almond liqueur, ground almonds and 45 ml (3 tbsp) fresh cream into custard. Pour over raspberries, leave to cool.

9. Whip remaining cream until softly stiff.

10. Decorate with whirls of cream, almonds and reserved raspberries.

STRAWBERRY SENSATION TRIFLE

Preparation 25 mins **plus chilling**   *Serves 6*

1 large jam Swiss roll
30 ml (2 tbsp) Kirsch liqueur
450 g (1 lb) strawberries, hulled and halved
150 ml (¼ pint) white wine
30 ml (2 tbsp) lemon juice
75 g (3 oz) caster sugar
300 ml (10 fl oz) fresh double cream
chopped pistachio nuts and sliced
    strawberries to decorate

1. Slice Swiss roll and arrange in a large glass bowl. Pour over Kirsch.

2. Place strawberries on top.

3. Put wine, lemon juice and sugar in a bowl.

4. Add cream and whip until mixture is softly stiff and holds its shape.

5. Pour over strawberries, cover and refrigerate for about 2 hours.

6. Decorate with nuts and strawberry slices.

TROPICAL TRIFLE

Preparation 45 mins   *Serves 6*

50 g (2 oz) strawberries, sliced
2 bananas, peeled and sliced
1 kiwi fruit, peeled and sliced
2 apples, cored and diced
1 mango, peeled, stoned and diced
225 g (8 oz) can pineapple chunks in
    natural juice, drained
juice of ½ lemon
75 g (3 oz) ratafia biscuits
50 ml (2 fl oz) white wine, sherry or fruit juice
150 ml (5 fl oz) fresh whipping cream
225 g (8 oz) Greek-style yogurt

1. Combine prepared fruit in a large bowl with lemon juice to prevent browning.

2. Place biscuits in base of a glass dish, pour over wine and leave to soak for 5 minutes.

3. Spoon fruit salad over biscuits, reserving a few pieces for decoration.

4. Whip cream until softly stiff, fold into yogurt and spoon over fruit.

5. Decorate with reserved fruit.

TRIPLE DECKER DESSERT

Preparation 15 mins **plus chilling**   *Serves 6*

400g (14oz) can black cherry pie filling
150g (5oz) fromage frais
150ml (5 fl oz) fresh double cream, whipped
30ml (2 tbsp) clear honey
50g (2oz) crunchy nut cornflakes

1. Divide cherry pie filling between 6 small dishes.

2. In a bowl, mix fromage frais, cream and honey together.

3. Spoon on top of pie filling.

4. Place cornflakes in a plastic bag and gently crush.

5. Sprinkle over the desserts.

6. Chill if desired before serving.

ALMOND & APRICOT FLAN

Preparation 35 mins **Cooking** 45 mins   *Serves 6*

short crust pasty
    made with 100g (4oz) flour (page 364)
30ml (2 tbsp) apricot jam
75g (3oz) butter
75g (3oz) caster sugar
1 egg
25g (1oz) cake crumbs (from plain cake)
50g (2oz) ground almonds
25g (1oz) self raising flour
15ml (1 tbsp) fresh milk
410g (14.4oz) can apricot halves, drained
150ml (5 fl oz) fresh double cream
6 glacé cherries

1. Roll out pastry on a floured work surface.

2. Use to line a 15–18cm (6–7 inch) flan tin.

3. Spread base with jam.

4. Cream butter with sugar until light and fluffy, then beat in egg.

5. Stir in cake crumbs and almonds. Fold in flour alternately with milk.

6. Transfer to pastry case and smooth top with a knife.

7. Bake at 220°C (425°F) Mark 7 for 15 mins.

8. Reduce temperature to 180°C (350°F) Mark 4 and bake for a further 30 mins.

9. Remove from flan tin and leave until cold.

10. Just before serving, cover top of cold flan with apricot halves.

11. Whip cream until softly stiff and use to decorate with glacé cherries.

LEMON MERINGUE PIE

Preparation 25 mins **Cooking** 1 hr   *Serves 4–6*

short crust pastry
    made with 175g (6oz) flour (page 364)
30ml (2 tbsp) cornflour
50g (2oz) sugar
grated rind and juice of 2 large lemons
150ml (¼ pint) water
2 egg yolks
15g (½oz) butter
meringue topping made with 2 egg whites
    (page 215)

1. Roll out pastry on a floured work surface. Use it to line a 20.5cm (8 inch) fluted flan ring resting on a lightly greased baking sheet.

2. Prick well all over, line with aluminium foil (to prevent pastry rising as it cooks).

3. Bake at 200°C (400°F) Mark 6 for 15 minutes.

4. Remove foil. Return flan to oven. Bake for a further 15 minutes or until crisp and golden. Remove from oven.

5. To make filling, put cornflour, sugar and lemon rind into a basin. Mix to a smooth paste with a little of the cold water.

6. Heat remaining water with lemon juice. Combine with paste then return to pan.
To microwave: Heat water with lemon juice for 1 minute. Combine with paste and return to microwave.

7. Cook, stirring, until mixture comes to the boil and thickens. Simmer for 3 minutes.
To microwave: Cook for 2–3 minutes, stirring frequently, until mixture thickens and boils.

8. Beat in yolks and butter. Cook gently for a further minute then pour into flan case.
To microwave: Beat in yolks and butter. Cook for 30 seconds then pour into flan case.

9. Pile meringue on top. Bake as directed for meringue topping (page 215).

10. Serve very cold.

BERRY FLAN Ⓕ

Preparation 40 mins **plus chilling**
Cooking 35 mins *Serves 6*

sweet flan pastry
  made with 175 g (6 oz) flour (page 365)
1 egg yolk
25 g (1 oz) caster sugar
15 g (½ oz) flour
2.5 ml (½ tsp) vanilla essence
150 ml (¼ pint) fresh milk
450 g (1 lb) raspberries, strawberries or
  loganberries
30 ml (2 tbsp) redcurrant jelly, melted
150 ml (5 fl oz) fresh double cream
15 ml (1 tbsp) fresh milk
15 ml (1 tbsp) icing sugar, sifted
10 ml (2 tsp) orange juice or sherry

1. Roll out pastry on a floured work surface. Use it to line a 18 cm (7 inch) fluted flan ring resting on a lightly greased baking sheet. Prick well all over.

2. Line with aluminium foil (to prevent pastry rising as it cooks).

3. Bake at 200°C (400°F) Mark 6 for 15 minutes.

4. Remove foil. Return flan to oven. Bake for a further 15 minutes (or until crisp and golden). Remove and cool.

5. Beat egg yolk and sugar together until thick and light.

6. Stir in flour and vanilla and gradually blend in milk.

7. Pour into a small saucepan and cook, stirring, until mixture comes to the boil and thickens. Simmer for 3 minutes.

8. Remove from heat and cool.

9. When completely cold, spread over base of flan case, cover with berries and brush with melted redcurrant jelly.

10. Beat cream and milk together until thick. Stir in sugar and orange juice or sherry.

11. Pipe or spoon mixture over fruit filling.

12. Chill for 30 minutes before serving.

Variation

GRAPE FLAN Ⓕ

Follow recipe and method for berry flan (left) but omit soft fruit and use halved and seeded black and green grapes. Brush with melted apricot jam instead of redcurrant jelly.

BERRY FLAN

BAKED SOURED CREAM CHEESECAKE

Preparation 30 mins **plus chilling**
Cooking 1 hr 20 mins   *Serves 10*

50 g (2 oz) butter, melted
100 g (4 oz) digestive biscuits, crushed
1.25 ml (¼ tsp) ground cinnamon
450 g (1 lb) cream cheese, softened
150 g (5 oz) sugar
3 eggs, beaten
grated rind of 1 lemon
30 ml (2 tbsp) lemon juice
7.5 ml (1½ tsp) vanilla essence
300 ml (10 fl oz) soured cream
grated lemon and lime rind to decorate

1. Mix together melted butter, biscuit crumbs and cinnamon.

2. Press into base of a greased loose-bottomed 20.5 cm (8 inch) cake tin.

3. Cook at 180°C (350°F) Mark 4 for 10 minutes.

4. Beat together cream cheese and 100 g (4 oz) sugar, gradually beat in eggs.

5. Stir in lemon rind, juice and vanilla essence.

6. Pour into tin and bake for 1 hour or until centre is firm to touch.

7. Remove from oven and increase temperature to 230°C (450°F) Mark 8.

8. Mix together remaining sugar and soured cream, spread over cheesecake, bake for 8 minutes, until set.

9. Remove from oven and cool in tin.

10. Remove from tin and chill until ready to serve.

11. Decorate with lemon and lime rind.

PIÑA COLADA CHEESECAKE

Preparation 30 mins **plus chilling**   *Serves 8*

50 g (2 oz) butter, melted
100 g (4 oz) digestive biscuits, crushed
25 g (1 oz) desiccated coconut
135 g (4¾ oz) packet pineapple jelly
225 g (8 oz) skimmed milk soft cheese, softened
150 g (5 oz) natural yogurt
30 ml (2 tbsp) coconut rum liqueur
150 ml (5 fl oz) fresh whipping cream
fresh pineapple and kiwi fruit to decorate

CITRUS CHEESECAKE

1. Mix butter, biscuit crumbs and coconut together. Press into base of a greased loose-bottomed 20.5 cm (8 inch) cake tin and chill.

2. Dissolve jelly in 150 ml (¼ pint) hot water, cool slightly.
To microwave: Cook jelly in 150 ml (¼ pint) water for about 2 minutes. Stir well until dissolved.

3. Beat together cheese, yogurt and rum. Gradually stir in jelly and mix well.

4. Whip cream until softly stiff and fold into cheese mixture.

5. Pour on to biscuit base and chill until set.

6. Remove from tin and decorate with fresh sliced fruit.

Variation

PEACH CHEESECAKE

Follow recipe and method for piña colada cheesecake (left) but omit desiccated coconut and liqueur. Use a peach jelly and add 2 chopped peaches to cheese mixture. Decorate with sliced peaches.

PEACHY CHEESE SLICE

Preparation 25 mins **plus chilling**
Cooking 5 mins   *Serves 7*

11 g (0.4 oz) sachet gelatine
45 ml (3 tbsp) water
7 moist cereal bars
350 g (12 oz) curd cheese
25 g (1 oz) icing sugar
150 g (5 oz) peach yogurt
410 g (14.4 oz) can peach slices in natural juice, drained
1 egg white
lime slices to decorate

1. Sprinkle gelatine over water in a small bowl. Leave to stand for 10 minutes.

2. Dissolve gelatine over a pan of hot water. Leave to cool.
To microwave: Cook for about 30 seconds, stirring every 10 seconds, until dissolved. Leave to cool.

3. Line a 900 g (2 lb) loaf tin with non-stick baking paper. Arrange cereal bars across base, covering it completely.

4. Beat together cheese, sugar and yogurt until smooth.

5. Reserve 4 peach slices for decoration, chop remainder and stir into cheese mixture with cooled gelatine.

6. Whisk egg white until stiff and fold into peach mixture.

7. Pour into loaf tin and chill until set.

8. Turn out on to a serving plate and decorate with reserved peaches and lime.

CITRUS CHEESECAKE

Preparation 45 mins **plus chilling**
Cooking 5 mins   *Serves 8*

225 g (8 oz) plain chocolate digestive biscuits, crushed
40 g (1½ oz) butter, melted
15 g (½ oz) gelatine
60 ml (4 tbsp) water
225 g (8 oz) full fat soft cheese
3 eggs, separated
50 g (2 oz) caster sugar
grated rind and juice of 2 lemons
300 ml (10 fl oz) fresh whipping cream
100 g (4 oz) lemon curd
150 ml (5 fl oz) fresh double cream, whipped
lemon strips and angelica to decorate

1. Mix biscuit crumbs and butter together, press into base of a greased loose-bottomed 20.5 cm (8 inch) cake tin.

2. Chill for 30 minutes until firm.

3. Sprinkle gelatine over water in a small bowl. Leave to stand for 10 minutes.

4. Dissolve gelatine over a saucepan of hot water. Leave to cool.
To microwave: Cook for about 30 seconds, stirring every 10 seconds, until dissolved. Cool.

5. In a large bowl, blend together soft cheese, egg yolks, sugar, lemon rind and juice.

6. Whip whipping cream until softly stiff.

7. Add gelatine and fold in whipped cream.

8. Beat egg whites until stiff and fold into mixture.

9. Pour into prepared tin, spoon on lemon curd and swirl with end of a sharp knife. Chill until set.

10. Remove from tin and decorate with piped double cream, lemon and angelica.

CHOCOLATE MOUSSE CUPS

Preparation 20 mins **plus cooling**
Cooking 5 mins   *Serves 6*

90 g (3½ oz) plain chocolate
50 ml (2 fl oz) fresh milk
200 ml (7 fl oz) fresh whipping cream
100 g (4 oz) strawberries, sliced
6 chocolate cups

1. Melt chocolate in a bowl over a pan of hot water.
To microwave: Break up chocolate and place in a bowl.

2. Heat milk until boiling, then whisk into chocolate. Leave to cool.
To microwave: Add milk and cook on MEDIUM (50%) for about 2 minutes, stirring twice, until melted. Leave until cool.

3. Whip 150 ml (5 fl oz) cream until softly stiff and fold into cool chocolate mixture.

4. Reserve 6 strawberry slices, place remainder in chocolate cups.

5. Spoon in chocolate cream and smooth over tops.

6. Whip remaining cream and use to decorate with reserved strawberries.

POTS-AU-CHOCOLAT

Preparation 15 mins **plus chilling**
Cooking 5 mins   *Serves 4*

75 g (3 oz) plain chocolate
25 g (1 oz) butter
3 eggs, separated
15 ml (1 tbsp) warm water
75 ml (3 fl oz) fresh double cream
chocolate flakes to decorate

1. Break up chocolate and place in a basin standing over a saucepan of hot water.
To microwave: Break up chocolate and place in a bowl.

2. Add butter and leave until both have melted, stirring once or twice.
To microwave: Add butter and cook on MEDIUM (50%) for about 2 minutes, stirring twice, until both have melted.

3. Beat in egg yolks. When smooth, remove from heat and stir in warm water.

4. Beat egg whites to a stiff snow and gently fold into chocolate mixture.

5. Spoon into 4 individual dishes and chill.

6. Just before serving, decorate each with cream, whipped until lightly stiff, and chocolate flakes.

POTS-AU-CHOCOLAT

Variation
POTS-AU-CHOCOLAT WITH BRANDY OR RUM

Follow recipe and method for pots-au-chocolat (left) but omit water. Use instead 15ml (1 tbsp) lukewarm brandy or rum.

CHOCOLATE GINGER ROULADE   Ⓕ

Preparation 40 mins **plus cooling**
Cooking 30 mins   *Serves 6–8*

60 ml (4 tbsp) cocoa powder
150 ml (¼ pint) fresh milk
5 eggs, separated
150 g (5 oz) caster sugar
300 ml (10 fl oz) fresh double cream, whipped
30 ml (2 tbsp) ginger preserve jam
icing sugar, preserved stem ginger and chocolate shapes to decorate

1. Mix cocoa powder and milk in a pan and heat gently until dissolved, leave to cool.
To microwave: Mix cocoa powder and milk in a jug and cook for 1–2 minutes, stirring occasionally, until dissolved. Leave to cool.

2. Whisk egg yolks and sugar together until pale and fluffy, then whisk in cooled milk mixture.

3. Whisk egg whites until stiff, fold into cocoa mixture.

4. Spoon into a greased and lined 33×23 cm (13×9 inch) Swiss roll tin and bake at 180°C (350°F) Mark 4 for 20–25 minutes until risen and firm.

5. Turn out on to greaseproof paper and cover with a warm, damp tea towel, leave to cool for 20 minutes. Cut off and discard outside edges.

6. Reserve a third of the cream, fold ginger preserve into remainder and spread on to sponge, roll up carefully.

7. Dust with icing sugar then decorate with reserved cream, pieces of ginger and chocolate shapes.

CHOCOLATE ORANGE CHARLOTTE

Preparation 1 hr **plus chilling**
Cooking 10 mins   *Serves 8*

15 g (½ oz) gelatine
45 ml (3 tbsp) water
175 g (6 oz) plain chocolate
300 ml (½ pint) fresh milk
30 ml (2 tbsp) orange brandy
2 eggs, separated
50 g (2 oz) soft light brown sugar
grated rind and juice of 2 oranges
300 ml (10 fl oz) fresh double cream, whipped
about 30 Langues de Chat biscuits
chocolate triangles and grated orange rind to decorate

1. Sprinkle gelatine over water in a small bowl. Leave to stand for 10 minutes.

2. Dissolve gelatine over a pan of hot water. Leave to cool.
To microwave: Cook for 20–30 seconds, stirring every 10 seconds until dissolved. Cool.

3. Break up chocolate and place in a small pan with milk.
To microwave: Break up chocolate and place in a bowl with milk.

4. Gently heat until melted. Stir in orange brandy.
To microwave: Cook on MEDIUM (50%) for 3–4 minutes, stirring twice, until melted. Stir in orange brandy.

5. Beat egg yolks and sugar together until creamy, then blend in chocolate mixture.

6. Return to pan and heat gently, stirring until thickened.

7. Stir in gelatine, orange rind and juice. Cool.

8. Fold in two-thirds of cream.

9. Whisk egg whites until stiff and fold into mixture.

10. Pour into a lightly greased loose bottomed, deep 19 cm (7½ inch) cake tin and chill until set.

11. Turn out on to a plate. Arrange biscuits around sides.

12. Decorate with remaining cream, chocolate triangles and orange rind.

PROFITEROLES Ⓕ

Preparation 30 mins **Cooking** 30 mins *Serves 4*

choux pastry made with 65 g (2½ oz) flour
  (page 368)
300 ml (10 fl oz) fresh double cream
30 ml (2 tbsp) fresh milk
45 ml (3 tbsp) icing sugar, sifted
luxury chocolate sauce (page 243)

1. Pipe or spoon 20 equal amounts of choux pastry – well apart – on greased baking sheets.

2. Bake at 220°C (425°F) Mark 7 for 25 minutes or until golden and well puffed.

3. Remove from oven. Make a small slit in side of each one.

4. Return to oven (with heat switched off) for a further 5 minutes for puffs to dry out. Cool on a wire cooling rack.

5. About 1 hour before serving, whip cream and milk together until softly stiff. Stir in sugar.

6. Halve puffs and fill with cream.

7. Pile in a pyramid shape in a shallow serving dish.

8. Serve with warm chocolate sauce.

STRAWBERRY CHOUX RING Ⓕ

Preparation 30 mins **plus chilling**
Cooking 45 mins *Serves 5–6*

choux pastry made with 65 g (2½ oz) flour
  (page 368)
300 ml (10 fl oz) fresh double cream
30 ml (2 tbsp) fresh milk
5 ml (1 tsp) vanilla essence
75 g (3 oz) icing sugar, sifted
350 g (12 oz) fresh strawberries, sliced

1. Using a piping bag and 1 cm (½ inch) plain piping tube, pipe pastry in a thick 18 cm (7 inch) ring on a greased baking sheet.

2. Bake at 200°C (400°F) Mark 6 for 15 mins.

3. Reduce to 180°C (350°F) Mark 4. Bake for a further 30 mins or until well puffed and golden. Cool on a wire cooling rack.

4. About 1 hour before serving, cut ring in half horizontally.

5. Whisk cream and milk together until softly stiff. Gently stir in vanilla, 50 g (2 oz) icing sugar and sliced strawberries.

6. Pile mixture into bottom half of ring. Replace top and dredge with remaining icing sugar. Chill before serving.

SWISS TOFFEE APPLE

Preparation 30 mins **plus chilling**
Cooking 15 mins   *Serves 6*

900 g (2 lb) cooking apples, peeled, cored
  and sliced
150 g (5 oz) sugar
30 ml (2 tbsp) water
150 ml (5 fl oz) fresh double cream
150 ml (5 fl oz) fresh single cream
50 g (2 oz) butter
30 ml (2 tbsp) golden syrup
100 g (4 oz) cornflakes

1. Place apples in a saucepan with
100 g (4 oz) sugar and water and cook until
soft.
*To microwave: Place apples in a bowl with
100 g (4 oz) sugar and water. Cover and cook
for about 7 minutes, stirring occasionally,
until soft.*

2. Strain off any juice from apples then
liquidise fruit or press through a sieve to
make a thick purée. Add a little of the juice
if necessary.

3. Place apples in a serving dish and leave
until cold.

4. Whip creams together until softly stiff,
then spread over apple.

5. Melt butter and golden syrup together.

6. Add remaining sugar and cornflakes, stir
quickly to coat flakes.

7. Scatter over cream and chill before
serving.

PINEAPPLE ROMANOFF

Preparation 25 mins **plus** 2 hrs **chilling** *Serves 4*

1 large fresh pineapple
45 ml (3 tbsp) Curaçao
225 g (8 oz) fresh strawberries
300 ml (10 fl oz) fresh double cream
75 g (3 oz) icing sugar, sifted
grated rind and juice of ½ lemon

1. Cut pineapple in half lengthways, cutting
through leafy crown as well. (Each half
should have its own crown.)

2. Remove and discard core. Gently scoop
out flesh and cut into cubes.

3. Place pineapple cubes into a bowl, mix
with Curaçao and chill for at least 2 hours.

4. About 1 hour before serving, slice all but
4 strawberries.

5. Whip cream until softly stiff then stir in
sugar, lemon rind and juice, pineapple
cubes and juices and sliced strawberries.

6. Mix well, spoon into pineapple halves and
chill for at least 30 minutes.

7. Just before serving, decorate with
remaining whole strawberries.

DEVONSHIRE ALMOND DREAMS

Preparation 15 mins **plus** 4½ hrs **chilling**
Cooking 5 mins   *Serves 4*

225 ml (8 fl oz) milk
50 ml (2 fl oz) Devonshire Royal Cream
  Liqueur
25 ml (1 fl oz) almond flavoured liqueur
45 ml (3 tbsp) sugar
50 ml (2 fl oz) water
15 g (½ oz) gelatine
150 ml (5 fl oz) fresh double cream
fresh whipped cream and melted
  chocolate to decorate

1. Place milk, liqueurs, sugar and water in a
saucepan. Bring to the boil. Simmer for
2–3 minutes until sugar has dissolved.
*To microwave: Place milk, liqueurs, sugar
and water in a jug. Cook for 2–3 minutes,
stirring frequently, until sugar dissolves.*

2. Stir in gelatine and whisk until dissolved.
*To microwave: Leave to cool for a minute or
two then whisk in gelatine until dissolved.*

3. Pour into a bowl and chill for 30 minutes
or until mixture begins to thicken.

4. Whip cream until softly stiff and fold into
chilled mixture.

5. Pour into 4 individual glass dishes and
chill for 4 hours.

6. Decorate with whipped cream and drizzle
with melted chocolate to serve.

IRISH COFFEE MOUSSE

Preparation 30 mins **plus chilling**
Cooking 3 mins   Serves 4–6

11g (0.4oz) sachet gelatine
45ml (3tbsp) water
2 eggs, separated
50g (2oz) sugar
30ml (2tbsp) coffee essence
30ml (2tbsp) Irish whiskey
300ml (10floz) fresh double cream
coffee beans to decorate

1. Sprinkle gelatine over water in a small bowl. Leave to stand for 10 minutes.

2. Dissolve gelatine over a pan of hot water. Leave to cool.
To microwave: Cook for 20–30 seconds, stir every 10 seconds, until dissolved. Cool.

3. Whisk together egg yolks, sugar and coffee essence until thick, creamy and leaves a trail.

4. Fold in whiskey and gelatine.

5. Softly whip cream, fold half into coffee mixture.

6. Whip egg whites until stiff, fold into mousse, spoon into a serving bowl or glasses.

7. Chill until set.

8. Top with remaining cream and decorate with coffee beans to serve.

CHOCOLATE BRANDY ROLL

Preparation 20 mins **plus chilling**
Cooking 15 mins   Serves 4–6

100g (4oz) plain chocolate
25g (1oz) custard powder
15g (½oz) sugar
300ml (½pint) fresh milk
200g (7oz) packet chocolate chip cookies
45ml (3tbsp) brandy or rum
300ml (10floz) fresh double cream
1 orange & chocolate triangles to decorate

1. Break up chocolate and place in a small bowl. Melt over a pan of hot water.
To microwave: Break up chocolate and place in a bowl. Cook on MEDIUM (50%) for 2–3 minutes, stirring twice, until melted.

2. Blend custard powder and sugar with a little milk.

3. Bring remaining milk to the boil and pour on to custard mixture, stirring well.
To microwave: Heat remaining milk for

IRISH COFFEE MOUSSE

2–3 minutes until boiling and pour on to custard mixture, stirring well.

4. Return to saucepan, bring to the boil stirring. Cook for 1 minute.
To microwave: Cook for 1 minute.

5. Stir chocolate into custard pour into a basin, cover with dampened greaseproof paper.

6. Dip each biscuit into brandy or rum.

7. Sandwich together with cold chocolate custard to form a roll.

8. Chill overnight to allow biscuits to soften.

9. Whip cream until softly stiff.

10. Spread cream over biscuit roll.

11. Decorate with slices of orange and chocolate triangles.

JUNKET

Preparation 5 mins **plus** 2 hrs **setting**
Cooking 3 mins   *Serves 4–6*

568 ml (1 pint) Pasteurised
   (or Channel Island) fresh milk
10 ml (2 tsp) caster sugar
5 ml (1 tsp) rennet essence
ground nutmeg

1. Put milk and sugar into a saucepan and warm to blood heat. The temperature should be no more than 37°C (98°F). (To test this, dip tip of the little finger in milk. It should feel comfortably warm, neither hot nor cold.)
To microwave: Put milk and sugar into a bowl or jug and heat for about 2 minutes or to blood heat. Stir once during heating and again after heating. To test for correct temperature – see conventional method.

2. Gently stir in rennet.

3. Pour into a serving dish, sprinkle with nutmeg and leave for 1½–2 hours at room temperature.

4. After junket has set, it can be chilled.

Sterilised and UHT milk are **not** suitable for junket making as the junkets will not set satisfactorily.
Junket should not be disturbed until it is served as once cut the whey separates from the curds.
Ensure that the rennet is not old as it loses it setting properties with age.

Variation

RUM OR BRANDY JUNKET

Follow recipe and method for junket (left) but add 30 ml (2 tbsp) rum or brandy to milk.

FROZEN DESSERTS

ICE CREAM

When making ice cream remember to turn on the fast freeze button an hour before placing mixture in the freezer.

Ice cream will freeze faster in a shallow container and if the sides or base are in contact with the freezer.

Do not whip the cream before adding to the other ingredients if you are freezing the mixture in an electrical ice cream maker. If the mixture has been heated, allow it to cool then chill for 30 minutes in the refrigerator before freezing.

When serving allow the ice cream or sorbet to soften slightly for 30–40 minutes in the refrigerator. This makes it easier to scoop and allows the flavour to develop. If the mixture has been frozen in small moulds allow only 5–10 minutes in the refrigerator before serving.

DAIRY ICE CREAM   ⓕ

Preparation 15 mins **plus freezing**   *Serves 6*

568 ml (1 pint) fresh double cream
60 ml (4 tbsp) fresh milk
90 g (3½ oz) icing sugar, sifted
10 ml (2 tsp) vanilla essence

1. Pour cream and milk into a well-chilled bowl and beat both together until softly stiff.

2. Stir in icing sugar and vanilla essence. Pour into a freezer container.

3. Freeze for 45 minutes or until ice cream has frozen about 1 cm (½ inch) around sides.

4. Transfer to a chilled bowl, break up with a fork and stir gently until smooth.

5. Return to a clean container and freeze for 2 hours or until firm.

Variations

CHOCOLATE CHIP DAIRY ICE CREAM   ⓕ

Follow recipe and method for dairy ice cream (left) but stir in 100 g (4 oz) coarsely grated plain chocolate before freezing.

STRAWBERRY OR RASPBERRY DAIRY ICE CREAM   ⓕ

Follow recipe and method for dairy ice cream (left). Stir in 450 g (1 lb) puréed strawberries or raspberries before freezing.

COFFEE DAIRY ICE CREAM   ⓕ

Follow recipe and method for dairy ice cream (left) but add 30 ml (2 tbsp) instant coffee granules mixed with 30 ml (2 tbsp) hot water (then left to go cold) instead of vanilla.

ORANGE DAIRY ICE CREAM   ⓕ

Follow recipe and method for dairy ice cream (left) but reduce sugar by 30 ml (2 tbsp) and omit vanilla. Add 15 ml (1 tbsp) grated orange rind and 30 ml (2 tbsp) orange brandy.

PRESERVED GINGER DAIRY ICE CREAM   ⓕ

Follow recipe and method for dairy ice cream (left) but reduce sugar by 30 ml (2 tbsp) and omit vanilla. Stir in 75 g (3 oz) finely chopped preserved stem ginger and 30 ml (2 tbsp) ginger syrup.

ALMOND DAIRY ICE CREAM   ⓕ

Follow recipe and method for dairy ice cream (left) but add 5 ml (1 tsp) of almond essence instead of vanilla. Before second freezing, stir in 25 g (1 oz) toasted, finely chopped almonds.

INSTANT ICE CREAM (F)

Preparation 10 mins   *Serves 4*

The fruit must be frozen hard in small pieces to make this recipe

225 g (8 oz) frozen raspberries or strawberries
40 g (1½ oz) icing sugar
100 ml (4 fl oz) fresh whipping cream, chilled
biscuits or meringue nests to serve

1. Place frozen fruit in a food processor and process until finely chopped.

2. Add icing sugar and process until mixed.

3. Add cream and process until soft and creamy.

4. Serve immediately with crisp biscuits or in a meringue nest.

ITALIAN ICE CREAM (F)

Preparation 20 mins **plus freezing**
Cooking 3 mins   *Serves 4*

2 egg yolks
50 g (2 oz) icing sugar, sifted
10 ml (2 tsp) vanilla essence
300 ml (10 fl oz) fresh double cream
30 ml (2 tbsp) fresh milk

1. Put egg yolks and sugar into a double saucepan (or basin standing over a saucepan of gently simmering water). Beat until thick and creamy.

2. Remove from heat. Continue beating until cool, then stir in vanilla.

3. Pour cream and milk into a chilled bowl and beat until softly stiff.

4. Gently fold into beaten egg yolks and sugar then transfer to a freezer container.

5. Freeze for 45 minutes or until frozen about 1 cm (½ inch) around sides.

6. Turn into a chilled bowl, break up gently with a fork then stir until smooth.

7. Return to a clean container and freeze for 1½–2 hours or until firm.

PRESERVED GINGER DAIRY ICE CREAM

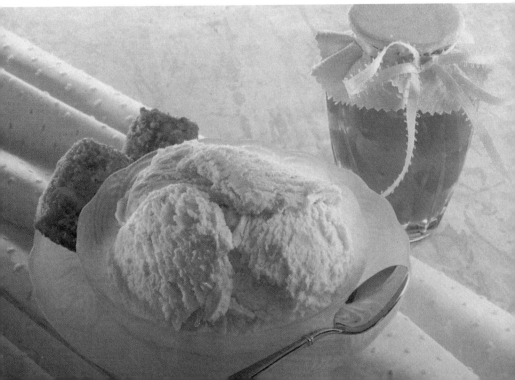

SNOWDRIFT ICE CREAM ⓕ

Preparation 20 mins **plus freezing**   *Serves 6*

2 egg whites
50 g (2 oz) caster sugar
75 ml (5 tbsp) water
1.25 ml (¼ tsp) cream of tartar
5 ml (1 tsp) golden syrup
5 ml (1 tsp) vanilla essence
150 ml (5 fl oz) fresh double cream
300 ml (10 fl oz) fresh soured cream
30 ml (2 tbsp) Tia Maria liqueur
100 g (4 oz) coloured glacé cherries,
   chopped

1. Place egg whites, sugar, water, cream of tartar, syrup and vanilla essence in a large bowl.

2. Whisk together until thick and smooth.

3. Whip double cream until softly stiff and fold into egg white mixture.

4. Fold in soured cream, liqueur and cherries.

5. Pour into a freezer container and freeze until half frozen.

6. Stir with a fork, breaking up ice crystals.

7. Cover and freeze until firm.

SNOWDRIFT ICE CREAM

APPLE ICE ⓕ

Preparation 25 mins **plus freezing**
Cooking 5 mins   *Serves 4*

4 eating apples
grated rind and juice of ½ lemon
30 ml (2 tbsp) brandy
25 g (1 oz) sugar
150 ml (5 fl oz) fresh double cream
chocolate leaves to decorate

1. Cut top off apples. Carefully hollow out flesh leaving a 1 cm (½ inch) shell.

2. Brush cut surfaces with lemon juice.

3. Place chopped flesh in a pan with lemon rind and 15 ml (1 tbsp) water. Cook until tender.
To microwave: Place chopped flesh in a bowl with lemon rind and 15 ml (1 tbsp) water. Cover and cook for 3–4 minutes, stirring occasionally, until tender.

4. Purée until smooth. Stir in brandy and sugar, leave to cool.

5. Whip cream until softly stiff.

6. Fold cream into cooled purée, pour into a container and freeze for 1 hour.

7. Beat mixture until smooth, freeze until half frozen.

8. Spoon mixture into apple cups. Open freeze until solid.

9. Place each apple in a plastic bag, seal and freeze.

10. Remove from freezer 30 minutes before serving.

11. Serve decorated with chocolate leaves.

PEACH MELBA

Preparation 10 mins   *Serves 4*

175 g (6 oz) raspberries
icing sugar
4 scoops Italian ice cream (page 295)
4 peach halves, fresh or canned

1. Purée raspberries, then sieve to remove seeds.

2. Add sufficient sifted icing sugar to sweeten to taste.

3. Place a scoop of ice cream into 4 sundae glasses.

4. Top with a peach half and raspberry sauce.

5. Serve immediately.

BANANA SPLITS

Preparation 20 mins   *Serves 4*

150 ml (5 fl oz) fresh double cream
4 large bananas
dairy ice cream made with
   300 ml (10 fl oz) fresh double cream
   (page 294)
25 g (1 oz) walnuts, chopped
4 glacé cherries
hot luxury chocolate sauce (page 243)
   or hot fudge sauce (page 245)

1. Whip cream until softly stiff.

2. Peel bananas and split lengthways. Quickly sandwich together with spoonfuls of ice cream.

3. Stand on 4 individual plates then top with whipped cream.

4. Sprinkle with nuts and put a whole cherry in centre of each.

5. Serve immediately with chocolate or fudge sauce.

297

RICH CHOCOLATE ICE CREAM Ⓔ

Preparation 25 mins **plus freezing**
Cooking 5 mins *Serves 4*

100g (4oz) plain chocolate
2 eggs
50g (2oz) caster sugar
10ml (2tsp) vanilla essence
300ml (10floz) fresh double cream

1. Break up chocolate. Melt in a basin standing over a saucepan of hot water. Cool. *To microwave: Break up chocolate into a bowl and cook on MEDIUM (50%) for 2–3 minutes, stirring twice, until melted.*

2. Place eggs and sugar in a double saucepan (or basin standing over a saucepan of hot water). Whisk until thick and creamy.

3. Remove from heat. Continue whisking until mixture is cool.

4. Stir in cooled chocolate and vanilla.

5. Whip cream until softly stiff and fold into chocolate mixture.

6. Pour into a freezer container and freeze for 45 minutes or until frozen 1cm (½inch) around sides.

7. Turn into a chilled bowl, break up with a fork then stir until smooth.

8. Return to a clean container and freeze for 1½–2 hours or until firm.

CHOCOLATE ORANGE ICE CREAM Ⓔ

Preparation 25 mins **plus freezing**
Cooking 20 mins *Serves 4–6*

450ml (15floz) fresh single cream
3 egg yolks
100g (4oz) caster sugar
150ml (5floz) fresh whipping cream, whipped
100g (4oz) chocolate polka dots
90ml (6tbsp) orange brandy
grated rind of 1 orange

1. Heat single cream to simmering point. Do not boil.

2. Beat egg yolks and sugar in a large bowl until thick and pale yellow in colour.

3. Pour on hot cream, stirring constantly.

4. Strain mixture into a heavy based saucepan and stir over a low heat, until custard thickens to coat the back of a wooden spoon (do not allow to curdle), this takes about 20 minutes.

5. Allow to cool.

6. Whip whipping cream until softly stiff.

7. Fold cream, chocolate dots, orange brandy and grated orange rind into custard.

8. Pour into a freezer container and freeze for 1 hour.

9. Stir with a fork, breaking up ice crystals.

10. Return to freezer and repeat after 1 hour.

11. Cover and freeze until firm.

KULFI Ⓔ

Preparation 20 mins **plus chilling and freezing**
Cooking 45 mins *Serves 4*

568ml (1pint) fresh Channel Islands milk
3 cardamom pods
450ml (15floz) fresh double cream
30ml (2tbsp) honey
50g (2oz) almonds, chopped
25g (1oz) pistachio nuts, chopped

1. Place milk and cardamoms in a heavy based saucepan. Bring to the boil and simmer until reduced to 450ml (¾pint).

2. Reduce heat and stir in cream. Continue to heat, stirring frequently until reduced to 568ml (1pint).

3. Remove cardamoms, stir in honey, almonds and half of pistachios.

4. Pour into a freezer container and leave until cold.

5. Freeze for 1 hour or until frozen about 1cm (½inch) around sides.

6. Turn into a chilled bowl and mash with a fork to break up ice crystals.

7. Either return to freezer container or divide between 4 small dariole moulds, cover and freeze until firm.

8. Serve sprinkled with remaining chopped pistachios.

TORTONI ⒠

Preparation 30 mins **plus freezing** *Serves 4*

150 ml (5 fl oz) fresh double cream
150 ml (5 fl oz) fresh single cream
25 g (1 oz) icing sugar
50 g (2 oz) almond macaroons,
   finely chopped
40 g (1½ oz) ratafia biscuits, crumbled
30 ml (2 tbsp) Marsala or sweet sherry
2 egg whites
a little melted chocolate

1. Combine creams and sugar and whisk together until softly stiff.

2. Refrigerate for 1 hour.

3. Stir macaroons, half the ratafias and Marsala or sherry into chilled cream.

4. Whisk egg whites to a stiff snow and fold into cream mixture.

5. Turn mixture into a lightly oiled 1.25 litre (2¼ pint) mould or large loaf tin. Freeze until firm.

6. Turn Tortoni out of mould and sprinkle with remaining ratafia crumbs to coat.

7. Decorate with melted chocolate drizzled over surface and serve immediately.

BAKED ALASKA

Preparation 15 mins **Cooking** 3 mins *Serves 4–6*

1 × 18 cm (7 inch) sponge flan case or a
   single layer of sponge cake
30 ml (2 tbsp) brandy or sherry
meringue topping,
   made with 3 egg whites (page 215)
dairy ice cream made with
   300 ml (10 fl oz) fresh double cream
   (page 294)
glacé fruits to decorate (optional)

1. Put flan or cake on to an ovenproof plate or dish.

2. Moisten with brandy or sherry.

3. Make meringue topping.

4. Spoon ice cream in a mound on top of cake.

5. Swirl meringue completely over cake and ice cream or pipe it over with a large star-shaped tube and piping bag.

6. Stud with fruits (if used) then bake at 230°C (450°F) Mark 8 for 1–3 minutes, until meringue just starts turning gold.

7. Serve immediately.

TORTONI

FAVOURITE MERINGUE DESSERT 🄵

Preparation 20 mins **plus freezing**   *Serves 6*

300 ml (10 fl oz) fresh double cream
30 ml (2 tbsp) Grand Marnier or Kirsch
   liqueur (optional)
100 g (4 oz) meringue shells, crumbled
225 g (8 oz) raspberries
50 g (2 oz) icing sugar

1. Lightly oil a 1.1 litre (2 pint) pudding basin.

2. Whip cream with liqueur until softly stiff.

3. Stir in meringues.

4. Spoon into basin. Cover with aluminium foil and freeze until firm.

5. Press raspberries through a sieve and sweeten to taste with icing sugar.

6. Turn frozen meringue dessert out and leave for about 1 hour before serving so it is only lightly frozen.

7. Serve a little of sauce spooned over dessert and remainder in a jug.

FROZEN RASPBERRY MOUSSE 🄵

Preparation 30 mins **plus freezing**   *Serves 4*

150 ml (¼ pint) sweetened raspberry purée,
   made from fresh or canned fruit
10 ml (2 tsp) lemon juice
25 g (1 oz) icing sugar, sifted
150 ml (5 fl oz) fresh double cream
15 ml (1 tbsp) fresh milk
2 egg whites
raspberries and sprigs of mint to decorate

1. Prepare 4 ramekin dishes with paper collars as for soufflés on page 214.

2. Sieve purée and discard seeds.

3. Stir in lemon juice and icing sugar.

4. Whip cream and milk until softly stiff.

5. Whisk egg whites to a stiff snow.

6. Fold cream and egg whites alternately into fruit mixture.

7. Spoon into ramekins, freeze until firm.

8. Remove from freezer 30 minutes before serving.

9. To serve remove paper collars and decorate with raspberries and mint.

FROZEN RASPBERRY MOUSSE

TANGY FRUIT SORBET Ⓕ

Preparation 15 mins **plus freezing**
Cooking 5 mins   *Serves 6*

175 g (6 oz) granulated sugar
6 mint leaves or 2.5 ml (½ tsp) dried mint
juice of 1 small lemon
grated rind and strained juice of
   1 medium orange
1 egg white
25 g (1 oz) caster sugar
orange slices to decorate

1. Put granulated sugar, 150 ml (¼ pint)
water and mint into a pan.
*To microwave: Put granulated sugar,
150 ml (¼ pint) water and mint into a bowl.*

2. Cook over a low heat and stir until sugar
dissolves.
*To microwave: Cook for about 2 minutes,
stirring once or twice. Stir well until sugar
dissolves.*

3. Remove from heat and strain. Stir in
300 ml (½ pint) water, lemon juice, orange
rind and juice.

4. Mix well. Pour into a freezer container and
chill until cold.

5. Freeze for 1 hour or until mixture has half
frozen.

6. Beat egg white to a stiff snow. Add caster
sugar. Continue whisking until white is very
stiff and shiny.

7. Pour fruit mixture into a chilled bowl.
Whisk until smooth.

8. Gently fold in beaten egg white.

9. Return to a clean container. Freeze for
45 minutes and whisk again.

10. Pour back into container. Freeze for
1½–2 hours or until firm.

11. Spoon into small dishes and decorate
with orange slices.

12. Serve immediately.

Variations

LEMON SORBET Ⓕ

Follow recipe and method for tangy fruit
sorbet (left) but omit mint, orange rind and
juice. Instead use the grated rind and juice
of 4 lemons.

STRAWBERRY SORBET Ⓕ

Follow recipe and method for tangy fruit
sorbet (left). Omit mint, orange rind and
juice. Use 450 g (1 lb) strawberries, puréed,
instead.

HOME
BAKING

BATH BUNS PAGE 345 · QUICK BROWN BREAD PAGE 340
WEST COUNTRY FLAN PAGE 372 · CHERRY CAKE PAGE 318 · RING DOUGHNUTS PAGE 335
VANILLA REFRIGERATOR BISCUITS AND VARIATIONS PAGE 354

CAKES

PREPARATION OF CAKE TINS

Materials for lining

Use greaseproof paper, brushed with melted butter, non-stick baking paper which will not require greasing, or a tin with a non-stick finish which will not need lining before use.

Sponge Cakes

Grease tins, then dust with flour.

Sandwich Cakes

Grease tins then line bottoms of tins with a round of greaseproof paper and grease this.

Fruit Cakes and Rich Mixtures

Grease and line whole tin. For mixtures requiring a long cooking period, use double-thickness greaseproof paper to prevent any overcooking of the outside of the cake.

To line a Swiss Roll tin

1. Cut a piece of greaseproof paper 5cm (2inch) larger all round than tin. Place tin on it and cut from each corner of paper to corner of tin.

2. Grease tin and put in paper so that it fits closely and overlaps at corners. Grease all paper surfaces.

To line a deep tin

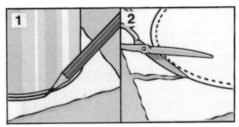

1. Place tin on a piece of greaseproof paper and draw round base.

2. Cut piece of greaseproof paper just inside pencil mark.

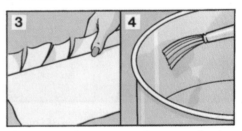

3. Cut a strip of greaseproof paper to the size of the depth of the tin, plus 5cm (2inch) longer and deeper. Then make a 2.5cm (1inch) fold along length of strip and cut diagonally up to the fold at 1.5cm (½inch) intervals.

4. Grease inside the tin with melted butter.

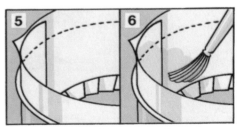

5. Insert the strip of greaseproof paper, ensuring that the snipped part lies flat against the base of the tin. Place base circle in position.

6. Grease all paper surfaces.

To ALMOND PASTE A CELEBRATION CAKE

The almond paste acts as a foundation for Royal icing to prevent the rich fruit cake from staining the white surface. The cake should have a flat surface for the almond paste to go on.

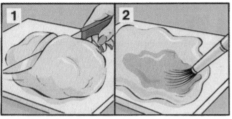

1. Dredge the working surface with a little sifted icing sugar. Knead the almond paste into a ball and divide in half.

2. Roll out one half to fit the top of the cake and then brush the almond paste with a little warmed and sieved apricot jam.

3. Place the cake upside down on the almond paste, press firmly, trim edges and then carefully place the right way up.

4. Measure the circumference and depth of the cake with a piece of string. If the cake is round, cut remaining almond paste into two and roll out each until the correct shape to encircle the cake. If the cake is square, divide the almond paste into four.

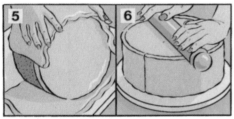

5. Brush almond paste with sieved apricot jam and place on the cake as for top.

6. Use a rolling pin to ensure that the sides and top have a neat finish.

Leave the cake for a week before icing.

To ROYAL ICE A CELEBRATION CAKE

Before icing the cake be sure that the almond paste has been allowed to dry.

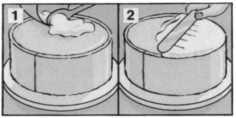

1. Stand the cake on a suitable silver board, 5 cm (2 inch) larger than the base of the cake. Place on an icing turntable, upturned mixing bowl or cake tin. Spoon a little Royal icing over the almond paste.

2. Spread with a palette knife evenly across the top of the cake and at the same time burst any air bubbles.

3. With a warm steel rule, draw the rule at an angle firmly across the cake to obtain a smooth surface. Remove surplus icing. Allow to dry for 24 hours.

4. Repeat this process for the sides of the cake, holding the steel rule vertically against the side of the cake.

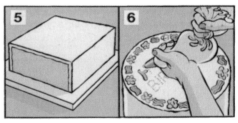

5. For a square cake, the two opposite sides should be iced and allowed to dry before icing the other two sides. Apply two or three more thin layers of icing to the surface until a good finish is obtained.

6. Decorate according to the occasion to be celebrated.

To FONDANT ICE A CELEBRATION CAKE

Royal icing is usually used to cover rich fruit cake which has already been coated with almond paste or marzipan. It may also be used to pipe onto or to attach decorations to a fondant iced cake.

Fondant icing, also called sugar paste, can be used to cover sponge, madeira, light fruit or rich fruit cakes.

Fondant icing is soft and pliable. It can be rolled out like almond paste to cover cakes or moulded to make edible decorations. It gives a softer texture and appearance than royal icing to decorated cakes and it remains softer to cut.

It is available as plain white in small blocks from supermarkets. Colour can be kneaded into fondant icing to colour it or it can be bought already coloured from specialist cake decorating shops.

The cake may be covered with almond paste or marzipan before covering with fondant icing. If not, the fondant icing should be 0.5 cm (¼ inch) thick and any crevices padded with fondant first to ensure as smooth a surface as possible.

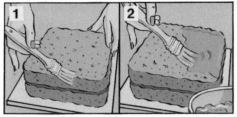

1. If unmarzipaned, use a dry pastry brush to brush away any crumbs on the surface of the cake. Place on a cake board.

2. Brush cake with boiled apricot jam (if marzipaned use cold boiled water).

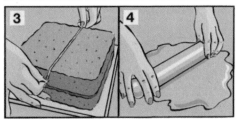

3. Using either a piece of string or a rolling pin measure both sides and top of cake.

4. Roll out fondant icing on a work surface lightly dusted with sieved icing sugar to

about the measured size of the cake. Keep turning the icing to prevent it sticking and do not use too much icing sugar or it will dry the icing. Never leave rolled fondant or it will dry out and crack.

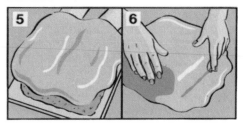

5. Lift fondant with both hands underneath onto centre of cake. Gradually slide hands out draping fondant over cake.

6. If it is a square cake use the palm of your hand to fit and smooth corners before the sides making sure that the sides are flat and not pleated.

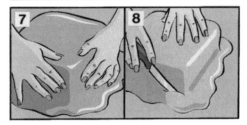

7. Dust ringless hands with icing sugar or cornflour and gently smooth over top and down sides of cake to smooth icing and ease out any air bubbles or creases.

8. Cut away any surplus icing from base of cake.

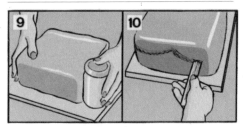

9. Finish by rolling a flat sided jar around cake.

10. If decorating the cake with crimping, do it while the fondant is still soft, otherwise cover with a dry tea towel and leave until dry and firm for decoration.

DO NOT store in an airtight container or leave in a cold damp room or the icing will absorb moisture.

VICTORIA SANDWICH Ⓕ

Preparation 25 mins **Cooking** 30 mins *Serves 6*

100g (4oz) butter, softened
100g (4oz) caster sugar
2 eggs
100g (4oz) self raising flour, sifted
45ml (3tbsp) jam
icing sugar, sifted (optional)

1. Prepare two 18cm (7inch) sandwich tins (page 303).
To microwave: Grease and base-line a 20.5cm (8inch) round cake dish.

2. Cream butter and sugar together until very pale in colour, light in texture and fluffy.

3. Beat in eggs, one at a time, adding 15ml (1tbsp) flour with each one.

4. Gently fold in remaining flour with a metal spoon.
To microwave: Gently fold in remaining flour with a metal spoon. Fold in 45ml (3tbsp) milk.

5. Transfer to prepared tins and smooth tops with a knife.
To microwave: Transfer to prepared dish and smooth top with a knife.

6. Bake at 180°C (350°F) Mark 4 for 25–30 minutes, or until well risen, golden brown and firm.
To microwave: Place dish on a low microwave rack and cook, uncovered, for about 6 minutes or until surface is still slightly moist and a wooden cocktail stick, inserted in centre, comes out clean.

7. Leave in tins for 2–3 minutes. Turn out on to a wire cooling rack.
To microwave: Allow to stand for 3 minutes. Turn out on to a wire cooling rack lined with non-stick baking paper.

8. Strip off paper and leave until cold.

9. When cold sandwich together with jam.
To microwave: Split and sandwich with jam.

10. Dust cake with icing sugar.

Variations

JAM & CREAM SANDWICH Ⓕ

Follow recipe and method for Victoria sandwich (left). When cakes are cold, sandwich together with 45ml (3tbsp) jam and 60ml (4tbsp) fresh double cream, whipped until thick. Dust with icing sugar.

JAM & CREAM SANDWICH

CHOCOLATE SANDWICH Ⓕ

Follow recipe and method for Victoria sandwich (left), but replace 25 g (1 oz) flour with 25 g (1 oz) cocoa powder.
Sandwich together with butter cream (page 329).

COFFEE SANDWICH Ⓕ

Follow recipe and method for Victoria sandwich (left), but add 10 ml (2 tsp) instant coffee granules dissolved in 15 ml (1 tbsp) warm water after beating in eggs. Sandwich together with butter cream (page 329).

SMALL ICED CAKES Ⓕ

Follow recipe and method for Victoria sandwich (left). Transfer equal amounts of mixture to 18 paper cases standing in 18 ungreased bun tins. Bake at 190°C (375°F) Mark 5 for 20–25 minutes, or until well risen and golden. Cool on a wire cooling rack. When completely cold cover tops with either butter cream or glacé icing (see Icings Section, page 326). Decorate with halved glacé cherries, pieces of angelica, chocolate buttons, grated chocolate, whole hazelnuts or walnut halves.

FAIRY CAKES Ⓕ

Follow recipe and method for Victoria sandwich (left). Stir 50 g (2 oz) currants or sultanas into mixture after beating in eggs. Transfer equal amounts to 18 paper cases standing in 18 ungreased bun tins. Bake at 190°C (375°F) Mark 5 for 20–25 minutes, or until well risen and golden. Cool on a wire cooling rack.

CHOCOLATE CHIP CAKES Ⓕ

Follow recipe and method for fairy cakes (above). Stir in 50 g (2 oz) chopped plain chocolate instead of currants or sultanas.

BUTTERFLY CAKES Ⓕ

Follow recipe and method for Victoria sandwich (left). Transfer equal amounts of mixture to 18 paper cases standing in 18 ungreased bun tins. Bake at 190°C (375°F) Mark 5 for 20–25 minutes, or until well risen and golden. Cool on a wire cooling rack. To make butterflies cut a slice off the top of each cake. Cut slices in halves, for wings. Place a little butter cream (page 329) on top of each cake. Put halved slices into icing at an angle to form wings. Dust lightly with sifted icing sugar.

SPONGE SANDWICH ⓕ

Preparation 30 mins **Cooking** 20 mins *Serves 6*

3 eggs
75g (3oz) caster sugar
75g (3oz) self raising flour, sifted twice
45ml (3tbsp) jam
60ml (4tbsp) fresh double cream, whipped

1. Prepare two 18cm (7inch) sandwich tins (see page 303). Dust sides of tins with flour.

2. Put eggs into a large bowl standing over a saucepan of hand-hot water.

3. Whisk for 2 minutes.

4. Add sugar. Continue whisking for a further 8–10 minutes (or until mixture is very light in colour, thick in texture – consistency of softly whipped cream – and at least double its original volume).

5. Remove bowl from saucepan. Continue whisking for a further 5 minutes or until egg mixture is cool.

6. Gently fold in flour with a large metal spoon.

7. Transfer to prepared tins.

8. Bake at 180°C (350°F) Mark 4 for 20 minutes or until well risen and golden.

9. Turn out on to a sheet of sugared greaseproof paper resting on a folded tea towel.

10. Carefully peel off lining paper. Leave until completely cold.

11. Sandwich together with jam and whipped cream.

If you are using an electric mixer no heat is required during whisking.

Variation

DEEP SPONGE CAKE ⓕ

Follow recipe and method for sponge sandwich (above) but use plain flour instead of self raising. Transfer mixture to a prepared 18cm (7inch) deep cake tin (see page 303). Bake at 180°C (350°F) Mark 4 for 40–45 minutes or until a wooden cocktail stick, inserted into centre, comes out clean. Leave until cold. Slice into 1 or 2 layers. Sandwich together with jam and cream.

SWISS ROLL ⓕ

Preparation 35 mins
Cooking 12 mins   *Serves 8–10*

3 eggs
75g (3oz) caster sugar
75g (3oz) self raising flour
60ml (4tbsp) jam or lemon curd, warmed

1. Prepare a 30.5×20.5cm (12×8inch) Swiss roll tin (see page 303).

2. Put eggs into a large bowl standing over a pan of hand hot water. Whisk for 2 minutes.

3. Add sugar and continue whisking for a further 8–10 minutes, or until mixture is very light in colour, thick in texture, consistency of softly whipped cream and at least double its original volume.

4. Remove bowl from saucepan. Continue whisking until egg mixture is cool.

5. Gently fold in flour with a large metal spoon. Transfer to prepared tin.

6. Bake at 200°C (400°F) Mark 6 for 10–12 minutes, or until well risen and firm.

7. Turn out on to a sheet of sugared greaseproof paper resting on a folded tea towel. Carefully peel off paper.

8. Cut away crisp edges with a sharp knife.

9. Spread quickly with warm jam.

10. Roll up tightly and hold in position for 1 minute. Cool on a wire cooling rack.

If you are using an electric mixer no heat is required during whisking.

Variations

CHOCOLATE SWISS ROLL ⓕ

Follow recipe and method for Swiss roll (above). Use 65g (2½oz) flour sifted twice with 15g (½oz) cocoa powder.

CREAM FILLED SWISS ROLL ⓕ

Follow recipe and method for Swiss roll (above). After trimming away crisp edges, roll up loosely with paper inside to prevent sticking. Cover with a damp tea towel and leave until completely cold. Unroll carefully, remove paper and fill with 150ml (5floz) softly whipped double cream. Roll up again and hold in position for about a minute.

BLACK FOREST GÂTEAU Ⓕ

Preparation 50 mins
Cooking 25 mins   *Serves 8–10*

150 g (5 oz) butter, melted
6 eggs
2.5 ml (½ tsp) vanilla essence
225 g (8 oz) caster sugar
50 g (2 oz) flour, sifted twice
50 g (2 oz) cocoa powder, sifted
60 ml (4 tbsp) Kirsch liqueur
568 ml (1 pint) fresh double cream
397 g (14 oz) can black cherry pie filling
75 g (3 oz) fresh or canned black cherries, stoned
grated chocolate or chocolate vermicelli

1. Grease and flour bases and sides of three, 20.5 cm (8 inch) sandwich tins.

2. Strain melted butter through muslin or see page 240 for how to clarify butter.

3. Whisk together eggs, vanilla essence and sugar over a saucepan of hand-hot water until mixture is thick and texture of softly whipped cream (about 8–10 minutes).

4. Remove bowl from saucepan, continue whisking for a further 5 minutes.

5. Gently fold in flour, cocoa powder and melted clarified butter, using a metal spoon.

6. Divide mixture between prepared tins.

7. Bake at 180°C (350°F) Mark 4 for 10–15 minutes.

8. Remove from oven and cool for 5 minutes in tins, then place on a wire cooling rack to cool thoroughly.

9. Prick cooled sponge cakes all over with a skewer.

10. Spoon Kirsch over cakes and allow to rest for 5 minutes.

11. Whip cream until softly stiff.

12. Sandwich cakes together with some of the whipped cream and pie filling.

13. Spread top and sides with cream.

14. Arrange cherries in centre of cake and decorate with swirls of cream.

15. Gently press grated chocolate or chocolate vermicelli around sides of cake.

16. Serve at once.

CREAM FILLED CHOCOLATE SWISS ROLL

Chocolate layer cake Ⓕ

Preparation 30 mins
Cooking 40 mins   *Serves 8–10*

100 g (4 oz) self raising flour
30 ml (2 tbsp) cocoa powder
100 g (4 oz) butter
100 g (4 oz) caster sugar
25 g (1 oz) golden syrup
2.5 ml (½ tsp) vanilla essence
2 eggs
20 ml (4 tsp) fresh milk
300 ml (10 fl oz) fresh double cream or
    butter cream (page 329)

1. Prepare a deep 20.5 cm (8 inch) round cake tin (see page 303).
To microwave: Grease and base-line a 20.5 cm (8 inch) round cake dish.

2. Sift flour twice with cocoa.

3. Cream butter, sugar, syrup and essence together until very pale in colour, light in texture and fluffy.

4. Beat in eggs, one at a time, adding 15 ml (1 tbsp) of sifted dry ingredients with each one.

5. Fold in milk and remaining dry ingredients with a metal spoon.
To microwave: Fold in 60 ml (4 tbsp) milk and remaining dry ingredients with a metal spoon.

6. Transfer to prepared tin and smooth top with a knife.
To microwave: Transfer to prepared dish and smooth top with a knife.

7. Bake at 180°C (350°F) Mark 4 for 35–40 minutes, or until a wooden cocktail stick, inserted into centre of cake, comes out clean.
To microwave: Place dish on a low microwave rack. Cook, uncovered, for 6–7 minutes, until surface is still slightly moist and a wooden cocktail stick, inserted into centre, comes out clean.

8. Turn out on to a wire cooling rack, strip off paper and leave until cool.
To microwave: Allow to stand for 5 minutes, then turn out on to a wire cooling rack lined with non-stick baking paper. Strip off paper and leave until cold.

9. Cut cake into 2 or 3 layers.

10. Fill and cover top with either fresh double cream, whipped until thick, or butter cream (page 329).

Chocolate brownies Ⓕ

Preparation 20 mins **Cooking** 30 mins   *Makes 8*

100 g (4 oz) plain chocolate
75 g (3 oz) butter
175 g (6 oz) dark brown soft sugar
3 eggs, beaten
150 g (5 oz) self raising flour
25 g (1 oz) cocoa powder
50 g (2 oz) chopped mixed nuts
175 g (6 oz) curd cheese
grated rind and juice of ½ orange
25 g (1 oz) icing sugar, sifted

1. Grease and base-line a 28×23 cm (11×9 inch) tin.

2. Break chocolate up and melt 75 g (3 oz) with butter in a bowl over a saucepan of hot water.

3. Stir in sugar and gradually beat in eggs.

4. Sift flour and cocoa together and fold into chocolate mixture with nuts.

5. Spoon into prepared tin.

6. Bake at 180°C (350°F) Mark 4 for 30 minutes.

7. Cool in tin, then turn out.

8. Mix curd cheese, orange rind, juice and icing sugar together and spread over cake.

9. Melt remaining chocolate and pipe on top to decorate.

10. Cut into 8 pieces.

Chocolate marble cake Ⓕ

Preparation 25 mins **Cooking** 1½ hrs   *Serves 8*

225 g (8 oz) butter
225 g (8 oz) caster sugar
3 eggs
350 g (12 oz) self raising flour
salt
200 ml (7 fl oz) fresh milk
25 g (1 oz) cocoa powder

1. Grease and line a 20.5cm (8inch) round cake tin.
2. Cream together butter and sugar.
3. Add eggs one at a time, beating well.
4. Fold in flour, salt and milk.
5. Divide mixture into two bowls, add cocoa to one and mix well.
6. Spoon mixtures alternately into prepared cake tin to achieve the "marbled" effect.
7. Bake at 170°C (325°F) Mark 3 for 1½ hours, or until well risen.
8. Cool and turn on to a wire cooling rack.

CHOCOLATE TRUFFLE CAKE

Preparation 40 mins **Cooking** 1¼ hrs   *Serves 12*

425g (15oz) plain chocolate
90g (3½oz) butter
150g (5oz) caster sugar
10ml (2tsp) instant coffee granules
4 eggs, separated
40g (1½oz) flour
25g (1oz) ground hazelnuts or almonds, toasted
300ml (10floz) fresh double cream
strawberries for decoration

1. Grease and line a 21.5cm (8½inch) cake tin.
2. Break up 150g (5oz) chocolate and place in a bowl over a pan of hot water, heat until melted.
3. Cream together butter and sugar until pale and fluffy.
4. Dissolve coffee granules in 30ml (2tbsp) hot water. Beat into butter mixture with melted chocolate and egg yolks.
5. Whisk egg whites until stiff, fold in to mixture.
6. Fold in flour and hazelnuts. Pour into prepared cake tin.
7. Bake at 170°C (325°F) Mark 3 for 1¼ hours.
8. Cool in tin for 15 minutes, then on a wire cooling rack.
9. Place cream in a small pan, heat until bubbling around edges.
10. Remove from heat and stir in remaining broken up chocolate.
11. Stand covered until chocolate melts, mix well then chill until firm enough to hold a peak, about 1½ hours.
12. Cover top and sides with icing and swirl with a spoon.
13. Decorate with strawberries to serve.

CHOCOLATE TRUFFLE CAKE

CARROT CAKE

CARROT CAKE Ⓕ

Preparation 35 mins **Cooking** 1¼ hrs   *Serves 8*

225 g (8 oz) self raising flour
5 ml (1 tsp) baking powder
150 g (5 oz) light brown soft sugar
50 g (2 oz) walnuts, chopped
50 g (2 oz) raisins
100 g (4 oz) carrots, grated
2 ripe bananas, peeled and mashed
2 eggs
150 ml (¼ pint) oil
65 ml (2½ fl oz) fresh double cream
50 g (2 oz) icing sugar, sifted
75 g (3 oz) full fat soft cheese, softened
2.5 ml (½ tsp) vanilla essence
chopped walnuts to decorate

1. Grease and line a 20.5 cm (8 inch) deep round cake tin.
To microwave: Grease and base-line a 2 litre (3½ pint) ring mould.

2. Sift together flour and baking powder into a bowl and stir in sugar.
To microwave: Sift together flour and baking powder into a bowl and stir in sugar, making sure there are no lumps.

3. Add nuts, raisins, carrots and bananas, stir to mix.

4. Add eggs and oil, beat until well mixed.

5. Pour into prepared tin and bake at 180°C (350°F) Mark 4 for 1½ hours or until firm to the touch.
To microwave: Pour into prepared mould and place on a low microwave rack. Cook, uncovered, for about 9 minutes until surface is still slightly moist and a wooden cocktail stick, inserted in the cake, comes out clean.

6. Remove from tin and cool on a wire cooling rack.
To microwave: Allow to stand for 5 minutes, then turn out on to a wire cooling rack lined with non-stick baking paper. Strip off paper and allow to cool.

7. Whip cream until softly stiff.

8. Cream icing sugar, cheese and vanilla essence together. Fold in cream.

9. Spread over top of cake and sprinkle with walnuts.

LEMON & ALMOND RING Ⓕ

Preparation 45 mins
Cooking 40 mins   *Serves 8*

100 g (4 oz) butter
100 g (4 oz) caster sugar
5 ml (1 tsp) grated lemon rind
2 eggs
100 g (4 oz) self raising flour, sifted
50 g (2 oz) blanched and finely chopped
    almonds
lemon glacé icing made with 225 g (8 oz)
    icing sugar (page 327)
small leaves cut from angelica and
    crystallised lemon slices, to decorate

1. Brush base and sides of a 900 ml (1½ pint)
ring tin with melted butter.
To microwave: Brush base and sides of a
1.4 litre (2½ pint) ring mould with melted
butter.

2. Cream butter with sugar and lemon rind
until light and fluffy.

3. Beat in eggs, one at a time, adding
15 ml (1 tbsp) of sifted flour with each one.

4. Stir in almonds.

5. Fold in remaining flour with a metal
spoon.
To microwave: Fold in remaining flour with
a metal spoon. Fold in 30 ml (2 tbsp) milk.

6. Transfer to prepared tin. Bake at
180°C (350°F) Mark 4 for 35–40 minutes, or
until a wooden cocktail stick, inserted into
centre of cake, comes out clean.
To microwave: Transfer to prepared mould
and place on a low microwave rack. Cook,
uncovered, for 5–6 minutes until surface is
still slightly moist and a wooden cocktail
stick, inserted in cake, comes out clean.

7. Leave in tin for 2 or 3 minutes. Turn out
on to a wire cooling rack.
To microwave: Allow to stand for 5 minutes,
then turn out on to a wire cooling rack lined
with non-stick baking paper.

8. When cake is cold pour icing over top and
allow to run down sides.

9. Leave undisturbed until icing has set.

10. Decorate with angelica and crystallised
lemon slices.

Variations

COFFEE & HAZELNUT RING Ⓕ

Follow recipe and method for lemon and
almond ring (left). Use hazelnuts instead of
almonds. Coat ring with coffee glacé icing
(page 327) instead of lemon. When icing is
set decorate with about 12 whole hazelnuts.

ORANGE & WALNUT RING Ⓕ

Follow recipe and method for lemon and
almond ring (left). Use walnuts instead of
almonds. Coat ring with orange glacé icing
(page 327) instead of lemon. When icing is
set decorate with walnut halves.

BANANA & PECAN CAKE Ⓕ

Preparation 30 mins
Cooking 1 hr   *Serves 16*

100 g (4 oz) butter
225 g (8 oz) sugar
3 eggs, separated
225 g (8 oz) peeled, ripe bananas, mashed
150 g (5 oz) buttermilk
225 g (8 oz) flour
10 ml (2 tsp) baking powder
175 g (6 oz) sultanas
90 g (3½ oz) shelled pecan nuts

1. Grease and line a 20.5 cm (8 inch) square
cake tin.

2. Cream together butter and sugar until
smooth.

3. Beat in egg yolks, mashed banana and
buttermilk. Mix well.

4. Add flour, baking powder and sultanas,
beat until smooth.

5. Whisk egg whites until stiff and fold into
cake batter.

6. Pour into prepared cake tin and arrange
nuts on top in rows.

7. Bake at 180°C (350°F) Mark 4 for 1 hour.

8. Cool in tin for 10 minutes before turning
out on to a wire cooling rack.

9. Cut into squares or slices to serve.

RICH FRUIT CAKE   Ⓕ

Preparation 40 mins
Cooking 4½ hrs   *Serves 8–10*

225 g (8 oz) flour
5 ml (1 tsp) mixed spice
2.5 ml (½ tsp) ground cinnamon
2.5 ml (½ tsp) ground nutmeg
5 ml (1 tsp) cocoa powder
175 g (6 oz) butter
175 g (6 oz) soft brown sugar
15 ml (1 tbsp) black treacle
5 ml (1 tsp) *each* grated orange and
    lemon rind
4 eggs
550 g (1¼ lb) mixed dried fruit (currants,
    sultanas and raisins)
100 g (4 oz) chopped mixed peel
50 g (2 oz) chopped walnuts or blanched
    almonds
50 g (2 oz) dates, chopped
50 g (2 oz) glacé cherries, chopped
15 ml (1 tbsp) fresh milk

1. Prepare a 20.5 cm (8 inch) round or
18 cm (7 inch) square cake tin (see page 303).

2. Sift flour with spice, cinnamon, nutmeg
and cocoa.

3. Cream butter with sugar, treacle and
orange and lemon rind.

4. Beat in eggs, one at a time, adding
15 ml (1 tbsp) of sifted dry ingredients with
each one.

5. Stir in currants, sultanas, raisins, chopped
peel, nuts, dates and cherries.

6. Fold in dry ingredients alternately with
milk.

7. Transfer to prepared tin and smooth top
with a knife.

8. Bake at 150°C (300°F) Mark 2 for
4–4½ hours, or until a skewer, inserted into
centre of cake, comes out clean.

9. Leave in tin for 15 minutes. Turn out on to
a wire cooling rack.

10. When completely cold, wrap in
aluminium foil and store in an airtight
container until needed.

ICED CHRISTMAS CAKE

Preparation 1 hr **plus** 1 week
standing   *Serves 8–10*

1 rich fruit cake (left)
60 ml (4 tbsp) apricot jam, melted
almond paste made with 275 g (10 oz)
    ground almonds (page 326)
Royal icing made with 2 egg whites
    (page 326)
Christmas cake ornaments to decorate

1. Brush top and sides of cake with melted
jam.

2. Turn almond paste on to a sugared
surface (either sifted icing or caster). Roll out
about half into a 20.5 cm (8 inch) round or
18 cm (7 inch) square. Use to cover top of
cake. See page 304.

3. Roll out remaining paste into a strip –
same depth as cake – and wrap round sides.

4. Press edges and joins well together with
fingers dipped in caster sugar.

5. When almond paste has set (overnight)
wrap cake loosely in aluminium foil. Leave
at least 1 week before icing.

6. To ice cake, stand on a suitable silver
board.

7. Spread Royal icing thickly and evenly
over top and sides.

8. Flick icing upwards with back of a
teaspoon so that it stands in soft peaks.

9. Decorate with Christmas ornaments. Leave
cake undisturbed overnight while icing
hardens.

Variation

ICED CELEBRATION CAKE

Follow recipe and method for iced Christmas
cake (above). To flat ice the cake follow
directions to Royal ice a celebration cake
(page 304). Decorate according to the
occasion to be celebrated.

FAMILY FRUIT CAKE

Preparation 25 mins
Cooking 1½ hrs
Serves 8

225g (8oz) self raising flour
100g (4oz) butter
100g (4oz) caster sugar
100g (4oz) mixed dried fruits
5ml (1tsp) grated lemon rind
1 egg
75ml (5tbsp) fresh milk

1. Prepare a 15cm (6inch) round cake tin or a 450g (1lb) loaf tin.

2. Sift flour into a bowl.

3. Rub butter into flour until mixture resembles fine breadcrumbs.

4. Add sugar, fruit and lemon rind.

5. Mix to a batter with egg and milk.

6. Stir with a metal spoon until evenly combined. Do not beat.

7. Transfer to prepared tin.

8. Bake at 180°C (350°F) Mark 4 for 1¼–1½ hours, or until a wooden cocktail stick, inserted into centre, comes out clean.

9. Leave in tin for 5 minutes. Turn out on to a wire cooling rack.

10. Peel off paper. Store cake in an airtight container when cold.

Variations

SULTANA & ORANGE CAKE

Follow recipe and method for family fruit cake (left). Use 100g (4oz) sultanas instead of mixed fruit and orange rind instead of lemon.

DATE & WALNUT CAKE

Follow recipe and method for family fruit cake (left). Sift 5ml (1tsp) mixed spice with flour. Add 75g (3oz) chopped dates and 25g (1oz) chopped walnuts instead of mixed fruit. Omit lemon rind.

CHERRY & GINGER CAKE

Follow recipe and method for family fruit cake (left). Using 50g (2oz) each chopped glacé cherries and chopped preserved ginger instead of mixed fruit.

COCONUT & LEMON CAKE

Follow recipe and method for family fruit cake (left). Omit fruit. Add 50g (2oz) desiccated coconut with sugar and increase lemon rind to 10ml (2tsp).

FAMILY FRUIT CAKE

MICROWAVE FRUIT CAKE RING   Ⓕ

Preparation 30 mins **Cooking** 50 mins *Serves 16*

This fruit cake has a different texture to a baked one. The shape makes it easy to slice and it looks very attractive, covered with marzipan and icing, as a last minute celebration cake. It may be made up to a week before serving or freezing.

500 g (1 lb 2 oz) mixed dried fruit
150 ml (¼ pint) orange or apple juice
250 g (9 oz) flour
5 ml (1 tsp) mixed spice
5 ml (1 tsp) ground ginger
5 ml (1 tsp) ground nutmeg
175 g (6 oz) butter
175 g (6 oz) dark soft brown sugar
4 eggs
30 ml (2 tbsp) black treacle
50 g (2 oz) walnuts, chopped
100 g (4 oz) glacé cherries, chopped
45 ml (3 tbsp) fresh milk

1. *Grease and base line a 2 litre (3½ pint) microwave ring mould.*

2. *To microwave: Put dried fruit and orange or apple juice in a bowl. Cover and cook for 5 minutes.*

3. *Sift flour with spice, ginger and nutmeg.*

4. *Cream butter with sugar until light and fluffy.*

5. *Gradually beat in eggs, one at a time, adding 15 ml (1 tbsp) of sifted dry ingredients with each one.*

6. *Stir in warm fruit and juice with remaining ingredients and mix well. (The mixture will be quite wet.)*

7. *Transfer to prepared mould and smooth top with a knife.*

8. *To microwave: Place on a low microwave rack. Cook, uncovered, on MEDIUM-LOW (30%) for 45–50 minutes until a wooden cocktail stick, inserted in cake, comes out clean.*

9. *Allow to stand for 20 minutes then turn out on to a wire cooling rack lined with non-stick baking paper.*

10. *Strip off paper and allow to cool (the moist surface will dry as it cools).*

FRUIT & HONEY CAKE

Preparation 30 mins
Cooking 25 mins   *Serves 6–8*

225 g (8 oz) butter, softened
225 g (8 oz) clear honey
4 eggs
100 g (4 oz) wholemeal self raising flour
100 g (4 oz) self raising flour
150 ml (5 fl oz) fresh whipping cream
225 g (8 oz) Greek-style yogurt
fresh fruit to decorate

1. Prepare two 20.5 cm (8 inch) sandwich tins (see page 303).

2. Cream butter and honey together until pale and creamy.

3. Beat in eggs separately with a spoonful of flour and fold in remaining flours.

4. Divide between prepared tins.

5. Bake at 180°C (350°F) Mark 4 for 25 minutes, or until firm to the touch.

6. Cool in tins for 5 minutes, then cool on a wire cooling rack.

7. Whip cream until softly stiff.

8. Fold cream into yogurt and sandwich cakes together with half the mixture and half the fruit.

9. Decorate with remaining cream mixture and fruit.

CIDER APPLE CAKE   Ⓕ

Preparation 30 mins
Cooking 35 mins   *Serves 9*

100 g (4 oz) butter
100 g (4 oz) sugar
2 eggs, beaten
75 g (3 oz) wholemeal self raising flour
75 g (3 oz) self raising flour
45 ml (3 tbsp) medium dry cider
50 g (2 oz) sultanas
5 ml (1 tsp) ground cinnamon
100 g (4 oz) English Cheddar, grated
2 eating apples, cored and sliced
30 ml (2 tbsp) apricot jam, melted

1. Cream butter and sugar together until pale and creamy.

FRUIT & HONEY CAKE

2. Beat in eggs gradually. Then fold in flours, cider, sultanas, cinnamon and 75g (3oz) cheese.

3. Spoon into a greased and lined 20.5cm (8inch) square tin.

4. Arrange apple slices in 3 lines, pressing down gently.

5. Sprinkle over remaining cheese and bake at 180°C (350°F) Mark 4 for 35 minutes until well risen and firm to touch.

6. Transfer to a wire cooling rack.

7. Brush with apricot jam and leave to cool before cutting into squares.

MARMALADE CAKE   Ⓕ

Preparation 20 mins
Cooking 1½ hrs   *Serves 6–8*

225g (8oz) flour
pinch of salt
15ml (1 tbsp) baking powder
100g (4oz) butter
50g (2oz) caster sugar
2.5ml (½ tsp) grated orange rind
2 eggs, beaten
45ml (3 tbsp) orange marmalade
30–45ml (2–3 tbsp) fresh milk

1. Prepare a 18cm (6inch) round cake tin (see page 303) or a 450g (1lb) loaf tin.

2. Sift flour, salt and baking powder into a bowl.

3. Rub in butter finely.

4. Add sugar and orange rind.

5. Mix to a fairly soft batter with eggs, marmalade and milk.

6. Transfer to prepared tin. Bake at 180°C (350°F) Mark 4 for 1¼–1½ hours or until a wooden cocktail stick, inserted into centre, comes out clean.

7. Leave in tin for 5 minutes. Turn out on to a wire cooling rack.

8. Peel off paper. Store cake in an airtight container when cold.

Variation

MARMALADE & WALNUT CAKE   Ⓕ

Follow recipe and method for marmalade cake (left). Add 50g (2oz) chopped walnuts with sugar.

MUNCHKIN CAKES (F)

Preparation 25 mins **plus cooling**
Cooking 30 mins   *Makes 16*

100 g (4 oz) butter
100 g (4 oz) sugar
1 egg, beaten
grated rind and juice of ½ orange
200 g (7 oz) self raising flour
100 ml (4 fl oz) fresh milk
75 g (3 oz) apricot jam
75 g (3 oz) plain chocolate, melted
crystallised orange and lemon slices

1. Melt butter and sugar in a pan over a low heat, cool for 2 minutes, stir occasionally. *To microwave: Cook butter and sugar for about 1½ minutes, stirring occasionally, until melted. Cool for 2 minutes, stirring occasionally.*

2. Add egg and orange rind, beat well. Fold in flour, gradually add milk then orange juice.

3. Spoon into paper bun cases and bake at 180°C (350°F) Mark 4 for 25–30 minutes, until well risen and golden brown.

4. Scoop out centre of each bun when cool, place a spoon full of jam in hollow.

5. Replace lid and ice with melted chocolate. Top with an orange or lemon slice.

CHERRY CAKE (F)

Preparation 35 mins
Cooking 1 hr   *Serves 8*

100 g (4 oz) glacé cherries
225 g (8 oz) self raising flour
50 g (2 oz) semolina
150 g (5 oz) butter
100 g (4 oz) caster sugar
5 ml (1 tsp) grated lemon rind
2.5 ml (½ tsp) vanilla essence
2 eggs, well beaten
45 ml (3 tbsp) fresh milk

1. Prepare a 18 cm (7 inch) round cake tin (see page 303).

2. Cut cherries into quarters.

3. Wash thoroughly to remove syrup.

4. Dry well. Mix with 15 ml (1 tbsp) measured flour.

5. Sift remaining flour and semolina into a bowl.

6. Rub butter into flour until mixture resembles fine breadcrumbs.

7. Add sugar, lemon rind and cherries.

8. Mix vanilla, eggs and milk to a stiff batter.

9. Stir briskly, without beating, until well mixed. Transfer to prepared tin.

10. Bake at 180°C (350°F) Mark 4 for 1 hour, or until a wooden cocktail stick, inserted into centre of cake, comes out clean.

11. Leave in tin for 5 minutes. Turn out on to a wire cooling rack.

12. Peel away paper. Store in an airtight tin.

RICH BUTTER CAKE (F)

Preparation 25 mins
Cooking 1¾ hrs   *Serves 8–10*

175 g (6 oz) butter, softened
175 g (6 oz) caster sugar
3 eggs
225 g (8 oz) flour
30 ml (2 tbsp) fresh milk
7.5 ml (1½ tsp) baking powder

1. Prepare a 20.5 cm (8 inch) round cake tin (see page 303).

2. Cream butter with sugar thoroughly for 3–4 minutes, until light and fluffy.

3. Beat in eggs, one at a time, adding 15 ml (1 tbsp) of flour with each one. Beat in milk with 15 ml (1 tbsp) of flour.

4. Sieve remaining flour together with baking powder. Gently fold in with a large metal spoon.

5. Transfer to prepared tin and smooth top with a knife.

6. Bake at 170°C (325°F) Mark 3 for 1½–1¾ hrs, or until a wooden cocktail stick, inserted into centre of cake, comes out clean.

7. Leave in tin for 5 minutes. Turn out on to a wire cooling rack.

8. Carefully peel off paper when cake is cold.

9. Store cake in an airtight container.

The creaming of the butter and caster sugar must be done very thoroughly to build as much air as possible into the mixture.

Variations
DUNDEE CAKE   ⓕ

Follow recipe and method for rich butter cake (left). Cream butter and sugar with grated rind of 1 small orange. After beating in eggs, stir in 50g (2oz) ground almonds, 100g (4oz) *each* currants, sultanas and raisins and 50g (2oz) chopped mixed peel. Before baking cake, cover top of mixture with 25–50g (1–2oz) blanched and split almonds. Bake at 150°C (300°F) Mark 2 for 2½–3 hours, or until a wooden cocktail stick, inserted into centre, comes out clean.

GENOA CAKE   ⓕ

Follow recipe and method for rich butter cake (left). Cream butter and sugar with 5ml (1tsp) grated lemon rind. After beating in eggs, stir in 100g (4oz) *each* currants, sultanas and chopped mixed peel, 50g (2oz) finely chopped glacé cherries and 25g (1oz) finely chopped almonds. Before baking cake, cover top of mixture with 25–50g (1–2oz) blanched and split almonds. Bake at 150°C (300°F) Mark 2 for 2½–3 hours, or until a wooden cocktail stick, inserted into centre of cake, comes out clean.

FROSTED WALNUT CAKE   ⓕ

Follow recipe and method for rich butter cake (left). Stir in 50g (2oz) finely chopped walnuts after beating in eggs. When cake is cold, cut into 2 layers. Sandwich together with American boiled frosting (page 328). Quickly swirl remaining frosting over top and sides. Decorate with 25–50g (1–2oz) walnut halves.

TRADITIONAL MADEIRA CAKE   ⓕ

Follow recipe and method for rich butter cake (left). Cream butter and sugar with grated rind of 1 medium lemon. Before baking cake arrange 2 strips of candied citron or lemon rind on top of cake.

GINGER CAKE   ⓕ

Follow recipe and method for rich butter cake (left). Sift flour with 5ml (1tsp) ground ginger. Add 75g (3oz) chopped preserved ginger after beating in eggs.

FROSTED WALNUT CAKE

SPICE CAKE Ⓕ

Preparation 30 mins **Cooking** 30 mins *Serves 6*

100 g (4 oz) butter
100 g (4 oz) sugar
1 egg, beaten
200 g (7 oz) self raising flour
5 ml (1 tsp) baking powder
2.5 ml (½ tsp) *each* ground nutmeg, ground
   cinnamon, ground cloves and allspice
150 ml (¼ pint) fresh milk
5 ml (1 tsp) vanilla essence
100 g (4 oz) marzipan
75 g (3 oz) lemon curd
icing sugar to decorate

1. Grease and line 2×18 cm (7 inch) sandwich tins.

2. Cream butter and sugar together until pale and fluffy.

3. Gradually beat in egg, then add dry ingredients alternately with milk and vanilla essence. Mix until smooth.

4. Divide mixture between prepared sandwich tins and bake at 190°C (375°F) Mark 5 for 30 minutes.

5. Cool in tins before turning out.

6. Roll out marzipan into a 18 cm (7 inch) circle.

7. Sandwich cakes together with marzipan and lemon curd. Dust top with icing sugar.

RIPON SPICE LOAF Ⓕ

Preparation 30 mins
Cooking 1¾ hrs *Makes 2 loaves*

225 g (8 oz) butter
275 g (10 oz) sugar
3 eggs, beaten
50 g (2 oz) chopped mixed peel
50 g (2 oz) glacé cherries, chopped
225 g (8 oz) currants
225 g (8 oz) raisins
450 g (1 lb) flour
150 ml (¼ pint) fresh milk
50 g (2 oz) ground almonds
15 ml (1 tbsp) baking powder
15 ml (1 tbsp) mixed spice
butter to serve (optional)

1. Grease and line 2×900 g (2 lb) loaf tins.

2. Cream together butter and sugar until pale and fluffy.

3. Add eggs gradually. Toss fruit in a little flour and stir into mixture with milk and almonds.

4. Add remaining ingredients and fold in.

5. Divide mixture between prepared loaf tins and bake at 150°C (300°F) Mark 2 for 1¾ hours.

6. Cool in tins for 15 minutes, then turn out and cool on a wire cooling rack.

7. When cold store in an airtight container.

8. Serve sliced and buttered, if desired.

APRICOT & PRUNE TEABREAD Ⓕ

Preparation 20 mins **Cooking** 1 hr *Serves 12*

275 g (10 oz) granary flour
12.5 ml (2½ tsp) baking powder
7.5 ml (1½ tsp) mixed spice
75 g (3 oz) butter
100 g (4 oz) no-soak prunes,
   stoned and chopped
75 g (3 oz) unsalted peanuts,
   roughly chopped
75 g (3 oz) soft brown sugar
100 g (4 oz) no-soak dried apricots,
   chopped
200 ml (7 fl oz) fresh milk
1 egg, beaten
butter to serve (optional)

1. Place flour, baking powder and mixed spice in a bowl.

2. Rub butter into flour until mixture resembles fine breadcrumbs.

3. Stir in prunes, peanuts, sugar and apricots.

4. Add milk and egg, mix well.

5. Turn into a greased 900 g (2 lb) loaf tin and bake at 180°C (350°F) Mark 4 for 1 hour until an inserted skewer comes out clean.

6. Leave to cool in tin.

7. Serve sliced with butter if desired.

PARADISE LOAF   Ⓕ

Preparation 15 mins **Cooking** 45 mins *Serves 12*

This is a very moist cake
100 g (4 oz) flour
5 ml (1 tsp) baking powder
50 g (2 oz) desiccated coconut
175 g (6 oz) sugar
1 egg, beaten
150 ml (¼ pint) fresh milk
100 g (4 oz) butter, melted
grated rind and juice of 1 orange
75 g (3 oz) curd cheese
30 ml (2 tbsp) orange juice
10 ml (2 tsp) icing sugar
50 g (2 oz) tropical fruit and nut mix

1. Grease and line a 900 g (2 lb) loaf tin.

2. Place flour, baking powder, coconut, sugar, egg, milk and melted butter in a food processor and process for about 30 seconds or until smooth.

3. Add orange rind and juice and mix in.

4. Pour into prepared tin and bake at 180°C (350°F) Mark 4 for 45 minutes.

5. Cool in tin before turning out.

6. Cream together curd cheese, remaining orange juice and icing sugar. Spread over top of loaf when cold.

7. Decorate with fruit and nut mix.

8. Cut into slices to serve.

GOLDEN COCONUT PYRAMIDS   Ⓕ

Preparation 15 mins **plus** 20 mins **standing**
Cooking 30 mins   *Makes 16*

2 eggs
225 g (8 oz) desiccated coconut
150 g (5 oz) caster sugar
6 glacé cherries, quartered

1. Line 1 or 2 ungreased baking sheets with non-stick baking paper.

2. Beat eggs well. Stir in coconut and sugar.

3. Leave to stand for 20 minutes.

4. Dip hands in cold water. Shape mixture into 16 pyramids, use egg cup as a guide.

5. Place on sheets, top with piece of cherry.

6. Bake at 180°C (350°F) Mark 4 for 25–30 minutes until pale gold.

7. Remove from sheets and cool on a wire cooling rack.

8. Store in an airtight container when cold.

SUNSHINE BARS 🅕

Preparation 25 mins **plus** 15 mins **standing**
Cooking 40 mins   *Makes 10*

This moist cake has no sugar added

150 ml (¼ pint) fresh milk
100 g (4 oz) stoned dried dates, chopped
175 g (6 oz) wholemeal self raising flour
2.5 ml (½ tsp) baking powder
2.5 ml (½ tsp) ground cinnamon
1 egg, beaten
50 g (2 oz) butter, melted
grated rind and chopped flesh of 1 orange

1. Grease and line an 18 cm (7 inch) square tin.

2. Warm milk in a small saucepan.
To microwave: Heat milk in a small bowl or jug for 1 minute.

3. Add dates to milk and stand for 15 minutes.

4. Mix together flour, baking powder and spice in a bowl.

5. Beat egg, melted butter and orange rind into milk.

6. Stir into dry ingredients with orange flesh and mix well.

7. Spoon into prepared tin.

8. Bake at 180°C (350°F) Mark 4 for 40 minutes, until risen and golden brown. Cool on a wire cooling rack.

9. Store in an airtight container for no longer than 2 days. Serve cut into fingers.

FAMILY TRAY BAKE 🅕

Preparation 30 mins **Cooking** 35 mins *Makes 16*

100 g (4 oz) butter
225 g (8 oz) flour
100 g (4 oz) sugar
100 g (4 oz) dried mixed fruit
15 ml (1 tbsp) baking powder
2.5 ml (½ tsp) ground nutmeg
2 eggs, beaten
150 ml (¼ pint) fresh milk

1. Grease a 28×18 cm (11×7 inch) cake tin.

2. Rub butter into flour. Add sugar, fruit, baking powder and nutmeg, stir in.

3. Mix in eggs and gradually stir in milk.

4. Turn into prepared cake tin.

5. Bake at 180°C (350°F) Mark 4 for 35 minutes, until lightly browned and firm.

6. Cool on a wire cooling rack.

7. Cut into fingers to serve.

CHERRY & WALNUT MUFFINS (F)

Preparation 20 mins **Cooking** 25 mins *Makes 12*

150 g (5 oz) plain flour
150 g (5 oz) wholemeal flour
12.5 ml (2½ tsp) baking powder
2.5 ml (½ tsp) salt
50 g (2 oz) brown sugar
75 g (3 oz) glacé cherries, chopped
50 g (2 oz) walnuts, chopped
1 egg
225 ml (8 fl oz) fresh milk
50 g (2 oz) butter, melted

1. Place flours, baking powder, salt, sugar, cherries and walnuts in a bowl and mix well.
2. Lightly whisk together egg, milk and butter.
3. Stir into dry ingredients and mix until evenly blended.
4. Spoon into 12 greased muffin tins or 12 paper cases.
5. Bake at 200°C (400°F) Mark 6 for 25 minutes.
6. Cool in tins for 5 minutes before turning out.

BRAN MUFFINS (F)

Preparation 30 mins **Cooking** 25 mins *Makes 6*

50 g (2 oz) bran
300 ml (½ pint) fresh milk
50 g (2 oz) caster sugar
50 g (2 oz) butter
1 egg
50 g (2 oz) raisins
100 g (4 oz) wholemeal flour
2.5 ml (½ tsp) salt
15 ml (1 tbsp) baking powder
butter to serve (optional)

1. Soak bran in milk for 10 minutes.
2. Cream together sugar and butter until light and fluffy.
3. Beat in egg, raisins, bran and milk.
4. Lightly fold in flour, salt and baking powder.
5. Grease 6 muffin tins or place 12 paper cases in 12 ungreased bun tins.
6. Divide mixture between them and bake at 200°C (400°F) Mark 6, for 25 minutes.
7. Serve warm with butter, if desired.

BRAN MUFFINS, CHERRY & WALNUT MUFFINS

PARKIN Ⓕ

Preparation 35 mins
Cooking 1 hr   *Serves 10*

225 g (8 oz) flour
2.5 ml (½ tsp) salt
5 ml (1 tsp) *each* mixed spice, ground
    cinnamon and ground ginger
5 ml (1 tsp) bicarbonate of soda
225 g (8 oz) medium oatmeal
175 g (6 oz) black treacle
150 g (5 oz) butter
100 g (4 oz) soft brown sugar
150 ml (¼ pint) fresh milk
1 egg, beaten

1. Prepare an 18 cm (7 inch) square cake tin.
*To microwave: Grease and base-line a
2 litre (3½ pint) ring mould.*

2. Sift flour, salt, spice, cinnamon, ground
ginger and bicarbonate of soda into a bowl.

3. Add oatmeal and make a well in centre.

4. Put treacle, butter, sugar and milk into a
saucepan. Stir over a low heat until butter
has melted.
*To microwave: Put treacle, butter, sugar and
milk into a bowl or jug. Cook for
3–4 minutes, stirring occasionally, until
butter has melted.*

5. Pour into well and add egg.

6. Stir mixture briskly, without beating, until
smooth and evenly combined.

7. Transfer to prepared tin. Bake at
180°C (350°F) Mark 4 for 1 hour, or until a
wooden cocktail stick, inserted into centre,
comes out clean.
*To microwave: Transfer to prepared mould
and place on a low microwave rack. Cook,
uncovered, for about 7 minutes or until
surface is still slightly moist and a wooden
cocktail stick, inserted into cake, comes out
clean.*

8. Cool on a wire cooling rack.
*To microwave: Allow to stand for 5 minutes,
then turn out on to a wire cooling rack lined
with non-stick baking paper.*

9. Store, without removing paper, in an
airtight container for about 1 week before
cutting.
*To microwave: Store, wrapped in non-stick
baking paper and overwrapped in foil, for
2–3 days before cutting.*

GINGERBREAD Ⓕ

Preparation 30 mins
Cooking 1 hr   *Serves 6–8*

175 g (6 oz) flour
10 ml (2 tsp) ground ginger
5 ml (1 tsp) mixed spice
2.5 ml (½ tsp) bicarbonate of soda
100 g (4 oz) golden syrup
25 g (1 oz) butter
25 g (1 oz) soft brown sugar
1 egg, beaten
15 ml (1 tbsp) black treacle
30 ml (2 tbsp) fresh milk

1. Prepare a 15 cm (6 inch) cake tin (see
page 303).
*To microwave: Grease and base-line a
1.4 litre (2½ pint) ring mould.*

2. Sift flour, ginger, spice and bicarbonate of
soda into a bowl. Make a well in centre.

3. Put syrup, butter and brown sugar into a
saucepan. Stir over a low heat until butter
has melted.
*To microwave: Put syrup, butter and brown
sugar into a bowl or jug. Cook for
1–1½ minutes until butter has melted.*

4. Pour into well with egg, treacle and milk.

5. Stir briskly, without beating, until well
combined.

6. Transfer to prepared tin. Bake at
180°C (350°F) Mark 4 for 1 hour, or until a
wooden cocktail stick, inserted into centre,
comes out clean.
*To microwave: Transfer to prepared mould
and place on a low microwave rack. Cook,
uncovered, for 4–5 minutes until surface is
still slightly moist and a wooden cocktail
stick, inserted in the cake, comes out clean.*

7. Turn out on to a wire cooling rack.
*To microwave: Allow to stand for 5 minutes,
then turn out on to a wire cooling rack lined
with non-stick baking paper.*

8. Remove paper when gingerbread is cold.

STREUSAL CAKE   Ⓕ

Preparation 30 mins
Cooking 40 mins   *Makes 15 pieces*

100 g (4 oz) butter
175 g (6 oz) caster sugar
1 egg
150 ml (¼ pint) fresh milk
225 g (8 oz) self raising flour
75 g (3 oz) soft brown sugar
5 ml (1 tsp) ground cinnamon
50 g (2 oz) chopped mixed nuts

1. Grease and line a 28×18 cm (11×7 inch) cake tin.
2. Cream 75 g (3 oz) butter and sugar until light and fluffy.
3. Beat in egg and milk.
4. Fold in 200 g (7 oz) flour.
5. Place half the mixture in a prepared cake tin.
6. Rub remaining butter into brown sugar, cinnamon and remaining flour.
7. Stir in nuts and sprinkle half over mixture in tin.
8. Cover with remaining cake mixture, then remaining nut mixture.
9. Bake at 180°C (350°F) Mark 4 for 35–40 minutes.
10. Cool in the tin then cut into bars to serve.

ROCK CAKES   Ⓕ

Preparation 20 mins **Cooking** 20 mins *Makes 10*

225 g (8 oz) self raising flour
100 g (4 oz) butter
75 g (3 oz) caster sugar
100 g (4 oz) mixed dried fruit
1 egg, beaten
10–20 ml (2–4 tsp) fresh milk

1. Sift flour into a bowl.
2. Rub butter into flour until mixture resembles fine breadcrumbs.
3. Add sugar and fruit.
4. Mix to a very stiff batter with beaten egg and milk.
5. Place 10 spoonfuls of mixture, in rocky mounds, on a well-greased baking sheet (allow room between each one as they spread slightly).
6. Bake at 200°C (400°F) Mark 6 for 15–20 minutes.
7. Cool on a wire cooling rack.

ICINGS

ROYAL ICING

Preparation 25 mins
Sufficient to cover top and sides of an
18–20.5 cm (7–8 inch) cake

2 egg whites
450 g (1 lb) icing sugar, sifted
2.5 ml (½ tsp) lemon juice
2–3 drops of glycerine

1. Beat egg whites until foamy.

2. Gradually beat in icing sugar, lemon juice and glycerine (glycerine prevents icing from becoming too hard to cut).

3. Continue beating hard for 5-7 minutes, or until icing is snowy-white and firm enough to stand in straight points when spoon is lifted out of bowl.

4. If too stiff, add a little more egg white or lemon juice. If too soft, beat in a little more sifted icing sugar.

5. If coloured icing is required, beat in a few drops of food colouring.

It is best to use Royal icing a day after is it made to give air bubbles time to disperse.

Always keep icing in an airtight, rigid plastic container until ready for use.

Variation

ROYAL ICING FOR PIPING

Follow recipe and method for Royal icing (above). Omit glycerine and make up ¼-½ quantity only.

ALMOND PASTE

Preparation 15 mins
Sufficient to cover top and sides of a 20.5–23 cm
(8–9 inch) rich fruit cake fairly thickly

275 g (10 oz) ground almonds
225 g (8 oz) icing sugar, sifted
225 g (8 oz) caster sugar
1 egg plus 2 egg yolks
5 ml (1 tsp) lemon juice
2.5 ml (½ tsp) vanilla essence

1. Combine almonds with both sugars.

2. Mix to a fairly stiff paste with remaining ingredients.

3. Turn out on to a board or table covered with sifted icing sugar. Knead lightly with fingertips until smooth, crack-free and pliable.

GLACÉ ICING

Preparation 10 mins
Sufficient to cover top of an
18–20.5 cm (7–8 inch) cake

225 g (8 oz) icing sugar, sifted
30 ml (2 tbsp) hot water

1. Put sugar into a bowl. Gradually add water.

2. Stir briskly until smooth and thick enough to coat back of spoon without running off.

3. If too thick, add a little more water; if too thin, stir in more sifted icing sugar. If liked, colour with a few drops of food colouring.

4. Use immediately.

Do not disturb cake until icing has set, or cracks will form.

Variations

COCOA GLACÉ ICING

Follow recipe and method for glacé icing (above) but omit 15 ml (1 tbsp) water. Mix 30 ml (2 tbsp) cocoa powder with 30 ml (2 tbsp) boiling water and stir into icing.

ORANGE OR LEMON GLACÉ ICING

Follow recipe and method for glacé icing (left). Add 5 ml (1 tsp) very finely grated orange or lemon rind to sifted sugar. Mix with 30 ml (2 tbsp) strained and warmed orange or lemon juice instead of water. If liked, colour with orange or lemon food colouring.

COFFEE GLACÉ ICING

Follow recipe and method for glacé icing (left). Dissolve 10 ml (2 tsp) instant coffee granules in hot water before adding to sugar.

ROSEWATER OR ORANGE FLOWER GLACÉ ICING

Follow recipe and method for glacé icing (left). Use 10 ml (2 tsp) rosewater or orange flower water and 20 ml (4 tsp) hot water in place of 30 ml (2 tbsp) hot water.

CHOCOLATE GLACÉ ICING

Preparation 10 mins **Cooking** 5 mins
Sufficient to cover top and sides of an 18–20.5 cm (7–8 inch) cake

50 g (2 oz) plain chocolate
15 g (½ oz) butter
30 ml (2 tbsp) warm water
2.5 ml (½ tsp) vanilla essence
115 g (4½ oz) icing sugar, sifted

1. Break up chocolate and put, with butter and water, into a basin standing over a saucepan of hot water.
2. Leave until melted, stirring once or twice.
3. Add vanilla. Gradually beat in icing sugar.
4. Use immediately.

MOCHA GLACÉ ICING

Follow recipe and method for chocolate glacé icing (above). Add 10 ml (2 tsp) instant coffee granules to chocolate, butter and water in basin.

LEMON GLACÉ ICING, LEMON AND ALMOND RING (PAGE 313)

SEVEN MINUTE FROSTING

Preparation 5 mins **Cooking** 7 mins
*Sufficient to fill and cover top and sides of
a 2 layer 20.5 cm (8 inch) sandwich cake*

165 g (5½ oz) granulated sugar
2.5 ml (½ tsp) cream of tartar
pinch of salt
2 egg whites
75 ml (3 fl oz) water
5 ml (1 tsp) vanilla essence

1. Place sugar, cream of tartar, salt, egg whites and water in a large bowl.
2. Place over a pan of hot water and beat with a hand held electric mixer for about 7 minutes, until mixture thickens sufficiently to stand in peaks.
3. Remove from pan and add vanilla.
4. Continue beating for 2–3 minutes.
5. Use to fill and spread over cake. Swirl with a palette knife or back of a spoon.

Variations

CARAMEL FROSTING

Follow recipe and method for seven minute frosting (above). Use soft brown sugar in place of granulated sugar.

COCONUT FROSTING

Follow recipe and method for seven minute frosting (above). Add 50 g (2 oz) desiccated coconut to finished frosting.

AMERICAN BOILED FROSTING

Preparation 10 mins **Cooking** 10 mins
*Sufficient to fill and cover top and sides of three
18 cm (7 inch) sandwich cakes or one deep
18–20.5 cm (7–8 inch) cake, cut into two layers*

This frosting is best made using a sugar thermometer and a table top electric mixer.
450 g (1 lb) granulated sugar
150 ml (¼ pint) water
2 egg whites
pinch of cream of tartar
5 ml (1 tsp) vanilla essence

1. Put sugar and water into a saucepan. Stir over a low heat until sugar dissolves.
2. Bring to the boil. Cover pan and boil for 1 minute.
3. Uncover. Continue to boil fairly briskly, without stirring, for a further 5 minutes (or until a small quantity of mixture, dropped into a cup of very cold water, forms a soft ball when gently rolled between finger and thumb.) Temperature on a sugar thermometer should be 116°C (240°F).
4. Meanwhile, beat egg whites and cream of tartar to a very stiff snow.
5. When sugar and water have boiled for required amount of time, pour on to egg whites in a slow, steady stream, beating all the time.
6. Add vanilla. Continue beating until frosting is cool and thick enough to spread.
7. Quickly use to fill cake (it is important to work quickly: frosting hardens rapidly once it has cooled).
8. Swirl remainder over top and sides.

COFFEE FUDGE FROSTING

Preparation 10 mins **Cooking** 5 mins
*Sufficient to fill and cover top and sides of a
2 layer, 18 cm (7 inch) sandwich cake*

50 g (2 oz) butter
100 g (4 oz) soft brown sugar
45 ml (3 tbsp) coffee essence
15 ml (1 tbsp) fresh single cream
225 g (8 oz) icing sugar, sifted

1. Put butter, sugar, coffee essence and cream into a saucepan.
2. Stand over a low heat, stirring, until butter melts and sugar dissolves.
3. Bring to the boil. Boil briskly for 3 minutes only.
4. Remove from heat. Gradually stir in icing sugar.
5. Beat until smooth. Continue beating for a further 5 minutes, or until frosting has cooled and is stiff enough to spread.

COFFEE FUDGE FROSTING

BUTTER CREAM Ⓕ

Preparation 10 mins
*Sufficient to fill and cover top of a 2 layer,
18 cm (7 inch) sandwich cake*

100 g (4 oz) butter, softened
225 g (8 oz) icing sugar, sifted
30 ml (2 tbsp) fresh milk
few drops of vanilla essence

1. Beat butter until soft.
2. Gradually beat in sugar and milk.
3. Continue beating until light and fluffy.
4. Stir in vanilla, chill until a little thicker.

Variations

COFFEE BUTTER CREAM Ⓕ

Follow recipe and method for butter cream
(above) but omit vanilla essence and milk.
Dissolve 15 ml (1 tbsp) instant coffee granules
in a little water and use in place of milk.

CHOCOLATE BUTTER CREAM

Follow recipe and method for butter Ⓕ
cream (above) but omit vanilla essence.
Beat in 50 g (2 oz) melted and cooled
plain chocolate with sugar and only
10 ml (2 tsp) milk.

ORANGE BUTTER CREAM Ⓕ

Follow recipe and method for butter cream
(left) but omit vanilla essence. Beat
5 ml (1 tsp) finely grated orange rind with
butter before adding sugar and milk. If
liked, colour pale orange with orange food
colouring.

CHOCOLATE ICING

Preparation 15 mins **Cooking** 2 mins
*Sufficient to fill and cover top of a 2 layer,
18 cm (7 inch) sandwich cake.*

65 g (2½ oz) butter
45 ml (3 tbsp) fresh milk
25 g (1 oz) cocoa powder, sieved
5 ml (1 tsp) vanilla essence
225 g (8 oz) icing sugar, sieved

1. Place butter and milk in a small
saucepan. Heat until butter has melted.
2. Pour into a bowl and blend in cocoa and
vanilla essence.
3. Stir in icing sugar and beat until smooth.
4. Either use immediately to give a smooth,
glossy finish or allow to thicken for a butter
cream type finish.

SCONES

Do **not** use pasteurised or other heat-treated milk, which has turned sour, for scone making. The souring may have been caused by other than natural souring processes. Instead use half milk with soured cream, yogurt or buttermilk.

Freshly baked scones should be pulled gently apart with fingers. Cutting spoils the texture and makes them doughy. As scones stale quickly it is preferable to make and eat them on the same day.

ALL-PURPOSE SCONES Ⓕ

Preparation 25 mins
Cooking 10 mins   *Makes 7–8*

225 g (8 oz) self raising flour
2.5 ml (½ tsp) salt
50 g (2 oz) butter
150 ml (¼ pint) fresh milk
extra milk for brushing
butter, fresh cream, jam or cheese
    to serve

1. Sift flour and salt into a bowl.

2. Rub butter into flour until mixture resembles fine breadcrumbs.

3. Add milk all at once. Mix to a soft, but not sticky, dough with a knife.

4. Turn on to a lightly floured work surface. Knead quickly until smooth.

5. Roll out to about 1 cm (½ inch) thick.

6. Cut into 7 or 8 rounds with a 6.5 cm (2½ inch) biscuit cutter.

7. Transfer to a greased baking sheet. Brush tops with milk.

8. Bake at 230°C (450°F) Mark 8 for 7–10 minutes or until well risen and golden.

9. Cool on a wire cooling rack.

10. Serve with butter or whipped cream and jam, or butter and cheese.

If using plain flour instead of self raising use 12.5 ml (2½ tsp) baking powder to 225 g (8 oz) flour.

Variations

CHEESE SCONES Ⓕ

Follow recipe and method for all-purpose scones (left). Sift 5 ml (1 tsp) dry mustard and a pinch of cayenne pepper with flour and salt. Mix in 50 g (2 oz) grated English Cheddar before adding milk.

SULTANA SCONES Ⓕ

Follow recipe and method for all-purpose scones (left). Add 50 g (2 oz) sultanas and 25 g (1 oz) sugar before adding milk.

DATE & WALNUT SCONES Ⓕ

Follow recipe and method for all-purpose scones (left). Add 25 g (1 oz) chopped dates, 15 g (½ oz) chopped walnuts and 25 g (1 oz) sugar before adding milk.

HONEY SCONES Ⓕ

Follow recipe and method for all-purpose scones (left). Mix to a dough with 15 ml (1 tbsp) clear honey (slightly warmed) and 105 ml (7 tbsp) milk. Serve warm.

WHOLEMEAL SCONES Ⓕ

Preparation 25 mins
Cooking 10 mins   *Makes 7–8*

100 g (4 oz) wholemeal flour
100 g (4 oz) flour
15 ml (1 tbsp) baking powder
2.5 ml (½ tsp) salt
40 g (1½ oz) butter
150 ml (¼ pint) fresh milk
extra milk for brushing
butter to serve

1. Sift flours, baking powder and salt into a bowl.

2. Rub butter into flour until mixture resembles fine breadcrumbs.

3. Add milk all at once. Mix to a soft, but not sticky, dough with a knife.

4. Turn on to a lightly floured work surface. Knead quickly until smooth.

5. Roll out to about 1 cm (½ inch) thickness. Cut into 7 or 8 rounds with a 6.5 cm (2½ inch) biscuit cutter.

6. Transfer to a greased baking sheet. Brush tops with milk.

7. Bake at 230°C (450°F) Mark 8 for 7–10 minutes, or until well risen and golden.

8. Cool on a wire cooling rack.

9. Serve with butter.

SOURED CREAM SCONES Ⓕ

Preparation 25 mins
Cooking 10 mins   *Makes 7–8*

225 g (8 oz) self raising flour
2.5 ml (½ tsp) salt
40 g (1½ oz) butter
60 ml (4 tbsp) fresh soured cream
60 ml (4 tbsp) fresh milk
extra milk for brushing
butter and jam to serve

1. Sift flour and salt into a bowl.

2. Rub butter into flour until mixture resembles fine breadcrumbs.

3. Add cream and milk all at once. Mix to a soft, but not sticky, dough with a knife.

4. Turn out on to a lightly floured work surface. Knead quickly until smooth.

5. Roll out to about 1 cm (½ inch) thickness.

6. Cut into 7 or 8 rounds with a 6.5 cm (2½ inch) biscuit cutter.

7. Transfer to a greased baking sheet. Brush tops with milk.

8. Bake at 230°C (450°F) Mark 8 for 7–10 minutes or until well risen and golden.

9. Cool on a wire cooling rack.

10. Serve with butter and jam.

Variations

YOGURT SCONES Ⓕ

Follow recipe and method for soured cream scones (left) but use 60 ml (4 tbsp) natural yogurt instead of soured cream.

BUTTERMILK SCONES Ⓕ

Follow recipe and method for soured cream scones (left). Use 150 ml (¼ pint) buttermilk instead of soured cream and milk.

DROPPED SCONES   Ⓕ

Preparation 10 mins **Cooking** 3 mins   *Serves 4*

225 g (8 oz) self raising flour
2.5 ml (½ tsp) salt
15 ml (1 tbsp) caster sugar
1 egg
300 ml (½ pint) fresh milk
25–50 g (1–2 oz) butter, melted
butter, jam, or honey to serve

1. Sift flour and salt into a bowl. Add sugar.

2. Mix to a smooth creamy batter with whole egg and half the milk.

3. Stir in remaining milk.

4. Brush a large heavy frying pan with melted butter. Heat.

5. Drop small rounds of scone mixture (about 12 in all), from a spoon, into pan.

6. Cook until bubbles show on surface (2½–3 minutes).

7. Carefully turn over with a knife. Cook for a further 2 minutes.

8. Pile scones in a clean, folded tea-towel to keep warm and moist.

9. Serve immediately with butter and jam, or honey.

POTATO SCONES   Ⓕ

Preparation 35 mins
Cooking 5 mins   *Makes about 10*

450 g (1 lb) potatoes
10 ml (2 tsp) salt
50 g (2 oz) butter
100 g (4 oz) flour
butter to serve

1. Cook potatoes in boiling water for about 20 minutes, until soft.
To microwave: Cut potatoes into cubes and cook with 60 ml (4 tbsp) water, covered, for 6–9 minutes, stirring once or twice, until tender.

2. Drain and mash well.

3. Add salt and butter, then work in flour, to make a stiff mixture.

4. Turn on to a floured work surface, knead lightly, then roll out to 0.5 cm (¼ inch) thickness.

5. Cut into circles with a 4 cm (2 inch) cutter.

6. Cook on a greased hot griddle or thick based frying pan, for 4–5 minutes, on each side, until golden brown.

7. Serve hot, spread with butter.

GRANARY HERB SCONES  F

Preparation 25 mins **Cooking** 10 mins *Makes 6*

225g (8oz) granary flour
15ml (1tbsp) baking powder
2.5ml (½tsp) dried oregano
50g (2oz) butter
150ml (¼pint) fresh milk
extra milk for brushing
butter for spreading
sliced cheese and salad to serve

1. Place flour, baking powder and oregano in a bowl.

2. Rub butter into flour until mixture resembles fine breadcrumbs.

3. Add milk and mix to a soft, but not sticky, dough.

4. Roll out on a floured work surface to about 1.5cm (¾inch) thick and cut out 6 triangles.

5. Place on a greased baking sheet and brush tops with milk.

6. Bake at 230°C (450°F) Mark 8 for 10 minutes, or until well risen and golden.

7. Serve fresh with butter, cheese and salad.

CHEESE & GRAIN SCONES F

Preparation 20 mins **Cooking** 10 mins *Makes 16*

225g (8oz) soft grain flour
15ml (1tbsp) baking powder
pinch of salt
50g (2oz) butter
75g (3oz) Red Cheshire cheese, crumbled
150ml (¼pint) fresh milk
sesame or poppy seeds

1. Place flour, baking powder and salt in a bowl.

2. Rub in butter until mixture resembles fine breadcrumbs.

3. Stir in cheese.

4. Add milk and mix to a soft dough.

5. Roll out on a floured work surface to 1cm (½ inch) thick and cut out with a 5cm (2 inch) cutter.

6. Place on a greased baking sheet and brush tops with milk. Sprinkle with sesame or poppy seeds.

7. Bake at 230°C (450°F) Mark 8 for 10 minutes.

GRANARY HERB SCONES

ORKNEY PANCAKES (F)

Preparation 30 mins **plus** 2 hours **standing**
Cooking 15 mins   *Makes 20*

175 g (6 oz) fine oatmeal
300 ml (10 fl oz) fresh soured cream
1 egg, beaten
30 ml (2 tbsp) golden syrup
75 g (3 oz) self raising flour
pinch of salt
5 ml (1 tsp) bicarbonate of soda
200 ml (7 fl oz) fresh milk
butter and jam to serve

1. Mix together oatmeal and soured cream, cover and stand for 2 hours.

2. Mix in egg, syrup, flour, salt and bicarbonate of soda.

3. Stir in sufficient milk to give a thick batter consistency.

4. Heat a griddle or frying pan until hot, then drop large spoonfuls of mixture onto griddle.

5. Cook until bubbles show on surface, turn and cook for a further 2 minutes.

6. Cook remaining mixture in batches.

7. Serve buttered with jam, if desired.

RASPBERRY SHORTCAKES

Preparation 35 mins **Cooking** 20 mins   *Serves 4*

225 g (8 oz) self raising flour
2.5 ml (½ tsp) salt
50 g (2 oz) butter
25 g (1 oz) caster sugar
150 ml (¼ pint) fresh milk
extra milk for brushing
150 ml (5 fl oz) fresh double cream,
  softly whipped
225 g (8 oz) raspberries
45 ml (3 tbsp) icing sugar, sifted (optional)

1. Sift flour and salt into a bowl.

2. Rub butter into flour until mixture resembles fine breadcrumbs.

3. Stir in sugar, add milk and mix to a soft, but not sticky dough with a knife.

4. Turn out on to a lightly floured work surface. Knead quickly until smooth.

5. Roll out to about 2.5 cm (1 inch) thickness. Cut into 4 rounds with a 7.5 cm (3 inch) cutter.

6. Stand on a greased baking sheet and brush tops with milk.

7. Bake at 220°C (425°F) Mark 7 for 15–20 minutes, until well risen and golden.

RASPBERRY SHORTCAKES

8. Transfer to a wire cooling rack. Leave until lukewarm.

9. Pull apart gently with fingers and spread with cream.

10. Sandwich together with raspberries mixed with sugar if used.

11. Serve warm.

APPLE & CINNAMON SCONES Ⓕ

Preparation 30 mins **plus cooling**
Cooking 20 mins   *Makes 10*

350 g (12 oz) cooking apples, peeled, cored
   and chopped
225 g (8 oz) self raising flour
2.5 ml (½ tsp) salt
7.5 ml (1½ tsp) ground cinnamon
50 g (2 oz) butter
25 g (1 oz) sugar
150 ml (¼ pint) fresh milk
extra milk for brushing
25 g (1 oz) demerara sugar
150 ml (¼ pint) fresh double or whipping
   cream

1. Cook apples in a little water until soft, mash well or purée. Allow to cool.
To microwave: Cook apples with 30 ml (2 tbsp) water, covered, for 3–4 minutes until soft. Mash well or purée and allow to cool.

2. Sieve flour, salt and 5 ml (1 tsp) cinnamon into a bowl.

3. Rub in butter until mixture resembles fine breadcrumbs. Stir in sugar.

4. Make a well in centre, add milk and one third of apple.

5. Mix until mixture forms a dough.

6. Knead quickly on a floured work surface then roll out to 1.5 cm (¾ inch) thick.

7. Cut out with a 5 cm (2 inch) cutter.

8. Place on a greased baking sheet.

9. Brush tops with milk and sprinkle with demerara sugar and remaining cinnamon.

10. Bake at 230°C (450°F) Mark 8 for 30 minutes or until golden brown.

11. Cool, split in half and sandwich together with remaining apple and whipped cream.

RING DOUGHNUTS Ⓕ

Preparation 30 mins
Cooking 3 mins   *Makes 20*

350 g (12 oz) self raising flour
1.25 ml (¼ tsp) salt
2.5 ml (½ tsp) ground cinnamon
2.5 ml (½ tsp) mixed spice
100 g (4 oz) butter
50 g (2 oz) caster sugar
1 egg
150 ml (¼ pint) fresh milk
deep fat or oil for frying
extra caster sugar

1. Sift flour, salt, cinnamon and spice into a bowl.

2. Rub butter into flour until mixture resembles fine breadcrumbs.

3. Add sugar.

4. Beat egg with milk. Add, all at once, to dry ingredients.

5. Mix to a soft, but not sticky, dough with a knife.

6. Turn out on to a lightly floured work surface. Knead quickly until smooth.

7. Roll out to 1 cm (½ inch) thickness.

8. Cut into rounds with a 5 cm (2 inch) biscuit cutter. Remove centres with a 2.5 cm (1 inch) cutter. Re-roll and cut into more rings.

9. Fry, a few at a time, in hot fat or oil for 2–3 minutes, turning once.

10. Remove from pan. Drain thoroughly on absorbent kitchen paper.

11. Toss in caster sugar.

12. Serve while still warm.

Variation

SQUARE DOUGHNUTS Ⓕ

Follow recipe and method for ring doughnuts (above). But roll out into a rectangle 0.5 cm (¼ inch) thick. Cut into 4 cm (1½ inch) squares before frying.

MOCK CHELSEA BUNS

Preparation 35 mins **Cooking** 20 mins *Makes 8*

225g (8oz) self raising flour
75g (3oz) butter
25g (1oz) sugar
150ml (¼pint) fresh milk
25g (1oz) butter
100g (4oz) currants
50g (2oz) demerara sugar
25g (1oz) mixed peel
25g (1oz) glacé cherries, chopped
5ml (1tsp) mixed spice

1. Sieve flour into a bowl and rub in butter until mixture resembles fine breadcrumbs.

2. Add sugar and mix in milk to give a soft dough.

3. Melt butter and stir in currants, demerara sugar, mixed peel, cherries and spice. Mix well.

4. Roll out dough on a floured work surface to 25.5×30.5cm (10×12inches).

5. Sprinkle fruit mixture over dough to within 1cm (½inch) of edge. Dampen edges of dough with water.

6. Starting from a longer edge, roll up and cut into 8.

7. Place cut sides down in a greased 23cm (9inch) round loose-bottomed tin, to form a ring – with one round in centre.

8. Bake at 200°C (400°F) Mark 6 for 15–20 minutes.

Variation

SUGAR & SPICE RINGS

Follow recipe and method for mock Chelsea buns (left). Omit filling ingredients. Instead brush 25 g (1oz) melted butter over rolled-out dough. Mix together 50g (2oz) caster sugar, 5ml (1tsp) ground cinnamon and 50g (2oz) currants and sprinkle over dough.

MOCK CHELSEA BUNS

BREADS

Flour

For best results (especially for bread-making) use a strong plain flour which, with kneading, develops quickly into a firm elastic dough to produce goods with a large volume and a light open texture. A good quality household plain flour will also give good results.

Yeast

Fresh or dried yeast can be used. Fresh yeast should be creamy in colour, firm to touch and easy to break. It can be stored in a refrigerator for 4–5 days. It can also be frozen in small amounts. Fresh yeast is often available from bakers and health food shops.

Dried yeast can be used instead of fresh yeast and will keep up to 6 months if stored in an airtight container.

Allow 7g (¼oz) or 10ml (2tsp) dried yeast for every 15g (½oz) fresh yeast recommended in a recipe.

To reconstitute dried yeast, dissolve 5ml (1tsp) of sugar in a little of the measured liquid, which should be warm. Sprinkle the yeast on top. Leave in a warm place until frothy (about 10 minutes) and add to the dry ingredients with the rest of the warm liquid.

Sachets of fast action dried yeast are also available. This is added straight to the flour and not reconstituted in liquid. It also contains bread improvers which speed up the action of the yeast. This means that the dough requires only one kneading and rising. One sachet of fast action dried yeast is sufficient for 700g (1½lb) flour.

Kneading & Rising

All doughs must be kneaded thoroughly after mixing to ensure a good rise and even texture.

To allow time for the yeast to work, the dough must be risen at least once before baking. The dough must be covered or placed in a lightly greased polythene bag during rising to prevent a skin forming on the surface.

The rising time varies with temperature and type of dough – it will take about 1 hour in a warm place or 1½–2 hours at room temperature 18–21°C (65–70°F).

To save time the dough may be made up the night before and left to rise for 8–12 hours (overnight) in a cold room or refrigerator. The dough should then be allowed to reach room temperature before shaping.

Richer doughs take longer to rise than plain ones and give best results when given a slow rise.

Once risen all mixtures must be kneaded quickly to make the dough firm and ready for shaping.

Testing for Baking

When cooked, loaves, etc. shrink slightly from the sides of the tin, sound hollow when tapped underneath with the knuckles and have golden brown crusts.

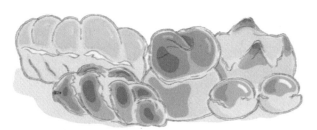

WHITE BREAD   Ⓕ

Preparation 25 mins **plus rising**
Cooking 40 mins   *Makes 2 loaves*

450g (1 lb) strong plain flour
10 ml (2 tsp) salt
15 g (½ oz) butter
15 g (½ oz) fresh yeast
   or 10 ml (2 tsp) dried yeast
300 ml (½ pint) lukewarm water
milk or beaten egg for brushing

1. Sift flour and salt into a bowl.

2. Rub in butter.

3. Mix fresh yeast to a smooth and creamy liquid with a little of the warm water. Blend in remaining water. If using dried yeast dissolve 5 ml (1 tsp) sugar in warm water and sprinkle yeast on top. Leave to stand for 10 minutes in a warm place until frothy.

4. Add all at once to dry ingredients. Mix to a firm dough, adding more flour if needed, until dough leaves sides of bowl clean.

5. Turn out on to a lightly floured work surface. Knead thoroughly for 10 minutes.

6. Cover with a greased polythene bag and leave to rise until doubled in size.

7. Turn out on to a lightly floured work surface and knead until firm. Cut into 2 equal-sized pieces.

8. Shape each to fit a 450 g (1 lb) loaf tin. Brush tin with melted butter then put in dough.

9. Cover and leave to rise until dough doubles in size and reaches top of tin.

10. Brush with milk or beaten egg and milk. Bake at 230°C (450°F) Mark 8 for 30–40 minutes, or until loaf shrinks slightly from sides of tin and crust is golden brown.

11. Cool on a wire cooling rack.

Variation

WHITE BREAD ROLLS   Ⓕ

Follow recipe and method for white bread (left). After first rising, divide dough into 12 equal-sized pieces and shape into round rolls, miniature plaits, knots and tiny cottage loaves. Put on to greased baking sheets, cover and leave to rise until doubled in size. Brush with milk or beaten egg and milk. Sprinkle with poppy or sesame seeds if desired. Bake at 230°C (450°F) Mark 8 for 20–25 minutes or until brown and crisp. Cool on a wire cooling rack.

WHOLEMEAL BREAD Ⓕ

Preparation 40 mins **plus rising**
Cooking 45 mins   *Makes 2 loaves*

700 g (1½ lb) wholemeal flour
10 ml (2 tsp) salt
7.5 ml (1½ tsp) caster sugar
25 g (1 oz) butter
20 g (¾ oz) fresh yeast
  or 15 ml (1 tbsp) dried yeast
300 ml (½ pt) lukewarm water
150 ml (¼ pint) fresh milk, lukewarm
salted water

1. Place flour, salt and sugar in a bowl and rub in butter.

2. Mix fresh yeast to a smooth and creamy liquid with a little of the warm water. If using dried yeast dissolve 5 ml (1 tsp) sugar in warm water and sprinkle yeast on top. Leave to stand for 10 minutes in a warm place until frothy.

3. Mix dry ingredients with yeast liquid, milk and sufficient of remaining water to make a firm dough that leaves sides of bowl clean.

4. Turn out on to a lightly floured work surface. Knead thoroughly for 10 minutes or until dough is smooth and elastic and no longer sticky.

5. Cover and leave until doubled in size.

6. Turn out on to a floured work surface. Knead well and cut in half.

7. Shape each piece to fit a 900 g (2 lb) loaf tin. Brush tins with melted butter then put in dough.

8. Brush tops of loaves with salted water. Cover and leave to rise until dough reaches tops of tins.

9. Bake at 230°C (450°F) Mark 8 for 40–45 minutes or until loaves shrink slightly from sides of tins.

10. Turn out and cool on a wire cooling rack.

Variation
COBURG ROLLS Ⓕ

Follow recipe and method for wholemeal bread (left). After first rising, divide dough into 18 equal-sized pieces and shape into round rolls. Place onto greased baking sheets and make 2 cuts to form a cross on top of each roll. Brush with salted water. Cover and leave to rise until doubled in size. Bake at 220°C (425°F) Mark 7 for 20–25 minutes.

WHOLEMEAL BREAD

QUICK WHITE BREAD Ⓕ

Preparation 20 mins **plus rising**
Cooking 35 mins   *Makes 1 loaf*

The quick method of bread making shortens the time of making to about 1¼ hours.

By adding a small amount of ascorbic acid (vitamin C) to the warm yeast liquid, it is possible to eliminate the first rising of the dough.

Ascorbic acid (vitamin C) tablets are available from most large chemists in 25 mg, 50 mg and 100 mg sizes.

It is recommended that fresh yeast be used with this method as dried yeast tends to prolong the time required for rising.

25 g (1 oz) fresh yeast
400 ml (14 fl oz) lukewarm water
25 g tablet of ascorbic acid (vitamin C)
700 g (1½ lb) strong plain flour
15 g (½ oz) salt
5 ml (1 tsp) sugar
15 g (½ oz) butter
milk or beaten egg for brushing

1. Blend together fresh yeast and warm water together. Crush tablet into yeast liquid.

2. Put flour, salt and sugar into a bowl. Rub in butter. Add yeast liquid, mix thoroughly until dough leaves side of bowl clean.

3. Turn on to a lightly floured work surface and knead for about 10 minutes.

4. Shape to fit a 900 g (2 lb) loaf tin. Brush tin with melted butter then place dough in tin.

5. Cover with lightly greased polythene and leave in a warm place until almost doubled in size.

6. Remove polythene, brush with milk or egg. Bake at 230°C (450°F) Mark 8 for 30–35 minutes.

Variation

QUICK BREAD ROLLS Ⓕ

Follow recipe and method for quick white bread (above) to step 4. Divide dough into 18–20 equal-sized pieces and shape into round rolls. Place on a greased baking sheet, cover and leave to rise until almost doubled in size. Remove cover, brush rolls with milk or beaten egg and milk. Bake at 230°C (450°F) Mark 8 for 15–20 minutes.

QUICK BROWN BREAD Ⓕ

Preparation 30 mins **plus rising**
Cooking 40 mins   *Makes 2 loaves*

225 g (8 oz) wholemeal flour
225 g (8 oz) strong plain flour
10 ml (2 tsp) salt
10 ml (2 tsp) granulated sugar
15 g (½ oz) butter
15 g (½ oz) fresh yeast
    or 10 ml (2 tsp) dried yeast
150 ml (¼ pint) lukewarm water
150 ml (¼ pint) fresh milk, lukewarm
salted water
30 ml (2 tbsp) cracked wheat
    or crushed cornflakes

1. Place flours, salt and sugar into a bowl.

2. Rub in butter finely.

3. Mix fresh yeast to a smooth and creamy liquid with a little of the warm water. Blend in remaining water and milk. If using dried yeast dissolve 5 ml (1 tsp) sugar in warm water and milk. Sprinkle yeast on top. Leave to stand for 10 minutes in a warm place until frothy.

4. Add all at once to dry ingredients. Mix to a fairly soft dough that leaves sides of bowl clean.

5. Turn out on to a floured work surface. Knead for 10 minutes, or until smooth and elastic.

6. Cut into 2 and shape each to fit a 450 g (1 lb) loaf tin.

7. Brush tins with melted butter. Put in dough.

8. Brush tops of loaves with salted water. Sprinkle with cracked wheat (if available) or crushed cornflakes.

9. Cover and leave to rise until loaves have doubled in size and spring back when pressed lightly with a floured finger.

10. Bake at 230°C (450°F) Mark 8 for 30–40 minutes.

11. Turn out and cool on a wire cooling rack.

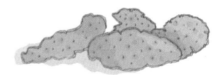

SODA BREAD Ⓕ

Preparation 20 mins
Cooking 35 mins   *Makes 1 loaf*

350 g (12 oz) wholemeal flour
100 g (4 oz) flour
5 ml (1 tsp) salt
5 ml (1 tsp) bicarbonate of soda
50 g (2 oz) butter
225 ml (8 fl oz) fresh milk
150 g (5 oz) natural yogurt
flour to dust
butter to serve

1. Mix together flours, salt and bicarbonate of soda. Rub in butter until mixture resembles fine breadcrumbs.

2. Add milk and yogurt and mix to a soft dough. Knead lightly.

3. Shape into a round and place on a greased baking sheet.

4. Score bread with a deep cross and dust with flour. Bake at 220°C (425°F) Mark 7 for 50 minutes.

5. When cool, slice and serve with butter.

This bread is best eaten on the day it is made.

CHEESE & ONION BREAD Ⓕ

Preparation 25 mins **plus rising**
Cooking 40 mins   *Makes 1 loaf*

280 g (10 oz) packet of bread mix
25 g (1 oz) dried sliced onions, crushed
100 g (4 oz) Sage Derby cheese, grated
200 ml (7 fl oz) fresh milk, lukewarm
butter to serve

1. Place bread mix in a bowl, stir in dried onions and cheese.

2. Stir in sufficient milk to make a soft dough.

3. Knead on a lightly floured work surface for 5 minutes until smooth and elastic.

4. Shape into a round and place on a greased baking sheet.

5. Cut top of dough to make a criss-cross pattern, cover with greased polythene and leave in a warm place for 30 minutes or until doubled in size.

6. Brush with a little milk and bake at 220°C (425°F) Mark 7 for 30–40 minutes or until well risen and golden brown.

7. Cool on a wire cooling rack.

8. Serve warm or cold spread with butter.

MILK LOAF Ⓕ

Preparation 45 mins **plus rising**
Cooking 50 mins   *Makes 2 loaves*

15 g (½oz) fresh yeast
  or 10 ml (2 tsp) dried yeast
5 ml (1 tsp) sugar
200 ml (7 fl oz) fresh milk, lukewarm
450 g (1 lb) strong plain flour
5 ml (1 tsp) salt
50 g (2 oz) butter
1 egg, beaten
extra milk for brushing

1. Stir yeast and sugar into milk. If using dried yeast leave to stand for 5 mins.

2. Put one third of flour into a large bowl. Add yeast liquid, mix well. Leave in a warm place for 20 mins or until frothy.

3. Meanwhile, sift remaining flour and salt into a bowl. Rub in butter then add, with beaten egg, to yeast mixture. Mix well.

4. Turn out on to a lightly floured work surface. Knead for 10 mins or until dough loses its stickiness.

5. Cover, leave to rise until doubled in size.

6. Turn out on to a floured work surface. Knead lightly. Cut into 2.

7. Shape each to fit a 450 g (1 lb) loaf tin. Brush tins with melted butter. Put in dough.

8. Cover and leave to rise until dough doubles in size and reaches top of tins.

9. Brush with milk. Bake at 190°C (375°F) Mark 5 for 45–50 mins or until loaf shrinks slightly from sides of tin and crust is golden.

10. Cool on a wire cooling rack.

Variation

POPPY SEED PLAITS Ⓕ

Follow recipe and method for milk loaf (above). After dough has risen for first time, turn out on to floured work surface, knead lightly and cut in half. Cut each half into 3 pieces. Shape each piece into a long thin roll and plait together to give two plaited loaves. Stand on greased and floured baking sheets. Brush with a little beaten egg. Sprinkle with poppy seeds. Cover and leave to rise until doubled in size. Bake at 190°C (375°F) Mark 5 for 45–50 mins or until bases of loaves sound hollow when tapped and tops and sides are lightly brown. Cool on a wire cooling rack.

HOT CROSS BUNS Ⓕ

Preparation 1¼ hrs **plus rising**
Cooking 25 mins   *Makes 12*

450 g (1 lb) strong plain flour
50 g (2 oz) caster sugar
25 g (1 oz) fresh yeast
  or 20 ml (4 tsp) dried yeast
150 ml (¼ pint) fresh milk, lukewarm
60 ml (4 tbsp) lukewarm water
5 ml (1 tsp) salt
5 ml (1 tsp) mixed spice
2.5 ml (½ tsp) ground cinnamon
100 g (4 oz) currants
50 g (2 oz) chopped mixed peel
50 g (2 oz) butter, melted and cooled
1 egg, beaten
50 g (2 oz) granulated sugar
45 ml (3 tbsp) fresh milk

1. Sift 100 g (4 oz) flour into a bowl. Add 5 ml (1 tsp) caster sugar.

2. Blend fresh yeast with milk and water. If using dried yeast dissolve 5 ml (1 tsp) sugar in milk and water and sprinkle yeast on top. Leave to stand for 10 mins in a warm place until frothy.

3. Add to sifted flour and sugar.

4. Mix well and leave for 20–30 mins or until frothy.

5. Meanwhile sift remaining flour, salt and spices into another bowl. Add remaining caster sugar, currants and peel. Toss lightly together.

6. Add to yeast mixture with butter and beaten egg. Mix to a fairly soft dough that leaves sides of bowl clean.

7. Turn out on to a floured work surface and knead for 5 mins or until dough is smooth and no longer sticky.

8. Cover, leave to rise until doubled in size.

9. Turn out on to a floured work surface. Knead lightly and divide into 12 equal-sized pieces.

10. Shape each into a round bun. Stand well apart on lightly greased and floured baking sheet.

11. Cover and leave to rise for 30 mins or until dough feels springy when pressed lightly with a floured finger.

12. Cut a cross on top of each with a sharp knife. Bake at 220°C (425°F) Mark 7 for 20–25 minutes.

13. Make glaze by dissolving granulated sugar in milk and boiling for 2 minutes.

14. Transfer buns to a wire cooling rack and brush twice with glaze.

CURRANT BREAD Ⓕ

Preparation 30 mins **plus rising**
Cooking 40 mins   *Makes 2 loaves*

450 g (1 lb) strong plain flour
5 ml (1 tsp) salt
25 g (1 oz) butter
25 g (1 oz) caster sugar
100 g (4 oz) currants
25 g (1 oz) fresh yeast
   or 20 ml (4 tsp) dried yeast
150 ml (¼ pint) lukewarm water
150 ml (¼ pint) fresh milk, lukewarm
clear honey or golden syrup

1. Sift flour and salt into a bowl, rub in butter. Add sugar and currants, mix together.

2. Mix fresh yeast to a smooth and creamy liquid with a little of the warm water. Blend in remaining water and milk. If using dried yeast dissolve 5 ml (1 tsp) sugar in warm water and milk. Sprinkle yeast on top. Leave to stand for 10 minutes in a warm place until frothy.

3. Add all at once to dry ingredients. Mix to a firm dough, adding a little extra flour if necessary, until dough leaves sides of bowl clean.

4. Turn out on to a lightly floured work surface. Knead for 10 minutes or until dough is smooth and elastic.

5. Cut into 2 equal-sized pieces. Shape each to fit a 450 g (1 lb) loaf tin.

6. Brush tins with melted butter and put in dough.

7. Cover and leave to rise until dough reaches tops of tins.

8. Bake at 220°C (425°F) Mark 7 for 30–40 minutes.

9. Turn out on to a wire cooling rack. Glaze tops of hot loaves by brushing with a wet brush dipped in clear honey or golden syrup.

10. Leave until cold before cutting.

CURRANT BREAD

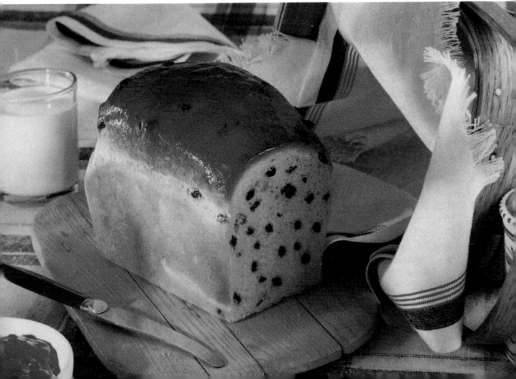

STOLLEN Ⓕ

Preparation 35 mins **Cooking** 52 mins *Serves 12*

700g (1½lb) flour
25g (1oz) butter
7g (¼oz) sachet fast action dried yeast
65g (2½oz) caster sugar
pinch of salt
grated rind of 1 lemon
5ml (1tsp) *each* ground cardamom and
  ground mace
175g (6oz) dried mixed fruit
300ml (½pint) fresh milk, lukewarm
2 eggs, beaten
30ml (2tbsp) rum
50g (2oz) marzipan
50g (2oz) butter, melted
icing sugar sieved to dust

1. Sift flour into a bowl, rub in butter.

2. Add yeast, sugar, salt, lemon rind, spices and fruit.

3. Stir in milk, eggs and rum.

4. Mix to form a soft dough and knead lightly on a lightly floured work surface.

5. Divide dough in half, shape into 2 rectangles 18×7.5cm (7×3inch).

6. Shape marzipan into a roll 18cm (7inch) long.

7. Place roll down centre of one rectangle of dough.

8. Fold dough over to encase marzipan. Seal edges, put sealed edge underneath.

9. Roll remaining dough into a roll same length as the other one.

10. Place two rolls close together on a baking sheet.

11. Cover and leave to rise for 20–30 minutes or until doubled in size.

12. Bake at 240°C (475°F) Mark 9 for 2 minutes. Reduce temperature to 170°C (325°F) Mark 3 for 50 minutes.

13. Brush with melted butter, dust with icing sugar.

14. Serve sliced.

STOLLEN

BATH BUNS Ⓕ

Preparation 1¼ hrs **plus rising**
Cooking 25 mins   *Makes 14*

450g (1lb) strong plain flour
25g (1oz) caster sugar
25g (1oz) fresh yeast
  or 20ml (4tsp) dried yeast
150ml (¼pint) fresh milk, lukewarm
60ml (4tbsp) lukewarm water
5ml (1tsp) salt
175g (6oz) sultanas
50g (2oz) chopped mixed peel
50g (2oz) butter, melted and cooled
1 egg, beaten
beaten egg mixed with a little water
coarsely crushed cube sugar

1. Sift 100g (4oz) flour into a bowl. Add 5ml (1tsp) sugar.

2. Blend fresh yeast with milk and water. If using dried yeast dissolve 5ml (1tsp) sugar in milk and water and sprinkle yeast on top. Leave to stand for 10 minutes in a warm place until frothy.

3. Add to sifted flour and sugar.

4. Mix well and leave for 20–30 minutes or until frothy.

5. Meanwhile, sift remaining flour and salt into another bowl.

6. Add remaining sugar, sultanas and peel. Toss lightly together.

7. Add to yeast mixture with butter and beaten egg. Mix to a fairly soft dough that leaves sides of bowl clean.

8. Turn out on to a floured work surface and knead for 5 minutes or until dough is smooth and no longer sticky.

9. Cover and leave to rise until doubled in size.

10. Turn out on to a floured work surface. Knead lightly.

11. Put 14 spoonfuls of dough on to a lightly greased and floured baking sheet.

12. Cover and leave to rise for 20 minutes or until dough feels springy when pressed lightly with a floured finger.

13. Brush with egg and water, sprinkle with crushed sugar and bake at 220°C (425°F) Mark 7 for 20–25 minutes.

14. Cool on a wire cooling rack.

CHELSEA BUNS Ⓕ

Preparation 1 hr **plus rising**
Cooking 25 mins   *Makes 9*

15g (½oz) fresh yeast
  or 10ml (2tsp) dried yeast
25g (1oz) sugar
75ml (3floz) fresh milk, lukewarm
225g (8oz) strong plain flour
2.5ml (½tsp) salt
40g (1½oz) butter
1 egg, beaten
50g (2oz) soft brown sugar
75g (3oz) dried fruit
25g (1oz) mixed peel
clear honey to glaze (optional)

1. Stir yeast and 2.5ml (½tsp) sugar into milk. If using dried yeast leave to stand for 5 minutes.

2. Mix in 50g (2oz) flour and leave in a warm place for about 20 minutes or until frothy.

3. Mix together remaining flour, salt and remaining sugar. Rub in 25g (1oz) butter.

4. Stir egg and yeast batter into flour and mix to a soft dough.

5. Turn onto a floured work surface and knead until smooth and no longer sticky.

6. Cover and leave to rise until doubled in size, about 1 hour.

7. On a floured work surface, roll out into a rectangle 30×23cm (12×9inch).

8. Melt remaining butter and brush over dough.

9. Sprinkle on brown sugar and fruit.

10. Roll up dough, like a Swiss roll, starting from longest side.

11. Cut roll into nine equal slices.

12. Place close together cut side down in a greased 18cm (7inch) square tin.

13. Cover and leave to prove until doubled in size and buns have joined together, about 40 minutes.

14. Bake at 220°C (425°F) Mark 7 for 20–25 minutes or until golden brown.

15. Place on a wire cooling rack to cool.

16. Glaze with clear honey if desired.

MALT LOAVES Ⓕ

Preparation 40 mins **plus rising**
Cooking 45 mins   *Makes 2 loaves*

75 g (3 oz) malt extract
30 ml (2 tbsp) black treacle
25 g (1 oz) butter
450 g (1 lb) strong plain flour
5 ml (1 tsp) salt
225 g (8 oz) sultanas
25 g (1 oz) fresh yeast
    or 20 ml (4 tsp) dried yeast
175 ml (6 fl oz) lukewarm water
clear honey

1. Put malt extract, treacle and butter into a pan. Heat through gently. Leave to cool.

2. Sift flour and salt into bowl. Add sultanas and toss lightly together.

3. Mix fresh yeast to a smooth and creamy liquid with a little of the water. Blend in remaining water. If using dried yeast dissolve 5 ml (1 tsp) sugar in warm water and sprinkle yeast on top. Leave to stand for 10 mins in a warm place until frothy.

4. Add to dry ingredients with cooled malt mixture. Work to a soft dough that leaves sides of bowl clean.

5. Turn out on to a floured work surface. Knead until dough is smooth and elastic.

6. Cut into 2 equal-sized pieces. Shape each to fit a 450 g (1 lb) loaf tin.

7. Brush tins with melted butter and put in dough. Cover and leave to rise until loaves double in size, this could take up to 5 hours.

8. Bake at 200°C (400°F) Mark 6 for 40–45 mins.

9. Turn out on to a wire cooling rack. Glaze tops of hot loaves with a wet brush dipped in honey. Leave until cold before cutting.

BARA BRITH Ⓕ

Preparation 45 mins **plus rising**
Cooking 1¼ hrs   *Makes 1 loaf*

5 ml (1 tsp) sugar
150 ml (¼ pint) fresh milk, lukewarm
15 ml (1 tbsp) dried yeast
400 g (14 oz) strong plain flour
5 ml (1 tsp) salt
5 ml (1 tsp) mixed spice
75 g (3 oz) butter
75 g (3 oz) demerara sugar
450 g (1 lb) mixed dried fruit
1 egg, beaten
clear honey to glaze

1. Dissolve sugar in warm milk. Sprinkle on yeast and leave for 10 minutes in a warm place or until frothy.

2. Sieve flour and salt into a bowl with spice.

3. Rub in butter, stir in sugar and dried fruit.

4. Pour yeast liquid and egg into mixture, mix until dough leaves sides of bowl clean.

5. Knead on a floured work surface for about 10 minutes until smooth and elastic.

6. Place in a greased polythene bag, leave until doubled in size.

7. Knead dough for 2 minutes, then shape to fit a greased 900g (2lb) loaf tin.

8. Cover, leave to rise above top of tin, then bake at 180°C (350°F) Mark 4 for 1¼ hours.

9. Turn on to a wire cooling rack and glaze with honey while still warm.

MUFFINS   Ⓕ

Preparation 40 mins **plus rising**
Cooking 10 mins   *Makes 12*

450g (1lb) strong plain flour
5ml (1tsp) salt
25g (1oz) fresh yeast
  or 20ml (4tsp) dried yeast
150ml (¼pint) fresh milk, lukewarm
90ml (6tbsp) lukewarm water
1 egg, beaten
25g (1oz) butter, melted
flour or semolina to dust
butter to serve

1. Sift flour and salt into a bowl.

2. Mix fresh yeast to a smooth and creamy liquid with a little milk. Blend in remaining milk and water. If using dried yeast dissolve 5ml (1tsp) sugar in warm milk and water and sprinkle yeast on top. Leave to stand for 10 minutes in a warm place until frothy.

3. Add to dry ingredients with beaten egg and melted butter. Mix to a fairly soft dough.

4. Turn out on to a well floured work surface. Knead for 10 minutes or until dough is smooth and no longer sticky.

5. Cover, leave to rise until doubled in size.

6. Turn out on to a floured work surface. Knead lightly and roll out to 1cm (½inch) thickness.

7. Cut into 12 rounds with a 8.5cm (3½inch) biscuit cutter. Transfer to a well-floured baking sheet. Dust with flour or semolina.

8. Cover, leave to rise until doubled in size.

9. Either bake at 230°C (450°F) Mark 8 for 5 minutes each side or cook in a frying pan for about 7 minutes each side until golden.

10. Remove from oven. Cool on a wire rack.

11. To serve, cut in half and toast on both sides. Butter thickly and serve hot.

DOUGHNUTS   Ⓕ

Preparation 1¼ hrs **plus rising**
Cooking 10 mins   *Makes 8*

15g (½oz) fresh yeast
  or 10ml (2tsp) dried yeast
90ml (6tbsp) fresh milk, lukewarm
2.5ml (½tsp) caster sugar
225g (8oz) strong plain flour
1.25ml (¼tsp) salt
15g (½oz) butter, melted and cooled
1 egg, beaten
20ml (4tsp) red jam
deep fat or oil for frying
60ml (4tbsp) caster sugar
5ml (1tsp) ground cinnamon

1. Blend fresh yeast with milk and sugar. If using dried yeast dissolve sugar in milk and sprinkle yeast on top. Leave to stand for 10 mins in a warm place until frothy.

2. Sift 50g (2oz) flour into a bowl then add yeast liquid.

3. Mix well, leave for 20–30 mins, until frothy.

4. Sift remaining flour and salt together, add to yeast mixture with butter and egg.

5. Mix to a soft dough, leaving bowl clean.

6. Turn out on to a floured work surface and knead for 5 mins or until dough is smooth and no longer sticky.

7. Cover, leave to rise until doubled in size.

8. Turn out on to a floured work surface, knead lightly, divide into 8 equal-sized pieces.

9. Shape into balls. Cover and leave to rise for 30 mins or until dough feels springy when pressed lightly with a floured finger.

10. Press a hole in each ball with a finger. Put in about 2.5ml (½tsp) jam.

11. Pinch up edges of dough so that jam is completely enclosed. Deep fry doughnuts in hot fat or oil for 4 mins.

12. Drain on absorbent kitchen paper.

13. Mix remaining sugar with cinnamon and coat doughnuts with it.

347

SWEDISH TEA RING Ⓕ

Preparation 1 hr **plus rising**
Cooking 25 mins   *Serves 12*

15 g (½ oz) fresh yeast
 or 10 ml (2 tsp) dried yeast
25 g (1 oz) sugar
75 ml (3 fl oz) fresh milk, lukewarm
225 g (8 oz) strong plain flour
2.5 ml (½ tsp) salt
40 g (1½ oz) butter
1 egg, beaten
50 g (2 oz) soft light brown sugar
10 ml (2 tsp) cinnamon
glacé icing made with 100 g (4 oz) icing
 sugar (page 326)
glacé cherries, walnuts and angelica to
 decorate

1. Stir yeast and 2.5 ml (½ tsp) sugar into milk. If using dried yeast leave to stand for 5 minutes.

2. Mix in 50 g (2 oz) flour and leave in a warm place for 20 minutes or until frothy.

3. Mix together remaining flour, salt and remaining sugar. Rub in 25 g (1 oz) butter.

4. Stir egg and yeast batter into flour and mix to a soft dough.

5. Turn on to a floured work surface and knead until smooth and no longer sticky.

6. Cover and leave to rise until doubled in size, about 1 hour.

7. On a floured work surface roll out dough into an oblong 23×38 cm (9×15 inch).

8. Melt remaining butter and brush over dough. Sprinkle with brown sugar and spice.

9. Roll up dough like a Swiss roll, starting from longest side.

10. Place on a greased baking sheet and form into a circle sealing ends together with a little milk or water.

11. Holding scissors at an angle of 45 degrees, cut almost completely through dough at 2.5 cm (1 inch) intervals. Turn cut sections on their sides so that pinwheel effect is seen.

12. Cover and prove until dough is light and fluffy, about 45 minutes.

13. Bake at 200°C (400°F) Mark 6 for 25 minutes or until golden. Cool on a wire cooling rack.

14. When cold, ice with glacé icing and decorate with glacé cherries, walnuts and angelica.

YORKSHIRE TEA CAKES Ⓕ

Preparation 40 mins **plus rising**
Cooking 20 mins   *Makes 6*

450 g (1 lb) strong plain flour
5 ml (1 tsp) salt
25 g (1 oz) butter
25 g (1 oz) caster sugar
50 g (2 oz) currants
15 g (½ oz) fresh yeast
 or 10 ml (2 tsp) dried yeast
300 ml (½ pint) fresh milk, lukewarm
extra milk for brushing
butter to serve

1. Sift flour and salt into a bowl and rub in butter.

2. Add sugar and currants. Toss lightly together.

3. Blend fresh yeast with milk. If using dried yeast dissolve 5 ml (1 tsp) sugar in warm milk and sprinkle yeast on top. Leave to stand for 10 minutes in a warm place until frothy.

4. Add all at once to dry ingredients.

5. Mix to a firm dough, adding a little extra flour if necessary, until dough leaves sides of bowl clean.

6. Turn out on to a lightly floured work surface. Knead for 10 minutes or until dough is smooth and elastic.

7. Cover and leave to rise until doubled in size.

8. Turn out on to a lightly floured work surface. Knead well and divide into 6 equal-sized pieces.

9. Roll each one out into a round cake 1 cm (½ inch) thick. Transfer to a greased baking sheet.

10. Brush tops with milk. Cover and leave to rise until almost doubled in size.

11. Bake at 200°C (400°F) Mark 6 for 20 minutes.

12. Cool on a wire cooling rack.

13. To serve, split open and spread thickly with butter. The tea cakes can also be split and toasted before being buttered.

CORNISH SPLITS   Ⓕ

Preparation 1¼ hrs **plus rising**
Cooking 25 mins   *Makes 14*

450g (1lb) strong plain flour
50g (2oz) caster sugar
25g (1oz) fresh yeast
   or 20ml (4tsp) dried yeast
150ml (¼pint) fresh milk, lukewarm
150ml (¼pint) lukewarm water
5ml (1tsp) salt
50g (2oz) butter, melted and cooled
jam and fresh whipped
   or clotted cream to serve

1. Sift 100g (4oz) flour into a bowl. Add 5ml (1tsp) sugar.

2. Blend fresh yeast with milk and water. If using dried yeast dissolve 5ml (1tsp) sugar in milk and water and sprinkle yeast on top. Leave to stand for 10 minutes in a warm place until frothy.

3. Add to sifted flour and sugar.

4. Mix well and leave for 20–30 minutes or until frothy.

5. Meanwhile, sift remaining flour and salt into another bowl.

6. Add remaining sugar.

7. Add to yeast mixture with butter. Mix to a fairly soft dough that leaves sides of bowl clean.

8. Turn out on to a floured work surface. Knead for 5 minutes or until dough is smooth and no longer sticky.

9. Cover and leave to rise until doubled in size.

10. Turn out on to a floured work surface. Knead lightly and divide into 14 equal-sized pieces.

11. Shape each into a round bun. Stand well apart on lightly greased and floured baking sheet.

12. Cover and leave to rise for 30 minutes or until dough feels springy when pressed lightly with a floured finger.

13. Bake at 220°C (425°F) Mark 7 for 20–25 minutes.

14. Cool on a wire cooling rack.

15. When cold split open and fill with jam and either fresh whipped or clotted cream.

BRIOCHES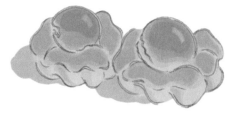

Preparation 35 mins **plus rising**
Cooking 10 mins   *Makes 8*

225 g (8 oz) strong plain flour
2.5 ml (½ tsp) salt
15 g (½ oz) caster sugar
15 g (½ oz) fresh yeast
   or 10 ml (2 tsp) dried yeast
30 ml (2 tbsp) lukewarm water
2 eggs, beaten
50 g (2 oz) butter, melted and cooled
extra beaten egg for brushing

1. Sift flour, salt and sugar into a bowl.

2. Mix fresh yeast to a smooth and creamy liquid with water. If using dried yeast dissolve 5 ml (1 tsp) sugar in warm water and sprinkle yeast on top. Leave to stand for 10 minutes in a warm place until frothy.

3. Add to dry ingredients with beaten eggs and butter.

4. Mix to a soft dough. Turn on to a floured work surface and knead for 5 minutes or until dough is smooth and no longer sticky.

5. Cover and leave to rise until doubled in size.

6. Turn out on to a floured work surface. Knead lightly.

7. Divide three-quarters of the dough into 8 equal-sized pieces.

8. Shape into balls. Put into well greased muffin tins or into 8.5 cm (3½ inch) fluted Brioche tins. Press a deep hole in centre of each one.

9. Divide remaining dough into 8 pieces. Roll into small balls and stand on top of holes.

10. Cover and leave to rise in a warm place for about 1 hour or until Brioches are light and well risen.

11. Brush gently with beaten egg. Bake at 230°C (450°F) Mark 8 for 10 minutes.

12. Transfer to a wire cooling rack.

13. Serve warm with butter.

BRIOCHES

BABAS   Ⓕ

Preparation 1½ hrs **plus rising**
Cooking 20 mins   *Makes 12*

25 g (1 oz) fresh yeast
   or 20 ml (4 tsp) dried yeast
90 ml (6 tbsp) fresh milk, lukewarm
225 g (8 oz) flour
2.5 ml (½ tsp) salt
25 g (1 oz) caster sugar
4 eggs, beaten
100 g (4 oz) butter, softened
100 g (4 oz) currants
60 ml (4 tbsp) golden syrup
30 ml (2 tbsp) rum
60 ml (4 tbsp) water
60 ml (4 tbsp) apricot jam
300 ml (10 fl oz) fresh double cream

---

1. Stir fresh yeast into milk. If using dried yeast add 2.5 ml (½ tsp) sugar and leave to stand for 5 minutes.

2. Mix yeast liquid and 50 g (2 oz) flour. Leave 20–30 minutes or until frothy.

3. Combine with remaining flour, salt, sugar, beaten eggs, butter and currants. Beat thoroughly for 5 minutes.

4. Brush 12 dariole moulds with melted butter and half fill with mixture.

5. Cover and leave to rise until moulds are two-thirds full.

6. Bake at 200°C (400°F) Mark 6 for 15–20 minutes.

7. Cool for 5 minutes. Turn out of moulds then transfer to a wire cooling rack with a baking sheet underneath.

8. Warm golden syrup with rum and water. Pour sufficient over babas to soak them well.

9. Heat jam slowly with 30 ml (2 tbsp) water. Strain. Brush thickly over babas then leave until cold.

10. Transfer to a serving dish. Serve with cream, whipped until thick.

Variation

SAVARIN   Ⓕ

Follow recipe and method for babas (left) but omit currants. Instead of using dariole moulds, half fill one well-greased 20.5 cm (8 inch) ring mould or two 15 cm (6 inch) moulds with mixture. After mixture has risen, bake at 200°C (400°F) Mark 6 for 20 minutes. Turn out on to a dish and prick with a skewer. Soak with hot syrup made by dissolving 90 ml (6 tbsp) granulated sugar in 150 ml (¼ pint) water and 45 ml (3 tbsp) rum or white wine. Serve hot or cold with fresh fruit and whipped cream.

CATHERINE WHEELS Ⓕ

Preparation 50 mins **plus rising**
Cooking 25 mins   *Makes 9*

175 g (6 oz) full fat soft cheese
6 spring onions, chopped
4 bacon rashers, crisply grilled and
    chopped
15 ml (1 tbsp) wholegrain mustard
280 g (10 oz) packet of bread mix
200 ml (7 fl oz) fresh milk, lukewarm

1. In a bowl, mix soft cheese with spring onions, bacon pieces and mustard.

2. Place bread mix in a bowl, stir in sufficient milk to make a soft dough.

3. Knead on a lightly floured work surface for 5 minutes until smooth and elastic.

4. Roll out into a rectangle 30.5×23 cm (12×9 inch).

5. Spread cheese mixture over dough and roll up like a Swiss roll from longest edge.

6. Cut into 9 thick slices and arrange in a greased 18 cm (7 inch) square tin.

7. Cover with greased polythene, leave in a warm place for 30 minutes, until doubled.

8. Bake at 220°C (425°F) Mark 7 for 25 minutes.

ONION ROLLS Ⓕ

Preparation 30 mins **plus rising**
Cooking 25 mins   *Makes 8*

450 g (1 lb) strong plain flour
10 ml (2 tsp) salt
75 g (3 oz) butter
15 g (½ oz) fresh yeast
    or 10 ml (2 tsp) dried yeast
300 ml (½ pint) fresh milk, lukewarm
45 ml (3 tbsp) dried sliced onions

1. Sift flour and salt into a bowl and rub in 25 g (1 oz) butter.

2. Blend fresh yeast with a little of the milk and stir into flour with remaining liquid. If using dried yeast dissolve 5 ml (1 tsp) sugar in warm milk and sprinkle yeast on top. Leave to stand for 10 minutes in a warm place until frothy. Stir into flour.

3. Knead for 10 minutes. Place dough in a clean bowl, cover with greased polythene, leave to rise in a warm place until doubled.

4. Melt remaining butter, add dried onions. Pour into a 23 cm (9 inch) round cake tin.

5. Divide dough into 8. Shape into rolls.

6. Turn rolls in butter to coat and then arrange 7 around the edge of tin to form a ring. Place remaining roll in centre.

7. Cover, leave to rise until doubled in size.

8. Bake at 220°C (425°F) Mark 7 for 20–25 minutes until golden brown.

CHAPATTIS Ⓓ

Preparation 20 mins **plus standing**
Cooking 25 mins   *Makes 8*

225 g (8 oz) wholemeal flour
175 ml (6 fl oz) lukewarm water
extra flour for rolling
butter

1. Place flour in a bowl and stir in water.

2. Knead dough on a floured work surface until fairly soft and pliable.

3. Replace dough in a bowl and cover. Leave to stand for 15–30 minutes.

4. Divide dough into 8 even sized pieces.

5. Dip in flour, roll out to 0.25 cm (⅛ inch) thick and 12.5 cm (5 inch) diameter.

6. Cook in a pre-heated, frying pan. When small bubbles appear on surface, turn chapatti over and repeat. Press edges down with a palette knife. It is cooked when both sides have brown spots on surface.

7. Remove from pan, spread with butter.

8. Serve immediately.

NAAN BREAD Ⓓ

Preparation 35 mins **plus rising**
Cooking 5 mins   *Makes 6*

1 egg, beaten
2.5 ml (½ tsp) salt
5 ml (1 tsp) baking powder
5 ml (1 tsp) sugar
7.5 ml (1½ tsp) dried yeast
60 ml (4 tbsp) natural yogurt
50 g (2 oz) butter, melted
450 g (1 lb) strong plain flour
200 ml (7 fl oz) fresh milk, lukewarm
sesame seeds

1. Beat egg with salt, baking powder, sugar, yeast, yogurt and half of the butter.

2. Stir in flour and add milk gradually. Knead until smooth, cover and leave in a warm place until doubled in size.

3. Knead for a minute. Divide into 6 balls. Flatten and roll balls into tear drop shapes about 0.5 cm (¼ inch) thick. Leave for 5–10 mintues.

4. Brush with remaining butter, sprinkle with sesame seeds and grill for 2 minutes on each side, until cooked and lightly brown.

5. Serve hot.

NAAN BREAD

BISCUITS

PLAIN BISCUITS ⓕ

Preparation 30 mins **plus** 30 mins **chilling**
Cooking 15 mins   *Makes 30*

225 g (8 oz) self raising flour
pinch of salt
150 g (5 oz) butter
100 g (4 oz) caster *or* sifted icing sugar
beaten egg to mix

1. Sift flour and salt into a bowl.

2. Rub in butter finely and add sugar.

3. Mix to a very stiff dough with beaten egg.

4. Turn out on to a lightly floured work surface. Knead gently until smooth.

5. Put into a polythene bag or wrap in aluminium foil. Chill for 30 minutes.

6. Roll out fairly thinly. Cut into about 30 rounds with a 5 cm (2 inch) plain or fluted biscuit cutter.

7. Transfer to greased baking sheets. Prick biscuits well with a fork.

8. Bake at 180°C (350°F) Mark 4 for about 12–15 minutes, or until pale gold.

9. Leave to cool for 2–3 minutes. Transfer to a wire cooling rack.

10. Store in an airtight container when cold.

Variations

ALMOND BISCUITS ⓕ

Follow recipe and method for plain biscuits (above). Add 50 g (2 oz) ground almonds with sugar, and 2.5 ml (½ tsp) almond essence with egg.

CHERRY BISCUITS ⓕ

Follow recipe and method for plain biscuits (above). Add 50 g (2 oz) finely chopped glacé cherries with sugar.

CURRANT BISCUITS ⓕ

Follow recipe and method for plain biscuits (above). Add 50 g (2 oz) currants with sugar.

SPICE BISCUITS ⓕ

Follow recipe and method for plain biscuits (left). Sift 7.5 ml (1½ tsp) mixed spice with flour and salt.

WALNUT BISCUITS ⓕ

Follow recipe and method for plain biscuits (left). Add 40 g (1½ oz) finely chopped walnuts with sugar and 2.5 ml (½ tsp) vanilla essence with egg.

VANILLA REFRIGERATOR BISCUITS ⓕ

Preparation 30 mins **plus chilling**
Cooking 12 mins   *Makes 45*

225 g (8 oz) flour
5 ml (1 tsp) baking powder
100 g (4 oz) butter
175 g (6 oz) caster sugar
5 ml (1 tsp) vanilla essence
1 egg, beaten

1. Sift together flour and baking powder.

2. Rub in butter finely.

3. Add sugar. Mix to a dough with vanilla and beaten egg.

4. Shape into a long sausage. Transfer to a length of aluminium foil.

5. Wrap foil round 'sausage' and twist ends. Work backwards and forwards to form a roll about 5 cm (2 inch) in diameter.

6. Refrigerate for one hour.

Shaping and baking
The full quantity of mixture makes about 45 biscuits. For only 10 or so, slice these very thinly from roll and stand (well apart to allow for spreading) on a greased baking sheet. Bake at 190°C (375°F) Mark 5 for 10–12 minutes or until pale gold. Cool on a wire cooling rack. Store in an airtight container when cold. Remainder of roll can be returned to refrigerator and left – up to about a week – until required.

A SELECTION OF PLAIN BISCUITS

Variations

COCONUT REFRIGERATOR BISCUITS ⓕ

Follow recipe and method for vanilla refrigerator biscuits (left). Add 50g (2oz) desiccated coconut with sugar.

CHOCOLATE REFRIGERATOR BISCUITS ⓕ

Follow recipe and method for vanilla refrigerator biscuits (left). Add 50g (2oz) finely grated plain chocolate with sugar.

GINGER REFRIGERATOR BISCUITS ⓕ

Follow recipe and method for vanilla refrigerator biscuits (left). Omit vanilla. Sift 7.5ml (1½tsp) ground ginger and 2.5ml (½tsp) mixed spice with flour and baking powder.

RAISIN REFRIGERATOR BISCUITS ⓕ

Follow recipe and method for vanilla refrigerator biscuits (left). Add 50g (2oz) chopped raisins with sugar.

BUTTER DIGESTIVE BISCUITS ⓕ

Preparation 20mins **Cooking** 20mins *Makes 12*

75g (3oz) wholemeal flour
15g (½oz) flour
1.25ml (¼tsp) salt
2.5ml (½tsp) baking powder
15g (½oz) oatmeal
40g (1½oz) butter
40g (1½oz) caster sugar
45ml (3tbsp) fresh milk

1. Sift flours, salt and baking powder into a bowl. Add oatmeal.
2. Rub in butter finely. Add sugar.
3. Mix to a stiff paste with milk.
4. Turn out on to a lightly floured work surface. Knead well.
5. Roll out thinly. Cut into 12 rounds with a 6.5cm (2½inch) fluted biscuit cutter.
6. Transfer to a greased baking sheet and prick well.
7. Bake at 190°C (375°F) Mark 5 for 15–20 minutes, or until light gold.
8. Transfer to a wire cooling rack.
9. Store in an airtight container when cold.

BUTTER WHIRLS Ⓕ

Preparation 25 mins
Cooking 25 mins   *Makes 16–18*

175 g (6 oz) butter, softened
50 g (2 oz) icing sugar, sifted
2.5 ml (½ tsp) vanilla essence
175 g (6 oz) flour
8 or 9 glacé cherries, halved

1. Cream butter with sugar and vanilla until light and fluffy.

2. Stir in flour.

3. Transfer mixture to a piping bag fitted with a star-shaped large piping tube.

4. Pipe 16–18 flat whirls on to greased baking sheets. Put half a cherry on each one.

5. Bake at 170°C (325°F) Mark 3 for 20 minutes, or until pale gold.

6. Leave to cool for 5 minutes. Transfer to a wire cooling rack.

7. Store in an airtight container when cold.

BUTTER WHIRLS

OATIE BISCUITS Ⓕ

Preparation 30 mins **Cooking** 20 mins *Makes 30*

175 g (6 oz) butter
150 g (5 oz) soft brown sugar
1 egg
60 ml (4 tbsp) fresh milk
40 g (1½ oz) raisins
25 g (1 oz) hazelnuts, chopped and toasted
275 g (10 oz) wholemeal self raising flour
75 g (3 oz) rolled oats

1. Cream butter and sugar together until light and fluffy.

2. Beat in egg and milk.

3. Add raisins and hazelnuts.

4. Fold in flour to make a fairly stiff dough.

5. Form 30 balls and roll each one in oats.

6. Place on greased baking sheets, allow room for them to spread.

7. Flatten each biscuit slightly.

8. Bake at 180°C (350°F) Mark 4 for 15–20 minutes until golden brown.

9. Cool on a wire cooling rack.

10. Store in an airtight container.

FLAPJACKS

FLAPJACKS 🅕

Preparation 20 mins **Cooking** 30 mins *Makes 24*

100 g (4 oz) butter
75 g (3 oz) golden syrup
75 g (3 oz) soft brown sugar
225 g (8 oz) rolled oats

1. Put butter, syrup and sugar into a saucepan and stand over low heat until melted.
To microwave: Put butter, syrup and sugar into a large bowl or jug. Cook for 2 minutes until melted.

2. Stir in oats and mix well.

3. Spread into a greased 20.5×30.5 cm (8×12 inch) Swiss roll tin, and smooth top with a knife.
To microwave: Spread into a greased and base-lined 23 cm (9 inch) round shallow dish. Smooth top with a knife.

4. Bake at 180°C (350°F) Mark 4 for 30 minutes.
To microwave: Cook for 4½–5 minutes.

5. Leave in tin for 5 minutes, then cut into 24 fingers.
To microwave: Leave in dish for 5 minutes, then cut into thin wedges.

6. Remove from tin when cold.
To microwave: Remove from dish when cold.

7. Store in an airtight container.

CHOCOLATE DROPS 🅕

Preparation 20 mins
Cooking 17 mins   *Makes 18–20*

100 g (4 oz) butter, softened
50 g (2 oz) caster sugar
2.5 ml (½ tsp) vanilla essence
90 g (3½ oz) flour
15 g (½ oz) cocoa powder

1. Cream butter with sugar and essence until light and fluffy.

2. Stir in flour sifted with cocoa powder.

3. Drop 18–20 teaspoons of mixture, well apart, onto a greased baking sheet.

4. Bake at 190°C (375°F) Mark 5 for 17 minutes.

5. Leave on sheet for 1 or 2 minutes before transferring to a wire cooling rack.

6. Store in an airtight container when cold.

SOURED CREAM BISCUITS Ⓕ

Preparation 30 mins **plus** 1 hr **chilling**
Cooking 15 mins   *Makes 35*

100g (4oz) butter, softened
175g (6oz) caster sugar
50g (2oz) light soft brown sugar
2.5ml (½tsp) ground cinnamon
1 egg
100g (4 floz) fresh soured cream
5ml (1tsp) grated lemon rind
175g (6oz) flour
2.5ml (½tsp) baking powder
1.25ml (¼tsp) bicarbonate of soda
1.25ml (¼tsp) salt
ground cinnamon to decorate

1. Cream together butter, sugars, cinnamon and egg until light and fluffy.

2. Add soured cream and lemon rind and beat until well blended.

3. Gradually beat in dry ingredients.

4. Refrigerate for 1 hour, then drop spoonfuls of mixture on to baking sheets covered with non-stick baking paper, allow room for them to spread.

5. Sprinkle a little cinnamon on top of each biscuit.

6. Bake at 190°C (375°F) Mark 5 for 10–15 minutes, or until lightly brown.

7. Cool on a wire cooling rack.

8. Store in an airtight container.

CREAM CHEESE COOKIES Ⓕ

Preparation 25 mins **Cooking** 10 mins *Makes 36*

175g (6oz) butter
100g (4oz) sugar
175g (6oz) cream cheese
225g (8oz) self raising flour
75g (3oz) ground almonds
75g (3oz) no-soak dried apricots, chopped
75g (3oz) chocolate chips

1. Beat together butter, sugar, cheese, flour and almonds. Mix well.

2. Stir in apricots and chocolate chips.

3. Place spoonfuls of mixture on to baking sheets covered with non-stick baking paper and press down lightly with a fork.

4. Bake at 220°C (425°F) Mark 7 for 10 mins.

5. Cool for 2 mins on baking sheets then lift off and cool on a wire cooling rack.

6. Store in an airtight container.

CHOCOLATE CHERRY COOKIES Ⓕ

Preparation 25 mins
Cooking 20 mins   *Makes 18–20*

100g (4oz) butter, softened
50g (2oz) caster sugar
2.5ml (½tsp) vanilla essence
25g (1oz) glacé cherries, finely chopped
25g (1oz) plain chocolate, finely chopped
100g (4oz) flour, sifted

1. Cream butter, sugar and vanilla until fluffy.

2. Add cherries and chocolate. Stir in flour.

3. Put 18–20 teaspoons of mixture, well apart, on to a greased baking sheet.

4. Bake at 190°C (375°F) Mark 5 for 15–20 minutes.

5. Leave to cool for 1 or 2 minutes before transferring to a wire cooling rack.

6. Store in an airtight container when cold.

Variation

DATE COOKIES Ⓕ

Follow recipe and method for chocolate cherry cookies (above). Add 50g (2oz) very finely chopped dates instead of chocolate and cherries.

COFFEE WALNUT COOKIES Ⓕ

Preparation 20 mins
Cooking 20 mins   *Makes 18–20*

100g (4oz) butter, softened
50g (2oz) caster sugar
50g (2oz) walnuts, finely chopped
100g (4oz) flour
10ml (2tsp) instant coffee powder

1. Cream butter with sugar until light and fluffy.

2. Add walnuts. Stir in flour sifted with coffee powder.

3. Put 18–20 teaspoons of mixture, well apart, on a greased baking sheet.

4. Bake at 190°C (375°F) Mark 5 for 15–20 minutes.

5. Leave to cool for 1 or 2 minutes before transferring to a wire cooling rack.

6. Store in an airtight container when cold.

RICH SHORTBREAD   (F)

Preparation 25 mins **Cooking** 40 mins   *Makes 8*

100g (4oz) butter, softened
50g (2oz) caster sugar
150g (5oz) flour
25g (1oz) semolina
extra caster sugar

1. Cream butter and sugar together until light and fluffy.

2. Using a fork, gradually stir in flour and semolina.

3. Draw mixture together with fingertips. Press into a lightly greased 18cm (7 inch) sandwich tin.
To microwave: Draw mixture together with fingertips. Press into a greased and base-lined 18cm (7 inch) flan dish.

4. Prick well all over. Either pinch up edges with finger and thumb or ridge with prongs of a fork.
To microwave: Prick well all over.

5. Bake at 170°C (325°F) Mark 3 for about 40 minutes, or until colour of pale straw.
To microwave: Cook for about 4 minutes or until set.

6. Leave in tin for 5 minutes.
To microwave: Leave in dish for 5 minutes.

7. Cut into 8 triangles. Dredge with extra caster sugar. Remove from tin when cold.
To microwave: Cut into 8 triangles. Dredge with extra caster sugar. Remove from dish when cold.

8. Store in an airtight container.

Variation
SHORTBREAD ROUNDS   (F)

Follow recipe and method for rich shortbread (left). Instead of placing in tin roll out dough and cut out rounds with a 5cm (2inch) biscuit cutter. Place on a greased baking sheet and cook for about 15–20 minutes, or until colour of pale straw.

CHOCOLATE CHERRY COOKIES

GINGERBREAD MEN

FRUIT & SESAME SQUARES

Preparation 10 mins **Cooking** 30 mins *Makes 18*

50 g (2 oz) sesame seeds
175 g (6 oz) medium oatmeal
90 ml (6 tbsp) clear honey
100 g (4 oz) butter, melted
50 g (2 oz) soft brown sugar
50 g (2 oz) no-soak dried apricots, chopped
25 g (1 oz) raisins

1. Place sesame seeds in a saucepan and gently heat for 2–3 minutes to 'toast' seeds. *To microwave: Place sesame seeds in a shallow heatproof dish and cook for about 5 minutes, stirring every minute, until golden brown.*

2. Add remaining ingredients and mix well.

3. Spoon into a greased 28 × 18 cm (11 × 7 inch) Swiss roll tin. Press mixture down and smooth surface level.

4. Bake at 180°C (350°F) Mark 4 for 20–25 minutes.

5. Cool in tin for a few minutes, then cut into squares.

6. Allow to cool completely before removing from tin and storing in an airtight container.

PEANUT CRISPS   Ⓕ

Preparation 25 mins **Cooking** 12 mins *Makes 24*

50 g (2 oz) flour
1.25 ml (¼ tsp) bicarbonate of soda
50 g (2 oz) butter, softened
25 g (1 oz) caster sugar
50 g (2 oz) soft brown sugar
2.5 ml (½ tsp) vanilla essence
50 g (2 oz) peanut butter
1 egg

1. Sift together flour and bicarbonate of soda.

2. Cream together butter with sugars, vanilla and peanut butter until very light and fluffy.

3. Beat in egg then stir in dry ingredients.

4. Drop 24 teaspoons of mixture, 2.5 cm (1 inch) apart, on to ungreased baking sheets.

5. Bake at 180°C (350°F) Mark 4 for 10–12 minutes.

6. Cool for 1 or 2 minutes before transferring to a wire cooling rack.

7. Allow to cool completely before storing in an airtight container.

GINGERBREAD MEN 🅕

Preparation 25 mins **plus cooling**
Cooking 15 mins   *Makes 4–6*

100 g (4 oz) flour
50 g (2 oz) soft brown sugar
5 ml (1 tsp) ground ginger
50 g (2 oz) butter
15 ml (1 tbsp) fresh milk
30 ml (2 tbsp) black treacle
currants to decorate

1. Place flour, sugar and ginger in a bowl and mix together. Make a well in centre of dry ingredients.

2. Put butter, milk and treacle into a small saucepan and heat gently until butter has melted. Remove from heat and cool for 2–3 minutes.
To microwave: Put butter, milk and treacle into a bowl or jug and cook for 1 minute, until butter has melted. Allow to cool for 2–3 minutes.

3. Pour butter mixture into dry ingredients and mix with a wooden spoon to a soft ball.

4. Leave mixture to cool until firm to touch.

5. Roll out on a floured work surface until 0.5 cm (¼ inch) thick. Cut out with a gingerbread man biscuit cutter.

6. Transfer to a greased baking sheet using a palette knife or fish slice. Allow room for them to spread.

7. Decorate with currants for eyes, nose and buttons.

8. Bake at 180°C (350°F) Mark 4 for 10–15 minutes.

9. Leave to cool for 3 minutes. Transfer to a wire cooling rack and leave until cold.

GINGER SNAPS 🅕

Preparation 25 mins
Cooking 10 mins   *Makes 26–30*

100 g (4 oz) self raising flour
5 ml (1 tsp) ground ginger
1.25 ml (¼ tsp) mixed spice
50 g (2 oz) butter
40 g (1½ oz) caster sugar
15 ml (1 tbsp) black treacle, melted
fresh milk to mix

1. Sift flour, ginger and spice into a bowl.

2. Rub in butter finely.

3. Add sugar. Mix to very stiff paste with treacle and milk.

4. Roll out very thinly and cut into 26–30 rounds with a 5 cm (2 inch) biscuit cutter.

5. Transfer to greased baking sheets.

6. Bake at 180°C (350°F) Mark 4 for 10 minutes.

7. Leave to cool for 1–2 minutes before transferring to a wire cooling rack.

8. Store in an airtight container when cold.

SYRUP BITES 🅕

Preparation 35 mins **plus** 30 mins **standing**
Cooking 15 mins   *Makes 24*

100 g (4 oz) self raising flour
75 g (3 oz) rolled oats
25 g (1 oz) desiccated coconut
100 g (4 oz) butter
125 g (5 oz) caster sugar
30 ml (2 tbsp) golden syrup
5 ml (1 tsp) bicarbonate of soda
15 ml (1 tbsp) fresh milk

1. Combine flour with oats and coconut.

2. Put butter, sugar and syrup into a saucepan. Very slowly bring to the boil, stirring all the time.

3. Remove from heat. Add bicarbonate of soda dissolved in milk.

4. Pour hot mixture on to dry ingredients. Mix thoroughly. Leave on one side for 30 minutes or until firm.

5. Break off 24 pieces of mixture and roll into marbles.

6. Transfer to greased baking sheets, leaving room between each one to allow for spreading.

7. Bake at 180°C (350°F) Mark 4 for 15 minutes.

8. Leave to cool for 1 or 2 minutes before transferring to a wire cooling rack.

9. Store in an airtight container when cold.

ALMOND MACAROONS

ALMOND MACAROONS   Ⓕ

Preparation 25 mins **Cooking** 25 mins *Makes 18*

2 egg whites
100 g (4 oz) ground almonds
225 g (8 oz) caster sugar
15 g (½ oz) ground rice
2.5 ml (½ tsp) vanilla essence
2.5 ml (½ tsp) almond essence
a little extra egg white
9 blanched and split almonds

1. Brush one or two baking sheets with melted butter. Line with rice paper.

2. Beat egg whites until foamy but not stiff.

3. Add almonds, sugar, ground rice and essences. Beat well.

4. Pipe or spoon 18 mounds of mixture, well apart, on to prepared baking sheets. Brush with egg white.

5. Put half an almond in middle of each one.

6. Bake at 170°C (325°F) Mark 3 for 20–25 minutes, or until pale gold.

7. Leave to cool for 5 minutes. Carefully lift off, remove rice paper from edges.

8. Cool on a wire cooling rack.

9. Store in an airtight container when cold.

BRANDY SNAPS   Ⓕ

Preparation 30 mins
Cooking 8 mins **per batch**   *Makes 16*

50 g (2 oz) butter
50 g (2 oz) granulated sugar
65 g (2½ oz) golden syrup
50 g (2 oz) flour
5 ml (1 tsp) ground ginger
10 ml (2 tsp) lemon juice

1. Put butter, sugar and syrup into a saucepan. Stand over a low heat until melted.

2. Sift together flour and ginger.

3. Add to melted mixture with lemon juice.

4. Drop 20 ml (4 tsp) of mixture (well apart to allow for spreading) on to a large greased baking sheet.

5. Bake at 170°C (325°F) Mark 3 for 8 minutes.

6. Leave for 1 minute. Lift off with a palette knife.

7. Roll quickly and loosely round greased handle of a wooden spoon.

8. Leave until firm and slide off handle.

9. Repeat with remaining mixture.

Variation

BRANDY SNAPS WITH CREAM

Follow recipe and method for brandy snaps (left). When cold whip 150 ml (5 fl oz) fresh double cream and pipe into brandy snaps before serving.

FLORENTINES Ⓕ

Preparation 40 mins **plus cooling**
Cooking 10 mins   *Makes 12*

82 g (3¼ oz) butter
60 ml (4 tbsp) fresh milk
100 g (4 oz) icing sugar, sifted
40 g (1½ oz) flour
75 g (3 oz) chopped mixed peel
50 g (2 oz) glacé cherries, finely chopped
75 g (3 oz) flaked almonds
5 ml (1 tsp) lemon juice
100 g (4 oz) plain chocolate

1. Cover two large baking sheets with non-stick baking paper.

2. Put 75 g (3 oz) butter, milk and sugar into a saucepan. Stand over a low heat until butter melts.

3. Remove from heat. Stir in flour, peel, cherries, almonds and lemon juice.

4. Leave on one side until completely cold.

5. Spoon equal amounts of mixture (well apart to allow for spreading) on to baking sheets.

6. Bake at 190°C (375°F) Mark 5 for 10 minutes, or until pale gold.

7. Leave until lukewarm. Carefully lift off baking sheets.

8. Cool completely on a wire cooling rack.

9. Melt chocolate and remaining butter in a basin standing over a saucepan of hot water.

10. Put a heaped teaspoonful on to each florentine.

11. Spread evenly with a knife.

12. Mark wavy lines with a fork on each one. Leave until chocolate hardens before serving.

13. Store in an airtight container, layered between non-stick baking paper.

FLORENTINES

PASTRY

Home-made Pastry

When a recipe calls for a certain weight of pastry, the weight refers to the amount of flour used and not to the total amount of pastry. For example, if a recipe says you need 100g (4oz) shortcrust pastry, it means you start off with 100g (4oz) flour and then add all the other ingredients.

Bought Pastry

When a recipe calls for a certain weight of bought pastry, this **does** refer to total weight. Thus if a recipe says you need 225g (8oz) puff pastry, you should buy 225g (8oz) puff pastry.

When cooking flans or quiches place a baking sheet in the oven to preheat. Place the flan tin on to the hot baking sheet to cook. This ensures a fully cooked pastry base.

SHORTCRUST PASTRY Ⓕ

Preparation 25 mins

For sweet and savoury flans, pies, tarts and tartlets, pasties, patties, turnovers, etc.

225g (8oz) flour
1.25ml (¼tsp) salt
100g (4oz) butter
cold water to mix; allow between
** 5–7.5ml (1–1½tsp) per 25g (1oz) of flour**

1. Sift flour and salt into a bowl.
2. Add butter. Cut into flour with a knife then rub in with fingertips. The mixture should look like fine breadcrumbs.
3. Sprinkle water over crumbs. Mix to a stiff crumbly-looking paste with a round-ended knife.
4. Draw together with fingertips, turn out on to a lightly floured work surface. Knead quickly until smooth and crack-free.
5. Roll out and use as required.
6. If not to be used immediately, transfer to a polythene bag or wrap in aluminium foil and refrigerate.

The usual cooking temperature is
200–220°C (400–425°F) Mark 6–7.

Variations

RICH SHORTCRUST PASTRY Ⓕ

For same dishes as shortcrust pastry. Follow recipe and method for shortcrust pastry (left) but use 150g (5oz) butter and mix with 20–25ml (4–5tsp) cold water. Transfer to a polythene bag or wrap in aluminium foil and chill for at least 30 minutes before rolling out and using.

NUT PASTRY

For flans, pies and turnovers etc. Follow recipe and method for shortcrust pastry (left) but stir in 25g (1oz) very finely chopped walnuts, hazelnuts, peanuts or cashew nuts before adding water. If using salted nuts, omit salt.

WHOLEMEAL SHORTCRUST PASTRY Ⓕ

Preparation 30 mins **plus** 5 mins **chilling**

100g (4oz) wholemeal flour
100g (4oz) self raising wholemeal flour
pinch of salt
100g (4oz) butter
100ml (4floz) water

1. Place flours, salt and butter in a bowl.
2. Using a fork, cut butter into flour, alternatively rub butter into flour, until mixture resembles fine breadcrumbs.
3. Add water and mix with a round-ended knife to a soft dough.
4. Draw together with fingertips.
5. Leave dough in bowl and refrigerate for 5 minutes.
6. Roll out and use as required.

The usual cooking temperature is
200–220°C (400–425°F) Mark 6–7.

CHEESE PASTRY Ⓕ

Preparation 25 mins

For savoury biscuits, straws, pies and flans

100 g (4 oz) flour
1.25 ml (¼ tsp) dry mustard
1.25 ml (¼ tsp) salt
shake of cayenne pepper
65 g (2½ oz) butter
50 g (2 oz) English Cheddar, grated
1 egg yolk
10–15 ml (2–3 tsp) cold water

1. Sift flour, mustard, salt and cayenne pepper into a bowl.

2. Cut butter into flour, and rub in until mixture resembles breadcrumbs.

3. Add cheese and mix ingredients together.

4. Mix to a stiff paste with egg yolk and water.

5. Turn out on to a floured work surface. Knead quickly until smooth and crack-free.

6. Wrap in a polythene bag or foil.

7. Chill for 30 minutes before using.

The usual cooking temperature is 200°C (400°F) Mark 6.

SWEET FLAN PASTRY Ⓕ

Preparation 30 mins **plus** 30 mins **chilling**

For sweet flans, tarts, tartlets, small and large pies

1 egg yolk
10 ml (2 tsp) icing sugar, sifted
100 g (4 oz) flour
pinch of salt
65 g (2½ oz) butter
5–10 ml (1–2 tsp) cold water

1. Mix egg yolk and sugar well together.

2. Sift flour and salt into a bowl.

3. Add butter, cut into flour with a knife, then rub in with fingertips until mixture resembles fine breadcrumbs.

4. Mix to a very stiff paste with yolk, sugar and water.

5. Turn out on to a lightly floured work surface. Knead quickly until smooth.

6. Wrap in a polythene bag or foil.

7. Chill for at least 30 minutes before rolling out and using.

The usual cooking temperature is 190°C (375°F) Mark 5.

ALMOND SLICES (PAGE 370) USING SHORTCRUST PASTRY (PAGE 364)

FLAKY PASTRY   Ⓕ

Preparation 35 mins **plus chilling**

For sweet and savoury pies, patties, turnovers and sausage rolls

175 g (6 oz) butter
225 g (8 oz) flour
1.25 ml (¼ tsp) salt
150 ml (¼ pint) chilled water
5 ml (1 tsp) lemon juice

1. Divide butter into 4 equal portions. Chill 3 portions.

2. Sift flour and salt into a bowl.

3. Rub in unchilled portion of butter.

4. Mix to a soft dough with water and lemon juice. Turn out on to a floured work surface. Knead thoroughly.

5. Put into a polythene bag or wrap in aluminium foil. Chill for 30 minutes.

6. Roll out on a floured work surface into a 0.5 cm (¼ inch) thick rectangle, measuring about 45.5×15 cm (18×6 inch).

7. Using tip of a knife, dot second portion of butter (in small flakes) over top and middle third of rectangle to within 2.5 cm (1 inch) of edges. Dust lightly with flour.

8. Fold in three, envelope style, by bringing bottom third over middle third and folding top third over.

9. Seal open edges by pressing firmly together with a rolling pin. Put into a polythene bag or wrap in aluminium foil and chill for 15 minutes.

10. Remove from bag or unwrap. With folded edges to left and right, roll out again into a 45.5×15 cm (18×6 inch) rectangle.

11. Cover with third portion of butter as before. Fold, seal and chill.

12. Repeat again, adding last portion of butter and chill.

13. Roll out again. Fold and seal, return to polythene bag or wrap in aluminium foil. Chill for at least 30 minutes before rolling out to 0.5 cm (¼ inch) thickness and using.

14. After shaping, let dishes, etc. rest 30 minutes in cool before baking.

The usual cooking temperature is 220°C (425°F) Mark 7.

PUFF PASTRY   Ⓕ

Preparation 50 mins **plus chilling**

For vol-au-vents, cream horns and Mille feuilles

225 g (8 oz) butter
225 g (8 oz) flour
1.25 ml (¼ tsp) salt
5 ml (1 tsp) lemon juice
chilled water to mix

1. Shape butter into a 1.5 cm (¾ inch) brick.

2. Sift flour and salt into a bowl. Mix to a soft paste with lemon juice and water.

3. Knead well on a floured work surface.

4. Roll out into a rectangle measuring 30×15 cm (12×6 inch).

5. Stand butter on lower half of rectangle. Bring top half over so that butter is completely enclosed.

6. Press open edges firmly together with rolling pin. Put into a polythene bag or wrap in aluminium foil. Chill for 15 minutes.

7. Remove from bag. With fold on right, roll into a 45.5×15 cm (18×6 inch) rectangle.

8. Fold in three envelope style, by bringing bottom third over middle third and folding top third over. Seal edges, wrap and chill for 20 minutes.

9. Repeat, until pastry has been rolled, folded and chilled 7 times.

10. Return to polythene bag or wrap in aluminium foil. Chill for at least 30 minutes before rolling out to 0.5 cm (¼ inch) thickness and using.

11. After shaping, let dishes, etc. rest 30 minutes in cool before baking.

The usual cooking temperature is 230°C (450°F) Mark 8.

ROUGH PUFF PASTRY   Ⓕ

Preparation 1 hr **plus chilling**

For same dishes as Flaky Pastry (left)

225 g (8 oz) flour
1.25 ml (¼ tsp) salt
175 g (6 oz) butter
150 ml (¼ pint) chilled water
5 ml (1 tsp) lemon juice

ECCLES CAKES (PAGE 371) USING FLAKY PASTRY (PAGE 366)

1. Sift flour and salt into a bowl.

2. Cut butter into tiny dice.

3. Mix together water and lemon juice.

4. Add butter to flour.

5. Using a knife, mix to a fairly soft crumbly paste with water and lemon juice. Take care not to cut or break down butter any further.

6. Draw together with fingertips. Turn out on to a floured work surface and shape into a block.

7. Roll into a 0.5cm (¼inch) thick rectangle, measuring about 45.5×15cm (18×6inch). Fold in three, envelope style, by bringing bottom third over middle third and folding top third over.

8. Seal open edges by pressing firmly together with rolling pin.

9. Give pastry a quarter turn so that folded edges are to right and left.

10. Roll out. Fold and turn three more times.

If possible, put folded pastry into a polythene bag or wrap in aluminium foil and chill for about 15 minutes between rollings.

The usual cooking temperature is 220°C (425°F) Mark 7.

SUET CRUST PASTRY

Preparation 10 mins

For sweet and savoury roly-polys, boiled and steamed puddings and dumplings

225g (8oz) self raising flour
2.5ml (½tsp) salt
100g (4oz) shredded suet
about 150ml (¼pint) cold water to mix

1. Sift flour and salt into a bowl.

2. Add suet and mix ingredients lightly together.

3. Mix to a soft dough with water.

4. Turn out on to a floured work surface. Knead until smooth and roll out to about 0.25cm (⅛inch) thickness.

5. Use immediately as required.

This pastry can be steamed or baked.

Variation

DUMPLINGS

Follow recipe and method for suet crust pastry (above) but use half the quantities. Divide into 8 pieces and shape into small balls. Add to soups, stews or casseroles and cook for 15–20 minutes.

HOT WATER CRUST PASTRY

Preparation 30 mins
plus 30 mins **standing**

For raised pies such as pork, veal, veal and ham and game

350 g (12 oz) flour
2.5 ml (½ tsp) salt
1 egg yolk
60 ml (4 tbsp) fresh milk
60 ml (4 tbsp) water
25 g (1 oz) butter
75 g (3 oz) lard

1. Sift flour and salt into a bowl and warm slightly. Make a well in centre.

2. Beat yolk with 15 ml (1 tbsp) milk and pour into well.

3. Pour remaining milk and water into a saucepan. Add butter and lard. Heat slowly until melted. Bring to a brisk boil.

4. Pour into well. Mix with a wooden spoon until ingredients are well blended.

5. Turn out on to a floured work surface. Knead quickly until smooth.

6. Put into a bowl standing over a saucepan of hot water. Cover with a clean tea-towel and leave to rest for 30 minutes.

7. Roll out warm pastry to 0.5 cm (¼ inch) thickness and use as required.

8. When making pies, cut off a piece for lid first. Leave it (covered with a tea towel) in bowl over hot water.

The usual cooking temperature is 220°C (425°F) Mark 7, reducing to 180°C (350°F) Mark 4.

CHOUX PASTRY ⒡

Preparation 30 mins

For sweet and savoury buns and éclairs, etc.

65 g (2½ oz) flour
pinch of salt
150 ml (¼ pint) water
50 g (2 oz) butter
2 eggs, well beaten

1. Sift flour and salt twice.

2. Put water and butter into a saucepan. Heat slowly until butter melts, then bring to a brisk boil.

CHOCOLATE ECLAIRS

3. Remove from heat and tip in all the flour.

4. Stir briskly until mixture forms a soft ball and leaves sides of pan clean.

5. Remove from heat and cool slightly. Add eggs very gradually, beating hard until mixture is smooth, shiny and firm enough to stand in soft peaks when lifted with a spoon.

6. Use immediately. Otherwise leave in saucepan and cover with a lid to prevent pastry drying out.

The usual cooking temperature is 200–220°C (400–425°F) Mark 6–7.

CHEESE AIGRETTES

Preparation 10 mins **Cooking** 15 mins *Makes 20*

50 g (2 oz) English Cheddar, finely grated
choux pastry made with 65 g (2½ oz) flour (left)
deep fat or oil for frying

1. Beat 25 g (1 oz) cheese into choux pastry.

2. Drop about 20 equal amounts, from a teaspoon, into hot fat or oil.

3. Fry for about 5 minutes or until aigrettes are golden and well puffed.

4. Remove from pan and drain on absorbent kitchen paper.

5. Transfer to a serving dish. Sprinkle with remaining cheese.

6. Serve hot.

CHEESE & WALNUT PUFFS

Preparation 30 mins **Cooking** 40 mins *Makes 20*

choux pastry made with 65 g (2½ oz) flour (left)
75 g (3 oz) cream cheese
50 g (2 oz) Blue Stilton cheese, crumbled
15 ml (1 tbsp) fresh milk
25 g (1 oz) chopped walnuts

1. Using a teaspoon, place 20 equal amounts of pastry on to a greased and lightly floured baking sheet.

2. Bake at 200°C (400°F) Mark 6 for 20 minutes.

3. Reduce temperature to 170°C (325°F) Mark 3. Bake for a further 20 minutes.

4. Cool on a wire cooling rack.

5. Just before serving, beat cream cheese, Stilton and milk well together. Stir in nuts.

6. Cut puffs in half. Fill bottom halves with cheese mixture. Replace tops.

7. Serve immediately (if left to stand too long, the pastry softens slightly).

Variation

CHEESE & PRAWN PUFFS

Follow recipe and method for cheese and walnut puffs (left). Use 75 g (3 oz) chopped peeled prawns instead of Stilton. Stir in 2.5 ml (½ tsp) grated lemon rind instead of walnuts.

CHOCOLATE ECLAIRS 🅕

Preparation 15 mins
Cooking 40 mins   *Makes 12*

choux pastry made with 65 g (2½ oz) flour (left)
300 ml (10 fl oz) fresh double cream
30 ml (2 tbsp) fresh milk
cocoa glacé icing made with
    175 g (6 oz) icing sugar (page 326)

1. Fit a piping bag with a 1 cm (½ inch) plain tube.

2. Fill bag with pastry. Pipe 12 × 10 cm (4 inch) lengths on to a greased baking sheet.

3. Bake at 200°C (400°F) Mark 6 for 10 mins.

4. Reduce temperature to 180°C (350°F) Mark 4. Bake for a further 20–25 mins or until eclairs are well puffed and golden.

5. Remove from oven and make a slit in the side of each one.

6. Return to oven for further 5 mins to dry out.

7. Cool on a wire cooling rack.

8. When completely cold slit each eclair along one side.

9. Whip cream with milk until softly stiff. Fill eclairs with cream.

9. Cover tops with icing. Leave until icing has set.

Alternatively ice with melted chocolate.

Variation

COFFEE ECLAIRS 🅕

Follow recipe and method for chocolate eclairs (above). Cover tops with coffee glacé icing (page 327) instead of cocoa.

ALMOND SLICES   Ⓕ

Preparation 30 mins **Cooking** 25 mins *Makes 12*

shortcrust pastry
   made with 225 g (8 oz) flour (page 364)
30 ml (2 tbsp) raspberry or apricot jam
100 g (4 oz) caster sugar
100 g (4 oz) icing sugar, sifted
175 g (6 oz) ground almonds
1 egg plus 1 egg white
2.5 ml (½ tsp) almond essence
25 g (1 oz) flaked almonds

1. Roll out pastry on a floured work surface to fit a 28×18 cm (11×7 inch) cake tin.

2. Use to line tin.

3. Cover base with jam.

4. Combine sugars with almonds.

5. Mix to a paste with whole egg, egg white and almond essence.

6. Cover jam with almond mixture, spreading it evenly with a knife.

7. Decorate with flaked almonds.

8. Bake at 200°C (400°F) Mark 6 for 25 minutes.

9. Cool on a wire cooling rack. Cut into 12 slices when cold.

CREAM HORNS   Ⓕ

Preparation 45 mins **plus** 30 mins **standing**
Cooking 20 mins   *Makes 12*

flaky pastry
   made with 225 g (8 oz) flour (page 366)
butter, melted
milk for brushing
granulated sugar
60 ml (4 tbsp) raspberry or strawberry jam
300 ml (10 fl oz) fresh double cream
icing sugar, sifted

1. Brush 12 cream horn tins with melted butter.

2. Roll out pastry thinly on a floured work surface. Cut into 12×2.5 cm (1 inch) strips, each about 30.5 cm (12 inch) long.

3. Moisten one side of each strip with water.

4. Starting at pointed end of each tin, wind pastry strip round. Make sure moistened side faces inwards and that the strip overlaps by about 0.5 cm (¼ inch).

5. Transfer to a damp baking sheet. Chill for 30 minutes.

6. Bake at 220°C (425°F) Mark 7 for 10–15 minutes.

7. Remove from oven. Brush with milk and sprinkle with sugar.

8. Return to oven. Bake for a further 2 minutes.

9. Transfer to a wire cooling rack. Cool for about 5 minutes.

10. Carefully remove tins. Leave horns until completely cold.

11. Put 5 ml (1 tsp) of jam into each one. Fill with cream, whipped until thick and sweetened to taste with icing sugar.

ECCLES CAKES   Ⓕ

Preparation 45 mins
Cooking 20 mins   *Makes 8*

15 g (½ oz) butter, softened
25 g (1 oz) currants
25 g (1 oz) chopped mixed peel
10 ml (2 tsp) soft brown sugar
1.25 ml (¼ tsp) mixed spice
flaky pastry
    made with 100 g (4 oz) flour (page 366)
milk for brushing
extra caster sugar

1. Mix softened butter with currants, peel, sugar and spice. Mix well.

2. Roll out pastry on a floured work surface.

3. Cut into 8 rounds with an 8.5 cm (3½ inch) biscuit cutter.

4. Put a heaped teaspoon of fruit mixture on to centre of each one.

5. Moisten edges of pastry with water.

6. With fingertips, draw up edges of each round so that they meet in the centre, completely enclosing filling.

7. Press well together to seal. Turn each cake over.

8. Roll out until fruit just shows through.

9. Make 3 slits in top of each with a sharp knife.

10. Brush with milk. Sprinkle thickly with caster sugar.

11. Bake at 230°C (450°F) Mark 8 for 15 minutes.

12. Cool on a wire cooling rack.

MINCE PIES   Ⓕ

Preparation 25 mins
Cooking 25 mins   *Makes 12*

shortcrust pastry *or* rich shortcrust pastry
    (page 364) made with 225 g (8 oz) flour
350 g (12 oz) mincemeat
beaten egg for brushing
icing sugar, sifted
brandy butter (page 245) to serve

1. Roll out pastry on a floured work surface.

2. Cut 12 rounds with an 8.5 cm (3½ inch) biscuit cutter and 12 rounds with a 6.5 cm (2½ inch) biscuit cutter.

3. Use larger rounds to line deep bun tins.

4. Put equal amounts of mincemeat in each.

5. Top with remaining rounds and brush with beaten egg.

6. Bake at 220°C (425°F) Mark 7 for 20–25 minutes or until golden brown.

7. Remove from tins and dredge thickly with sifted icing sugar. Serve with brandy butter.

APPLE TURNOVERS   Ⓕ

Preparation 25 mins **Cooking** 40 mins *Makes 6*

rough puff pastry *or* flaky pastry
    (page 366) made with 225 g (8 oz) flour
225 g (8 oz) cooking apples, peeled, cored
    and sliced
50 g (2 oz) caster sugar
lightly beaten egg white
extra caster sugar

1. Roll out pastry on a floured work surface and cut into 6×10 cm (4 inch) squares.

2. Mix apples with sugar. Put equal amounts on to centres of each square.

3. Moisten edges of pastry with cold water. Fold each in half to form a triangle, completely enclosing fruit.

4. Press edges together to seal. Flake by cutting lightly with back of a knife then 'ridge' with a fork.

5. Transfer on to a baking sheet. Brush with egg white and sprinkle with sugar.

6. Bake at 220°C (425°F) Mark 7 for 20 mins.

7. Reduce to 180°C (350°F) Mark 4 and bake for a further 20 mins.

WEST COUNTRY FLAN (F)

Preparation 30 mins **Cooking** 50 mins *Serves 8*

shortcrust pastry
    made with 225 g (8 oz) flour (page 364)
100 g (4 oz) fresh clotted cream
30 ml (2 tbsp) sugar
2.5 ml (½ tsp) ground cinnamon
1 egg, beaten
15 ml (1 tbsp) cornflour
2 eating apples, cored, sliced and dipped
    in lemon juice
25 g (1 oz) apricot jam, melted

1. Roll out pastry on a floured work surface and use to line a 23 cm (9 inch) flan tin.

2. Bake blind at 180°C (350°F) Mark 4 for 15 minutes.

3. Blend together cream, sugar, cinnamon, egg and cornflour.

4. Pour into flan case.

5. Arrange sliced apples in flan case and bake for a further 35 minutes until set.

6. Remove from oven and brush with melted jam.

7. Serve hot or cold.

SAUSAGE ROLLS (F)

Preparation 30 mins **Cooking** 20 mins *Makes 10*

rough puff pastry
    made with 225 g (8 oz) flour (page 366)
225 g (8 oz) sausagemeat or skinless
    sausages
beaten egg for brushing

1. Roll out pastry on a lightly floured work surface into a long strip about 10 cm (4 inch) wide.

2. Roll sausagemeat into a roll as long as pastry. Place in centre of pastry.

3. Brush edges of pastry with water. Fold over pastry and seal longest edge well.

4. Cut into 10 pieces and place on baking sheets.

5. Make 2 cuts in tops of pastry and brush with beaten egg.

6. Bake at 230°C (450°F) Mark 8 for 20 minutes or until golden brown.

Variations

SAUSAGE & APPLE ROLLS

Follow recipe and method for sausage rolls (left). Peel, core and grate 1 eating apple and mix with sausagemeat before using.

TOMATO SAUSAGE ROLLS

Follow recipe and method for sausage rolls (left). Mix 30 ml (2 tbsp) tomato purée with sausagemeat before using.

MEAT & VEGETABLE PASTIES (F)

Preparation 30 mins **Cooking** 65 mins *Serves 4*

175 g (6 oz) rump steak
100 g (4 oz) ox liver *or* kidney
1 medium onion, chopped
1 large potato, diced
15 ml (1 tbsp) water
salt and freshly ground pepper
shortcrust pastry
    made with 225 g (8 oz) flour (page 364)
milk for brushing

1. Cut steak and liver or kidney into very small pieces.

2. Combine with onion, potato, water and seasoning.

3. Divide pastry into 4 equal-sized pieces.

4. On a floured work surface, roll out each into a 15 cm (6 inch) round.

5. Moisten edges with water.

6. Put equal amounts of filling into centres of each.

7. Fold rounds in half over filling to form semi-circles.

8. Press edges well together to seal. Ridge with a fork.

9. Transfer to a lightly greased baking sheet.

10. Brush with milk.

11. Bake at 220°C (425°F) Mark 7 for 20 minutes.

12. Reduce to 170°C (325°F) Mark 3. Bake for a further 45 minutes.

13. Serve hot or cold.

Quiche lorraine Ⓔ

Preparation 30 mins
Cooking 55 mins   *Serves 4–5*

shortcrust pastry
   made with 225 g (8 oz) flour (page 364)
100 g (4 oz) streaky bacon
150 ml (¼ pint) fresh milk
150 ml (5 fl oz) fresh single cream
3 eggs, beaten
salt and freshly ground pepper
large pinch of ground nutmeg

1. Roll out pastry on a floured work surface. Use to line a 20.5 cm (8 inch) flan tin.

2. Cut bacon into strips. Fry lightly in its own fat until soft but not crisp.

3. Drain thoroughly on absorbent kitchen paper. Place in base of pastry case.

4. Heat milk and cream to just below boiling point. Combine with beaten eggs.

5. Season to taste and add nutmeg. Pour into pastry case.

6. Bake at 200°C (400°F) Mark 6 for 10 minutes.

7. Reduce temperature to 170°C (325°F) Mark 3, bake for a further 35–45 minutes until set.

Leek flan Ⓔ

Preparation 30 mins **Cooking** 35 mins   *Serves 6*

shortcrust pastry
   made with 225 g (8 oz) flour (page 364)
225 g (8 oz) smoked streaky bacon, chopped
4 leeks, sliced and quartered
100 g (4 oz) Caerphilly cheese, crumbled
3 eggs
225 ml (8 fl oz) fresh milk
freshly ground pepper

1. Roll out pastry on a floured work surface and use to line a 28×20.5 cm (11×8 inch) rectangular flan tin.

2. Bake blind at 200°C (400°F) Mark 6 for 10 minutes.

3. Cook bacon in a non-stick frying pan until browned, remove and add leeks. Cook until soft.

4. Place bacon, leeks and cheese in flan case.

5. Beat together eggs and milk, season and pour into flan.

6. Bake at 180°C (350°F) Mark 4 for 25 minutes or until set.

7. Cut into squares, serve either hot or cold.

MIXED PEPPER FLAN

MIXED PEPPER FLAN   Ⓕ

Preparation 30 mins
Cooking 45 mins   *Serves 4–6*

wholemeal shortcrust pastry
   made with 225g (8oz) flour (page 364)
25g (1oz) butter
1 onion, sliced
3 peppers, assorted colours,
   seeded and sliced
1 garlic clove, crushed
2 eggs
150ml (5floz) fresh single cream
75ml (3floz) fresh milk
freshly ground pepper

1. Roll out pastry on a floured work surface
and use to line a 33×10cm (13×4inch)
rectangular flan tin.

2. Bake blind at 200°C (400°F) Mark 6 for
15 minutes.

3. Melt butter and fry onion, peppers and
garlic until soft but not brown.

4. Spoon into pastry case.

5. Beat together eggs, cream and milk.
Season to taste and pour over vegetables.

6. Reduce temperature to 180°C (350°F)
Mark 4 and cook for 30 minutes or until set.

MACKEREL & SWEETCORN FLAN   Ⓕ

Preparation 25 mins
Cooking 45 mins   *Serves 6*

wholemeal shortcrust pastry
   made with 225g (8oz) flour (page 364)
2 eggs
100g (4oz) cottage cheese
150ml (¼pint) fresh milk
175g (6oz) smoked mackerel fillets,
   skinned and flaked
100g (4oz) can sweetcorn, drained
30ml (2tbsp) chopped parsley

1. Roll out pastry on a floured work surface
and use to line a 23cm (9inch) flan tin.

2. Bake blind at 190°C (375°F) Mark 5 for
10 minutes.

3. Beat together eggs, cottage cheese and
milk.

4. Place mackerel and sweetcorn in flan
case.

5. Pour over egg mixture. Sprinkle with
parsley.

6. Bake for a further 35 minutes or until set.

7. Serve hot or cold.

BROCCOLI & BEAN FLAN Ⓕ

Preparation 35 mins **Cooking** 45 mins *Serves 6*

wholemeal shortcrust pastry
  made with 225g (8oz) flour (page 364)
100g (4oz) broccoli florets
300g (11oz) can red kidney beans, drained
100g (4oz) Double Gloucester cheese,
  grated
3 eggs
150ml (5floz) fresh single cream
150ml (¼pint) fresh milk

1. Roll out pastry on a floured work surface and use to line a 23cm (9inch) flan tin.

2. Bake blind at 200°C (400°F) Mark 6 for 10 minutes.

3. Cook broccoli florets in boiling water for 2–3 minutes. Drain well.

4. Arrange in base of flan case with kidney beans and cheese.

5. Beat eggs, cream and milk together and pour into flan case.

6. Bake for a further 35 minutes until set.

7. Serve hot or cold.

CRUNCHY SPINACH FLAN Ⓕ

Preparation 30 mins **Cooking** 1 hr *Serves 4*

75g (3oz) branflakes, crushed
75g (3oz) wholemeal flour
15g (½oz) sesame seeds
75g (3oz) butter, melted
150ml (¼pint) fresh milk
2 eggs
150g (5oz) curd cheese
75g (3oz) spinach, cooked, drained and
  chopped
50g (2oz) bacon, grilled and chopped

1. Mix branflakes, flour and sesame seeds together in a bowl.

2. Stir in melted butter and mix well until coated.

3. Press into base and up sides of a 20.5cm (8inch) flan tin to form a case.

4. Bake blind at 190°C (375°F) Mark 5 for 15 minutes.

5. Mix together milk, eggs, cheese, spinach and bacon.

6. Pour into flan case and bake for 45 minutes or until set.

BROCCOLI & BEAN FLAN

PRESERVES CONFECTIONERY DRINKS

PRESERVES

Fruit for jam making should be firm, under-ripe or only just ripe and fresh. Over-ripe fruit lacking in acid or pectin, or both, never makes satisfactory jam since it will not set properly. Low pectin fruits such as strawberries need lemon juice or bottled pectin to help them set. Preserving sugar is also available and it contains natural pectin. The fruit should be cleaned, prepared as for other cooking purposes and as dry as possible.

Choose a good quality jam pan or a strong, roomy saucepan with a heavy base to prevent the jam from sticking and burning. To allow room for the jam to boil vigorously, the pan should be about half full when the sugar has been added – it is a mistake to try to make too much jam at once.

To microwave: **Use a very large, heatproof bowl and no more than 1.4kg (3lb) fruit. Use equal quantities of sugar to fruit. Most soft fruit needs no additional liquid. Fruit with skins may need about 15ml (1tbsp) water for each 450g (1lb). When following a conventional recipe which uses liquid, halve the quantity for the microwave.**

Scum should never be removed until the jam is made as continuous skimming is wasteful and unnecessary. A small piece of butter rubbed over the bottom of the pan helps to reduce foaming and prevent sticking. When boiling has finished, remove scum with a metal spoon.

Add the sugar only when the fruit is well cooked and broken down, then boil the jam rapidly until setting point is reached.

To microwave: **Add the sugar only when the fruit is cooked. Then cook uncovered until setting point is reached. If the jam bubbles up so much that it may boil over, lower the power level to MEDIUM (50%).**

To test for setting, pour a scant teaspoonful of the jam on to a cold saucer and leave for 1 minute. Setting point has been reached if the surface sets and crinkles when pushed with the finger. Remove the jam from the heat while this test is being made, otherwise it may boil too rapidly and the setting point may be missed. A sugar thermometer will register about 105°C (220°F) once setting point has been reached.

To microwave: **If using a sugar thermometer, make sure it is suitable for use in a microwave. Alternatively test the jam regularly with an ordinary sugar thermometer but do not leave it in the jam during cooking.**

After removing the scum, allow the jam to cool off slightly before pouring into perfectly clean, dry, warm jars. To prevent strawberries or other whole fruits rising in the jars, cool the jam in the pan until a thin skin begins to form, then stir gently before potting.

Jars should be filled to the brim with hot jam to allow for the considerable shrinkage that takes place during cooling. After filling, press a well-fitted waxed disc on the surface of the jam in each jar and wipe the rim carefully with a hot, damp cloth. Cover the jam either while it is still very hot or completely cold.

Label the jam and date; store in a dry, dark, cool, ventilated cupboard.

Note When following the recipes given, slight alterations in the quantities of ingredients will sometimes be advisable. More water may be necessary if large quantities of jam are made or if slow cooking is used. If the fruit is of very good quality, the quantity of fruit may be reduced slightly whereas if the fruit is wet or over-ripe more may be needed.

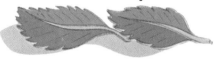

STRAWBERRY JAM

Preparation 30 mins
Cooking 35 mins   *Makes about 2.3 kg (5 lb)*

1.6 kg (3½ lb) strawberries, hulled
juice of 1 large lemon
1.4 kg (3 lb) granulated sugar
15 g (½ oz) butter

1. Put strawberries, lemon juice and sugar into a large saucepan.

2. Heat slowly, stirring all the time, until sugar dissolves.

3. Bring to the boil. Boil briskly for 10–15 mins or until setting point is reached.

4. Draw pan away from heat. Stir in butter to disperse scum.

5. Leave jam to cool off in pan until skin forms on surface.

6. Stir gently, pot and cover.

MIXED FRUIT JAM

RASPBERRY JAM

Preparation 10 mins
Cooking 20 mins   *Makes about 2.3 kg (5 lb)*

1.4 kg (3 lb) raspberries
1.4 kg (3 lb) granulated sugar
15 g (½ oz) butter

1. Put fruit into a large saucepan and crush finely with back of a wooden spoon.

2. Simmer gently for 5 minutes.

3. Add sugar and stir until dissolved.

4. Bring to the boil. Boil briskly for 5–7 minutes or until setting point is reached.

5. Draw pan away from heat. Stir in butter to disperse scum.

6. Pot and cover.

PLUM JAM

Preparation 10 mins
Cooking 1 hr   *Makes about 2.3 kg (5 lb)*

1.4 kg (3 lb) washed plums
450 ml (¾ pint) water
1.4 kg (3 lb) granulated sugar
15 g (½ oz) butter

1. Put plums into a saucepan and add water.

2. Bring to the boil, cover pan and reduce heat.

3. Simmer gently until fruit is tender about 10–20 minutes.

4. Add sugar and stir until dissolved.

5. Bring jam to the boil. Boil briskly for 10–15 minutes or until setting point is reached. Remove stones with a perforated spoon as they rise to the surface.

6. Draw pan away from heat. Stir in butter to disperse scum.

7. Pot and cover.

MIXED FRUIT JAM

Preparation 10 mins
Cooking 1 hr   *Makes about 2.3 kg (5 lb)*

1.4 kg (3 lb) mixed soft fruit, such as raspberries, strawberries, gooseberries, rhubarb and redcurrants
150 ml (¼ pint) water
1.4 kg (3 lb) granulated sugar
15 g (½ oz) butter

1. Place fruit in a saucepan with water.

2. Bring to the boil, reduce heat and cover pan.

3. Simmer gently for 10–15 minutes, crushing fruit against sides of pan until it is soft and pulpy.

4. Add sugar and heat slowly, stirring all the time, until sugar dissolves.

5. Bring to the boil. Boil briskly for 10–15 minutes until setting point is reached.

6. Draw pan away from heat. Stir in butter to disperse scum.

7. Pot and cover.

BLACKCURRANT JAM

Preparation 30 mins
Cooking 55 mins   *Makes about 2.3 kg (5 lb)*

900 g (2 lb) stemmed and washed blackcurrants
900 ml (1½ pint) water
1.4 kg (3 lb) granulated sugar
15 g (½ oz) butter

1. Put blackcurrants into a large saucepan and add water.

2. Bring to the boil, cover pan and reduce heat.

3. Simmer gently until fruit is tender about 45 minutes.

4. Add sugar and stir until dissolved. Bring to the boil. Boil briskly for 5–10 minutes or until setting point is reached.

5. Draw pan away from heat. Stir in butter to disperse scum.

6. Pot and cover.

Variation

GOOSEBERRY JAM

Follow recipe and method for blackcurrant jam (left). Use gooseberries instead of blackcurrants and halve the quantity of water. Boil for 10–15 minutes or until setting point is reached.

DRIED APRICOT JAM

Preparation 20 mins plus soaking
Cooking 1 hr   *Makes about 1.4 kg (3 lb)*

450 g (1 lb) dried apricots
900 ml (1½ pint) water
450 g (1 lb) granulated sugar
75 g (3 oz) blanched and split almonds
juice of 1 large lemon
15 g (½ oz) butter

1. Snip apricots into smallish pieces with kitchen scissors. Cover with extra cold water and leave to soak overnight.

2. Drain, put into a saucepan and add 900 ml (1½ pint) water.

3. Bring to the boil, lower heat and cover pan. Simmer gently for about 45 minutes or until fruit is tender.

4. Add sugar, almonds and lemon juice. Heat slowly, stirring all the time, until sugar dissolves.

5. Bring to the boil. Boil briskly until setting point is reached.

6. Draw pan away from heat. Stir in butter to disperse scum.

7. Pot and cover.

THICK ORANGE MARMALADE

Preparation 30 mins **plus standing**
Cooking 2½ hrs   *Makes about 2.3 kg (5 lb)*

700 g (1½ lb) Seville (or bitter) oranges
1.7 litres (3 pint) water
juice of 1 lemon
1.4 kg (3 lb) granulated sugar
15 g (½ oz) butter

1. Scrub oranges well.

2. Put, without slicing, into a large saucepan.

3. Pour in water and bring to the boil.

4. Reduce heat and cover pan. Simmer very gently for 1½–2 hours or until skins of fruit are soft and can be pierced easily with a fork or skewer.

5. Lift oranges out of pan. Cool slightly and chop coarsely.

6. Collect pips and tie in a muslin bag.

7. Return chopped oranges to pan with lemon juice and bag of pips.

8. Add sugar and heat slowly, stirring all the time, until sugar dissolves.

9. Bring to the boil. Boil steadily until setting point is reached.

10. Draw pan away from heat. Stir in butter to disperse scum.

11. Leave marmalade in saucepan until a skin forms on surface.

12. Stir gently.

13. Pot and cover.

MICROWAVE MARMALADE

Preparation 40 mins **plus** 15 mins **standing**
Cooking about 40 mins
                    Makes about 1.1 kg (2½ lb)

2 lemons
900 g (2 lb) Seville (or bitter) oranges
900 ml (1½ pint) boiling water
900 g (2 lb) sugar
knob of butter

1. *To microwave: Warm lemons for 1 minute. Halve and squeeze their juice into a very large heatproof bowl.*

2. *Remove outer rind (not the pith) of oranges, shred and reserve.*

3. *To microwave: In a food processor, chop oranges (including the pips). Add mixture to lemon juice with BOILING water. Cover and cook for 14 minutes.*

4. *Tip into a sieve and press out all juice. Discard contents of sieve.*

5. *To microwave: Add orange rind to juice and cook for 13–15 minutes, stirring occasionally until rind is tender.*

6. *To microwave: Add sugar and stir until dissolved. Cook uncovered for about 10 minutes, stirring once or twice, until setting point is reached.*

7. *Stir in butter, then remove any scum.*

8. *Allow marmalade to cool for about 15 minutes, then pot and cover.*

LEMON CURD

Preparation 30 mins
Cooking 30 mins   *Makes about 550 g (1¼ lb)*

100 g (4 oz) butter
225 g (8 oz) granulated sugar
3 eggs plus 1 yolk, beaten together
grated rind and juice of 3 lemons

1. Melt butter in a double saucepan or a basin standing over a saucepan of gently simmering water.

2. Add sugar, eggs and extra yolk and lemon rind and juice.

3. Cook gently without boiling until curd thickens sufficiently to coat back of a spoon. (This is important because if overheated the mixture may curdle and separate.)

4. Pour into clean, dry and warm jars and cover as for jam.

Store in a cool place. Use within 2 weeks

Variation

ORANGE CURD

Follow recipe and method for lemon curd (above). Instead of all lemons, use 2 medium oranges and 1 medium lemon.

Microwave lemon curd

Preparation 35 mins **plus** 5 mins **standing**
Cooking about 10 mins *Makes about 900g (2 lb)*

grated rind and juice of 4 lemons
100 g (4 oz) butter, diced
450 g (1 lb) caster sugar
4 eggs, beaten

1. *To microwave: Mix together lemon rind and juice, butter and sugar in a large heatproof bowl. Cook for about 4 minutes until butter melts. Stir well.*

2. *Stir in eggs.*

3. *To microwave: Cook for 5–6 minutes, whisking every minute, until curd is thick and creamy.*

4. *Stand for 5 minutes, whisk occasionally.*

5. *Pot and cover.*

Store in a cool place. Use within 2 weeks.

Variation

Microwave orange curd

Follow recipe for microwave lemon curd (above). Use 1 one lemon and 2 large oranges.

Microwave raspberry jam

Preparation 10 mins
Cooking 14–17 mins *Makes about 2.3 kg (5 lb)*

This recipe gives the basic method for making jam in the microwave. When using other fruits, please check the notes on page 377 too.

1.4 kg (3 lb) raspberries
1.4 kg (3 lb) caster sugar
knob of butter

1. *To microwave: Put fruit into a very large, heatproof bowl and cook uncovered for 4–5 minutes, stirring once or twice, until just soft.*

2. *To microwave: In another bowl, warm sugar for 3 minutes, then stir into hot fruit. Stir well until sugar dissolves.*

3. *To microwave: Cook uncovered for 10–12 minutes, stirring occasionally, until setting point is reached.*

4. *Stir in butter then remove any scum.*

5. *Allow jam to cool slightly, then pot and cover.*

LEMON CURD

CONFECTIONERY

MILK FUDGE Ⓕ

Preparation 10 mins **plus setting**
Cooking 30 mins   *Makes about 50 pieces*

300 ml (½ pint) fresh milk
450 g (1 lb) granulated sugar
100 g (4 oz) butter
2.5 ml (½ tsp) vanilla essence

1. Pour milk into a saucepan. Bring slowly to the boil.

2. Add sugar and butter.

3. Heat slowly, stirring all the time, until sugar dissolves and butter melts.

4. Bring to the boil. Cover pan with lid. Boil for 2 minutes.

5. Uncover and continue to boil steadily, stirring occasionally, for a further 10–15 minutes or until a little of the mixture, dropped into a cup of cold water, forms a soft ball when rolled gently between finger and thumb. Temperature on a sugar thermometer, if used, should be 116°C (240°F).

6. Remove from heat. Stir in vanilla. Leave mixture to cool for 5 minutes.

7. Beat fudge until it just begins to lose its gloss and is thick and creamy.

8. Transfer to a greased 18 cm (7 inch) square tin.

9. Mark into squares when cool. Cut up with a sharp knife when firm and set.

10. Store in an airtight container.

Variations

CHERRY FUDGE Ⓕ

Follow recipe and method for milk fudge (above). Add 50 g (2 oz) chopped glacé cherries with vanilla.

CHOCOLATE FUDGE Ⓕ

Follow recipe and method for milk fudge (above). Melt 100 g (4 oz) grated plain chocolate in milk before adding sugar and butter.

WALNUT FUDGE Ⓕ

Follow recipe and method for milk fudge (left). Add 50 g (2 oz) chopped walnuts with vanilla.

SYRUP TOFFEE

Preparation 5 mins **plus setting**
Cooking 30 mins   *Makes about 550 g (1¼ lb)*

75 ml (5 tbsp) water
100 g (4 oz) golden syrup
10 ml (2 tsp) vinegar
450 g (1 lb) granulated sugar
50 g (2 oz) butter

1. Pour water and syrup into a saucepan. Bring to the boil.

2. Add vinegar, sugar and butter. Heat slowly, stirring, until sugar dissolves and butter melts.

3. Bring to the boil. Cover pan. Boil gently for 2 minutes.

4. Uncover. Continue to boil, stirring occasionally, for 8–10 minutes or until a little of the mixture, dropped into a cup of cold water, forms a very hard ball when rolled between finger and thumb. Temperature on sugar thermometer, if used, should be 138°C (280°F).

5. Pour into a greased 15 cm (6 inch) square tin. Leave until hard.

6. Turn out on to a board. Break up with a small hammer or rolling pin.

Variation

NUT TOFFEE

Follow recipe and method for syrup toffee (above). Cover base of a greased tin with 100 g (4 oz) blanched almonds or 100 g (4 oz) sliced Brazil nuts before pouring in toffee.

EVERTON TOFFEE

Preparation 5 mins **plus setting**
Cooking 30 mins   *Makes about 450g (1 lb)*

60 ml (4 tbsp) water
100 g (4 oz) butter
350 g (12 oz) demerara sugar
30 ml (2 tbsp) golden syrup
15 ml (1 tbsp) black treacle

1. Put all ingredients into a saucepan.

2. Heat slowly, stirring, until butter melts and sugar dissolves.

3. Bring to the boil. Cover pan. Boil gently for 2 minutes.

4. Uncover and continue to boil, stirring occasionally, for 10–15 minutes or until a little of the mixture, dropped into cup of cold water, separates into hard and brittle threads. Temperature on a sugar thermometer, if used, should be about 138°C (280°F).

5. Pour into a greased 15 cm (6 inch) square tin. Leave until hard.

6. Turn out on to a board. Break up with a small hammer or rolling pin.

7. Store in an airtight container between greaseproof paper.

BUTTERSCOTCH

Preparation 5 mins **plus setting**
Cooking 25 mins   *Makes about 450g (1 lb)*

150 ml (¼ pint) water
450 g (1 lb) demerara sugar
50 g (2 oz) butter

1. Pour water into a saucepan and bring to the boil.

2. Add sugar and butter. Heat slowly, stirring, until sugar dissolves and butter melts.

3. Bring to the boil. Cover pan and boil gently for 2 minutes.

4. Uncover and continue to boil, without stirring, for about 8–12 minutes or until a little of the mixture, dropped into a cup of cold water, separates into hard brittle threads. Temperature on sugar thermometer, if used, should be about 138°C (280°F).

5. Pour into a greased 15 cm (6 inch) square tin.

6. Mark into squares or bars when almost set with a buttered knife.

7. Break up when hard and wrap in waxed paper if desired.

8. Store in an airtight container.

HONEYCOMB

Preparation 5 mins **plus setting**
Cooking 20 mins   *Makes about 350g (12oz)*

As honeycomb does not keep well and very quickly becomes sticky it should be made and eaten on the same day.

45 ml (3 tbsp) clear honey
250g (9oz) sugar
60 ml (4 tbsp) water
25g (1oz) butter
5 ml (1 tsp) vinegar
5 ml (1 tsp) bicarbonate of soda

1. Put honey, sugar, water, butter and vinegar into a saucepan.

2. Heat slowly, stirring, until sugar dissolves and butter melts.

3. Bring to the boil. Cover pan and boil gently for 2 minutes.

4. Uncover and continue to boil, without stirring, for about 5 minutes or until a little of the mixture, dropped into a cup of cold water, separates into hard and brittle threads. Temperature on a sugar thermometer, if used, should be about 149°C (300°F).

5. Remove pan from heat. Stir in bicarbonate of soda – mixture will rise in pan.

6. Pour into a small greased tin.

7. Break up into pieces when set.

PEPPERMINT CREAMS

Preparation 15 mins **plus setting**   *Makes 20*

225g (8oz) ready-to-roll fondant icing
few drops of peppermint essence
green food colouring (optional)
icing sugar

1. Gradually knead peppermint essence and food colouring, if used, into fondant icing.

2. Roll out on a work surface dusted with icing sugar to 0.25 cm (⅛ inch) thick.

3. Cut into rounds with a 2.5 cm (1 inch) biscuit cutter.

4. Leave for 24 hours until firmer.

Variation

CHOCOLATE PEPPERMINT CREAMS

Follow recipe and method for peppermint creams (left). Half dip the rounds in melted plain chocolate and leave to set on non-stick baking paper.

COCONUT ICE   Ⓕ

Preparation 15 mins **plus setting**
Cooking 25 mins   *Makes about 50*

65 ml (2½ fl oz) fresh milk
65 ml (2½ fl oz) water
450g (1 lb) granulated sugar
15g (½ oz) butter
100g (4oz) desiccated coconut
2.5 ml (½ tsp) vanilla essence
pink food colouring

1. Pour milk and water into a saucepan. Bring to the boil.

2. Add sugar and butter. Heat slowly, stirring, until sugar dissolves and butter melts.

3. Bring to the boil. Cover pan and boil gently for 2 minutes.

4. Uncover and continue to boil, stirring occasionally for 7–10 minutes or until a little of the mixture, dropped into cup of cold water, forms a soft ball when rolled gently between finger and thumb. Temperature on sugar thermometer, if used, should be 116°C (240°F).

5. Remove from heat. Add coconut and vanilla.

6. Beat briskly until mixture is thick and creamy looking.

7. Pour half into a 18 cm (7 inch) square tin lined with non-stick baking paper.

8. Quickly colour remainder pale pink with food colouring.

9. Spread over white layer.

10. Leave in the cool until firm and set.

11. Cut into squares.

MARSHMALLOWS

Preparation 30 mins **Cooking** 15 mins *Makes 48*

350g (12oz) cornflour
700g (1½lb) icing sugar
225g (8oz) granulated sugar
7.5ml (1½tsp) liquid glucose
215ml (7½floz) water
15g (½oz) gelatine
1 egg white
pink food colouring (optional)

1. Sift cornflour and icing sugar together and spoon into 2 Swiss roll tins.

2. Using 2 eggs make 24 shallow dents in cornflour mixture in each tin, leaving 1 egg in mixture when making next hollow so that sides do not collapse.

3. Place granulated sugar, liquid glucose and water in a large saucepan. Heat gently until sugar has dissolved.

4. Bring to the boil and continue boiling until a little mixture, dropped into a cup of cold water forms a hard ball when rolled between finger and thumb.

Temperature on a sugar thermometer, if used, should be 121°C (250°F).

5. Meanwhile sprinkle gelatine over 50ml (2floz) water in a small saucepan. Leave to stand for 5 mins. Then heat gently until dissolved.

To microwave: Meanwhile, sprinkle gelatine over 50ml (2floz) water in a small bowl. Leave to stand for 5 mins. Cook for about 30 secs, stirring every 10 secs, until dissolved.

6. In an electric mixer whisk egg white until stiff.

7. Remove syrup from heat. Slowly and carefully add gelatine, syrup will bubble up.

8. Pour syrup slowly on to egg white in a steady stream beating all the time until mixture becomes thick and stiff.

9. Add food colouring to half the mixture.

10. Spoon mixture into a large piping bag fitted with a 1cm (½inch) plain nozzle and carefully pipe into moulds.

11. Leave to stand for 1 hour until set. Sprinkle with a little cornflour mixture.

12. Remove from tin and dust off excess.

13. Store in an airtight container, not touching.

Alternatively omit steps 1 and 2. Pour mixture into a deep greased tin, allow to set. Cut into squares and toss in cornflour.

MARSHMALLOWS

CHOCOLATE ORANGE TRUFFLES, FRESH CREAM TRUFFLES

FRESH CREAM TRUFFLES Ⓕ

Preparation 45 mins **plus setting**
Cooking 5 mins   *Makes 36*

150 ml (5 fl oz) fresh double cream
350 g (12 oz) plain chocolate, broken up
30 ml (2 tbsp) liqueur
25 g (1 oz) unsalted butter
extra chocolate for dipping
grated white and plain chocolate for
    decoration

1. Heat cream in a small pan until boiling,
remove from heat and add chocolate, stir
until melted.
*To microwave: Pour cream into a bowl and
cook for about 2 minutes until boiling. Add
chocolate and stir until melted.*

2. Stir in liqueur and butter, mix until butter
has melted. Pour into a bowl.

3. Freeze until firm enough to hold its shape,
about 20 minutes.

4. Using a melon baller scoop out rounds
and place on to non-stick baking paper and
chill until firm.

5. Either roll each truffle in a little cool,
melted chocolate in your hands or dip into
melted chocolate.

6. Roll a third in grated white chocolate, a
third in grated plain chocolate and leave the
remainder plain.

7. Place in small paper cases and store in
refrigerator.

CHOCOLATE RUM TRUFFLES Ⓕ

Preparation 30 mins **plus chilling**
Cooking 5 mins   *Makes 36*

100 g (4 oz) plain chocolate
50 g (2 oz) butter
15 ml (1 tbsp) rum
25 g (1 oz) ground almonds
25 g (1 oz) stale cake crumbs
225 g (8 oz) icing sugar, sifted
drinking chocolate powder

1. Break up chocolate and put, with butter,
into a basin standing over a saucepan of hot
water.
*To microwave: Break up chocolate and put
into a bowl with butter.*

2. Leave until both have melted, stirring
occasionally.
*To microwave: Cook on MEDIUM (50%) for
2–3 minutes, stir occasionally, until melted.*

3. Add rum and mix well.

4. Work in remaining ingredients (except drinking chocolate).

5. Transfer mixture to a dish. Chill until firm, about 1½ hours.

6. Roll equal amounts of mixture into 36 balls.

7. Coat in drinking chocolate powder.

8. Transfer to small paper cases.

Alternatively omit rum and use a few drops of rum essence.

Variation

MOCHA TRUFFLES 🅕

Follow recipe and method for chocolate rum truffles (left). Omit rum and use 5–10 ml (1–2 tsp) coffee essence.

CHOCOLATE ORANGE TRUFFLES 🅕

Preparation 30 mins **plus setting**
Cooking 5 mins   *Makes 32*

225 g (8 oz) plain chocolate, broken up
75 g (3 oz) butter, cut into small pieces
50 g (2 oz) icing sugar, sifted
30 ml (2 tbsp) fresh double cream
grated rind of ½ orange
15 ml (1 tbsp) orange liqueur
75 g (3 oz) biscuits, crushed
drinking chocolate powder

1. Place chocolate in a bowl over a pan of hot water and heat until melted.
To microwave: Place chocolate in a bowl and cook on MEDIUM (50%) for 3–4 minutes, stirring occasionally, until melted.

2. Add butter and leave until melted.

3. Stir sugar, cream, orange rind, liqueur and biscuit crumbs into melted chocolate.

4. Leave until firm, then roll spoonfuls into balls.

5. Refrigerate until firm.

6. Roll in drinking chocolate powder before serving.

CHOCOLATE DIPPED STRAWBERRIES

Preparation 15 mins **plus setting**
Cooking 5 mins   *Makes about 12*

75 g (3 oz) plain chocolate
225 g (8 oz) strawberries

1. Cover a baking sheet with non-stick baking paper.

2. Break up chocolate and place in a small bowl.

3. Place over a saucepan of hot water and heat until melted.
To microwave: Cook on MEDIUM (50%) for 2–3 minutes, stirring occasionally, until melted.

4. Remove from the heat and stir.

5. Do not remove the leaves on strawberries. Dip into chocolate leaving part of the fruit uncovered.

6. Place on non-stick baking paper and leave until the chocolate is dry and set.

These are best eaten on the same day as they are made.

Alternatively use white chocolate.

CHOCOLATE NUT CLUSTERS

Preparation 20 mins **plus setting**
Cooking 5 mins   *Makes about 450g (1lb)*

175 g (6 oz) plain or milk chocolate
100 g (4 oz) unsalted peanuts
50 g (2 oz) flaked almonds
50 g (2 oz) hazelnuts

1. Cover a baking sheet with non-stick baking paper.

2. Break up chocolate and place in a bowl.

3. Place over a saucepan of hot water and heat until melted.
To microwave: Cook on MEDIUM (50%) for 3–4 minutes, stirring occasionally, until melted.

4. Remove from the heat and stir.

5. Stir in the nuts and mix until coated.

6. Drop spoonfuls of the mixture on to non-stick baking paper.

7. Leave until chocolate is dry and set. Store in an airtight container.

HOT DRINKS

When heating milk in a saucepan for hot drinks rinse the pan out with cold water first. This makes it easier to clean the pan afterwards.

Stirring milk whilst heating it in a saucepan helps to prevent a skin forming. Thus reducing the chances of the milk boiling over.

To microwave
The microwave is ideal for quickly heating drinks in the mug or cup in which they are to be served.

As with conventional heating, care should be taken when using the microwave, particularly when children are involved.

When heating *any* drinks in the microwave, to prevent them boiling over or erupting (even after being removed from the microwave):

☐ Use mugs with wide tops and sloping (rather than vertical) sides – tall, narrow mugs encourage spillover so do not use them

☐ Stir the drink before and during heating

☐ Take care not to over-heat the drink

HOT SHAKE

Preparation 3 mins **Cooking** 5 mins   *Serves 1*

300 ml (½ pint) fresh milk
milk shake syrup or powder to taste

1. Heat milk until hot, but not boiling in a saucepan.
To microwave: Pour milk into a large mug and cook for 3–4 minutes, stirring occasionally, until hot but not boiling.

2. Blend together with milk shake syrup or powder.
To microwave: Stir in the milk shake syrup or powder.

3. Serve immediately.

MALTED CHOCOLATE

Preparation 5 mins **Cooking** 5 mins   *Serves 1*

30 ml (2 tbsp) drinking chocolate powder
15 ml (1 tbsp) Ovaltine
300 ml (½ pint) fresh milk

1. Whisk together all ingredients in a small saucepan.
To microwave: Whisk together all ingredients and pour into a large mug.

2. Heat until almost boiling.
To microwave: Cook for 3–4 minutes, stirring occasionally, until almost boiling.

3. Pour into a mug to serve.
To microwave: Stir well and serve.

HOT MOCHA

Preparation 3 mins **Cooking** 3 mins   *Serves 1*

10 ml (2 tsp) drinking chocolate powder
10 ml (2 tsp) coffee granules
200 ml (7 fl oz) fresh milk
chocolate flake (optional)

1. Blend chocolate and coffee with a little cold milk.
To microwave: In a large mug, blend chocolate and coffee with a little cold milk.

2. Add to remaining milk and heat in a saucepan, whisking until hot.
To microwave: Stir in remaining milk and cook for 2–3 minutes, stirring occasionally, until hot.

3. Pour into a mug and serve with a chocolate flake, if used.
To microwave: Stir well and serve with a chocolate flake, if used.

REAL HOT CHOCOLATE

Preparation 10 mins **Cooking** 5 mins   *Serves 1*

25 g (1 oz) plain chocolate
pinch of ground nutmeg
200 ml (7 fl oz) fresh milk
30 ml (2 tbsp) whipped double cream
  (optional)
grated chocolate (optional)

1. Place chocolate, spice and milk in a saucepan.
To microwave: Place chocolate, spice and milk in a large mug.

2. Heat gently until chocolate dissolves. Do not boil.
To microwave: Cook for 2–3 minutes, stirring occasionally, until chocolate dissolves. Do not boil.

3. Pour into a mug, spoon cream on top and sprinkle with a little grated chocolate if used.
To microwave: Spoon cream on top and sprinkle with a little grated chocolate if used.

4. Serve immediately.

Alternatively use milk chocolate or orange flavoured chocolate, and omit nutmeg.

GINGERED WHITE CHOCOLATE

Preparation 10 mins **Cooking** 5 mins   *Serves 1*

300 ml (½ pint) fresh milk
25 g (1 oz) white chocolate, broken up
15 ml (1 tbsp) ginger wine
15 ml (1 tbsp) rum
ground nutmeg to serve

1. Place all ingredients except rum, in a small saucepan.
To microwave: Place all ingredients, except rum, in a large mug.

2. Heat, stirring until chocolate has melted and milk is hot.
To microwave: Cook for about 3 minutes, stirring occasionally, until chocolate has melted and milk is hot.

3. Pour into a mug, stir in rum and sprinkle with nutmeg to serve.
To microwave: Stir in rum and sprinkle with nutmeg to serve.

Alternatively for a non-alcoholic drink use stem ginger syrup and a few drops of rum essence.

REAL HOT CHOCOLATE, GINGERED WHITE CHOCOLATE

ORANGE & HONEY MILK

Preparation 5 mins **Cooking** 5 mins *Serves 1*

200 ml (7 fl oz) fresh milk
5 ml (1 tsp) clear honey
few drops of natural orange essence
orange colouring (optional)
grated orange rind to decorate

1. Heat milk in a small saucepan until almost boiling.
To microwave: Pour milk into a large mug and cook for 2–3 minutes, stirring occasionally, until almost boiling.

2. Pour into a mug and stir in honey, essence and colouring if used.
To microwave: Stir in honey, essence and colouring if used.

3. Serve decorated with orange rind.

EASTERN SPICED MILK

Preparation 3 mins **Cooking** 5 mins *Serves 1*

200 ml (7 fl oz) fresh milk
pinch of ground cinnamon
pinch of ground cardamom

1. Place milk and spices in a saucepan and heat until almost boiling, stir occasionally.
To microwave: Place milk and spices in a large mug and cook for 2–3 minutes, stirring occasionally, until almost boiling.

2. Pour into a mug and serve sprinkled with a little extra spice.
To microwave: Sprinkle with a little extra spice.

BLENDER CAPPUCCINO

Preparation 15 mins **Cooking** 5 mins *Serves 2*

300 ml (½ pint) fresh skimmed milk
175 ml (6 fl oz) very strong hot coffee
drinking chocolate powder

1. Heat milk until almost boiling.
To microwave: Pour milk into a jug and cook for 3–4 minutes until almost boiling.

2. Pour into a blender and process until frothy.

3. Pour black coffee into two cups.

4. Top up with milk and spoon some froth on to each one.

5. Sprinkle with drinking chocolate powder.

6. Serve immediately.

ORANGE & HONEY MILK, EASTERN SPICED MILK

IRISH COFFEE

Dutch Chocolate Cups

Preparation 20 mins **Cooking** 5 mins   *Serves 4*

300 ml (½ pint) fresh milk
150 ml (5 fl oz) fresh single cream
150 ml (¼ pint) water
75 g (3 oz) drinking chocolate powder
175 ml (6 fl oz) Advocaat
ground cinnamon

1. Pour milk, cream and water into a saucepan. Bring just to the boil.
To microwave: Pour milk, cream and water into a large jug. Cook for 4–5 minutes, stirring occasionally, until just boiling.

2. Remove from heat.

3. Whisk in drinking chocolate and Advocaat.

4. Pour into 4 cups.

5. Sprinkle lightly with cinnamon.

Irish Coffee

Preparation 20 mins   *Serves 1*

30 ml (2 tbsp) Irish whiskey
3 sugar cubes or 10 ml (2 tsp) brown sugar
freshly made strong coffee
fresh double cream

1. Warm a stemmed goblet or medium sized coffee cup with hot water. Quickly wipe dry.

2. Pour in whiskey, add sugar and fill with hot coffee to within 2 cm (1 inch) of rim.

3. Stir briskly to dissolve sugar.

4. Top up with cream, by pouring it into goblet or cup over back of a teaspoon.

5. Serve immediately.

Variations

French Coffee

Follow recipe and method for Irish coffee (above). Use brandy instead of whiskey.

Jamaican Coffee

Follow recipe and method for Irish coffee (above). Use rum instead of whiskey.

COLD DRINKS

THICK STRAWBERRY SHAKE

Preparation 10 mins   *Serves 1*

75 ml (3 fl oz) fresh milk, chilled
2 scoops of strawberry dairy ice cream

1. Place milk and ice cream in a blender and process until smooth.
2. Pour into a glass, add straws and serve immediately.

MILK SHAKE FLOAT

Preparation 5 mins   *Serves 1*

200 ml (7 fl oz) fresh milk, chilled
2 scoops of vanilla dairy ice cream
30 ml (2 tbsp) milk shake syrup
   (flavour to taste)

1. Whisk milk, 1 scoop of ice cream and syrup well together.
2. Pour into a glass.
3. Float remaining ice cream on top.

ICED COFFEE

Preparation 10 mins **plus chilling**   *Serves 3–4*

300 ml (½ pint) freshly made double
   strength black coffee
450 ml (¾ pint) fresh milk
sugar to taste
30 ml (2 tbsp) fresh double cream, whipped

1. Combine coffee with milk.
2. Sweeten to taste. Chill.
3. Pour into 3 or 4 tumblers just before serving.
4. Top each one with a swirl of lightly whipped cream.

MILK SHAKE FLOAT, FRUITY FRAIS

CHOCOLATE PEPPERMINT SIZZLERS

Preparation 15 mins **plus chilling**
Cooking 5 mins   *Serves 4*

75g (3oz) plain chocolate, grated
30ml (2tbsp) caster sugar
900ml (1½pint) fresh milk
5ml (1tsp) peppermint essence
30ml (2tbsp) fresh double cream, whipped
mint leaves

1. Slowly melt chocolate and sugar in 150ml (¼pint) milk.
To microwave: Put chocolate, sugar and 150ml (¼pint) milk into a large jug. Cook for about 2 minutes, stirring once, until chocolate melts and sugar dissolves. Stir well.
2. Stir in remaining milk with peppermint essence and chill.
3. Just before serving pour into 4 glasses.
4. Top each with cream and mint leaves.

CHOCOLATE GINGER FRAPPÉ

Preparation 15 mins   *Serves 4*

crushed ice
90ml (6tbsp) drinking chocolate powder
45ml (3tbsp) boiling water
900ml (1½pint) fresh milk, chilled
30ml (2tbsp) ginger wine
30ml (2tbsp) fresh double cream, whipped

1. Cover base of 4 tumblers with crushed ice.
2. Mix drinking chocolate to a smooth liquid with water.
3. Whisk in milk and ginger wine.
4. Pour into glasses.
5. Top each with cream. Serve immediately.

FRUITY FRAIS

Preparation 10 mins   *Serves 2*

150g (5oz) fromage frais
150ml (¼pint) orange juice
7.5ml (1½tsp) clear honey

1. Blend together all ingredients.
2. Pour into 2 glasses and serve.

TAJ TEMPTATION, NUTTY BANANA SHAKE

DRINKING YOGURT

Preparation 10 mins   *Serves 2*

300 ml (½ pint) fresh milk, chilled
150 g (5 oz) orange yogurt
100 ml (4 fl oz) orange juice
grated orange rind to decorate

1. Blend together milk, yogurt and orange juice,
2. Pour into 2 glasses and serve decorated with orange rind.

YOGURT STRAWBERRY COOLER

Preparation 10 mins   *Serves 2*

150 g (5 oz) strawberry yogurt
300 ml (½ pint) fresh milk, chilled
strawberries to decorate

1. Whisk yogurt and milk well together.
2. Pour into 2 glasses.
3. Decorate with strawberries to serve.

TAJ TEMPTATION

Preparation 10 mins   *Serves 2*

150 g (5 oz) natural yogurt
10 ml (2 tsp) clear honey
75 g (3 oz) pawpaw, peeled, seeded and chopped
1 medium banana, peeled and sliced
150 ml (¼ pint) fresh milk, chilled

1. Place all ingredients in a blender and process until smooth and frothy.
2. Pour into 2 glasses and serve.

NUTTY BANANA SHAKE

Preparation 10 mins   *Serves 2*

1 medium banana, peeled and sliced
150 g (5 oz) hazelnut yogurt
300 ml (½ pint) fresh milk, chilled
banana chips and chopped hazelnuts to decorate

1. Place banana, yogurt and milk in a blender and process until smooth and frothy.
2. Pour into a glass and decorate to serve.

TROPICAL TANTALISER

Preparation 10 mins   *Serves 2*

150 ml (¼ pint) fresh milk, chilled
65 g (2½ oz) exotic fruit yogurt
50 ml (2 fl oz) tropical fruit juice drink
desiccated coconut to serve

1. Blend together milk, yogurt and fruit drink.
2. Pour into 2 glasses and top with coconut.

RHUBARB & GINGER FROTH

Preparation 10 mins   *Serves 2*

300 ml (½ pint) fresh milk, chilled
65 g (2½ oz) rhubarb yogurt
5 ml (1 tsp) preserved stem ginger syrup
½ piece preserved stem ginger, chopped
1 scoop vanilla dairy ice cream
ground nutmeg to decorate

1. Place all ingredients except nutmeg in a blender and process until smooth and frothy.
2. Pour into 2 glasses and decorate with a little ground nutmeg before serving.

WHISKY CREAM LIQUEUR

Preparation 15 mins **plus chilling**   *Serves 4*

15 ml (1 tbsp) soft brown sugar
30 ml (2 tbsp) hot water
2.5 ml (½ tsp) vanilla essence
75 ml (3 fl oz) Drambuie
300 ml (10 fl oz) fresh single cream

1. Dissolve sugar in hot water.
To microwave: Place sugar and water in a small bowl and cook for 20–30 seconds. Stir to dissolve sugar.
2. Allow to cool.
3. Stir in vanilla essence, Drambuie and single cream.
4. Chill before serving.
This will keep for 4 days in a refrigerator.

Variation

COFFEE CREAM LIQUEUR

Follow recipe and method for whisky cream liqueur (above). Omit Drambuie and use 75 ml (3 fl oz) Tia Maria.

WHISKY CREAM LIQUEUR

Agar agar
Comes as powder, sticks or strands made from seaweed and used as a jelling agent.

Arrowroot
Can be used as a substitute for cornflour as a thickening agent in liquids, such as sauces. It gives a clear sauce.

Au gratin
Describes a dish which has been covered with sauce, sprinkled with breadcrumbs or cheese and finished by browning under the grill or in the oven. The low-sided dishes in which this is done are called gratin dishes.

Bain-marie
A shallow-side container which is half-filled with water kept just below boiling point. Containers of food are placed in it to keep warm or cook without overheating. A bain-marie is used for cooking custards and other egg dishes and keeping sauces warm. No special container is needed; a roasting tin will do.

Baking
Cooking in the oven using dry heat.

Baking Blind
Method used for cooking flans and tarts without their filllings. Line with greaseproof paper and fill with baking beans or rice.

Basting
Pouring the juices and melted fat over meat, poultry or game which is being roasted to keep it moist. Use a large spoon or a special bulb baster.

Béchamel
A basic which sauce; flavoured with onion, carrot, herbs and spices.

Beurre manié
Equal quantities of flour and butter kneaded together to form a paste. Used for thickening soups, stews and casseroles at the end of cooking.

Blanching
Immersing food quickly in boiling water to whiten it, as in sweetbreads, or to remove skin, e.g. peaches and tomatoes. Vegetables which are to be frozen and kept for a certain length of time are blanched to destroy enzymes and preserve the colour, flavour and texture.

Boling
Cooking in water or stock at 100°C (212°F).

Bombe
A spherical metal mould with a lid for shaping ice cream desserts.

Boning
Taking out the bones from meat or poultry, cutting the flesh as little as possible, so that it can be rolled or stuffed.

Bouquet garni
A small posy of herbs - usually a mixture of parsley stems, thyme and a bay leaf ties in muslin and used to flavour soups and stews.

Braising
Cooking method used for cuts of meat, poultry and game which are too tough to roast. It is also good for some vegetables. Use a pan or casserole with a tightly fitting lid so that little liquid is lost thorough evaporation. Place the meat on a bed of chopped vegetables (called a mirepoix), add sufficient liquid to cover the vegetables and cook on the hob or in the oven.

Brining
Immersing food in a strong salt and water solution.

Brioche
An enriched yeast dough mixture baked in the shape of a cottage loaf. French in origin and normally eaten warm for breakfast.

Brochette
A metal or wood skewer.

Broiling
American name for grilling.

Browning
Searing the outside surface of meat to seal in the juices.

Bruleé
Grilling a sugar crust on top of sweet dish to caramelise it.

Bulghur wheat
Pre-boiled cracked wheat. The only preparation it needs is soaking.

Canapé
Small appetisers, usually accompanied with drinks and often consisting of a topping on a bread or pastry base.

Cannelloni
Large pasta tubes, filled with savoury stuffings.

Caramel
A substance gained by heating sugar syrup very slowly until a rich brown colour.

Caramelise
To change sugar into caramel by gentle heating so it dissolves and turn brown.

Carbonade
A rich slew or braise of meat including beer.

Casserole
A dish with a well fitting lid used for cooking meat and vegetables, also applied to food cooked in this way.

Chantilly
Whipped cream which has been slightly sweentened and often flavoured with vanilla.

Chining
Severing the rib bones from the backbone by sawing through the ribs near to the spine. Joints such as loin or neck of

lamb, veal or pork are best chined as this makes them easier to crave into chops or cutlets after cooking

Chowder
An American dish somehwere between a soup and a stew, normally based on fish, e.g. clam chowder.

Clarifying
The process of extracting sediment or impurities, from a food. Butter and dripping may be clarified so that they can be used for frying at higher temperatures.

Clotting
A gentle heat applied to cream which results in the thick clotted cream of the south-west of England.

Cocotte
Small earthenware, ovenproof dish of single portion size. Also called a ramekin.

Coddling
A method for soft boiling eggs.

Compote
A mixture of fruit stewed in sugar and water. Served hot or cold.

Conserve
Jam containing whole fruits.

Cornstarch
American tern for cornflour.

Court bouillon
A seasoned stock in which meat, poultry, fish or vegetables are boiled or poached.

Couscous
A North African dish made from hard wheat semolina. Using a special double boiler, the meat and vegetables are cooked in the lower half and the semolina steamed in the top half.

Crêpe
French name for a pancake.

Crimping
Decorating the edges of a pie, tart or short bread by pinching it at regular intervals to provide a fluted effect. Also using special icing tools to decorate fondant iced cakes.

Croûtons
Small cubes of fried or toasted bread which are served with salads and soup.

Crudités
French name for a selection of raw spring onions, carrots, radishes and other vegetables served at the beginning of a lunch.

Curdle
To separate fresh milk or a sauce either by adding an acid such as lemon juice or by over heating. Also used to refer to creamed mixtures which have separated when the egg has been beaten in too quickly.

Dariole
Individual cup shaped mould used for making puddings, sweet and savoury jellies and creams.

Daube
Meat or vegetables which have been braised in stock, for several hours.

Deep-Frying
Frying food by placing it in deep hot fat or oil.

Dhal (Dal)
A spicy bean or lentil dish of Indian origin.

Dredge
To cover generously with sifted flour or sugar.

Dropping consistency
A term used to describe the correct texture of a cake or pudding mixture prior to cooking. Test for it by taking a spoonful of the mixture and holding the spoon on its side above the bowl. The mixture should fall off its own accord within 5 seconds.

En Croûte
A term describing food which is wrapped in pastry prior to cooking.

En papillote
To wrap food in aluminium foil or grease-proof paper for cooking and served in the parcel.

Entrée
Third course in a formal meal. Following the fish course. Main dish with vegetable garnish.

Escalope
A slice of meat such as veal, turkey or port cut from the top of the leg and normally egged and crumbed, then fried.

Farce
Alternative French name for stuffing.

Fermenting
A term used when enzyme activity changes a food consistency, e.g. when making bread, yogurt or wine.

Fillet
A name given to the undercut of a loin of beef, veal, pork or game, for boned breasts of poulltry and for boned slices of fish.

Filo
Greek or Middle Eastern pastry made in wafer thin sheets; also called strudel pastry.

Fine herbs
A mixture of chopped herbs, normally parsley, tarragon, chives and chervil.

Flambe
Flavouring a dish with alcohol which is then ignited so that the alcohol is evaporated. Traditionally done to Christmas Pudding and Crêpes Suzette.

Fluting
See crimping.

Folding in
(Cutting and folding) method of combining a whisked or creamed mixture with other ingredients so that it maintains its lightness. Used mainly for meringues, souffles and certain cake mixtures. Folding is done with a metal spoon.

Fondue
A dish cooked at the table over a fondue burner into which the diners dip food speared on long pronged fondue forks.

Frappé
A name given to iced drinks, creams amd fruit desserts.

Fricassée
White stew of chicken, rabbit, veal or vegetables. finished with cream and egg yolks, often served with boiled rice.

Frosting
American term for icing cakes, aslo the method of decorating the rim of a drinks glass.

Frying
A method of cooking food in hot fat or oil. There are two ways of frying. Shallow frying in a little fat in a shallow pan and deep frying where the food is totally immersed in oil.

Game chips
Potatoes sliced very thinly and fried.

Garam masala
An Indian combination of roasted spices, such as coriander seed, cumin, cloves, cardamom and cinnamon.

Gelatine
Animal-derived setting agent.

Ghee
Clarified butter extensively used in Indian cookery.

Gill
A liquid measure equivalent to 150ml (1/4 pint).

Glaze
Foods used to give glossy finish to sweet and savoury dishes to improve their appearance and sometimes flavour. Ingredients for glazes include beaten egg, egg white, milk and syrup.

Gluten
A constituent of wheat and other cereals. The amount present in varying flours produces the different textures of cakes and breads.

Griddle
A flat, heavy, metal plate used on top of the cooker for baking scones.

Hors d'oeuvre
Often used as a term for a starter but, really it means a selection of cold foods served together as an appetiser.

Hulling
Removing the stalk and leaves from soft fruits, e.g. strawberries.

Infusing
The method of transferring flavour to a liquid. Flavouring, herbs, spices or coffee beans are soaked in milk or water.

Julienne
Matchstick strips of vegetables, or citrus rind, commonly used as a garnish.

Junket
An English pudding made with sweetened and flavoured milk, which is then set with rennet.

Knead
To work dough with a pushing, pressing motion of the heel of the hands to develop the gluten in the flour.

Langues de chats
Literally means cats' tongues. Small thin flat crisp biscuits served with desserts.

Lukewarm
About blood heat, approcimately 37°C (98.4°F).

Marinating
Soaking meat, poultry or game in a combination of oil, wine, vinegar and flavourings to tenderise it and add flavour. The mixture is known as a marinade.

Mille feuilles
A French pastry made with thin crispy puff pastry and layered with cream and jam. Topped with icing and cut into slices.

Mornay
Béchamel sauce containg cheese. Also the name given to a dish coated with cheese sauce before grilling.

Meuniére
Applies to food cooked in butter, seasoned with salt, peper and lemon juice and finished with parsley. Often used for fish dishes.

Mocca (mocha)
A name which has come to mean a blend of chocolate and coffee.

Open-freeze
Foods frozen without wrapping until solid. Then wrapped and sealed for storage in the freezer.

Par-boiling
Boiling food for part of its cooking time before completing it by another method.

Parfait
Frozen dessert comprising whipped cream and fruit purée.

Paring
Thinly peeling or trimming vegetables or fruit.

Pasteurising
Sterilising milk by heating to 72°C (161°F) for 15 seconds to kill bacteria.

Pectin
Substance found in most fruit and some vegetables which is required for settng jams and jellies.

Pesto
A Italian sauce used for pasta or flavouring. Made from basil, garlic, pine nuts, parmesan cheese and olive oil.

Pith
In citrus fruit, the white cellular lining to the rind coating the flesh.

Poaching
Cooking food in an open pan covered with simmering, seasoned liquid.

Pot roasting
A method of cooking meat in a pan with fat and a small amount of liquid.

Pre-boiling
A term applied to pulses when they are

boiled rapidly for 15 minutes to destroy any toxins before further cooking.

Proving
The term used for standing bread dough to rise after shaping.

Ramekin
Individual round small soufflé ovenproof dish.

Ratafias
Boiling button-sized almond falvoured macaroons mainly served with puddings and cream sweets.

Reducing
Boiling a liquid to evaporate it and produce a more concentrared flavour.

Rendering
Obtaining fat from meat trimmings by cutting them into small pieces and heating in a cool oven at 150°C (300°F). Mark 2 until the fat runs out and can be strained.

Rennet
A substance used for making junket by coagulating milk obtained from the stomach of a suckling calf. Rennet is also available from fungal or bacterial origin, Rennet for domestic purposes can be purchased from a supermarket.

Roasting
Cooking meat in an oven or over an open fire.

Roe
Milt of the male fish, called soft roe. Eggs of the female fish, called hard roe. shellfish roe, called coral due to its colour.

Roulade
A name given to a meat, cake or soufflé mixture served in roll.

Roux
A mixture of equal amounts of fat and flour cooked together to produce the base of sauces.

Rubbing in
Method of incorporating fat into flour when a short texture is required for pastry, cakes or biscuits.

Satay
An Indonesian-style peanut sauce which is usually served with grilled beef, pork or chicken kebabs.

Sautéing
Cooking food in a small quantity of fat in a sauté pan (a frying pan with straight sides and a wide base), to brown the food quickly.

Scalding
Pouring boiling water over food to clean it, loosen hairs or remove the skin. Food should not be left in boiling water or it will begin to cook. It is also the term used for heating milk to just below boiling point, to delay souring or infuse it with another flavour.

Scalloping
Descorating the double edge of a pastry pie with small horizontal cuts which are pulled up with the back of a knife to form a scalloped effect.

Scoring
Cutting narrow parallel lines in the surface of food to improve its appearance or help it cook more quickly.

Searing
Browning meat quickly in a little hot fat prior o grilling or roasting.

Simmering
Keeping liquid just below boiling point.

Skimming
To reomove and discard froth, scum or fat from the surface of stock, gravy, stews and jam. Use either a skimmer, a spoon or absorbent kitchen paper.

Sousing
Cooking in brine or vinegar marinade.

Steaming
Cooking food in the steam of quickly boiling water.

Stewing
Long, slow cooking method where food is immersed in liquid which is kept at simmering point. Good for tenderising coarse meat and vegetables.

Stir-frying
A quickly method of frying in shallow fat. The food must be cut into small, even-sized pieces and moved around constantly until coated. Stir-fried food is normally cooked in a wok.

Sweating
Genlty cooking food (usually vegetables), coated in melted fat until the juices run.

Tenderising
Beating raw meat with a spiked mallet or rolling pin to break down fibres tenderising it for grilling or frying.

Tepid
About blood heat (see lukewarm).

Trivet
A metal stand on which dishes are stood.

Trussing
Tying or skewering into shape before cooking. Associated mainly with poultry and game.

Velouté
A white sauce made with chicken, veal or fish stock, or a soup of creamy consistency.

Vermicelli
Very thin strands of pasta or small sugar strands used to decorate cakes.

Widl rice
The seed of a North American grass. The grain is long and drak brown. It is cooked in the same way as rice and often served mixed with rice.

Wok
A Chinese pan used for stir-frying. The food cooks on the slopping sides of the pan as well as in the rounded or flat base.

Zest
The coloured outer layer of citrus fruit which contains vital oil.

F

E

G

T